CompTIA Strata Study Guide

CompTIA Strata Objectives

OBJECTIVE	CHAPTER
1.0 Technology and Computer Hardware Basics	
1.1 U.S. (1.1 FC0-U11 U.K.) Identify basic IT vocabulary	1, 2, 3
Processor speed/cores	
RAM	
Hard drives	
Networking	
1.2 U.S. (1.1 FC0-U21 U.K.) Demonstrate the proper use of the following devices:	3, 4
Monitors	
Desktop	
Server	
Portable	
1.3 U.S. (1.2 FC0-U21 U.K.) Explain the characteristics and functions of internal and external storage devices	2
CD/CD-RW drive	
DVD/DVD-RW drive	
Blu-Ray disk drive	
USB storage	
Multi-card reader and writer	
Hard drives	
Mobile media devices	
1.4 U.S. (1.3 FC0-U21 U.K.) Explain the characteristics and functions of peripheral devices	3
Digital camera	
Web camera	
Speaker	
Tuner	
Microphone	
Printer/scanner	
1.5 U.S. (1.4 FC0-U21 U.K.) Explain the characteristics and functions of input devices:	2
Keyboard	
Mouse	
Tablet	
Numeric keyboard	
Gamepad	

Sybex®
An Imprint of
WILEY

D1335950

OBJECTIVE	CHAPTER
1.6 U.S. (1.2 FCO-U11 U.K.) Identify the risks associated with upgrading the following technologies and equipment:	6, 7
Operating systems (open source and commercial)	
PC Speed/Storage Capability	
Applications	
Bandwidth and contention	
Automatic applications and operating system updates	
1.7 U.S. (1.3 FCO-U11 U.K.) Demonstrate the ability to set up a basic PC workstation	2, 3, 4
Identify differences between connector types:	
Monitor types	
Computer (desktop, tower, laptop, custom cases)	
Keyboard (keyboard layout, regionalization)	
Mouse (touchpad, optical, trackball)	
Printer (USB, wireless, networked)	
Voltage and power requirements	
Turn on and use the PC and peripherals	
2.0 Compatible Issues and Common Errors	
2.1 U.S. (2.1 FCO-U21 U.K.) Identify basic compatibility issues between:	3, 7
Processor performance	
RAM memory	
USB (1.1, 2.0)	
Firewire	
PS/2	
Ethernet	
Wireless networks	
2.2 U.S. (2.2 FCO-U21 U.K.) Recognize common operational problems caused by hardware	8
Critical error message or crash	
System lockup (freeze)	
Application will not start or load	
Cannot logon to network	
Driver/hardware compatibility	
Input device will not function	
2.3 U.S. (2.3 FCO-U21 U.K.) Demonstrate the ability to minimize risks	5
Data loss	
Loss of service	
Damage to equipment	
3.0 Software Installation and Functions	

Sybex®
An Imprint of
WILEY

Sybex®
An Imprint of
WILEY

NOTE

Exam objectives are subject to change at any time without prior notice and at CompTIA's sole discretion. Please visit CompTIA's website (www.comptia.org) for the most current listing of exam objectives.

Sybex®
An Imprint of
WILEY

CompTIA
Strata
Study Guide

CompTIA

Strata

Study Guide

Andrew Smith

Faithe Wempen

WILEY

John Wiley & Sons, Ltd.

Executive Commissioning Editor: Birgit Gruber
Senior Acquisitions Editor: Chris Katsaropolous
Assistant Editor: Ellie Scott
Development Editor: Gary Schwartz
Technical Editors: Aubrey Adams, and Dwight Silverman
Technical Proofreader: Richard Millet
Production Editor: Christine O'Connor
Copy Editor: Tiffany Taylor
Editorial Manager: Pete Gaughan
Production Manager: Tim Tate
Vice President and Executive Group Publisher: Richard Swadley
Vice President and Publisher: Neil Edde
UK Tech Publishing
    VP Consumer and Technology Publishing Director: Michelle Leete
    Associate Director–Book Content Management: Martin Tribe
    Associate Publisher: Chris Webb
    Associate Marketing Director: Louise Breinholt
    Marketing Executive: Kate Parrett
Project Manager 1: Laura Moss-Hollister
Associate Producer: Marilyn Hummel
Quality Assurance: Doug Kuhn
Book Designers: Judy Fung and Bill Gibson
Proofreader: Jen Larsen, Word One New York
Indexer: Robert Swanson

This edition first published 2012.

© 2012 John Wiley & Sons, Ltd

Registered office

John Wiley & Sons Ltd, The Atrium, Southern Gate, Chichester, West Sussex, PO19 8SQ, United Kingdom

For details of our global editorial offices, for customer service, and for information about how to apply for permission to reuse the copyright material in this book please see our website at www.wiley.com.

978-0-470-97742-2

A catalogue record for this book is available from the British Library.

Set in 9.5pt Sabon by MPS Limited, a Macmillan Company

Printed in UK by TJ International

Dear Reader,

Thank you for choosing *CompTIA Strata Study Guide*. This book is part of a family
of premium-quality Sybex books, all of which are written by outstanding authors who
combine practical experience with a gift for teaching.

Sybex was founded in 1976. More than 30 years later, we're still committed to producing
consistently exceptional books. With each of our titles, we're working hard to set a new
standard for the industry. From the paper we print on, to the authors we work with, our
goal is to bring you the best books available.

I hope you see all that reflected in these pages. I'd be very interested to hear your
comments and get your feedback on how we're doing. Feel free to let me know what you
think about this or any other Sybex book by sending me an email at nedde@wiley.com.
If you think you've found a technical error in this book, please visit http://sybex
.custhelp.com. Customer feedback is critical to our efforts at Sybex.

Best regards,

Neil Edde
Vice President and Publisher
Sybex, an Imprint of Wiley

Acknowledgments

Thank you to Chris Katsaropolous for asking me to be a part of this project and to the great editors at Sybex, including Gary Schwartz, Christine O'Connor, Aubrey Adams, Dwight Silverman, and Tiffany Taylor for making the editorial process run so smoothly.

—Faithe

To Shirley, Jeremy, and Victoria, yet again I am indebted to your patience. Thanks must go to colleagues, namely Nicky Moss and Richard Seaton, from whom I can always count on wise counsel. Finally, to the many educators out there working with CompTIA—keep up the enthusiasm; you are doing something worthwhile.

—Andrew

About the Authors

Andrew Smith works both as an academic for the UK Open University and a national senior examiner for a popular BTEC vocational information technology qualification. Having contributed to many texts on systems maintenance and networking, Andrew has both industrial and teaching experience on hardware and networking that spans more than 20 years.

Faithe Wempen a 20-year veteran of the computer book publishing industry, is the author of well over 120 books about computer hardware and software. Top-selling titles include *Office 2010 for Seniors for Dummies*, *A+ Certification Workbook for Dummies*, and the *Microsoft Office PowerPoint 2010 Official Academic Course*. In addition to her book-length works, Faithe has written over 50 online courses for Powered.com, which have educated over a quarter of a million online students on subjects such as PC repair, Office applications, and Windows optimization. She has also written technical articles for TechRepublic and CertCities, and her articles on Office have appeared in *Microsoft OfficePro* and *Microsoft Office Power User* magazines. Faithe is an adjunct instructor of Computer Information Technology at Indiana University/Purdue University at Indianapolis, where she has taught Microsoft Office applications, Information Technology Fundamentals, and Computer Hardware and Software Architectures. She has also done extensive in-house custom software training for small businesses.

About the Contributor

Rehan Bhana has 15 years' experience in information technology. Over the last decade, he has worked at a number of educational institutions across Europe. He directs several continuing professional development programs.

His passion for teaching and learning has been instrumental to the many students who have gone onto careers in computing after taking his courses. He is the academic lead for CompTIA, Microsoft, and Apple educational programs at his University in Birmingham, U.K., and he has a number of associated certifications. He holds a degree in systems engineering as well as educational qualifications including Microsoft Certified Trainer. He brings with him a wide range of curriculum design skills and realistic interactivity experience from the classroom.

Born in the warm heart of Africa, of Asian origins, and now living in a cosmopolitan society, Rehan is used to learning about different cultures and traditions. Beyond this, he is likely to be engrossed in quality time with his lovely wife and their two adorable children.

Contents at a Glance

Contents

Chapter   6   Installing and Configuring Software   213

Table of Exercises

Preface

There was a time where the discipline of information technology systems support was considered a mythical skill—to be practiced by a chosen few from a somewhat selective priesthood.

Fortunately, membership of this mysterious priesthood has become more accessible for everyone. With information technology having become less mysterious and more open, the opportunity for many individuals to take on the solemn responsibility of systems support specialist has been enhanced through the work of independent organizations such as CompTIA.

The skill of computer support once was definitely a dark art. This was made more confusing by the lack of suitable training and the absence of any internationally recognized certification accompanied by good training resources.

I have worked in the information systems support and networking industry for more than 20 years, and I have been involved in teaching for at least 15 years. I can see that the demands on IT professionals have increased at the same pace as the many developments in hardware and software.

It isn't unusual for information systems professionals to be expert in hardware, software, operating systems, and security while they are also expected to know about every new development on the market and be able to support all the old technologies in many organizations (and in homes, for that matter) at the same time.

Unfortunately, it isn't enough to have one skill and hope that the technology won't change. As you're reading this preface, some technology company somewhere has just announced a new release or revision to the phantasmagoria of techie toys you can plug into your personal computer.

If things aren't complicated enough, the advent of smartphones and tablet devices adds even more tools and technologies to the mix. But in the immortal words of Douglas Adams, "Don't Panic."

This book will introduce you to everything you need to know to get you started in supporting computers and all the related technologies in use. We'll keep everything as simple as possible while giving you all the tools you need to get started in the Information Systems Support profession and develop the knowledge required to help you toward the CompTIA Fundamentals of IT certification.

You'll also learn what you need to know to remain skilled as an information systems professional. Your education won't stop here, because you may work in an industry where it will continue, we hope forever. Also, consider that your experience with this book may lead you to higher-level certifications, such as the CompTIA A+ exam.

While reading this book, take the time to explore each technology discussed, and don't be afraid to experiment with your computer. You'll learn more and gain greater confidence if you learn by doing rather than trying to acquire experience by reading alone. Your practical skills will become a longer-term asset; the more you work on these, the better you'll become.

You won't need any special computer system to work with this book; the technology explored is available in most desktop or laptop systems. If you don't wish to damage your desktop, then feel free to install a virtual machine (explored in this book) and install your own version of Windows or Linux. You'll appreciate the experience as well as the freedom this provides.

Take the time to enjoy learning, and eventually you'll become one of the high priests of information technology.

—Andrew Smith

CompTIA Strata IT Fundamentals

- Designed for students just starting in IT, who lack the basic knowledge needed for a fundamental IT education or who need IT fundamentals to help them pass the CompTIA A+ exam.
- Covers knowledge of PC components, setting up a workstation, recognizing security risks, and preventive maintenance.

It Pays to Get Certified

In a digital world, digital literacy is an essential survival skill. Certification proves you have the knowledge and skill to solve business problems in virtually any business environment. Certifications are highly valued credentials that qualify you for jobs, increased compensation and promotion.

The CompTIA Strata IT Fundamentals certificate ensures a knowledge of PC components, functionality, compatibility, and related technology topics

- **Target Audience**—The Strata IT Fundamentals certificate is ideal for individuals and students preparing to enter the IT workforce and professionals changing careers to IT or technology-related fields.
- **Career Pathway**—The certificate can be a stepping stone to CompTIA's higher A+ certification, and with specialized experience, CompTIA Network+ and CompTIA Security+.
- **Job Roles**—include network and system administrator, sales engineer, account manager, and business development manager.

How Certification Helps Your Career

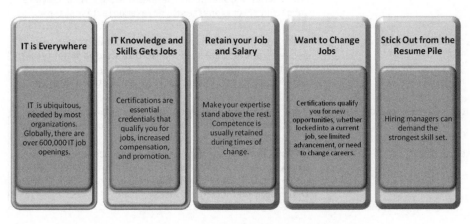

IT is Everywhere	IT Knowledge and Skills Gets Jobs	Retain your Job and Salary	Want to Change Jobs	Stick Out from the Resume Pile
IT is ubiquitous, needed by most organizations. Globally, there are over 600,000 IT job openings.	Certifications are essential credentials that qualify you for jobs, increased compensation, and promotion.	Make your expertise stand above the rest. Competence is usually retained during times of change.	Certifications qualify you for new opportunities, whether locked into a current job, see limited advancement, or need to change careers.	Hiring managers can demand the strongest skill set.

CompTIA Career Pathway

CompTIA offers a number of credentials that form a foundation for your career in technology and allow you to pursue specific areas of concentration. Depending on the path you choose to take, CompTIA certifications help you build upon your skills and knowledge, supporting learning throughout your entire career.

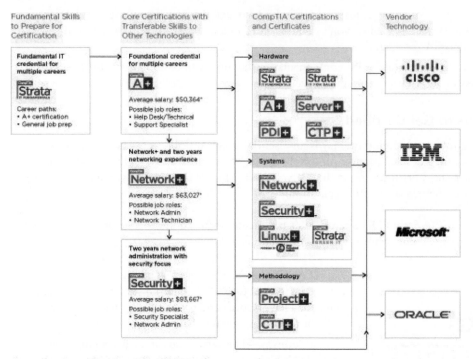

*Source: *Computerworld* Salary Survey 2010—U.S. salaries only

STEPS TO GETTING CERTIFIED AND STAYING CERTIFIED

1. Review Exam Objectives	▪ Review the certificate objectives to make sure you know what is covered in the exam. http://www.comptia.org/certifications/testprep/examobjectives.aspx
2. Practice for the Exam	▪ After you have studied for the certificate, take a free assessment and sample test to get an idea what type of questions might be on the exam. http://www.comptia.org/certifications/testprep/practicetests.aspx
3. Purchase an Exam Voucher	▪ Purchase your exam voucher on the CompTIA Marketplace, which is located at: www.comptiastore.com
4. Take the Test!	▪ Select a certificate exam provider and schedule a time to take your exam. You can find exam providers at the following link: http://www.comptia.org/certifications/testprep/testingcenters.aspx

Join IT Pro Community http://itpro.comptia.org	The free IT Pro online community provides valuable content to students and professionals. ▪ Career IT Job Resources ▪ Where to start in IT ▪ Career Assessments ▪ Salary Trends ▪ US Job Board ▪ Forums on Networking, Security, Computing and Cutting Edge Technologies ▪ Access to blogs written by Industry Experts ▪ Current information on Cutting Edge Technologies ▪ Access to various industry resource links and articles related to IT and IT careers

Content Seal of Quality

This courseware bears the seal of **CompTIA Approved Quality Content.** This seal signifies this content covers 100% of the exam objectives and implements important instructional design principles. CompTIA recommends multiple learning tools to help increase coverage of the learning objectives.

Why CompTIA?

- **Global Recognition**—CompTIA is recognized globally as the leading IT non-profit trade association and has enormous credibility. Plus, CompTIA's certifications are vendor-neutral and offer proof of foundational knowledge that translates across technologies.

- **Valued by Hiring Managers**—Hiring managers value CompTIA certification because it is vendor and technology independent validation of your technical skills.

- **Recommended or Required by Government and Businesses**—Many government organizations and corporations either recommend or require technical staff to be CompTIA certified. (e.g. Dell, Sharp, Ricoh, the US Department of Defense and many more)

- **Three CompTIA Certifications ranked in the top 10.** In a study by DICE of 17,000 technology professionals, certifications helped command higher salaries at all experience levels.

How to obtain more information

- **Visit CompTIA online**—www.comptia.org to learn more about getting CompTIA certified.
- **Contact CompTIA**—call 866-835-8020 ext. 5 or email questions@comptia.org
- **Join the IT Pro Community**—http://itpro.comptia.org to join the IT community to get relevant career information.
- **Connect with us:**

Introduction

Are you considering the benefits of a CompTIA Strata certificate for your career—or even just for your own benefit? Thousands of people today already have become Strata certified, demonstrating that they have the skills and knowledge required to install, use, and maintain computer hardware and software. This book will help you prepare to succeed at the Strata exams.

What Is Strata Certification?

The official CompTIA description of Strata is "an entry-level certificate that ensures a knowledge of PC components, functionality, compatibility, and related technology topics."

The exam covers the explanation of technology of computer hardware basics, compatibility issues and common errors, software installation and functions, and security risks and prevention. The exam also assesses the candidate's knowledge of Green IT and preventative maintenance of computers.

Candidate job roles include network and system administrator, sales engineer, account manager, and business development manager. Strata is for individuals and students preparing to enter the IT workforce and professionals changing careers to IT or technology-related fields. This certificate can be a stepping-stone to higher certifications, such as CompTIA A+, CompTIA Network+, and CompTIA Security+.

CompTIA is a non-profit information technology trade association. CompTIA's certifications are designed by subject matter experts from across the IT industry. Each CompTIA certification is vendor-neutral, covers multiple technologies, and requires demonstration of skills and knowledge widely sought after in the IT industry.

Differences in UK and US Exams

In the United States, Strata consists of a single exam:

- FC0-U41 CompTIA Strata IT Fundamentals

In the United Kingdom, Strata certification consists of two exams:

- FC0-U21 CompTIA Strata Fundamentals of Technology (UK only)
- FC0-U11 CompTIA Strata Fundamentals of PC Functionality (UK only)

The exam objectives are very similar, with the US exam encompassing most of the objectives for the two UK exams combined. There are minor differences between the objective sets for the two countries, and we point these out in the book where applicable.

What's the Test Like?

The US/International version of the test (FCO-U41) has 70 questions, and you have 120 minutes to complete it. A passing score is 70%, and it's available in English, Spanish, Portuguese, Japanese, German, Greek, Arabic, and Korean. This exam may be taken in any country except the UK

The UK version consists of two exams of 35 questions each: FC0-U11 and FC0-U21, and you have 60 minutes to complete each exam. A passing score is 70%. The exams are available only in English and may be taken only in the UK

To find a testing center near you, see:

```
http://certification.comptia.org/Training/testingcenters.aspx
```

Special Features in This Book

Each chapter begins with a list of the objectives. (See the next section, "Exam Content," for a comprehensive look at all the objectives in one place.) Within the chapter, information is arranged in logical ways, rather than in a strict objective-by-objective manner, because it makes for easier learning.

After you learn about a particular technology or technique, you'll have the opportunity to practice that skill in a hands-on exercise. Exercises walk you step by step through a process, such as updating a device driver or installing a drive. Most of the exercises assume that you're using Windows 7; Windows is the most popular operating system, and version 7 is the latest version at the time of this writing. In many cases, an earlier version of Windows will have similar steps. Where applicable, Mac and Linux procedures are also outlined. For example, when learning about issuing commands at a text-based command prompt, we've included the command equivalents for Windows, Mac, and Linux.

Each chapter also includes notes, with the extra information that you may need. For example, a note may tell you about a special limitation of a particular operating system or an extra command you can use as a shortcut to the main procedure.

At the end of each chapter is a quick summary section that reviews what you learned. There's also an "Exam Essentials" section that points out the important exam objectives for which you should be prepared by reading this chapter.

The final element of each chapter is a set of 20 review questions that test your understanding of the chapter material. Answers are provided after each question set, so you can quickly check your work.

Exam Content

Here are the objectives you'll be responsible for meeting on the Strata exam. In the following table, we've listed the US/International exam objectives on the left and matched up the equivalent objectives from the UK exams on the right, with the exam number for each section on the UK side.

FCO-U41 Strata IT Fundamentals	UK Exam Equivalents	Chapter
1.0 Technology and Computer Hardware Basics	1.0 Technology (FCO-U11)	
1.1 Identify basic IT vocabulary.	1.1 Identify basic IT vocabulary.	1
▪ Processor speed/cores	▪ Processor speed/cores	1
Single/Dual/Quad core	Single/Dual/Quad core	1
Intel based / Cell based / AMD based	Intel based/Cell based / AMD based	1
GHz vs. MHz	GHz vs. MHz	1
Processor cache size	Processor cache size	1
Bus speed (as it relates to motherboards, memory, and so on)	Bus speed (as it relates to motherboards, memory, and so on)	1
▪ RAM	▪ RAM	1
DDR, DDR2, DDR3	Single data rate, dual data rate, triple data rate	1
DIMMS vs. SODIMMS	DIMMS vs. SODIMMS	1
▪ Hard drives	▪ Hard drives	2
RPMs	RPMs	2
Cache size	Cache size	2
Flash based vs. traditional hard drives	Flash based vs. traditional hard drives	2
SATA, SCSI, IDE	SATA, SCSI, IDE	2
Internal vs. external	Internal vs. external	2
Local vs. network shares	Local vs. network shares	2
▪ Networking	▪ Networking	3
Wireless networking terms	Wireless networking terms	3
802.11a/b/g/n	802.11a/b/g/n	3
Bluetooth	Bluetooth	3
RF (Radio Frequency)	RF (Radio Frequency)	3
Interference	Interference	3
WAP (Wireless Access Point)	WAP (Wireless Access Point)	3
SSID	SSID	3
Wireless router	Wireless router	3

(continued)

FCO-U41 Strata IT Fundamentals	UK Exam Equivalents	Chapter
Ethernet technologies	Ethernet technologies	3
CAT5 connections and cables	CAT5, CAT5e connections and cables	3
Home plug (Ethernet over Power)	Home plug (Ethernet over Power)	3
Broadband router	Broadband router	3
DSL and cable modems	DSL and cable modems	3
Standard vs. crossover cables	Standard vs. crossover cables	3
Auto-negotiating (speed and duplex)	Auto-negotiating (speed and duplex)	3
Internet	Internet	3
Protocols	Protocols	3
▪ HTTP vs. HTTPS	▪ HTTP vs. HTTPS	3
▪ FTP	▪ FTP	3
▪ SSL	▪ SSL	3
▪ POP3	▪ POP3	3
▪ SMTP	▪ SMTP	3
▪ IMAP	▪ IMAP	3
▪ DNS	▪ DNS	3
▪ DHCP	▪ DHCP	3
▪ TCP/IP (IPv4 address, IPv6 address)	▪ TCP/IP (IPv4 address, IPv6 address)	3
Browser features	Browser features	3
▪ Plug-ins	▪ Plug-ins	3
▪ Customization (text sizes, text styles, and so on)	▪ Customization (text sizes, text styles, and so on)	3
▪ Anti-phishing features	▪ Anti-phishing features	3
▪ ActiveX and Java	▪ ActiveX and Java	3
▪ Cookies	▪ Cookies	3
▪ Internet Cache	▪ Internet Cache	3

FCO-U41 Strata IT Fundamentals	UK Exam Equivalents	Chapter
1.2 Demonstrate the proper use of the following devices:	1.1 Demonstrate the proper use of the following devices: (FTO-U21)	3, 4
▪ Monitors	▪ Monitors	3
Adjust monitor settings (brightness, contrast, and so forth)	Adjust monitor settings (brightness, contrast, and so forth)	3
▪ Desktop	▪ Desktop	4
▪ Server	▪ Server	4
▪ Portable	▪ Portable	4
Laptop	Laptop	4
PDA	PDA	4
Smartphone	Smartphone	4
Netbook	Netbook	4
1.3 Explain the characteristics and functions of internal and external storage devices	1.2 Explain the characteristics and functions of internal and external storage devices (FTO-U21)	2
▪ CD/CD-RW Drive	▪ CD/CD-RW Drive	2
▪ DVD/DVD-RW Drive	▪ DVD/DVD-RW Drive	2
▪ Blu-Ray Disk Drive	▪ Blu-Ray Disk Drive	2
▪ USB storage (solid state vs. magnetic disk)	▪ USB storage (solid state vs. magnetic disk)	2
▪ Multi-card reader and writer	▪ Multi card reader and writer	2
▪ Hard drives	▪ Hard drives	2
▪ Mobile media devices (for example, MP3 player or PDAs)	▪ Mobile media devices (for example, MP3 player or PDAs)	2
1.4 Explain the characteristics and functions of peripheral devices	1.3 Explain the characteristics and functions of peripheral devices (FTO-U21)	3
▪ Digital camera	▪ Digital camera	3

(continued)

FCO-U41 Strata IT Fundamentals	UK Exam Equivalents	Chapter
▪ Web camera	▪ Web camera	3
▪ Speaker	▪ Speaker	3
▪ Tuner	▪ Tuner	3
▪ Microphone	▪ Microphone	3
▪ Printer / scanner	▪ Printer / scanner	3
1.5 Explain the characteristics and functions of core input devices	1.4 Explain the characteristics and functions of core input devices (FTO-U21)	
▪ Keyboard	▪ Keyboard	2
▪ Mouse	▪ Mouse	2
▪ Tablet (touch screen)	▪ Tablet (touch screen)	2
▪ Numeric keypad	▪ Numeric keypad	2
▪ Gamepad	▪ Gamepad	2
Data loss	Data loss	
▪ PC Speed/storage capability	▪ PC Speed/storage capability	2
Compatibility issues	Compatibility issues	2
Upgrade issues	Upgrade issues	2
Bus differences	Bus differences	2
Hardware failure	Hardware failure	2
▪ Application	▪ Application	
Minimum requirements	Minimum requirements	6
Compatibility issues	Compatibility issues	6
▪ Bandwidth and contention	▪ Bandwidth and contention	6

FCO-U41 Strata IT Fundamentals	UK Exam Equivalents	Chapter
VoIP	VoIP	6
Streaming	Streaming	6
Web delivered services	Web delivered services	6
▪ Automatic application and operating system updates	▪ Automatic application and operating system updates	6
Risks of automatic updates	Risks of automatic updates	6
Risks of not using automatic updates	Risks of not using automatic updates	6
Risks of not using manufacturer websites	Risks of not using manufacturer websites	6
1.6 Identify the risks associated with upgrading the following technologies and equipment	1.2 Identify the risks associated with upgrading the following technologies and equipment (FCO-U11)	6, 7
▪ Operating systems (open source and commercial)	▪ Operating systems (open source and commercial)	6
Compatibility issues	Compatibility issues	6
Upgrade issues	Upgrade issues	6
Data loss	Data loss	6
▪ PC speed/storage capability	▪ PC speed/storage capability	7
Compatibility issues	Compatibility issues	7
Upgrade issues	Upgrade issues	7
Bus differences	Bus differences	7
Hardware failure	Hardware failure	7
▪ Application	▪ Application	6
Minimum requirements	Minimum requirements	6
Compatibility issues	Compatibility issues	6
▪ Bandwidth and contention	▪ Bandwidth and contention	
VoIP	VoIP	
Streaming	Streaming	
Web delivered services	Web delivered services	

(continued)

FCO-U41 Strata IT Fundamentals	UK Exam Equivalents	Chapter
▪ Automatic application and operating system updates	▪ Automatic application and operating system updates	6
Risks of automatic updates	Risks of automatic updates	6
Risks of not using automatic updates	Risks of not using automatic updates	6
Risks of not using manufacturer Websites	Risks of not using manufacturer Websites	6
1.7 Demonstrate the ability to set up a basic PC workstation	1.3 Demonstrate the ability to set up a basic PC workstation (FCO-U11)	2, 3, 4
▪ Identify differences between connector types	▪ Identify differences between connector types	2, 3, 4
DVI, VGA, HDMI	DVI, VGA, HDMI	3
USB, PS/2	USB, PS/2	2
FireWire	FireWire	3
Bluetooth and Wireless	Bluetooth and Wireless	3
Serial	Serial	3
Network connectors	Network connectors	3
PCMCIA	PCMCIA	4
ExpressCard	ExpressCard	4
3.5mm audio jack	3.5mm audio jack	3
Power connectors	Power connectors	4
▪ Monitor types	▪ Monitor types	3
▪ Computer (desktop, tower, laptop, custom cases)	▪ Computer (desktop, tower, laptop, custom cases)	4
▪ Keyboard (keyboard layout: regionalization)	▪ Keyboard (keyboard layout: regionalization)	2
▪ Mouse (touchpad, optical, trackball)	▪ Mouse (touchpad, optical, trackball)	2
▪ Printer (USB, wireless, networked)	▪ Printer (USB, wireless, networked)	3, 4
▪ Voltage and power requirements	▪ Voltage and power requirements	4
▪ Turn on and use the PC and peripherals	▪ Turn on and use the PC and peripherals	4

FCO-U41 Strata IT Fundamentals	UK Exam Equivalents	Chapter
2.0 Compatibility Issues and Common Errors	2.0 Compatibility Issues and Common Errors (FTO-U21)	
2.1 Identify basic compatibility issues between:	2.1 Identify basic compatibility issues between: (FTO-U21)	3, 7
▪ Processor performance	▪ Processor performance	7
▪ RAM memory	▪ RAM memory	7
▪ USB (1.1, 2.0)	▪ USB (1.1, 2.0)	7
▪ FireWire	▪ FireWire	7
▪ PS/2	▪ PS/2	7
▪ Ethernet	▪ Ethernet	3
▪ Wireless networks	▪ Wireless networks	3
2.2 Recognize common operational problems caused by hardware	2.2 Recognize common operational problems caused by hardware (FTO-U21)	8
▪ Critical error message or crash	▪ Critical error message or crash	8
▪ System lockup (freeze)	▪ System lockup (freeze)	8
▪ Application will not start or load	▪ Application will not start or load	8
▪ Cannot logon to network	▪ Cannot logon to network	8
▪ Driver / hardware compatibility	▪ Driver / hardware compatibility	8
▪ Input device will not function	▪ Input device will not function	8
2.3 Demonstrate the ability to minimize risks	2.3 Demonstrate the ability to minimize risks (FTO-U21)	5
▪ Data loss	▪ Data loss	5
▪ Loss of service	▪ Loss of service	5
▪ Damage to equipment	▪ Damage to equipment	5

(continued)

FCO-U41 Strata IT Fundamentals	UK Exam Equivalents	Chapter
3.0 Software Installation and Functions	2.0 Software Installation and Functions (FCO-U11)	
3.1 Conduct basic software installation, removal and/or upgrading.	2.1 Conduct basic software installation, removal and/or upgrading. (FCO-U11)	6, 10
▪ Follow basic installation/upgrade procedures	▪ Follow basic installation/upgrade procedures	6
Check PC meets minimum requirements	Check PC meets minimum requirements	6
Administrative Rights	Administrative Rights	6
Firewall access (unblocking ports for proper functionality)	Firewall access (unblocking ports for proper functionality)	6
▪ Configure the Operating System	▪ Configure the OS	6
Adjust basic settings (for example, volume, date, time, time zone)	Adjust basic settings (for example, volume, date, time, time zone)	6
User accounts	User accounts	6
Power settings (power save, sleep mode, and so on)	Power settings (power save, sleep mode, and so on)	10
Screen resolutions	Screen resolutions	6
▪ Documentation	▪ Documentation	6
Licensing (Commercial, Freeware, Shareware)	Licensing (Commercial, Freeware, Shareware)	6
Software registration	Software registration	6
▪ Digital Rights Management	▪ Digital Rights Management	6
▪ Software removal (clean un-installation)	▪ Software removal (clean un-installation)	6
▪ Re-installation (clean installation)	▪ Re-installation (clean installation)	6
3.2 Identify issues related to folder and file management	2.2 Identify issues related to folder and file management (FCO-U21)	5
▪ Create, delete, rename and move folders	▪ Create, delete, rename and move folders	5
Assign folder structure during installation	Assign folder structure during installation	5

FCO-U41 Strata IT Fundamentals	UK Exam Equivalents	Chapter
• Create, delete, rename, move and print files	• Create, delete, rename, move and print files	5
• Importance of following back-up guidelines and procedures	• Importance of following back-up guidelines and procedures	5
3.3 Explain the function and purpose of software tools	2.3 Explain the function and purpose of software tools (FCO-U21)	5
• Performance and error correction tools	• Performance and error correction tools	5
• Activity or event logging	• Activity or event logging	5
• Back-up tools	• Back-up tools	5
• Disk cleanup tools	• Disk cleanup tools	5
• File compression tools	• File compression tools	5
4.0 Security	3.0 Security (FCO-U11)	
4.1 Recognize basic security risks and procedures to prevent them.	3.1 Recognize basic security risks and procedures to prevent them. (FCO-U11)	9
• Identify Risks	• Identify Risks	9
Social Engineering	Social Engineering	9
Viruses	Viruses	9
Worms	Worms	9
Trojan Horses	Trojan Horses	9
Unauthorized Access	Unauthorized Access	9
Hackers	Hackers	9
Phishing	Phishing	9
Spyware	Spyware	9
Adware	Adware	9
Malware	Malware	9
Identity Fraud	Identity Fraud	9
File and folder sharing	File and folder sharing	9
Web browser risks	Web browser risks	9

(continued)

FCO-U41 Strata IT Fundamentals	UK Exam Equivalents	Chapter
Operating System vulnerability	Operating System vulnerability	9
Service packs	Service packs	9
Security updates	Security updates	9
Theft	Theft	9
Open or free networks	Open or free networks	9
▪ Identify prevention methods	▪ Identify prevention methods	3, 9
User awareness/education	User awareness/education	9
Anti-virus software	Anti-virus software	9
Ensure proper security certificate are used (SSL)	Ensure proper security certificate is used (SSL)	9
Wireless encryption (WPA/WEP)	Wireless encryption (WPA/WEP)	3, 9
Anti-spyware	Anti-spyware	9
File encryption	File encryption	9
Firewalls	Firewalls	9
Anti-spam software	Anti-spam software	9
Password best practice	Password best practice	9
Complexity (password construction)	Complexity (password construction)	9
Password confidentiality	Password confidentiality	9
Change frequency	Change frequency	9
Re-use	Re-use	9
Utilization	Utilization	9
▪ Identify access control methods	▪ Identify access control methods	9
Passwords and User ID	Passwords and User ID	9
Screensavers	Screensavers	9
Physical security of hardware	Physical security of hardware	9
Locks	Locks	9
Parental controls	Parental controls	9
Smart card	Smart card	9
Fingerprint reader	Fingerprint reader	9
One time password	One time password	9

FCO-U41 Strata IT Fundamentals	UK Exam Equivalents	Chapter
▪ Identify security threats related to the following:	▪ Identify security threats related to the following:	9
Media used for backup (theft or loss)	Media used for backup (theft or loss)	9
Screen visibility (shoulder surfing)	Screen visibility (shoulder surfing)	9
Cookies (can be stolen, stores passwords, browser tracking)	Cookies (can be stolen, stores passwords, browser tracking)	9
Pop-ups (automatic installations, click on links to malware)	Pop-ups (automatic installations, click on links to malware)	9
Accidental misconfiguration	Accidental misconfiguration	9
4.2 Recognize security breaches and ways to resolve them.	3.2 Recognize security breaches and ways to resolve them. (FCO-U11)	9
▪ Recognize the proper diagnostic procedures when infected with a virus	▪ Recognize the proper diagnostic procedures when infected with a virus	9
Run anti-virus scan	Run anti-virus scan	9
Quarantine virus when possible	Quarantine virus when possible	9
Escalate to IT professional when needed	Escalate to IT professional when needed	9
▪ Recognize the proper procedures to maintain a secure environment	▪ Recognize the proper procedures to maintain a secure environment	9
Regular antivirus and malware scans	Regular antivirus and malware scans	9
Application / operating system updates	Application / operating system updates	9
	3.3 Recognize IT related laws and guidelines (FCO-U11)	9
	Data Protection Act	10
	Copyright Act	10
	Computer Misuse Act	10
	Freedom of Information Act	10
5.0 Green IT and Preventative Maintenance		
5.1 Identify environmentally sound techniques to preserve power and dispose of materials.		10

(continued)

FCO-U41 Strata IT Fundamentals	UK Exam Equivalents	Chapter
▪ Environmentally hazardous substance disposal		10
Battery disposal		10
CRT disposal-replace with LCDs		10
Recycling of computers for reuse or parts		10
Toner disposal		10
Cleaning supply disposal		10
Materials that meet RoHS guidelines		10
▪ Power management (Power saving features)		10
Shutdown/power off procedures/policies at end of day		10
Automatic power off after 15 minutes of non-use (not in UK)		10
Shutdown scripts		10
▪ Power management PCs and lower power servers replace large desktops with energy efficient laptops and thin clients		10
5.2 Identify green techniques, equipment and procedures.		1, 3, 10
▪ Define Cloud computing (not in UK version)		10
Define Virtualization (Have more than one server running on a single piece of hardware)		10
Reduced power and cooling consumption		10
▪ Define VoIP and how it relates to Green IT (not in UK version)		10
▪ Duplex printing and use lower cost per page network printers		10

FCO-U41 Strata IT Fundamentals	UK Exam Equivalents	Chapter
▪ Terminal Servers		10
▪ Energy Star rating		10
▪ Use low power NAS (network attached storage) instead of file servers		10
▪ Solid State drives		3
▪ Green building infrastructure		10
Eliminate cool air leaks in server rooms		10
Proper spacing for cooling IT equipment		10
Energy efficient cooling fans-BIOS adjustable (not in UK version)		1
▪ Employee telecommuting		10
Reduced emissions		10
Reduced office space heating, lighting, and so forth .		10
	3.0 Health, Safety and Preventative Maintenance (FTO-U21)	
	3.1 Recognize safety hazards and identify corresponding guidelines (FTO-U21)	5, 10
	▪ Hazards	5
	▪ Fire	5
	▪ Flood	5
	▪ Electrical surges	5
	▪ Extreme storms	5
	▪ Environmental hazards	5
	▪ Guidelines	5
	▪ Use of ESD equipment	5
	▪ Use of tools and equipment	5
	▪ Electricity and safety	5

(continued)

FCO-U41 Strata IT Fundamentals	UK Exam Equivalents	Chapter
	▪ Hazardous substances	5, 10
	▪ Wire placement and safety	5
	▪ Environmental legislation and regulations (e.g. disposal of materials)	5, 10
5.3 Identify preventative maintenance products, techniques, and how to use them.	3.2 Identify preventative maintenance products, procedures, and how to use them (FTO-U21)	5
▪ Liquid cleaning compounds	▪ Liquid cleaning compounds	5
▪ Types of materials to clean contacts and connections	▪ Types of materials to clean contacts and connections	5
▪ Compressed air	▪ Compressed air	5
▪ Cleaning monitors	▪ Cleaning monitors	5
▪ Cleaning removable media devices	▪ Cleaning removable media devices	5
▪ Ventilation, dust and moisture control on the PC hardware interior	▪ Ventilation, dust and moisture control on the PC hardware interior	5
▪ Surge suppressors	▪ Surge suppressors	5
▪ Use of ESD equipment		5
▪ Wire placement and safety		5
	▪ Replacing printer consumables	5

Assessment Test

1. What is the type of most RAM used in most notebook computers?
    - **A.** SODIMM
    - **B.** DIMM
    - **C.** RIMM
    - **D.** SIMM

2. 24FF is an example of what numbering system?
    - **A.** Decimal
    - **B.** Octal
    - **C.** Binary
    - **D.** Hexadecimal

3. What is the large circuit board inside a computer called?
    - **A.** Expansion board
    - **B.** Motherboard
    - **C.** Memory
    - **D.** CPU

4. A megabyte is approximately how many bytes?
    - **A.** 10
    - **B.** 1000
    - **C.** 10,000
    - **D.** 1,000,000

5. QWERTY is a layout for what PC input device?
    - **A.** Mouse
    - **B.** Scanner
    - **C.** Keyboard
    - **D.** Monitor

6. Which is the newer hard-disk technology: PATA or SATA?
    - **A.** PATA
    - **B.** SATA
    - **C.** Both are equally new

7. How much data can a single-sided, single-layer DVD hold?

   A. 700 MB

   B. 1.4 GB

   C. 4.7 GB

   D. 9.4 GB

8. How is printer resolution measured?

   A. ppm

   B. dpi

   C. cps

   D. bps

9. What kind of printer uses powdered toner and a spinning drum?

   A. laser

   B. inkjet

   C. dot matrix

   D. thermal wax

10. What does LCD stand for?

   A. Liquid Carrier Duplex

   B. Long Course Data

   C. Liquid Crystal Display

   D. Lengthwise Crystal Data

11. In what type of environment would a P2P network be appropriate?

   A. Large business with multiple locations

   B. Large business in a single location

   C. Home office

   D. Internet

12. What type of connector does Cat5e cable have on each end?

   A. RS-232

   B. RJ-11

   C. RJ-14

   D. RJ-45

13. Most printers and other external devices connect to the PC using what interface?

   A. Legacy serial

   B. VGA

   C. PATA

   D. USB

14. In the United States, if your power supply has a 120v/220v switch on it, in what position should it be set?

    A. 120v

    B. 220v

    C. Halfway between the two settings

    D. None; this power supply cannot be used in the United States

15. What two possible connectors could be used for a monitor?

    A. HDMI and PATA

    B. DVI or VGA

    C. VGA or USB

    D. FireWire or SATA

16. What is the more common name for ESD?

    A. static electricity

    B. magnetic interference

    C. crosstalk

    D. refresh rate

17. How do you open a command prompt in Windows Vista or Windows 7?

    A. Click Start, and then click Prompt.

    B. Click Start, type cmd, and press Enter.

    C. Right-click the desktop and click DOS.

    D. Right-click the desktop and click Open Command Prompt.

18. What Windows utility lists the currently running applications and processes and enables you to shut down any that have stopped responding?

    A. System Utility Manager

    B. System Editor

    C. Device Manager

    D. Task Manager

19. On Windows and Mac systems, you can create two types of user accounts: standard and _____.

    A. Guest

    B. Administrator

    C. Full

    D. System

20. What kind of software is free, and users are encouraged to modify its code to help improve it?

    A. Freeware

    B. Shareware

    C. Open source

    D. Commercial

21. True or false: activating and registering software are the same thing.

    A. True

    B. False

22. What type of file helps the operating system interface with a hardware device?

    A. Driver

    B. Executable

    C. Server

    D. Client

23. In Windows Vista and higher, the _____ provides a numeric score indicating your computer's performance level.

    A. Device Manager

    B. System Configuration Editor

    C. Windows Experience Index

    D. Help and Support Center

24. How many drives can a SATA cable support?

    A. 1

    B. 2

    C. 7

    D. 255

25. What do you have to do to recover when you get a STOP error (aka blue screen of death) in Windows?

    A. Restart the application that crashed

    B. Unplug the keyboard and mouse

    C. Turn the computer off and back on again

    D. Reformat the hard disk

26. If an older application won't run in your new version of Windows, you may be able to use _____ mode to get it to run.

   A. Accessibility

   B. Standard

   C. Legacy

   D. Compatibility

27. What command can you type at a command prompt to get information about the network devices and their IP addresses?

   A. PING

   B. TRACERT

   C. CMD

   D. IPCONFIG

28. What is a K-slot for on a notebook computer?

   A. Memory card

   B. USB device

   C. Lock

   D. External keyboard

29. Which of these is an example of a strong password?

   A. 58WRxry%41x2

   B. Password

   C. QWERTY

   D. 0987654321

30. A(n) _____ is a plain-text file that a web page stores on your hard disk for tracking purposes.

   A. pop-up

   B. phish

   C. cookie

   D. worm

31. A(n) _____ is an application that appears to do something useful but is actually malware that harms your system or compromises your privacy.

   A. Virus

   B. Trojan horse

   C. Worm

   D. Bot

32. In what low-power mode does the computer shut off power to all components except RAM?

    A. Hibernate

    B. Kill

    C. RAM mode

    D. Sleep

33. What is duplexing?

    A. Reusing a CD or DVD

    B. Recapturing used toner

    C. Printing on both sides of the paper

    D. Setting up a virtual server

34. What is VoIP?

    A. Creating a secure channel through the Internet for data communications

    B. Using the Internet for telephone service

    C. Telecommuting

    D. Setting up a virtual server

35. Why should you not throw away toner in the regular trash?

    A. It is valuable and can be sold

    B. It is flammable

    C. It is carcinogenic

    D. It explodes when it gets wet

Answers to Assessment Test

1. **A.** Desktop RAM is mostly DIMM, and notebook RAM is mostly SODIMM. The smaller size of SODIMM makes it more appropriate for use in smaller computing devices. See Chapter 1, "Processing and Memory."

2. **D.** Whereas humans use mostly decimal numbering (0 through 9), computers use a combination of binary numbering (0 and 1) and hexadecimal numbering (0 through 9 plus A through F). See Chapter 1.

3. **C.** The motherboard is the main circuit board in the PC to which everything else connects. It contains the CPU, memory, and connectors to all the drives. See Chapter 1.

4. **D.** A megabyte, abbreviated MB, is one million bytes. Megabyte is a common measurement of computer storage, and also of RAM capacity. One thousand megabytes (or one billion bytes) is a gigabyte. See Chapter 1.

5. **C.** The term *QWERTY* comes from the first six letters on the first row of the keyboard layout. See Chapter 2, "Input and Storage Devices."

6. **B.** Serial ATA (SATA) is a newer interface for attaching hard disks to PCs. It is faster and the cables are thinner than Parallel ATA (PATA), the older technology that used ribbon cables. See Chapter 2.

7. **C.** DVDs hold 4.7 GB per side. Double-layer DVDs hold almost twice that much per side: 8.54 GB. See Chapter 2.

8. **B.** Printer quality is measured in dots per inch, or dpi; the higher the dpi, the smaller and closer together the dots that make up the image. See Chapter 3, "Peripherals and Networking."

9. **A.** A laser printer works much like a photocopier. It writes an image on a drum with electrical charges, and powdered toner, attracted to those charges, clings to the drum and then is fused to a piece of paper. See Chapter 3..

10. **C.** In a Liquid Crystal Display monitor, there are two polarized filters, between which are liquid crystals. The crystals twist when electricity passes through them, letting light pass through. This lights up an area of the screen. See Chapter 3.

11. **C.** P2P stands for peer-to-peer. This network type has no server; the client PCs share the burden of maintaining the network. P2P works best for small networks of fewer than 10 computers. See Chapter 3.

12. **D.** Most Ethernet cable, including Cat5, Cat5e, and Cat6, uses an RJ-45connector on each end. This looks like a telephone connector but is slightly wider and has eight wires (four twisted pairs). See Chapter 3.

13. D. The USB interface is a general-purpose interface used for a wide variety of devices, including keyboard, mouse, printer, scanner, modem, and so on. See Chapter 4, "Setting Up a Computer."

14. A. In the United States, 120v power is used. In Europe, 220v or 230v power is used. See Chapter 4.

15. B. Digital Video Interface (DVI) is the more modern digital monitor connector. Video Graphics Array (VGA) is the older analog connector. See Chapter 4.

16. A. Electrostatic discharge, or ESD, is also called static electricity. It is a threat to computer components because the voltage of the static shock can harm them. See Chapter 5, "Maintaining a Computer."

17. B. A command-prompt interface enables you to issue certain commands that aren't available in the graphical interface. The CMD command opens it. See Chapter 5.

18. D. Task Manager enables you to shut down unresponsive applications. To display task Manager, right-click the taskbar and choose Start Task Manager. See Chapter 5.

19. B. Use a standard account for users who should not be able to make changes that affect other users. Use an administrator account for users who should have full control. See Chapter 6, "Installing and Configuring Software."

20. C. Open source software is free to all, and everyone may modify it to help improve it. Linux is an example of such software. See Chapter 6.

21. B. Registering a product is usually optional; it provides your contact information to the maker. Activating a product locks it to your computer so that it cannot be installed elsewhere. No personal information is sent, and the process is not optional. See Chapter 6.

22. A. Device drivers translate instructions between devices and the OS. You can update a device driver if a newer version becomes available. See Chapter 7, "Updating and Upgrading Hardware."

23. C. The Windows Experience Index ranks your computer in five areas with a numeric score. The overall base score is the lowest of those five scores. See Chapter 7.

24. A. Unlike a PATA cable, which can take two drives, each SATA cable connects to one drive only. See Chapter 7.

25. C. A STOP error freezes the computer; you have to reboot to recover from it. See Chapter 8, "Troubleshooting Operational Problems."

26. D. Compatibility Mode can be set up for individual applications to simulate an earlier version of Windows. See Chapter 8.

27. D. IPCONFIG tells you each network adapter's status and IP address. It is available only at a command prompt. See Chapter 8.

28. C. It is for attaching a lock to secure a notebook computer physically to a location, such as a desk. K is short for Kensington, the maker of the lock. See Chapter 9, "Security and Access Control."

29. A. Strong passwords are long, varied, and unusual, and not easily guessable. See Chapter 9.

30. C. Cookies help a website remember your previous preferences or status. They are usually harmless, but some people prefer to disable them for additional privacy. Some websites will not work correctly without them. See Chapter 9.

31. B. Trojan horse applications may tell you that they are scanning for errors or improving your system, when they may actually be logging your keystrokes or spying on your browsing habits. See Chapter 9.

32. D. Sleep keeps RAM powered, so the computer uses very little power. Hibernate keeps nothing powered at all, so the computer uses no power. See Chapter 10, "Safe, Legal, and Green Computer Usage."

33. C. You can cut printing supply costs, and also help the environment, by using both sides of the paper in your printer. See Chapter 10.

34. B. VoIP can help decrease building costs by minimizing the wiring required for each office because it doesn't need a separate phone line and Internet line. See Chapter 10.

35. C. Toner not only is messy, but can also pose a health hazard. See Chapter 10.

CompTIA
Strata
Study Guide

Understanding Computer Hardware

Chapter

1

Processing and Memory

COMPTIA FUNDAMENTALS OF TECHNOLOGY (UK)
IT FUNDAMENTALS (USA)

OBJECTIVES COVERED IN THIS CHAPTER:

✓ **1.1 Identify basic IT vocabulary**

- Processor speed/cores

- RAM

Every computer, whether it's a high-speed supercomputer at a research facility or a hand-held game for children, has a processor—the component that performs math calculations. Every computer also has some type of random access memory (RAM), which is used for temporary data storage as data moves into and out of the processor.

In this chapter, you'll review the basics of processors and RAM. Having this information will help you evaluate these components in the computers you buy, use, and maintain.

Processors

Every computing device has a *central processing unit (CPU)*, more commonly known as a processor (or microprocessor). Processors are a part of mobile phones, gaming consoles, digital music players, and everything from automobiles to washing machines. Some computers even have multiple processors that share the computing load for faster performance.

Processors are integrated circuits containing millions of electronic components called transistors. *Transistors* are an important component in any electronic device, including a computer. Transistors are electrical gates that let power through or don't depending on their current state. They're the basis of binary processing—that is, processing based on things being in one of two states: on or off, 1 or 0.

At its most basic level, a processor's job is to do math. It accepts numbers as input, performs calculations on them, and delivers other numbers as output. It's mostly oblivious to the significance of those numbers; it just runs the instructions it has been given. It's a common misconception that the processor is the brain of the computer—it's not nearly as sophisticated as a human brain. It just does what it's told, like a hand-held calculator, but at incredibly high speed. The brains of the operation would more accurately be the *operating system (OS)*, which feeds the numbers to the processor and uses the results.

Different processors have different *instruction sets*—that is, different math calculations they can perform. The advanced processors in *personal computers (PCs)* have very large and complex instruction sets; the simple processors in items like appliances have fewer instruction sets. The OS must be written with the processor's instruction set in mind so it can send the right codes to activate the desired instructions.

Processors also vary in the number of bits they can accept and process as input. A *bit* is a binary digit, either 0 or 1. The more bits a processor can accept simultaneously, the faster it can work through the backlog of data to be processed. The earliest PCs had 8-bit or 16-bit processors; today, PCs have 32-bit or 64-bit processors. The higher the number of bits, the larger the word size the processor can accept. *Word size* refers to the amount of data that can simultaneously enter the processor in one operation.

RISC

Reduced instruction set computing (RISC) is based on the principle that having a simple instruction set for a processor improves performance. The logic is that the more you can ask of a complex processor, the slower it becomes. Thus a processor that is capable of a smaller set of tasks can complete them more quickly. The Advanced RISC Machine (ARM) is a popular processor found in many mobile computing devices, including cell phones and hand-held game machines. In contrast, most personal computer processors are considered complex instruction set computing (CISC), having a comparatively large instruction set for greater flexibility.

Processors work only with *binary* digits, so the OS translates all numbers to the binary numbering system in order to send them for processing. Humans most commonly use the *decimal* numbering system (digits 0 through 9). Computers typically use *hexadecimal* numbering (16 digits, 0 through 9 plus A through F) or *binary* numbering (2 digits, 0 and 1). Binary is used when interacting with the processor, and hexadecimal is used when the OS refers to memory addresses. Exercise 1.1 demonstrates how to convert between binary and other numbering systems.

EXERCISE 1.1

Convert Between Binary and Other Numbering Systems

1. In Windows 7, open the Calculator application.

2. Choose View ➤ Programmer to switch to Programmer view, as shown here. Notice that the Dec radio button is selected, indicating decimal numbering.

EXERCISE 1.1 *(continued)*

3. Enter the number **335**.

4. Click the Bin radio button. The number is converted to binary (101001111). Notice that all the number keys are disabled except 1 and 0.

5. Click the Hex radio button. The number is converted to hexadecimal (14F). Notice that all the number keys are active again, as are the A through F keys.

6. Click the Dec radio button again to return to decimal numbering.

7. Experiment on your own with more numbers. Close the Calculator app when you're finished.

Processor Brands

A variety of manufacturers produce processors that serve inside appliances and other non-computer devices. However, for personal computer processors, market competition has virtually eliminated all but two manufacturers, Intel and AMD.

Apple Macintosh computers used Motorola processors for many years but switched to Intel processors in mid-2006.

Intel Processors

Intel is the most popular brand of processors for personal computers. Since the company's founding in 1968, it has manufactured more than 50 different processors, plus graphics cards, motherboards, and various computer peripheral devices.

The original IBM PC and PC-XT computers ran on Intel processors (the 8088 and 8086, respectively). Later IBM models also used Intel processors, such as the PS/2 that used the 16-bit 80286 processor. In 1993, Intel released the original Pentium processor, the first commercially viable 32-bit CPU. It was followed by the Pentium 2 in 1997, the Pentium 3 in 1999, and the Pentium 4 in 2000.

Intel's current offerings include a 64-bit line called Intel Core, which includes the Core i3, Core i5, and Core i7. The Core i3 is an entry-level CPU, the Core i5 is midrange, and the Core i7 is a high-end product. As you might expect from the word *core* in the name, each of these is a multicore processor (containing from two to six cores, depending on the model, each of which functions as a processor in its own right).

Within Intel's Core lineup are many different versions of the i3, i5, and i7, for both desktop and laptop use, each with a different codename and combination of number of cores, L3 cache size, and socket type. For example, the brand name Core i3-5xx (where each x represents a digit), codenamed Clarkdale, has two cores and a 4 MB L3 cache and fits in an LGA 1156 socket. Some of the other codenames include Arrandale, Lynnfield, Gulftown and, the most recent of these, Sandy Bridge.

AMD Processors

Advanced Micro Devices (AMD) has been the strongest competitor to Intel in the PC processor market since the 1990s. AMD processors have historically been less expensive than Intel's, while offering roughly equivalent performance. Because AMD processors use a different instruction set than Intel's, they require motherboards specially designed for them. The *motherboard* is the large circuit board inside a PC to which everything else connects.

AMD's early CPU offerings included the K5, K6, K7, K8, and K9 processors, each of which competed directly with an Intel processor. AMD's current lineup includes the Phenom II, Athlon II, and Turion II lines.

Processor Sockets

Processors require the correct type of socket in the motherboard in which you're installing them. When buying a motherboard, make sure the processor socket is appropriate for the CPU you plan to use.

Sockets use various code names and numbering. The numbering is often based on the number of pins, or contacts, on the chip. For example, the LGA 1356 contains 1,356 pins.

In earlier times, a pin grid array (PGA) was the preferred style of processor socket. It consisted of a grid of tiny holes into which the tiny pins on the back of a CPU chip were secured. Figure 1.1 shows a PGA socket in a motherboard circa 2005.

FIGURE 1.1   Pin grid array (PGA) was a common type of processor socket until a few years ago.

Photo credit: Wikipedia® is a registered trademark of the Wikimedia Foundation, Inc., a non-profit organization. User:Berkut

However, in recent years, this design has been replaced by land grid array (LGA), a style that has no pins on the chip. Figure 1.2 shows an example of an LGA socket. In place of the pins are tiny pads of bare gold-plated copper that touch corresponding pins on the socket. The main advantage of LGA is size; the pads can be much smaller than a socketed pin, so the CPU can contain more connection lines to the motherboard without the size of the CPU socket becoming very large.

FIGURE 1.2   Most CPUs today use an LGA socket.

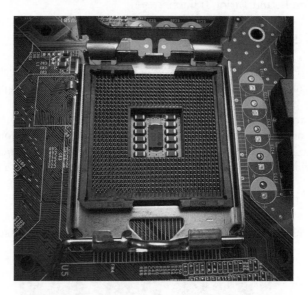

Photo credit: User Smial on de.wikipedia.

For mobile computers, where the processors and motherboards are very small, a different type of socket is used. It's either a very small PGA socket (such as the µPGA-989) or a ball grid array (BGA) socket, which is an updated type of PGA in which pins are replaced by balls of solder.

Processor Speed and Performance

Just as an automobile has unique performance features that single it out from the crowd, computer processors have specialized performance features that distinguish each model. In this section, you'll learn about some of the ways that processor performance is measured and enhanced.

We measure the speed of a processor in hertz (Hz), or cycles per second. Each time the internal clock of the processor completes a full cycle, a single Hz has passed. Modern processors operate at millions (*megahertz, MHz*) or billions (*gigahertz, GHz*) of cycles per second. The original IBM PC, released in 1981, operated at 4.77 MHz. Processor speeds have exponentially increased because then because of new technology advances, with some of the fastest processors today running at more than 3 GHz.

In Table 1.1, you can see a relative comparison of some single-processor clock speeds. Notice that the dates end at 2008. That's not a misprint; it's just that dual-core and quad-core processors have replaced single-processor models in recent years. You'll learn about those processors later in this chapter.

TABLE 1.1   Comparison of single-processor clock speeds

Speed	In Plain Numbers	Example Processor	Year Available (Estimate)
50 MHz	50,000,000	Intel 486	1993–1995
500 MHz	500,000,000	Intel Pentium 3	1999–2001
1.5 GHz	1,500,000,000	Intel Pentium 4	2000–2003
3 GHz	3,000,000,000	Intel Pentium 4	2005–2008

Don't confuse the number of cycles per second with *instructions per second (IPS)*, the number of instructions that a processor can complete per second. Many instructions carried out by processors take multiple internal clock cycles to execute. Many current systems compute in *millions of instructions per second (MIPS)*.

A processor's speed is related to its number of instructions per second, but other factors besides its speed can affect the number of instructions it can process per second. For example, a multicore CPU can process more instructions than a single-core, and other technology enhancements such as hyperthreading and efficient cache usage further enhance a processor's capability. As a point of reference, the Intel Core i7 Extreme Edition (quad core) runs at 3.3 GHz and processes 147,600 MIPS.

Another major contributor to the performance of any processor is the quality and speed of the motherboard that supports the processor. The motherboard's *system bus* (also called the *front-side bus*) is the pathway that delivers data to the processor. The speed at which this pathway operates is determined by the motherboard's front-side bus speed. The *system timer* on the motherboard determines this speed. Most motherboards can automatically adjust the speed of the timer based on the installed processor; on older models, it was necessary to set jumpers on the motherboard manually to indicate what processor type and speed was installed.

The word *bus* as it's used in computers comes from Latin; the original word was a shorthand version of *omnibus* or to "transport all." Here a bus can literally transport all data.

Processor Cache

Sometimes the processor sits idle through one or more cycles because the motherboard hasn't delivered any data to it to be processed. That happens for a variety of reasons. One of them is that some data has to travel all the way from the memory to the processor and, even though the motherboard's front-side bus is fast, it's not fast enough to keep up with the processor in delivering that data. Although system memory is probably less than 50 millimeters away from the processor, this could be 1,000 miles in terms of processor performance.

Therefore, to increase the instructions processed per second, computer manufacturers have looked for ways to keep frequently used data closer at hand to the processor, so it has to travel a shorter distance when it's called. That's the purpose of a cache. A *cache* is a temporary storage area located very near the processor and connected to it by an extremely high-speed pathway. It holds recently used data so the data doesn't have to be re-retrieved from RAM every time.

Modern processors include multiple cache levels. The Level 1 (L1) cache is the smallest, and it's on the processor die itself. In other words, it's an integrated part of the manufacturing pattern that's used to stamp the processor pathways into the silicon chip. You can't get any closer to the processor than that. The Level 2 (L2) cache is larger and almost as close—it's in the processor chip, but it's not usually part of the die (see Figure 1.3). Some processors also use a Level 3 (L3) cache. When the processor needs some data, it first checks the L1 cache and retrieves the data from there if possible. If not, the processor checks the L2 cache and then the L3 cache. If the data is none of those places, the processor retrieves it from RAM.

FIGURE 1.3   The L1 cache is on-die; the L2 cache is on-chip.

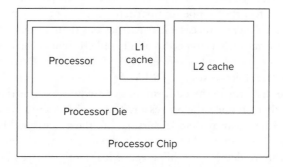

The original Pentium processor had 16 KB of L1 cache. (The L2 cache was on the motherboard, so the amount varied depending on the board.) In contrast, today's Intel Core i7 processors can have up to 12MB of cache. (A *megabyte*, abbreviated *MB*, is approximately one million *byte*s, or eight bits. A *bit* is a binary digit, either 0 or 1. You'll learn more about these measurements later in the chapter.) When processor manufacturers list cache sizes in their marketing materials, they typically list only the largest cache (that is, the highest numbered one). On multicore systems, the largest cache is shared among all the cores.

Multicore Processors

To keep making better and faster processors every year, manufacturers constantly have to find ways to increase the number of instructions per second. One way they have done this is to increase the complexity of the processor design. Another is to house multiple processors together and have them work in unison.

For many years, motherboards have been available that hold multiple, separate processors, each with its own slot on the motherboard. This technology is limited, though, because of the distance between the processors and the speed limitations on the bus pathways between them. As mentioned earlier, manufacturers found a solution to this by creating multicore processors that combine several processors into a single package. These processors look like one chip from the outside but actually have several separate processor cores inside.

Cell Microprocessors

Cell microprocessors are a hybrid between multiple-core processors and specialized systems (such as high-end graphics cards), created by a partnership between Sony, Toshiba, and IBM. The result is a system that is better equipped for simulation, imaging, and gaming solutions. Sony uses a cell microprocessor for its PlayStation 3 gaming system, with eight cells (or processors) running the console. The Xbox 360 differs in that it uses a three-core technology, the Xenon.

Motherboards are still available that hold more than one processor, especially boards designed for servers. By combining multiple multicore processors in a system, you can increase the processing power many times over. For example, if you have a single-core processor running at 3 GHz, a quad-core processor could elicit the combined potential of 12 GHz, and a board with four quad cores could theoretically have a processing potential equivalent of 48 GHz. Be advised, however, that in the transaction of commands between multiple processors, there is an inevitable loss in performance.

EXERCISE 1.2

Comparing Processors

Intel and AMD list their processors and specifications, including the cache size of each of their products. Visit http://ark.intel.com/Default.aspx and http://products.amd.com/en-us/DesktopCPUResult.aspx to identify current processors, their speeds (in GHz), cache sizes, and the numbers of cores and clock speeds per core.

Cooling Fans and Heat Sinks

With millions of transistors working in close proximity, processors generate heat. This is a result of one of the simpler laws of physics involving electrical energy. Heat is caused as the transistor restricts the flow of electrical current. The energy has to go somewhere, so it's released as heat. Heat generation is highest when a processor is busy, such as when it's drawing a complex graphic or juggling many applications at once.

Without external cooling, a processor would overheat and shut down almost immediately after the system started up. Therefore, all modern computers have some type of heat-displacement system. A cooling system can be either passive or active. A *passive cooling system* contains no moving parts; an *active cooling system* does something active to circulate either water or air to displace the heat.

The most common type of passive cooling system is a heat sink. A *heat sink* is a block of heat-conductive metal that touches the processor and draws the heat away from it. Some small, less powerful processors, such as the one in a cell phone or hand-held gaming device, can stay cool enough to function with only a passive heat sink. Figure 1.4 shows a passive heat sink that might be used to cool one of the nonprocessor chips on a motherboard, such as the main chip in the chipset that controls motherboard operations.

FIGURE 1.4   A passive heat sink

In today's PCs, passive cooling usually isn't enough for the processor to stay cool; a heat sink is combined with a fan that blows across it, further helping to dissipate the heat as it's drawn off. Figure 1.5 shows an example of an active heat sink.

FIGURE 1.5   An active heat sink

Photo credit: http://en.wikipedia.org/wiki/GNU_Free_Documentation_License Fir0002/Flagstaffotos

Active cooling systems require power to operate, increasing the amount of power required by the PC. Some computers have energy-efficient cooling fans that can be adjusted in the BIOS setup to operate only if the processor's temperature (as evaluated by an internal thermometer) is over a certain value.

NOTE   BIOS stands for Basic Input/Output System. It's software on a chip on the motherboard that controls the boot process and low-level hardware access. It has its own setup program, which you can access by pressing a specific key as the computer is booting. Watch onscreen as the computer boots for information about which key to press. Because it's stored on a read-only memory (ROM) chip, it's sometimes referred to as the ROM-BIOS. You'll learn about ROM later in this chapter.

Water can also be used as a coolant, instead of air from a fan. In a water-cooled system, a pump circulates water through tubing that runs between the components that generate heat. The tubing passes through passive heat sinks affixed to the chips (usually with a heat-conductive adhesive compound), carrying the heat away from the chips. The chips involved can include not only the main processor on the motherboard, but also the main processing chip on the graphics card and perhaps some of the other larger chips on the motherboard too. Water cooling is effective, and it allows systems that otherwise might run too hot to operate. However, water cooling can be expensive to set up, and a leak in the water cooling subsystem can ruin other components.

Can I Upgrade My Processor?

The relationship between the processor and the motherboard is very close, because they must work together seamlessly. Not only must the processor be physically compatible with the motherboard's processor socket, but the motherboard must also be aware of the processor's instruction set and the speed at which it can accept data. As a result, most motherboards support only a few processors, so upgrading to a significantly better processor without replacing the motherboard usually isn't possible.

Memory

Memory, generically speaking, is data storage that uses on/off states on a chip to record patterns of binary data (that is, data that consists of only 1s and 0s). Inside a memory chip is a grid of on/off switches. An on value represents 1, and an off value represents 0.

Memory can be either static or dynamic. *Static memory* (a.k.a. *nonvolatile memory*) doesn't require refreshing to maintain its contents. *Dynamic memory* (aka *volatile memory*) has to be constantly powered on to retain its contents.

Broadly speaking, all memory can be divided into one of two types: ROM and RAM. *Read-only memory (ROM)* chips store data *very* permanently; you can't make changes to their content at all. (It takes a special ROM-writing machine to write one.) This type of memory is always static. The basic startup instructions (BIOS) stored on your motherboard are typically stored on a ROM chip. So is the programming on simple electronic devices that will never need to be user-updated, like the computer on an exercise treadmill that stores various fitness programs. The main advantage of ROM is its reliability. It can never be accidentally changed or deleted. The disadvantages of ROM are that it's slow compared to RAM, and that you can't ever update it; you have to pull the chip out of the system and replace it. Because of these drawbacks, ROM isn't used as a PC's primary memory source; a PC has only a small amount of ROM.

Random access memory (RAM) can be written and rewritten on the device in which it's installed. It's called *random access* because the data is stored in whatever locations are available in it, and reading data back from it doesn't require that the data be in a certain storage location.

RAM can be either static or dynamic. *Static RAM (SRAM)*, also called flash RAM, is the type you use when you store files on a USB flash drive. Static RAM is nonvolatile; you can disconnect a flash RAM device and carry it with you, and the next time you connect it to a computer, the data will still be there. Most of the memory on a PC's motherboard is *dynamic RAM (DRAM)*, so when someone refers to a computer's memory or RAM, you can generally assume that they mean the DRAM on the motherboard. Dynamic RAM is volatile; when you turn off your computer, its content is gone.

The motherboard's RAM functions as a work area when the computer is on. The OS is loaded into it, as are any applications you have open and any data associated with those applications. The more free RAM in the computer, the larger the available workspace, so the more applications and data files you'll be able to have open at once.

Virtual Memory

Many OSs, including Microsoft Windows, use a tremendous amount of RAM as they operate, to the point that even a well-equipped PC might not have enough RAM to do everything that a user wants. To prevent the user from being denied an activity due to lack of available memory, these OSs employ *virtual memory* to take up the slack.

With virtual memory, a portion of the hard disk is set aside as a holding area for the contents of RAM. When there isn't enough space in RAM to hold the data that needs to be placed there, the OS's virtual memory management utility temporarily moves some of the least-recently used data in RAM onto the hard disk, making room for the new incoming data. Then, if an application calls for the data that was moved out, the virtual memory manager moves something *else* out and swaps the needed data back in again. Due to all this data swapping, the reserved area on the hard disk for virtual memory is sometimes called a *swap file*.

The main drawback of virtual memory is its speed, which is limited to the speed at which the hard drive can store and retrieve data. Compared to the speed of the processor and memory, the hard disk is very slow. Therefore, the less physical RAM available in a system, and the more that system has to rely on virtual memory, the more slowly applications will run on that system. That's why adding more RAM to a system is often a worthwhile upgrade.

EXERCISE 1.3

Assessing Your Computer's RAM and Virtual Memory

1. In Windows Vista or Windows 7, click Start and then right-click Computer and click Properties. (Alternately, open Control Panel, go to System and Security, and then go to System.)

2. In the System section of the page that appears, note the amount of Installed Memory (RAM). This is the total physical amount of RAM.

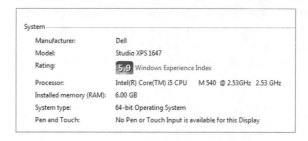

System

Manufacturer:	Dell
Model:	Studio XPS 1647
Rating:	**5.9** Windows Experience Index
Processor:	Intel(R) Core(TM) i5 CPU M 540 @ 2.53GHz 2.53 GHz
Installed memory (RAM):	6.00 GB
System type:	64-bit Operating System
Pen and Touch:	No Pen or Touch Input is available for this Display

3. In the bar at the left, click Advanced System Settings. The System Properties dialog box opens.

4. On the Advanced tab, in the Performance section, click Settings. The Performance Options dialog box opens.

5. Click the Advanced tab, and, in the Virtual Memory section, note the total paging file size for all drives. This is the amount of virtual memory set aside for the system's use.

6. Click the Change button. The Virtual Memory dialog box opens.

7. Click Cancel to close the dialog box without making any changes. (It's usually best to leave this setting to be automatically managed by the system.)

8. Click Cancel to close the Performance Options dialog box.

9. Click Cancel to close the System Properties dialog box.

10. Under the system heading, find the Rating line, and click Windows Experience Index. The Performance and Information Tools section of Control Panel opens.

11. Note the subscore next to Memory (RAM). If this number is the lowest of the subscores by a substantial amount, the computer's performance might be improved by adding more RAM. As shown here, the RAM has the highest score (6.8) of any component, so this system has adequate RAM.

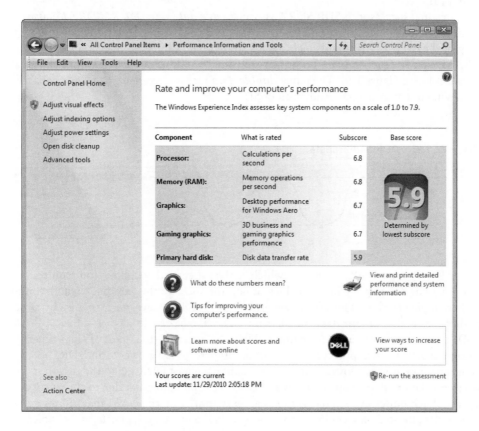

12. Close the Control Panel window.

Memory Bus Speeds

The pathway that delivers data to and from the memory is called a *memory bus*. Memory has a *bus width* that determines how many columns are in each row of storage. All the bits in a single row are read together as a single value, so the wider the memory bus width, the more data that can be read at once. For example, in memory with an 8-bit width, you might have a number like 01001100. In memory with a 32-bit width, you could have a number with up to 32 binary digits.

The memory bus also has a speed, which determines how quickly data will travel on its pathway. Memory on modern PCs is synchronized (that is, *synchronous*) with the system bus, which in turn is controlled by the system timer on the motherboard. The system timer determines the speed at which data enters the processor. Memory that operates at the same speed as the front-side bus is called *single data rate (SDR) synchronous dynamic read-only memory (SDRAM)*.

The original successor to SDR SDRAM was *double data rate (DDR) SDRAM*, also sometimes called DDR1. It makes higher transfer rates achievable by strictly controlling the timing of the electrical data and clock signals so that data can be *double-pumped* into the RAM: that is, pumped in on both the rising and the falling of each tick of the internal system clock (see Figure 1.6). The name *double data rate* is a reference to DDR's capability of achieving nearly twice the bandwidth of SDR.

FIGURE 1.6   DDR data transfer

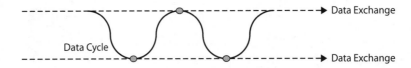

After DDR1 came DDR2 SDRAM, which enables greater throughput and requires lower power by running the internal clock at half the speed of the data bus, in addition to double-pumping the bus. This effectively multiplies the DDR1-level performance by two, so that there are a total of *four* data transfers per internal clock cycle.

DDR3 goes even further, once again doubling the data rate, to a total of eight times the original SDR throughput. It also uses about 30 percent less power than DDR2 modules because it uses a lower voltage. The main benefit of DDR3, and the reason it doubles the data rate, isn't due to a raw increase in the pumping, but due to the use of a deeper prefetch buffer. A *prefetch buffer* is an extra buffer on the RAM that allows quick access to data located on a common physical row in the memory. (A *buffer* is a simpler version of a cache.)

Generally speaking, most motherboards accept only one type of RAM: SDR, DDR, DDR2, or DDR3. Even if the motherboard is physically compatible with other types, it's programmed to work with RAM at a certain speed.

The Strata objectives also ask about triple data rate RAM, but there is no such thing—at least not by that name. The objectives are most likely referring to DDR3.

Physical Characteristics of RAM

There have been various sizes and shapes of RAM modules in PCs over the years Today, however, there are two basic physical types: *dual inline memory modules (DIMMs)*, used in desktop PCs, and *small-outline dual inline memory modules (SODIMMs)*, used in portable PCs. Both of these consist of small circuit boards with RAM chips mounted on them and a row of metal tabs (called *pins*) along one edge.

 The *dual* in DIMM refers to the fact that the module uses pins on both sides of the circuit board. If you count the pins (metal tabs) along one side of a DIMM, you'll count only half the prescribed number of pins. In contrast, earlier types of RAM, *single inline memory modules (SIMMs)*, had visible metal tabs on both sides of the modules. However, those tabs were wrapped around the bottom of the edge so they were effectively the same tab on both sides. SIMMs have been obsolete for many years; they had either 30 or 72 pins and were used in 486 and some early Pentium motherboards.

Figure 1.7 and Figure 1.8 show a DIMM and a SODIMM, respectively. The RAM modules slide into sockets on the motherboard, where the pins connect with corresponding pins in the socket. Table 1.2 and Table 1.3 list the pins for these RAM modules.

FIGURE 1.7   A DIMM

Photo credit: Martyn M aka Martyx.

FIGURE 1.8 A SODIMM

Attribution: Matthieu Riegler, Wikimedia Commons

TABLE 1.2 DIMM pins

DIMM Pins	Data Transfer	Notes
168	64 bit	Single data rate (SDR)
184	64 bit	Double data rate (DDR)
240	64 bit	DDR2, DDR3, and FB-DIMM

TABLE 1.3 SODIMM Pins

SODIMM Pins	Data Transfer	Notes
72	32 bit	FPM and EDO
100	32 bit	Used in printers
144	64 bit	SDR
200	64 bit	DDR and DDR2
204	64 bit	DDR3
214	64-bit	MicroDIMM, used for DDR2

In Table 1.3, the memory types FPM and EDO are old, obsolete types of RAM. Fast page mode (FPM) was a nonsynchronous type of RAM that had its own speed rating independent of the system bus, expressed in nanoseconds of latency (delay), such as 70 ns. Extended data out (EDO) was a type of RAM that needed to be refreshed with electricity less frequently than other RAM of its era, so it offered slightly better performance than standard RAM.

Different types of SDR and DDR DIMMs and SODIMMs may be similar or even identical in overall size and shape, and may even have the same number of pins. (For example, DDR2 and DDR3 DIMMs both have 240 pins.) To ensure that people don't install the wrong type of RAM, each type of RAM has a uniquely placed notch in the edge that contains the pins. That notch makes the RAM fit only in a slot that has a correspondingly placed spacer. Figure 1.9 compares DDR2 and DDR3 DIMMs; notice the difference in notch placement.

FIGURE 1.9   DDR2 and DDR3 memory modules

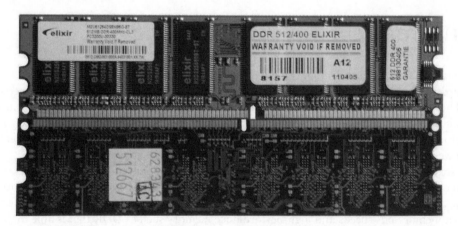

Photo credit: Jérôme BLUM.

EXERCISE 1.4

Determining the Type of RAM Installed

1. Look in the documentation that came with your computer to see if there is anything about the RAM specifications.

2. In the documentation, locate the information about installing a RAM upgrade. This will tell you where to find the RAM on your system.

3. Open the computer's case, and locate the RAM. Identify whether it's DIMM or SODIMM. (Most notebook PCs use SODIMM, and most desktop PCs use DIMM.) To avoid damaging it with static electricity, avoid touching it. If you need to touch it, touch the metal frame of the PC's case first. You'll learn more about preventing static electricity damage in Chapter 4, "Setting Up a Computer."

4. Examine the numbers or codes, if any, on the DIMM or SODIMM, looking for model numbers, speeds, or any other pertinent information.

5. Look at the data you gathered online to see if you can determine anything about the memory based on those numbers.

6. If you can't determine the RAM type by any of these methods, find the motherboard's brand and model number (look for this information printed on the motherboard itself). Then look up the motherboard online to see if information about its RAM requirements is available.

Summary

In this chapter, you learned about computer processors and their function in a personal computer. You learned how a processor's instruction set dictates the calculations it can perform and how processing is done using a binary numbering system inside the processor. You learned about Intel and AMD, the two major processor makers, and about PGA and LGA, two types of processor sockets. We discussed processor performance speeds and operations per second, and we looked at how caches and multicore processors improve system performance.

Next, we looked at memory. You learned the difference between static and dynamic memory, and between RAM and ROM. You learned how data is stored inside a memory chip, and how virtual memory swaps data into and out of physical memory. You learned about memory bus speeds and high-performance memory such as DDR that is able to perform multiple operations per clock tick. Finally, we compared the various physical types of memory modules that PCs can accept, including DIMMs and SODIMMs.

Exam Essentials

Know the most popular model names of Intel and AMD processors.   Intel's CPUs include the Pentium 4 and the Intel Core i3, i5, and i7. Within those lines, code names differentiate subtypes, such as Arrandale, Gulftown, and Sandy Bridge. AMD's processors include the Phenom II, Athlon II, and Turion II lines.

Understand CPU speed measurements.   Modern CPUs have core speeds measured in gigahertz (GHz); older CPU speeds were measured in megahertz (MHz). A CPU's core speed is related to, but not the same as, its operations per second, measured in millions of operations per second (MIPS).

Know about processor caches.   Caches improve performance by storing data that was recently used or is likely to be needed so it will be close at hand when the processor requests it. The L1 cache is an on-die cache in the CPU; it's the smallest and fastest cache. Close behind it is the L2 cache, which is on the CPU chip but not on the processor die itself. Some CPUs also have an L3 cache.

Understand the problems involved in upgrading a processor.   Not only must the new processor be physically compatible with the socket, but the motherboard must be aware of the instruction set and the speed at which it can accept data. As a result, most motherboards support only a few processors.

Understand RAM data rates.   RAM can either be synchronous with the motherboard's bus speed (single data rate, or SDR) or have double the data rate (DDR) by executing operations at both the top and the bottom of the clock tick. This is called double-pumping. DDR2 and DDR3 RAM go even further, effectively doubling and redoubling the data rates.

Understand the compatibility issues involved in upgrading RAM.   Most motherboards accept only one type of RAM at a certain data rate. This is partly due to physical compatibility, because different RAM types have different numbers of pins, and partly due to the way the memory bus operates on the motherboard.

Identify physical characteristics of RAM.   Most desktop systems today accept dual inline memory modules (DIMMs). Most notebook computers accept small-outline DIMMs (SODIMMs). Depending on the type, DIMMs may have from 168 to 240 pins; SODIMMs may have from 72 to 214 pins.

Review Questions

1. What is the function of a processor?

    A. To display graphics

    B. To manage user input

    C. To communicate with the operating system

    D. To do math

2. What type of device is most likely to have a RISC processor?

    A. Cell phone

    B. Notebook PC

    C. Desktop PC

    D. File server

3. Which of these numbers is a binary number?

    A. 159

    B. FFh

    C. 010110

    D. All of these are binary numbers

4. Which companies are the major manufacturers of PC processors today?

    A. Intel and IBM

    B. Apple and AMD

    C. Motorola and Apple

    D. Intel and AMD

5. What type of socket is used for most processors in modern systems?

    A. PGA

    B. LGA

    C. DIMM

    D. SODIMM

6. How is the core speed of a processor measured?

    A. Gigahertz (GHz)

    B. Millions of instructions per second (MIPS)

    C. Gigabytes (GB)

    D. Gigabits per second (Gbps)

7. The speed at which the motherboard sends and receives data to/from the processor is determined by the speed of the _____.

    A. Memory

    B. System timer

    C. Processor

    D. Hard disk

8. Which cache is closest to the processor and is checked first for data retrieval?

    A. L4

    B. L3

    C. L2

    D. L1

9. Multicore processors can have various numbers of cores. Which of these is the most likely number of cores a multicore processor might have?

    A. 1

    B. 4

    C. 32

    D. 256

10. In what type of device would you find a cell microprocessor?

    A. PlayStation 3

    B. Notebook PC

    C. Cell phone

    D. Desktop PC

11. An example of a passive cooling system is a _____.

    A. Fan

    B. Water-cooling pump

    C. Heat sink

    D. Air-conditioning compressor

12. What does BIOS stand for?

    A. Basic Information Operation Standard

    B. Boolean Input Operation System

    C. Builder's Information Overhead Standard

    D. Basic Input/Output System

13. Which type of memory is volatile and therefore loses its contents if not continuously powered by electricity?

   A. SRAM

   B. DRAM

   C. ROM

   D. CPU

14. When hard disk space is used to store data swapped out of physical RAM temporarily, it is known as _____.

   A. SRAM

   B. Virtual memory

   C. DRAM

   D. ROM

15. In the acronym SDRAM, what does the *S* stand for?

   A. Single

   B. Static

   C. Synchronous

   D. Simple

16. Compared to SDR SDRAM, what is the data transfer rate of DDR2 SDRAM?

   A. The same

   B. 2x

   C. 4x

   D. 8x

17. What type of RAM is most often used in notebook PCs?

   A. SODIMM

   B. SODRAM

   C. DIMM

   D. ROM

18. If you find a 184-pin DIMM, what kind of RAM can you assume it is?

   A. SDR

   B. DDR

   C. DDR2

   D. DDR3

19. A(n) _____ is an extra buffer in RAM that allows quick access to data located in a common physical row in the memory.

   A. BIOS

   B. L1 cache

   C. L2 cache

   D. Prefetch buffer

20. When it is said that a certain kind of RAM is *synchronous*, with what is it synchronized?

   A. Processor's internal core speed

   B. Motherboard's system bus speed

   C. Hard disk's data bus

   D. Other memory modules installed in the same PC

Answers to Review Questions

1. D. A processor may accomplish all those other tasks indirectly, with the help of software, but its core function is to do math. Numbers come in, are processed, and are outputted. What the software chooses to do with them is not the processor's concern.

2. A. A reduced instruction set computing (RISC) processor is a simple processor that has a small instruction set and can operate efficiently using that small set. RISC processors are often used in hand-held devices like cell phones.

3. C. A binary number consists of only 1 and 0 digits. Processors and memory use binary numbering to store data in a series of on/off transistors.

4. D. Intel and AMD are the two major manufacturers of PC processors.

5. B. Land grid array (LGA) is the most popular socket type for today's processors. PGA is a previous-generation socket that used pins on a processor that fit into holes on the socket. DIMM and SODIMM are types of RAM, not processors.

6. A. The core speed of a processor is measured in gigahertz. Core speed is not the same as the amount of data the processor can process per second, though; that's measured in MIPS. Gigabytes are a measurement of disk storage space or memory capacity. Gigabits per second is a measurement of data transport throughput, such as on a network.

7. B. The motherboard's system bus, or front-side bus, moves the data to/from the CPU at a rate set by the system timer on the motherboard. The memory, processor, and hard disk all have a maximum speed at which they can reliably operate, but those speeds do not determine the actual rate at which the system operates.

8. D. The L1 cache is built into the processor's die, so it is the closest of all caches. The L2 cache is on the processor chip but not on the die itself. An L3 cache, if present, is also on the chip but not on the die.

9. B. Multicore processors are typically either dual-core or quad-core; some even have six or eight cores. A processor with one core would not be considered multicore. There are currently no processors that have 32 or 256 cores.

10. A. A cell microprocessor is a hybrid between a multiple-core processor and a specialized system, well-equipped for imaging and gaming applications. Sony uses a cell microprocessor for its PlayStation 3 gaming system, with eight cells running the console.

11. C. A passive cooling system has no moving parts and uses no power to run. The only one of the options listed that fits these criteria is a heat sink.

12. D. BIOS stands for Basic Input/Output System. The BIOS chip on the motherboard contains the essential information it needs to start the computer and load the operating system into memory.

13. B. Static RAM (SRAM) is, by its definition, nonvolatile; it is used for flash RAM drives, for example. Dynamic RAM is the volatile type, used for the main memory in most computer systems. Read-only memory (ROM) is not only nonvolatile, but also not easily rewriteable without a special tool. The central processing unit (CPU) is not a type of memory.

14. B. Virtual memory, also called a swap file, consists of a hard disk file that is used to hold data that is swapped out of RAM temporarily until it is needed again and swapped back in. SRAM, DRAM, and ROM are all physical types of memory.

15. C. SDRAM is synchronous dynamic random access memory. *Synchronous* refers to the synchronization of its speed with that of the front-side bus. Do not confuse this with SRAM (static RAM) or SDR (single data rate).

16. C. If SDR is the baseline, then DDR (also known as DDR1) is 2x the speed, DDR2 is 4x the speed, and DDR3 is 8x the speed.

17. A. Small-outline DIMM (SODIMM) is typically used in notebook PCs. There is no such thing as SODRAM. Regular DIMMs are typically used in desktop PCs. ROM is not a type of RAM; it's read-only memory.

18. B. According to Table 1.2, a 184-pin DIMM is a double data rate (DDR) DIMM.

19. D. A deeper prefetch buffer is the primary reason why DDR3 is faster than DDR2 RAM. A BIOS chip is ROM. The L1 and L2 caches are on the processor, not on the RAM.

20. B. Synchronous RAM is synchronized with the system bus speed, which is in turn controlled by the motherboard's system timer.

Chapter

2

Input and Storage Devices

FUNDAMENTALS OF PC FUNCTIONALITY
FUNDAMENTALS OF PC TECHNOLOGY
OBJECTIVES COVERED IN THIS CHAPTER:

✓ **1.1 Identify basic IT vocabulary**

- Hard drives

✓ **1.2 U.K. / 1.3 U.S. Explain the characteristics and functions of internal and external storage devices**

✓ **1.3 Demonstrate the ability to set up a basic PC workstation**

- Identify differences between connector types

- USB, PS/2

- Keyboard

- Mouse

✓ **1.4 U.K. / 1.5 U.S. Explain the characteristics and functions of input devices**

You can have the greatest processor and best RAM in the world, but unless you give these devices directions as to what to do with themselves, you'll get nothing back. That's where input devices come in. They help you put data into a computer for processing.

In this chapter, we'll review the various types of devices that people use to give a computer instructions, including essential user-input tools like keyboards and mice. We'll also look at many of the technologies used for data storage and retrieval in a PC, such as hard disks, CDs, flash drives, and so on.

Core Input Devices

A variety of input devices exist for entering data into a computer. The oldest method that's still in use today is the alphanumeric keyboard. Some other types of input devices include the numeric keypad, mouse, touch screen, and game controller. In this section, we'll review the function of each of these input device types.

Keyboards

Computer keyboards are the descendants of typewriter keyboards. They enable users to enter text and numeric input for documents and other data files. Figure 2.1 shows a typical keyboard.

FIGURE 2.1   Computer keyboard

Photo credit: Microsoft (credit on copyright page)

Electronically, a keyboard is a grid of uncompleted circuits. When you press a number, letter, or symbol key, you lower a contact that completes the circuit and sends data to the PC. Different keys complete different circuits, resulting in different characters being sent to the computer.

Some keys are modifiers; they trigger a circuit that changes any other values sent while they're pressed. The Shift key is the most common example. When you press Shift by itself, nothing happens. But when you hold down Shift and press a letter key, an uppercase letter is sent, a different value than when the letter is typed by itself.

Other keys send function codes rather than letters or numbers. For example, the F1 key sends a code string to the PC that represents Function 1. What that entails depends on the operating system (OS) and/or the active application. For example, at a command prompt, pressing F1 has no effect, but within Windows, pressing F1 opens the Help system. If an application is active that has a function assigned to the F1 key, it grabs that input and interprets it as its own command.

In addition to the alphabetic, numeric, and symbol keys from the original typewriter layout, today's keyboards also contain a variety of special-purpose keys, including the following:

Function Keys   Labeled F1 through F12, these keys perform special functions, which vary depending on the application or OS in use. For example, in Windows and in most Windows-based applications, pressing F1 opens the Help system.

Esc   The Esc(ape) key typically cancels the action in process. Its exact use depends on the application; Esc commonly closes an open dialog box or cancels a special mode, for example.

Shift, Ctrl, and Alt   These modifier keys change what happens when some other key is pressed. Shift makes uppercase letters, for example. Ctrl and Alt have special uses depending on the application. Ctrl plus a letter may activate a shortcut; Alt typically opens or activates a menu bar.

Arrow Keys   Arrow keys enable you to move an onscreen cursor or insertion point in the up, down, right, or left direction.

Scrolling or Positioning Keys   In some programs, the Home and End keys move to the beginning or end of the document, and the Page Up and Page Down keys move up or down one screen.

Windows Key   This key, usually with a four-sectioned flag graphic on it, opens the Start menu in Windows.

Fn   Found only on notebook and other portable computers, this key is like an alternative version of the Ctrl key; when combined with some other key press, it performs a special command, usually hardware-related. For example, pressing Fn and the up-arrow key together might increase the display brightness.

Numeric Keypad   Standalone keyboards typically have a separate numeric keypad to the right of the main keypad layout. This is useful when you have to enter a lot of numeric data. The numeric keypad has two different functions: it can be used either to input numeric data or to move the onscreen cursor or insertion point. To toggle between those two modes, press the NumLock key. Notebook computer keyboards don't usually have a separate numeric keypad.

Different keyboards have different key layouts. QWERTY is the most common type. The QWERTY arrangement of the keys on a typewriter (whose name comes from the first six keys on the top row) was conceived to slow down typing enough to prevent jamming the metal arms of the typewriter, which struck a ribbon and transferred print characters to a piece of paper. Even though metal arms are long gone, this key layout is still used on computers today. Other layouts have been developed, such as the Dvorak layout, which enable faster typing once the user memorizes the key locations, but the QWERTY layout is so entrenched in our culture that other layouts have never caught on.

Most desktop keyboards today use a USB connection to attach to the computer as shown in Figure 2.2. As with other USB devices, a USB keyboard is hot pluggable, meaning that you can connect it to and disconnect it from the computer without shutting down the computer.

FIGURE 2.2 A USB connector

Photo credit: Andreas Frank

Older keyboards may use a PS/2 connector, which is a small round plug. Figure 2-3 shows a PS/2 connector. PS/2 connectors aren't hot pluggable, so you must shut down the computer before you connect or disconnect a PS/2 keyboard.

FIGURE 2.3 A PS/2 connector

Wireless keyboards are also available, which use either Bluetooth or some other short-range wireless technology to connect the keyboard to a small receiver/transmitter device that plugs into one of the PC's USB ports.

If you're working with the PC in a language other than English, you may have a keyboard that is specific to that language. The OS may identify the correct keyboard layout automatically, or you may need to specify a keyboard layout or a Region or Nationality setting in the OS to tell it the language in which you're working. The following exercise explores the keyboard layout and regional options in Windows 7.

Explore Keyboard Layout and Region Settings

1. In Windows 7, choose Start ➢ Control Panel ➢ Clock, Language, And Region (or Language And Region, depending on your version) ➢ Change Keyboards Or Other Input Methods. The Region And Language dialog box opens with the Keyboards And Languages tab displayed.

2. Click Change Keyboards. The Text Services And Input Languages dialog box opens.

3. On the General tab, open the Default Input Language drop-down list and examine the other choices available. Don't change the current selection. You may or may not have other options besides English (United States).

    If you don't have any other keyboard layout options, but you want to use a different country's keyboard layout, you need to install a language pack from Microsoft.

4. Click US in the Installed Services area under Keyboard. The Properties button becomes available, as shown here.

5. Click the Properties button. The Keyboard Layout Preview dialog box opens, showing the current keyboard layout.

6. Click Cancel to close the dialog box.

7. Click the Advanced Key Settings tab, and note the settings, as shown in the example here. Note that the Caps Lock key currently turns Caps Lock on/off, but you could choose instead to make the Shift key do that if you wanted. Notice also that the keyboard shortcut for switching input languages is currently set to Left Alt + Shift. You could use that shortcut to switch between languages if you had multiple language packs installed.

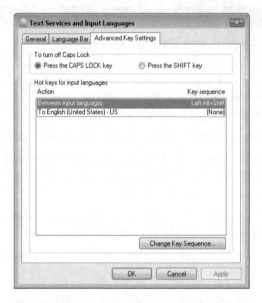

8. Click Cancel to close the Text Services And Input Languages dialog box.

9. Click Cancel to close the Region And Language dialog box.

10. Close all remaining open windows.

Numeric Keypads

In some business sectors, such as finance, accounting, and banking, computer users spend a lot of time entering numeric data. In such cases, a numeric keypad can be a big help. Users who are trained in the so-called "10-key" keypad usage can enter numbers much more swiftly with a numeric keypad than they can using the number keys above the letter keys on a standard keyboard.

Numeric keypads are built into most full-size keyboards for desktop PCs and can also be purchased as separate input devices.

Pointing Devices

A *pointing device* is an object that you move with your hand to control an onscreen pointer, or *cursor*. You move the pointer to communicate with the OS or application. Most pointing devices today use the USB interface; old mice may use a PS/2 connector like the one shown in Figure 2.3.

Being USB devices, they're usually *Plug and Play*, meaning the OS recognizes them immediately without any special software needed. However, to use the advanced features of the device, such as to custom-program its buttons, driver software may be required.

Mice

The oldest and still the most popular pointing device is the *mouse*. The mouse gets its name from its size and shape; it's approximately the size of a small rodent (or, if you prefer, of a bar of soap), and it traditionally has a cord (which looks somewhat like a tail) that connects it to the computer.

Mice use two main technologies: mechanical and optical. With a *mechanical mouse*, there is a rubber ball on the underside of the mouse. The ball rolls across the mouse pad or desktop, and, as it rolls, it moves past rollers or sensors inside the mouse that tell the onscreen pointer to move a corresponding amount on the screen in a corresponding direction.

With an *optical mouse*, there is no ball on the bottom; instead there is a *light-emitting diode (LED)* and *photodiodes* (light sensors) to detect movement. A *laser mouse* is like an optical mouse except that it uses an infrared laser instead of an LED. With either an optical or a laser mouse, the rate of change of motion signals the OS where the mouse is moving. Figure 2.4 shows a mechanical mouse with the top cover removed so that you can see what's going on inside. Figure 2.5 shows the underside of an optical mouse; the inside of an optical mouse contains no moving parts.

FIGURE 2.4   The inside workings of a mechanical mouse

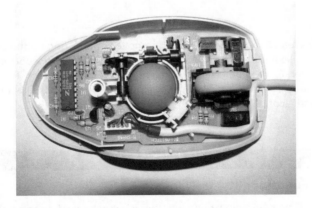

Photo credit: Gregory Badon

FIGURE 2.5 The underside of an optical mouse

Photo credit: www.dansdata.com

A mouse has buttons that you can press and release to act on whatever you're pointing at onscreen. Apple Macintosh computers can use a one or two-button mouse; Windows systems require the two-button variety. There may be a third (center) button on some models, or a scroll wheel for scrolling through windows. In Windows, the left mouse button is the main button, used for selecting; the right mouse button typically opens a context-sensitive menu.

WARNING   It's important to consider the surface on which you're using the mouse. Well-polished or glass desks may look nice, but they can inhibit your optical mouse from sending a clear signal to your OS. Although optical mice work on many different surfaces, many users prefer to use a nonreflective pad on which to move the mouse.

TIP   To clean a mechanical mouse, remove the lock ring on the bottom of the mouse and take out the ball. Then clean inside with a cotton swab and alcohol. If the ball is dirty, clean it with soap and water. To clean an optical mouse, clear away any dust and grime around the LED with a cotton swab and alcohol.

EXERCISE 2.2

Explore Mouse Functionality

1.   Turn your mouse over, and determine whether it's mechanical (with a ball) or optical (with an LED). If it's mechanical, rotate the lock ring holding the ball in, remove the ball, examine the cavity in which the ball sits, and then reassemble the mouse.

2. In Windows 7, choose Start ➤ Control Panel ➤ Hardware And Sound ➤ Devices And Printers ➤ Mouse. The Mouse Properties dialog box opens.

3. Click each of the tabs in the dialog box to explore the configurable options for your mouse. Here is an example of Mouse Properties, but your dialog box may look different depending on the type of mouse you have.

4. Drag the slider in the Double-Click Speed section of the Buttons tab, and then try double-clicking the folder icon to the right of the slider to test the new setting. Drag the slider back to its original position when finished.

5. On the Pointers tab, open the Scheme drop-down list and examine the alternate mouse pointer schemes available. Pick one and apply it (Apply button). Then change back to the originally-used pointer scheme.

6. Click the Pointer Options tab, and drag the slider in the Motion section to experiment with a different pointer speed. Click Apply, and move the mouse pointer around to see the result. Then set the pointer speed back to its original setting.

7. Click Cancel to close the dialog box, and close all open windows.

Touchpad

A *touchpad* (sometimes called a *trackpad*) is a pressure-sensitive surface across which you can run your finger to move the onscreen pointer. A touchpad for a Windows-based PC typically has buttons under it, corresponding to the right and left mouse buttons; most models also allow you to tap the touchpad surface to click or double-click. The MacBook touchpad shown in Figure 2.6 doesn't include buttons because on a Mac, no right-clicking is needed; Macs use a single-button pointing device, so tapping to click is all you need.

FIGURE 2.6   Touchpad on a Macintosh computer

Photo credit: Highway of Life, Wikimedia Commons

Touchpads take up less space to operate than mice, so they're commonly found on notebook computers.

Trackball

A *trackball* is something like an upside-down mechanical mouse. Its base stays stationary, and you roll the ball with your fingers to move the onscreen pointer. Figure 2.7 shows an example of a trackball. Trackballs require less space to operate than a mouse, and some people find them more comfortable to use. Trackballs are also more effective for pointing when precision is needed, such as when using graphics software.

FIGURE 2.7   A trackball

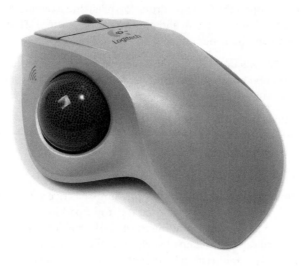

Touch Screen and Stylus Input

A *touch screen* is a pressure-sensitive video display. Touch screens are found at bank ATMs, airport check-in counters, mall kiosks, and many other locations where consumers need to interact with a video display without a keyboard or mouse.

Tablet computers are notebook computers that include touch-screen technology, either as a primary or secondary form of user input. Some tablet computers, like the Apple iPad, use the touch-screen capability for all input, including keyboarding. (A keyboard appears on the video display, and you touch the screen to type.) Others either have a built-in keyboard or can accept an attached keyboard and/or mouse via USB port.

Most touch screens made today are finger-touch activated, but earlier models, especially those made for Windows-based tablet PCs, used a technology called *pen computing*. With pen computing, the touch screen is activated only when touched by a special pen stylus that comes with the device. The stylus transmits a signal to sensors in the display's surface to make the connection; a plain finger-touch does nothing. Some gaming devices, like the Nintendo 3DS, also use this technology.

Game Controllers

Gaming consoles have input controllers specifically designed for game playing, which is one reason why the consoles are so popular with gaming enthusiasts. Similar controllers are also available for personal computers to make playing certain games easier and more enjoyable. For example, game controllers that are identical to those that come with popular gaming consoles are available for PCs, as are joysticks that make it easier to play flight simulator games.

Internal and External Storage Devices

After data enters the computer via an input device—then what? The incoming data is temporarily stored in RAM, but eventually it has to be saved to a storage device in order to preserve it. A variety of storage devices are available for personal computers, each with its own unique set of pros and cons in terms of speed, cost, portability, and convenience. In this section, you'll learn about some of the most popular storage devices available.

Storage space is measured in kilobytes (KB, thousands of bytes), megabytes (MB, millions of bytes), and gigabytes (GB, billions of bytes). The original storage device for a personal computer, the floppy disk, held between 360 KB and 1.44 MB, which seems laughably small nowadays. But at the time, entire applications could be stored on a single disk. Table 2.1 summarizes the various measurements of storage capacity and provides notes and examples. Notice that the multipliers aren't exact thousands, but multiples of 1,024. That's because of the binary nature of number storage in computers. For example, a kilobyte is 1,024 bytes, not exactly 1,000. The decimal value 1,024 is 10000000000 when converted to binary.

TABLE 2.1   Measurements of storage

Size	Equals	Example
Byte	8 bits	One character of text.
Kilobyte (KB)	1,024 bytes	A 1,000-character plain text file, or a tiny graphic (18x18 pixels), such as an icon.
Megabyte (MB)	1,024 KB	A 600×600 pixel photograph, or one minute of a music clip.
Gigabyte (GB)	1,024 MB	A full-length audio CD is about 800 MB (4/5 of one gigabyte); a two-hour DVD movie is about 4 GB.
Terabyte (TB)	1,024 GB	A large business database containing records of all financial transactions.
Petabyte (PB)	1,024 TB	All the data stored by the taxing authority of a large country, such as the U.S. Internal Revenue Service.

The various storage types you'll learn about in the rest of this chapter have their own capacity limitations. Table 2.2 summarizes these.

TABLE 2.2   Maximum storage capacities

Media Format	Largest (as of 2011)
Standard (mechanical) hard drive	3 TB
Solid-state drive	2 TB
USB flash drive	256 GB
Compact flash card	128 GB
CD	900 MB
Blu-ray	50 GB
Double-sided, double-density DVD	17.08 GB

ASCII and Unicode

Disks store data as binary numbers. Each character can be uniquely described by a certain combination of 1s and 0s. The set of codes that defines which character corresponds to which code is called American Standard Code for Information Interchange (ASCII). It was developed in the 1960s to achieve some standardization among different types of data-processing equipment. The numbers and letters familiar to our written language are known as the ASCII character set. The original ASCII standard called for 7-bit codes, so there were 128 combinations possible. In 1981, IBM introduced an 8-bit version called the extended ASCII character set for use on the IBM PC, which added another 128 combinations used for math, graphical, and foreign language characters, for a total of 256 combinations.

Nowadays, a different encoding system, called Unicode, is the predominantly used standard. Unicode consists of more than 109,000 characters covering multiple languages. Unicode can be implemented with different character encodings. The most common one is UTF-8, which is very similar to Extended ASCII, using the same one-byte values for the basic set of ASCII characters.

Floppy disk drives, once the most popular and affordable storage medium for PCs, are now obsolete. Very rarely will a new system come with a floppy disk drive, although you might occasionally encounter one in an old PC. You don't need to know anything about them for the Strata exam except that the acronym FDD stands for floppy disk drive.

Hard Drives

A *hard drive* (or hard disk) is a sealed stack of metal platters, each with a read-write head on a retractable arm that reads data from and writes data to the platters by magnetizing bits of iron oxide particles on the platters in patterns of positive and negative polarity. As a hard disk operates, the platters rotate at a high speed, and the read/write heads hover just over the disk surfaces on a cushion of air generated by the spinning.

Figure 2.8 shows the inside of a hard disk drive. You wouldn't normally see one this way because the metal box in which a hard disk is encased is permanently sealed; if you take it apart, you ruin it. The platters are typically 3.5" in diameter for full-size hard disk drives (for desktop PCs) and 2.5" for smaller hard disk drives used in notebook PCs.

FIGURE 2.8   Inside of a hard disk drive

Photo credit: Mfield, Matthew Field, http://www.photography.mattfield.com

Is the proper term *hard disk* or *hard drive*? Either is correct. The original disks in computers, floppy disks, were removable. A floppy drive was permanently mounted in the computer, and the floppy disks popped in and out of it. The drive and the disk were two separate pieces. Then along came hard disks, which are integrated with their drives. Because there is no separating them, a hard disk (the platters inside the metal case) and a hard drive (the casing and read-write heads that support and access the platters) aren't referred to separately. The entire thing is the *hard disk drive*, and that can be shortened to *hard disk* or *hard drive* equally appropriately.

A hard disk is typically an internal device, mounted inside the computer's case. However, external hard disks are also available, connected to the computer by a USB or FireWire (IEEE 1394) connector. Compared to other storage options, hard disks have a low cost per megabyte, a relatively fast read/write speed, and high reliability. Their main drawbacks are that they're fairly large and bulky and not very portable.

Hard disks today have capacities measured in hundreds of gigabytes or even terabytes; a typical hard disk in a notebook computer might have 500 gigabytes of storage, for example. The OS itself occupies one or two gigabytes of that, and the rest of the space is available for applications and data files. An older computer might have considerably less hard disk space than that—perhaps only 10 or 20 gigabytes.

EXERCISE 2.3

Get Hard Disk Information

1. In Windows 7, click Start ➢ Computer. A list of the drives on your PC appears.

2. Click the primary hard disk (C:) to select it, and look in the status bar at the bottom of the window. The hard disk's total size, space used, space free, and file system information appear. Here is an example, but your hard drive will have different specifications.

3. Right-click the hard disk, and click Properties. A Properties dialog box opens for that drive, as shown in the example here.

4. Examine the information about used space, free space, and capacity. It's the same as you saw earlier, but now you have an exact count and also a chart.

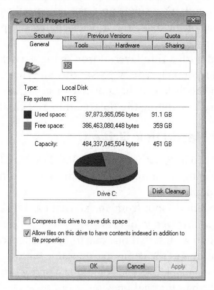

5. Click the Hardware tab. Information appears about all the disk drives, including your DVD/CD drive if you have one. Here you can see the brand name and model number of each drive.

6. Click Cancel to close the dialog box, and close the Computer window.

How Magnetic Disks Store Data

Magnetic storage, such as that used with a traditional hard disk, creates transitions by magnetizing areas of the disk with either a positive or a negative polarity. It then reads the transitions between the positive and negative areas as 1s and the lack of transitions as 0s.

The read/write head, although it's a single unit, actually performs two different functions: it magnetizes areas of the disk, and it reads changes in polarity and relays them to the drive controller.

The disk surface is coated with a thin layer of iron oxide particles. The read/write head has a wire coil around it, and electricity passes through that coil. The magnetic field polarizes the surface of the disk as either positive or negative. The flow of electricity through the wire then reverses, changing the polarization and creating a transition point.

Internal vs. External Hard Disk Drives

External hard drives connect to a PC either via a USB or FireWire (IEEE 1394) connector. They're easy to use; you just plug them in. External hard drives often require their own power source from an AC adapter.

It's possible to set up a system to boot from an external hard disk, so you can put the OS on an external hard disk. However, you'll lose performance doing so, because an external hard disk is usually slower than an internal one due to the bottleneck of the external cable and connector. In addition, it makes the computer unusable without the external drive, so if the external drive is missing or misplaced, the computer won't work. External hard disks are also more susceptible to theft than internal ones.

How much slower is an external drive than an internal one? Universal Serial Bus (USB) version 2.0 has a data rate of up to 480 megabits per second (Mbps). FireWire comes in at 400 Mbps. In contrast, Serial Advanced Technology Attachment (SATA), used for internal drives, can transfer data at between 1.5 and 6 Gbps.

Factors that Govern Hard Disk Speed

Speed of hard disk access is an important consideration in system performance, because a hard disk, being a mechanical device, is likely to be a bottleneck area. The processor and RAM can run much faster than the fastest hard disk, so they end up waiting around for the hard disk to supply the needed data.

As mentioned in the previous section, internal hard disks are much faster than external ones. Some other factors that affect hard disk speed are as follows:

Revolutions per Minute (RPM)   The faster the platters spin, the faster the read/write heads can read from them. RPMs on hard disks range from 5,400 to 15,000. Obviously, this isn't an issue on solid-state drives, which use static RAM to store the data rather than discs because there are no platters.

Cache Size   Just like a processor, a hard disk has a small, integrated RAM cache for storing data that was recently used or is probably about to be asked for. The larger the drive's cache size, the more it can anticipate the OS's requests. Both mechanical and solid-state drives have caches.

Types of Hard Drive Connectors

Internal hard disks connect to the motherboard via a cable that uses one of three types of connectors:

Parallel Advanced Technology Attachment (PATA)   An old-technology type of connector that uses a wide ribbon-like cable with 40 wires (see Figure 2.9). Until a few years ago, nearly all hard disks used this type of connector; now it's nearly obsolete. Multiple wires in the cable send data bits in parallel (that is, at the same time).

FIGURE 2.9   A PATA hard disk cable

Small Computer System Interface (SCSI)   Like PATA, SCSI is a parallel interface; it uses a ribbon cable that is very similar to the PATA cable shown in Figure 2.9 but slightly wider (50 or 68 wires). SCSI was very popular in high-end systems at one point because they were faster and you could chain many SCSI devices together on a single interface with a single controller board. SCSI is no longer popular in mainstream systems because SATA has most of its advantages and is cheaper.

Serial Advanced Technology Attachment (SATA)   SATA is a newer technology connector that uses a seven-wire plug. Data is sent serially (that is, one bit at a time). SATA drives have the fastest data-transfer capabilities of the three, and the thinner and less bulky cables enable better air flow in the case (see Figure 2.10).

FIGURE 2.10   A SATA hard disk cable

In addition, each drive requires a power supply connector. PATA and SCSI drives require one type of power connector, and SATA drives require another. So if you want to use an SATA hard disk, you must make sure not only that the motherboard supports SATA, but also that the PC's power supply does.

> Many people—and the Strata objectives—refer to PATA drives as IDE or EIDE, but that isn't exactly accurate. IDE stands for Integrated Drive Electronics, and it refers to any hard disk drive that has the controller for the drive on a circuit board in the drive itself. That includes both PATA and SATA drives. In EIDE, the E stands for *Enhanced*. The enhancement was added many years ago, so nowadays every IDE drive is an EIDE drive; the terms are therefore mainly synonymous. SCSI is different from EIDE, because the controller for a SCSI drive is on the SCSI controller card (or motherboard, if the motherboard has a SCSI connector on it, although that's rare).

Older motherboards typically support only PATA; newer motherboards support both PATA and SATA. (PATA connectors are typically included for backward compatibility, especially with other non–hard disk devices that use the same interface, like CD and DVD drives.) A few motherboards support SCSI, but usually SCSI support comes from an add-on circuit board installed in one of the motherboard's expansion slots.

Small hard disks (the type with 2.5" platters) designed for notebooks use a miniature version of the standard PATA connector, or they use the same standard SATA connector as a desktop PC hard disk drive.

Master/Slave Jumpers and PATA

The parallel ATA interface on a motherboard uses a 40-pin ribbon cable that has three connectors on it. One goes to the motherboard, and the other two—one in the middle of the cable and one at the other end—go to drives. If you have only one PATA drive, you use the connector at the far end of the cable, and the extra connector in the middle of the cable goes unused.

A PATA drive can be either the master (MA) or the slave (SL) on that cable. If there is only one drive on the cable, it's automatically the master, and you set its jumper to indicate that. (Some drives have a Single setting that's different from Master, to be used in a single-drive situation.) If there are two drives, you must set the jumper on one of the drives to Master and the jumper on the other drive to Slave. This tells the motherboard which is which. Alternatively, you can use a special cable that assigns mastery or slavery to a drive based on the connector into which it's plugged. (That's called Cable Select, or CS.) However, you must set the jumpers on each of the drives to the CS setting in order to use that feature, so you don't really save any time. When a newly installed PATA drive doesn't work, it's often because the jumpers aren't set correctly.

RAID Systems

For PCs in situations where the continued running of the hard disk is critical, such as a server on which many salespeople rely, it may be useful to implement a *RAID* system. (*RAID* stands for *redundant array of independent disks*.) A RAID system bundles multiple physical hard disks together to work as a team for increased performance, increased reliability, or both.

RAID 0 combines multiple drives to make one large drive. It offers faster disk access than a single volume because more read/write heads are reading or writing simultaneously. RAID 1 combines multiple drives also, but one drive is an exact copy of the others. If one drive physically fails, the data is all still safe and sound on the other ones.

RAID versions 2 through 6 (of which RAID 5 is the most popular) all do basically the same thing, with minor differences. They increase both performance and reliability by using at least three physical hard disks together and striping the data across all the drives using a parity-based error recovery method to ensure that if one drive fails, whatever it held can be reconstructed using the data from the remaining ones. In addition, striping data across multiple drives increases throughput performance.

In a nutshell, here's how parity-based error recovery works. Let's say that you have the binary number 101 to store, and you have four physical drives in your RAID. Each bit is stored on a different physical disk, and a parity bit is stored on yet another physical disk. The parity bit is set either to 1 (if the total of the other numbers summed is odd) or 0 (if the total is even). In this case, the total (1+1) is even, so the parity bit would be set to 0.

Now let's say that drive #2 of the set fails. Looking at the other data you have, you know that the first number is 1, the third number is 1, and the parity is even. With that information, you can deduce that the missing number is 0. Voilà, you've just reconstructed that bit. When RAID stripes data across multiple drives, it alternates which drive will hold the parity bit so that the data is evenly spread out across all drives. Then, if one of the drives ever needs to be replaced, a utility can reconstruct every bit that the old drive contained. That's the general concept, but in all except RAID 2, the data is striped in 64KB chunks, rather than individual bits. Working with larger blocks of data makes the operations go faster.

Low-Level Formatting

When a disk is manufactured, its surface is one large area. Before the disk can accept any data, an organizational structure must be imposed that uniquely names each physical location on the disk. That way, the drive controller can specify the exact physical spot where a given bit of data should be written or retrieved.

Here are the organizational units into which a disk is divided:

Heads   Almost all magnetic disks are double-sided. There is a separate read/write head for each side. On hard drives, there are usually multiple stacked platters, each with a top and bottom head.

Tracks   Each disk side is organized into concentric rings called *tracks*, like the rings on a cross-section of a tree. A high-capacity hard disk can have tens of thousands of tracks.

Cylinders   The read/write heads move in and out on a single actuator arm so that all the heads are in the same in-out position at all times. The stacks of tracks accessible at a given arm position is a cylinder. The number of cylinders a drive contains is the same as the number of tracks on a single disk side.

Sectors   The surface of the disk is further divided into pie slices made by lines that cross over the track lines. Where these lines intersect the track lines, they create small segments called *sectors*. Sectors are uniquely numbered, and they can be referred to by their numbers when their data is needed. Each sector holds 512 bytes on most disks.

This slicing up of the disk surface into logical organizational units is accomplished by a procedure known as low-level formatting. *Low-level formatting* determines the number and spacing of the tracks and the number and spacing of sectors per track. Together, these two factors determine the total number of sectors on the disk and therefore its storage capacity.

Hard disks are low-level formatted at the factory. A label on a hard drive casing reports the number of cylinders, heads, and sectors for the disk, sometimes abbreviated *CHS*. Another name for the drive's organizational characteristics is *geometry*. BIOS setup requires this information in order to communicate with the drive.

In the early days of hard disks, the CHS values reflected the physical reality of how a disk was low-level formatted. Today, however, that is no longer the case. A drive's CHS values don't necessarily refer to the exact physical arrangement on the drive, but to the logical way that the drive controller sees the drive as it communicates with it. For example, a drive's label might report that it has 16 heads (8 platters) when it actually has only 3 or 4.

Partitioning a Disk and Creating Logical Drives

An OS doesn't deal directly with the physical hard disk. Instead it deals with logical drives. A *logical drive* is a drive letter that has been assigned to a portion of a physical disk. A single physical disk can have multiple logical drives. The OS might see a C drive, a D drive, and an E drive, for example, all of which are part of a single physical disk drive.

To create these logical drives, you must first create *partitions*. At a minimum you need to create one *primary partition*. You can allocate all the space on the entire physical drive, or you can set aside some of the space for another partition. If you do set aside space, you can create an *extended partition* and then create additional logical drives on that partition. When you partition a physical drive, it creates a *master boot record (MBR)* that contains information about each partition and logical drive. The OS looks to the MBR to determine what drive letters you have.

Partitioning requires a disk management utility. Each OS comes with at least one such utility, and third-party partitioning utilities are also available. The Windows Setup program contains a partitioning and formatting utility and, within Windows, you can use the Disk Management utility (from Computer Management, as you'll see in the upcoming exercise) to partition and format drives. In earlier versions of Windows, a text-based utility called FDISK was used to manage partitions. If you're using the Windows Recovery Console, a similar program called DISKPART manages partitions.

A disk needs to be partitioned only once; you should repartition a drive only if you want to change the allocation of the disk space to the various drive letters. Repartitioning a drive, in most cases, will wipe out the current contents of the drive, so don't change the partitions on a drive that contains data you want to keep. Some third-party partitioning programs can do a nondestructive repartition—that is, can change the partition sizes without losing any data.

Computers that come with a hidden recovery partition are set up such that the single hard disk is split into two partitions, one of which contains the hidden backup files and the other of which contains the C: drive, the main drive that you work with when you access the computer's hard disk. The fact that there are two partitions isn't obvious until you run a recovery utility that accesses the hidden one.

High-Level Formatting

After you create the partitions and the logical drives, the OS sees them but can't read and write them because they haven't yet been high-level formatted. High-level formatting lays down an organization system that is compatible with the specific OS installed.

In Windows XP and higher, the predominantly used file system is NTFS. FAT32 is an older file system that is backward compatible with earlier Windows versions, such as Windows 98. For NTFS, high-level formatting entails creating a *master file table (MFT)* that contains pointers to the starting points of files and folders. It's essentially a table of contents for the logical drive. A *volume boot record* is also created, which stores information needed to boot from the drive, and a *root directory* (that is, a top-level folder).

To make addressing the various locations on the disk less complex, high-level formatting groups sectors into *clusters*, also called *allocation units*. It then addresses the various locations by cluster, rather than by individual sector. Depending on the size of the disk and the file system used, a cluster can contain anywhere from 1 to 128 sectors. Each sector holds 512 bytes, so an allocation unit can range from 512 bytes to 65,536 bytes.

After a disk has been partitioned, you can format it in Windows either using the Disk Management utility (covered in the next exercise) or from the Computer window. To do the latter, right-click the drive letter, select Format, and follow the prompts.

Formatting wipes out anything that the disk currently contains, so don't reformat a drive that contains anything you want to keep.

EXERCISE 2.4

Examining Partition and Formatting Settings

1. In Windows 7, click Start and type **Computer,** and then click Computer Management at the top of the Start menu. The Computer Management console opens.

2. In the left pane of the console, click Disk Management. Information about each disk drive appears. Yours will be different from the example shown here. What follows is an explanation of what you see in the example.

In the example, there is one physical disk (Disk 0, shown as one row in the lower pane), which is divided into three partitions.

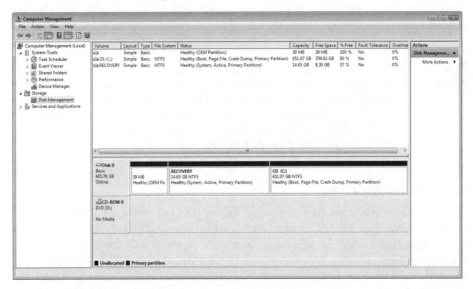

The first partition is an OEM partition. OEM stands for original equipment manufacturer; some computer companies use a hidden partition such as this one to store proprietary information for that model of computer.

The second partition, named RECOVERY, is the hidden partition on which the system recovery files are stored. This partition is the System partition, which means it contains the disk's boot sector (the sector that holds the boot data). It's also the Active partition, which means it's the first partition in which the system looks for the boot files. Only one partition can be active.

The third partition, named OS, has the drive letter C: assigned to it; it's the only one of the three partitions that is normally visible to the computer user. This partition is the Boot partition, meaning it contains the Windows startup files. It's also the Page File partition, meaning it's where the paging file is stored for virtual memory (as explained in Chapter 1, "Core Computer Hardware"), and the Crash Dump partition, meaning it's where information about system crashes will be written.

Each of the partitions appears in the example as Healthy, meaning it's operational. The OS and RECOVERY partitions show a file system of NTFS, meaning they have been formatted. The OEM partition may contain files in a proprietary file system that only the BIOS can understand; it isn't readable in Windows.

3. Examine your own partitions and logical drives. Don't make any changes.

4. Close the Computer Management window.

Creating Network Shares

When many people need access to the same data, system administrators may choose to place that data on a centrally accessible file server on a network. The folder containing the data is then made accessible to—that is, shared with—the people who need it. This is called a *network share*. You can also share folders on your own hard disk with others on a network.

Network shares can be set up as mapped drive letters, so that the folder being shared appears as a separate drive letter on the user's PC. For example, you might access a personnel folder for your company from the network as if it were drive P: on your system.

File servers only used to be for companies that had dedicated servers for their networks, but some wireless access points now come with *network attached storage (NAS),* and stand-alone NAS devices are also available. NAS is a hard drive configured to function as a network share, independently of any individual PC. You could use a NAS device to share music or video clips in your home, for example, or important client files in a small business.

As convenient as network sharing can be, it also has its risks. Any folder you make available on your local network can be accessed by anyone who gets access to that network. If you have an unsecured wireless network, anyone driving by your house with a laptop in their car could potentially snoop your files and even steal your private information. Chapter 9, "Security and Access Control," points out some ways to minimize the risks.

Many file-downloading services, such as BitTorrent, use local shares to enable the mass distribution and downloading of many different file formats. This peer-based system is incredibly powerful in principle, both for you as the file sharer and to unscrupulous hackers who seek to exploit your system. Unless you have developed adept networking security and system management skills, you're best advised to ensure that you don't open your hard drive to any file sharing beyond the local system you trust.

EXERCISE 2.5

Sharing a Folder on a Network

1. In Windows 7, click Start and then click Computer. Double-click the C: drive to open it.

2. Click New Folder. A new folder appears. For its name, type **Test Share** and press Enter.

3. Right-click the new folder, and click Properties. The Test Share Properties dialog box opens.

4. Click the Sharing tab.

5. Click the Share button. The File Sharing dialog box opens.

6. In the text box above the list of names, type **Everyone** as shown in the example here. Everyone is a system-defined group that includes all users.

7. Click the Add button. The Everyone group is added to the list of names.

8. Click the down arrow next to Read on the Everyone line as shown, opening a menu, and click Read/Write.

9. Click Share. A message appears that the folder is shared.

10. Click Done. The folder is now shared, and others on your network can access it.

11. Click Close to close the dialog box.

Compact Disc Drives

Compact discs (CDs) are widely used to distribute music, software, and video games. CDs, along with their relatives DVDs, are optical media, storing data in patterns of more and less reflective areas on a disc platter. CDs store data as a series of microscopic indentations, known as *pits* and *lands*. A pit is less reflective than a land, so when the light of the drive's laser hits a pit, less light reflects back to the sensor than when it hits a land. Whenever there is a transition between light levels, the drive electronics register that as a 1. Whenever enough time passes that there could have been a transition but there wasn't one, it registers that as a 0. And that's how binary data is stored and read on a CD.

Round discs like CDs and DVDs are discs (with a *c*). Square disks like floppy and hard disks are disks (with a *k*). Yes, technically inside a hard disk drive are round platters, but because you can't see or access them, the *k* moniker has stuck with hard disk drives in popular usage. Just remember: square=*k*, round=*c*.

CD drives that just read CDs, but don't write to them, are known as *CD-ROM drives*. (Recall from Chapter 1 that ROM stands for Read-Only Memory.) That's the type of drive we'll talk about first; later in this chapter, we'll get into the writeable and rewriteable varieties.

The first CD-ROMs could store 650 MB of data or play 74 minutes of analog audio. Later versions supported 800 MB or 90 minutes, which is the most common type found today. A high-capacity version is available (but not as widely used) that can hold 900 MB or 99 minutes.

CD Drive Speeds

CD drives can have different RPMs—that is, different speeds at which the discs spin. On a CD drive, the RPM and the amount of data it can access per second are directly related, so the faster the RPM, the faster the drive can deliver data. (This relationship is much more direct with CD drives than it is with hard disk drives, where a variety of other factors complicate the equation.)

CD speeds are defined in comparison to the original speed of a CD back when the technology was first invented in the 1980s. This original speed, known as 1x, is between 200 and 500 RPM. That range varies because the original CD drives used *constant linear velocity (CLV)*. The drives read data at a consistent speed, no matter which spot on the disk was being read at the time. Because the inner rings on a disk are much smaller than the outer ones, the speed at which the disk spun had to change when accessing different areas. The disk spun fastest when reading the inner rings, at 500 RPM. It spun slowest when reading the outer rings, at 200 RPM.

Later CD drives, including all writeable CD drives (covered later in this chapter), changed to a different technology known as *constant angular velocity (CAV)*. With CAV, the disc always spins at the same speed, and it's the reading speed that varies.

Table 2.3 lists some speeds and compares their maximum data rates and RPMs.

TABLE 2.3 CD speeds

Speed	Maximum Data Rate (Megabits per Second)	RPM	Technology
1x	1.23	200–500	CLV
2x	2.46	400–1,000	CLV
10x	9.83	800–2,000	CLV
20x	24.6	4,000	CAV
40x	49.2	7,200	CAV
56x	68.8	11,200	CAV

In addition to considering a drive's speed, you should also consider its access time. *Access time* is the amount of time that elapses between a PC's request for data from the CD and the drive's delivery of the first part of that data. This is mostly a measure of the drive's mechanical ability to move the head to the correct spot. Access time isn't directly related to the drive's rotational speed, although drives with faster speeds also tend to have superior mechanics. A 1x drive has a typical access time of around 400 milliseconds (ms). Today's best-performing drives have an access time of around 75 ms.

CD drives, like hard drives, have built-in caches for buffering data—the larger the cache, the more efficient the drive. A good CD drive should have at least a 512 KB cache.

CD and DVD Drive Interfaces

CD and DVD drives use the same connectors as hard disks do to the motherboard. Depending on the model, they can use PATA, SATA, or SCSI, which were described earlier in this chapter.

CD Writing Technologies

CD-ROMs are read-only, but there are two technologies for creating your own CDs: CD-R and CD-RW.

CD-R, which stands for *Compact Disc Recordable*, can be written to only once (except in the case of multisession writing, where the previous content isn't exactly erased, but ignored, and the new content shown in the disc's file listing instead). *CD-RW* or *Compact Disc Rewriteable* can be written to, erased, and reused many times, functioning somewhat like a flash RAM drive. CD-RW is a good choice when you need to store small amounts of data over time, such as a daily backup of a few critical files. CD-R is more compatible with stereo systems and other non-computer devices that play audio CDs, so it's a better choice when burning a CD to which you don't expect to make changes.

In today's PCs, all writeable CD drives can read and write both CD-R and CD-RW discs. CD-R blanks are less expensive than CD-RW blanks, so you may want to keep both on hand for different usages.

PCs don't contain the manufacturing equipment to create the pitted aluminum layer that exists on a mass-produced CD. The recording process for CD-R is made possible by the fact that CD readers don't actually touch the surface of the disc—they only look at it. Thus a home-recorded CD need not actually have the pits, as long as it appears to have them. CD-R blanks have a dye-and-metal coating that is, in its natural state, very shiny. The laser zaps certain areas of the disc to make it less shiny, and therefore less reflective.

The CD drive's sensor interprets a less-reflective area as a pit, regardless of whether the area is actually pitted. Once a spot on a CD-R disc is made less reflective, it can't be undone.

In contrast, CD-RW doesn't use a dye-and-metal coating. Instead it's coated with a metal alloy with reflective properties that change depending on the temperature to which it's heated. Three settings are used. The high write setting heats the alloy to around 1,112 degrees Fahrenheit, at which temperature it liquefies. Then it solidifies again and loses its reflective properties. The same spot can be reheated by the low write setting to a lower temperature (around 392 degrees Fahrenheit), causing it to revert to its original reflectivity. That is how an area is rewritten. The lowest power setting reads the data without changing it.

DVD Drives

DVD stands for *Digital Versatile Disc* or *Digital Video Disc*. DVDs may look a lot like CDs, but technologically they're much more advanced and hold much more data. DVD drives can also read CDs, so it's rare to find a CD-only drive these days; most optical drives can read and write both CDs and DVDs.

A single-sided, single-layer DVD holds 4.7 GB; when you double the layers, that amount approximately doubles, and when you double the sides on which the disc can be written, you double the capacity once again. Table 2.4 provides a quick summary

 A double-layer disc has two sets of optical media on top of each other. The upper layer is semi-translucent; that is, it will let through a certain level of light without altering its data, so that two sets of data can coexist in the same surface area. Double-layer discs are common in mass-produced video DVDs because they enable longer movies to be placed on a single DVD. Many PC DVD drives can read and write double-layer discs too.

TABLE 2.4 DVD capacity

Single Sided	Double Sided	Single Layer	Double Layer	Capacity (Gigabytes)
✓		✓		4.7
✓			✓	8.54
	✓	✓		9.4
	✓		✓	17.08

Aside from storing more data, the data-transfer rates are greater for DVD than for CD. For each rotation, the drive reads from a DVD about nine times the amount of data that it reads from a CD. Table 2.5 illustrates how DVD rotational speeds translate to data transfer rates.

TABLE 2.5 DVD speeds

Speed	Maximum Data Rate (Megabits per Second)
1x	10.8
2x	21.6
4x	43.2
10x	108
20x	216
24x	259.2

DVD writeable and rewriteable blanks are available in two formats: DVD+ and DVD-. The writeable-once versions are DVD+R and DVD-R; the rewriteable versions are DVD+RW and DVD-RW. These are two different and competing technologies for how the data is written to the disc. Most drives can write in either format.

 Some non-computer DVD players, especially older ones, may reject one format or the other, so you may want to test your DVD player to make sure it can read movies written to a certain type of DVD disc before investing in a large quantity of blanks.

Blu-Ray Disk Drives

Blu-ray discs (BD) are physically similar to DVDs but hold more data, so they're suitable for high-definition movies and high-volume data storage. A BD can hold 25 GB per layer and can have up to two layers for a total of 50 GB. Table 2.6 summarizes Blu-ray storage capacities.

TABLE 2.6   Blu-ray storage capacity

Size	Number of Layers	Capacity (Gigabytes)
8 cm	1	7.8
8 cm	2	15.6
12 cm	1	25
12 cm	2	50

Blu-ray technology uses blue light lasers instead of the red ones used for CD and DVD reading and writing. (Drives that support all of those standards have two separate lasers.) The laws of physics behind the shorter wavelength of blue light allow for at least 10 times more data to be stored on a Blu-ray disc than on a DVD. Depending on the speed of the drive, data throughput can range from 36 to 432 Mbps, as outlined in Table 2.7.

TABLE 2.7   Blu-ray speeds

Speed	Data Rate (Megabits per Second)
1x	36
2x	72
4x	144
8x	288
12x	432

Flash RAM Storage

So far in this chapter, we've looked mainly at mechanical drives—their technologies, interfaces, and specifications. Next we'll look at devices that use nonvolatile RAM to store data. They're technically not drives, but the term *drive* is widely used for them because consumers are accustomed to that term for any device that holds data.

As you learned in Chapter 1, some types of RAM are nonvolatile, meaning they continue to hold whatever you put in them until you make a change. Flash RAM gets its name from the way it's written and erased. It's a form of *electrically erasable programmable read-only memory (EEPROM)*, which is memory that, like read-only memory, can hold what you put in it indefinitely, but can also be erased and rewritten by a burst (flash) of electricity.

There are various sizes and packaging of flash RAM storage devices, but what they all have in common is that they're solid state; that is, they have no mechanical parts. As a result, they don't wear out from mechanical use, they aren't as susceptible to data loss from physical trauma, they're silent when operating, and they use much less electricity than their mechanical counterparts.

Some of the devices in this category include USB flash drives (aka memory sticks), memory cards, and solid-state hard disks. The following sections cover each of those device types.

USB Flash Drives

A *flash drive*, also called a *thumb drive*, is a thumb-sized device that stores data on memory chips rather than on magnetic or optical media (see Figure 2.11). These devices can hold up to 256 GB of data, and they're useful for transferring files between PCs and between computers and other electronic devices.

FIGURE 2.11   A USB flash drive

A USB flash drive's speed is limited to the speed of the USB data bus. There are different versions of USB, and each has a different maximum speed. Most PCs today have a USB 2.0 data bus, which transfers data at up to 480 Mbps. In contrast, a SATA data bus has a maximum speed of between 1.5 Gbps and 3 Gbps.

Because USB flash drives are physically small, very portable, and capable of retaining large quantities of data, they're considered by many industry experts to be a serious security risk. Some organizations prohibit staff from using these devices on their systems. There have been widely reported cases of USB flash drives being found in public places with sensitive data on them. Some USB flash drives come with additional encryption, rendering the data useless to anyone except the authorized user.

Flash Memory Cards and Readers

A *flash memory card* contains the same flash RAM as a USB flash drive except that it's in a different kind of packaging. Instead of being on a stick-like USB device, it's embedded in a thin plastic cartridge with metal contacts that fit up against the metal contacts in a card reader.

Many non-computer devices use flash RAM cards to store data for eventual transfer to a computer. For example, digital cameras, digital video recorders, and some medical devices such as blood pressure and blood sugar meters store their output on flash RAM cards.

Because there is no port built into a flash memory card, it must be placed in a card reader, which is like a disk drive except that it reads memory cards instead of disks. Some computers have built-in card readers, and you can also buy external card readers that connect to a PC's USB port. Built-in card readers typically use the same data bus as hard disks, so data transfer is fast. External card readers are limited to the USB data-bus speed, as are USB flash drives. Figure 2.12 shows an example of a card reader that supports multiple card types.

FIGURE 2.12   An external multicard reader

Photo credit: King of Hearts, Wikimedia Commons

Several different sizes and shapes of flash memory cards are available, each with its own specifications and features. Some card readers can accept only one type of card; others can read and write multiple card types. Some of the common card types include CompactFlash (CF), SmartMedia (SM), MultiMediaCard (MMC), Secure Digital (SD), Memory Stick, and xD. Figure 2.13 shows a Secure Digital card.

FIGURE 2.13   A Secure Digital memory card

Photo credit: Wirepath, Wikimedia Commons

 For a very complete comparison of the various types and subtypes of flash memory cards, including their exact sizes and features, see http:// en.wikipedia.org/wiki/Comparison_of_memory_cards.

Cards vary not only in their sizes, shapes, and capacities, but also in whether they implement these features:

Write-Protection   Some types have a write-protection switch that enables you to set them to read-only.

Digital Rights Management (DRM)   Some types support a form of security encryption that allows you to make files on the card private.

Mobile Media Devices

A variety of mobile devices employ flash RAM as their primary means of storage. Today's mobile devices include smart phones, hand-held gaming devices, music players, and more. They all run their own proprietary OSs and applications, but they all rely on the same basic nonvolatile RAM technology as a flash RAM device or solid-state drive to hold it.

Many devices are multifunction. For example, a typical smart phone serves not only as a mobile phone, but also as a scheduling organizer, a music player, and even a Global Positioning System (GPS) device.

Solid-State Hard Drives

A *solid-state hard drive* isn't really a drive, but it's called that for consistency with mechanical hard drive terminology. Its central storage component is flash RAM, the same as other flash RAM devices. It differs from other flash RAM devices primarily in the data bus it uses. Solid-state hard drives use the same fast SATA or PATA interface as mechanical hard drives, and they have similar caches and controllers to mechanical hard drives.

Solid-state drives offer many benefits over mechanical ones and have few drawbacks. The primary drawback at this writing is price; mechanical drives are less expensive for equivalent storage capacity. Table 2.8 summarizes the pros and cons of each technology.

TABLE 2.8   Solid-state vs. mechanical hard disk drives

Advantages Solid State	Mechanical	Disadvantages Solid State	Mechanical
Faster start-up time	Lower cost per megabyte	Higher cost per megabyte	Slower startup time
Faster access, because there is no seek time for a read/write head to locate data	Theoretically unlimited writes to media	Limited lifetime, based on number of writes	Head seek time a factor, mitigated by disc revolution speed
Silent operation, no moving parts	Still has greater storage capacity		Less resilient to shock and damage
Low heat output and power consumption			
High mechanical reliability (no moving parts)			
Resilient to shock and damage			
Large data density (per square centimeter)			

EXERCISE 2.6

Shopping for Hard Drives

Visit the websites of some hard disk drive manufacturers, and compare their least and most expensive mechanical and solid-state hard drives. Here are some sites to try:

Western Digital: www.wdc.com/en/products/catalog/

Seagate: www.seagate.com/www/en-us/products/internal-storage/

What conclusions can you draw from this research? What were the main differentiating factors between the drives?

Summary

In this chapter, you learned about keyboards and pointing devices, two of the most common input devices for personal computers. You learned about the special keys on a keyboard for functions and other shortcuts, and about mice, trackballs, and touch pads.

You also learned about storage devices, both the mechanical and the solid-state varieties. You learned how mechanical hard drives work, and how drives are partitioned and formatted to make them addressable. Then you learned the differences between various CD and DVD technologies and about the various types of flash RAM storage available, from solid-state hard disks to portable music players.

Exam Essentials

Identify the keys found on a standard keyboard.   Besides alphanumeric and symbol keys, keyboards have a Windows key, modifier keys like Ctrl, function keys, arrow keys and, in some cases, an Fn key or a numeric keypad.

List the units of storage measurement.   A byte is 8 bits; a kilobyte is 1,024 bytes. A megabyte is 1,024 KB, a gigabyte is 1,024 MB, and a terabyte is 1,024 GB.

Explain how a mechanical hard disk stores data.   Hard disks store data on metal platters that are charged with patterns of positive and negative polarity. The drives are low-level formatted at the factory to create cylinders, heads, and sectors (CHS), and then they're partitioned and high-level formatted by the end-user.

Understand the factors that govern hard disk performance.   Hard disk performance is affected by the speed limitations of the interface used (PATA, SCSI, or SATA for internal drives; USB or FireWire for external ones) as well as the revolutions per minute and cache size.

Know the difference between low-level formatting, partitioning, and high-level formatting.   Low-level formatting is done at the factory. Partitioning breaks up the disk space into multiple sections, each of which can be a logical drive with its own drive letter. Formatting places a file system on a logical drive that is compatible with the OS in use.

Differentiate between various types of optical media.   Know the differences in capacities and capabilities between CD formats (CD-ROM, CD-R, CD-RW), DVD formats (DVD-ROM, DVD-R, DVD+R, DVD-RW, DVD+RW), and Blu-ray.

Identify types of flash RAM storage.   Flash RAM stores data in static solid-state memory chips, so there are no moving mechanical parts in a flash device. Flash devices include USB flash drives, portable music players, flash memory cards, and solid-state hard drives.

Review Questions

1. Which of these is an example of a modifier key on a keyboard?
   A. Shift
   B. F1
   C. Esc
   D. Tab

2. On what type of computer is an Fn key most likely to be found?
   A. Server
   B. Notebook PC
   C. Desktop PC
   D. Cell phone

3. What does a PS/2 connector most resemble?
   A. A small round plug
   B. A coin-slot
   C. A wide set of metal pins
   D. A four-pronged rectangular block

4. How does an optical mouse record movement?
   A. With Bluetooth
   B. With radio frequency (RF) output
   C. With a rolling ball
   D. An LED and photodiodes (light sensors)

5. With pen computing, you must use a(n) _____ to touch the screen.
   A. Mouse
   B. Stylus
   C. Tablet
   D. Finger

6. Characters are stored in binary format in a computer using _____ coding.
   A. RTF
   B. TXT
   C. GB
   D. ASCII

7. Which of these would be a common capacity for a modern hard disk drive?

    A. 500 GB

    B. 500 MB

    C. 500 KB

    D. 500 TB

8. What is the most popular interface used for external hard disk drives?

    A. PS/2

    B. SATA

    C. PATA

    D. USB

9. How is the speed of the spinning platters in a hard disk measured?

    A. Megabytes

    B. RPM

    C. Milliseconds

    D. None of the above

10. Which type of hard disk interface is serial?

    A. PATA

    B. SCSI

    C. SATA

    D. All of the above

11. Which hard disk interface uses a wide ribbon-like cable with 40 wires?

    A. PATA

    B. SATA

    C. SCSI

    D. USB

12. What type of disk preparation creates the cylinders, heads, and sectors (CHS)?

    A. Low-level formatting

    B. Partitioning

    C. High-level formatting

    D. Packet writing

13. What Windows utility can you use to partition a disk drive?

- **A.** Disk Formatter
- **B.** Check Disk
- **C.** Disk Management
- **D.** Disk Partitioner

14. To make a folder or drive available to others on a network, right-click the drive's icon in the Computer window and click _____.

- **A.** Services
- **B.** Share
- **C.** Group
- **D.** Read/Write

15. How much data can a standard single-sided writeable CD-ROM hold?

- **A.** 100 MB
- **B.** 800 MB
- **C.** 4.7 GB
- **D.** 9 GB

16. A Blu-ray drive uses a(n) _____ laser, which has a shorter wavelength than the type used on a CD or DVD player.

- **A.** High-frequency
- **B.** Blue
- **C.** High-RPM
- **D.** Purple

17. Which of these is not a type of flash RAM storage device?

- **A.** Solid-state hard drives
- **B.** Memory cards
- **C.** Portable digital music players
- **D.** CD-ROM

18. Which of these is a type of memory card?

- **A.** VGA
- **B.** SD
- **C.** DDR
- **D.** PATA

19. Which of these is a disadvantage of solid-state drives over mechanical ones?

    A. Noisier

    B. More expensive

    C. Less durable

    D. Uses more power

20. What does DRM support add to a flash RAM device or card?

    A. Speed

    B. Ability to reformat

    C. Security

    D. Low power consumption

Answers to Review Questions

1. A. A modifier key is one that does nothing when pressed by itself but causes another key to produce a different value when held down as it is pressed.

2. B. The Fn key is found on notebook computers. It's an alternative version of the Ctrl key; when combined with some other key press(es), it performs some special command, usually hardware-related.

3. A. A PS/2 connector, which is an older connector for keyboards and mice, is small and round.

4. D. Bluetooth and RF are two technologies that are sometimes used for wireless mice, but they have no relationship to how an optical mouse measures movement. A rolling ball is used in a mechanical mouse. An LED is used in an optical mouse.

5. B. A pen-shaped stylus is used to interact with the screen on a pen computing device. It is not an actual pen, because it does not have ink in it.

6. D. ASCII coding assigns a unique 7-digit or 8-digit binary number to each character. RTF is a word-processing file format. TXT is a text file format. GB is an abbreviation for gigabytes.

7. A. Hard disks store hundreds of gigabytes (GB). A very old hard disk might store 500 MB. 500 TB is larger than today's hard disks would store. 500 KB is a very small amount—less than one floppy disk's worth of data.

8. D. USB is the interface used for most external devices, including hard disk drives. PS/2 is an older style connector for keyboards and mice. PATA and SATA are connectors for internal hard disk drives.

9. B. The speed of the platters' spinning is measured in revolutions per minute, or RPM. Megabytes are a measure of storage space. Milliseconds are a measurement of time.

10. C. SATA is Serial ATA, a serial technology. Both Parallel ATA and Small Computer System Interface are parallel.

11. A. Parallel ATA uses a 40-wire cable. SATA uses a thin cable (not a ribbon cable). SCSI uses a 50-wire or 68-wire ribbon cable. USB uses a thin cable (not a ribbon cable).

12. A. The drive's CHS values are determined by its low-level formatting, which is done at the factory where the drive is manufactured.

13. C. The Disk Management utility, accessible from the Computer Management window, enables you to check and change partition information for a drive.

14. B. Right-click a drive and click Share to open the drive's Properties dialog box and display the Share tab. From there you can choose to share the drive (or folder).

15. B. A CD can hold 650, 800, or 900 MB of data, depending on the type.

16. B. Blu-ray gets its name from the fact that it uses a blue laser.

17. D. CD-ROM is optical and digital, but not flash RAM based. It stores data in patterns of pits and lands on a reflective surface.

18. B. Secure Digital (SD) is one type of memory card. VGA is a video standard. DDR refers to a type of dynamic RAM. PATA is an interface for mechanical hard disks.

19. B. Solid-state drives are quieter, higher capacity, faster, and use less energy than mechanical drives. However, they are more expensive.

20. C. DRM stands for Digital Rights Management, which refers to security encryption. Different brands and types of flash RAM devices have different security technologies (or none).

Chapter

3

Peripherals and Networking

FUNDAMENTALS OF PC FUNCTIONALITY OBJECTIVES COVERED IN THIS CHAPTER:

✓ **1.1 Identify basic IT vocabulary**

- Networking

✓ **1.3 Demonstrate the ability to set up a basic PC workstation**

- Identify differences between connector types: DVI, VGA, HDMI; Bluetooth and Wireless; Network connectors; 3.5mm audio jack 3.1

- Monitor types

- Printer (USB, wireless, networked)

✓ **3.1 Recognize basic security risks and procedures to prevent them**

- Identify prevention methods: Wireless Encryption (WPA/WEP)

FUNDAMENTALS OF PC TECHNOLOGY OBJECTIVES COVERED IN THIS CHAPTER:

✓ **1.1 U.K. / 1.2 U.S. Demonstrate the proper use of the following devices**

- Monitors

✓ **1.3 U.K. / 1.4 U.S. Explain the characteristics and functions of peripheral devices**

- Digital camera

- Web camera

- Speaker

- Tuner

- Microphone
- Printer/scanner

✓ **2.1 Identify basic compatibility issues between**

- Ethernet
- Wireless networks

In addition to the essential internal components in a PC, many other devices and technologies contribute to your computer's usability and productivity. In this chapter, we'll explore the uses of several types of computer peripherals.

This chapter also delves into the technologies and standards used in computer networking, both local area networks and larger ones such as the Internet.

Peripheral Devices

There are two possible definitions of a *peripheral device* in the context of personal computers. One is a device that is external to the main body of the computer. Under this definition, printers, monitors, mice, keyboards, and external drives are all considered peripherals. The other definition is a device that isn't essential to the computer's functioning, regardless of its internal or external status. Under this definition, the monitor, keyboard, and pointing device (such as a mouse) aren't peripherals because they're essential, but a sound card installed inside the computer is peripheral because the computer can operate without it. The Strata exam objectives mostly use the first definition. However, two of the items Strata includes, speakers and microphones, rely on a sound card (or motherboard sound support) in order to function, so in this chapter we'll consider sound cards as peripherals too.

Printers

All printers perform the same basic function: they put image onto paper. To do this, they all must have certain subsystems that perform these tasks, more or less in this order:

1. Receive data from the PC. Each printer has at least one input interface. For most printers today, this is a USB or network connection. Older printers may use a parallel port or serial port.

2. Store the data in RAM. The printer contains a small amount of RAM that holds the incoming data while it's waiting for the printer's physical print mechanism to output it. Printers that print one line at a time (like an inkjet) have less memory than printers that compose an entire page before transferring it to paper (like a laser).

3. Convert the data into print instructions. Each printer has a motherboard and processor inside that accept the data and convert it to instructions to the mechanical parts that transfer the image to paper.

4. Feed the paper in and out. Inside each printer is a series of gears, rollers, grabbers, and so on, which feed the paper through the printer.

5. Store and dispense ink or toner. A printer needs some sort of colored material to create the image on the page. Inkjets use liquid ink; laser printers use dry toner.

6. Transfer the image to the paper. Liquid ink is squirted out of nozzles (jets) onto the page. The force that drives the jets may be either heat or electricity. With dry toner, the magnetic particles in the toner are attracted to a charged drum and then to the paper; then they pass through a head unit that melts the plastic particles so they stick to the paper.

One printer is distinguished from another in the following ways:

Cost   This includes not only the initial cost of the printer, but also the cost of the ink or toner and routine maintenance.

Quality   The primary measurement of quality is *dots per inch (dpi)*, or resolution. A printer with a higher dpi will produce text with crisper edges and more realistic-looking graphics.

Photo Printing   Some printers are specifically designed to reproduce photos on special shiny photographic paper. In addition to having a high dpi, they may also use special photo ink.

Speed   A printer's speed is measured in *pages per minute (ppm)*. Printers that print in either black and white or color typically have two separate ppm ratings. A printer's ppm is a theoretical maximum, and it will seldom be achieved in real-life use.

Paper Tray   Some printers hold more paper at once than others. Some have multiple paper trays, so you can keep different paper types loaded at once, such as letterhead and plain paper, or letter-sized and legal-sized.

Interfaces   Some printers have only a local interface, like USB; others optionally support a wired or wireless network interface.

Other Functions   Some printers are multifunction, meaning they can also scan and make copies. Some of them also can serve as fax machines.

Two main technologies are available today for consumer printers: inkjet and laser. The following sections look at each of these technologies in detail.

 This chapter covers the types of printers and their general characteristics. To learn how to configure and use a printer, including how to install a driver for one, see Chapter 4, "Setting Up a Computer."

Inkjet Printers

Inkjet printers are printers that squirt ink onto paper. There are between 21 and 256 nozzles for each of the four colors (cyan, yellow, magenta, and black) in the print head, depending on the brand and model; the print engine tells the jets to squirt out ink in different combinations and proportions for whatever colors are needed. Some photo printers have six or eight cartridges, because different types of ink are used in some print jobs.

There are two technologies for forcing ink out of the nozzles: thermal and piezoelectric.

Thermal inkjet printers heat the ink to about 400 degrees Fahrenheit, which creates vapor bubbles that force out the ink. This creates a vacuum inside the cartridge which, in turn, draws more ink into the nozzles. This technology is also called *bubble jet* printing. Because the heat tends to degrade the print heads over time, ink replacement cartridges for these models often include replacement print heads as well. These cartridges shouldn't be home-refilled because, by simply refilling the ink, you don't get the new print head you need.

In contrast, *piezoelectric inkjet*, or *piezo*, moves the ink with electricity instead of heat. The nozzles contain piezoelectric crystals, which change their shape when electricity is applied to them and force out the ink. Piezo technology is easier on the printer because it doesn't need a heating element, and it's better for the output because the ink is less prone to smearing.

Inkjet printers are *line printers*; they print the document in a series of horizontal passes as the print head moves vertically past the print head. Therefore an inkjet printer requires only a limited amount of RAM—just enough to hold a few fonts and a few lines' worth of data. Most inkjet printers don't even advertise the amount of RAM they contain because it isn't important.

Laser Printers

A *laser printer* works much like a photocopier. The main difference is that a photocopier scans a document to produce an image, whereas the laser printer receives digitized data from a computer.

A laser printer contains a large cylinder known as a *drum*, which carries a high negative electrical charge. The printer directs a laser beam to partially neutralize the charge in certain areas of the drum. When the drum rotates past a toner reservoir, the toner clings to the areas of lesser charge, and the page image is formed on the drum. Then the drum rotates past positively charged paper, and the toner jumps off onto the paper. The paper then passes through a fuser that melts the plastic particles of the toner so that it sticks to the paper.

Laser printers are available in color or monochrome models. To print in color, a laser printer must make four passes across the same page, laying down a different color each time. Such a printer has four separate toner cartridges: cyan, magenta, yellow, and black.

Although you're unlikely to do so, if you spill any toner, let it settle before you clean it up. Toner is a fine powder and is carcinogenic. A *carcinogen* is a product that, with long-term continued exposure, may cause cancer. The most prudent course of action is always to refer to the health and safety guidelines that come from the manufacturer.

Setting Up a Printer

Most printers today use a USB connection. Any full-size USB cable and port will work, but the fastest performance will come with a USB 2.0 or higher cable.

USB is a Plug and Play interface. Thus when you connect the printer to the computer, the computer will likely recognize the printer automatically and set it up for you. However, having the printer automatically set up isn't always a good thing! Some printers come with their own special software that makes them easier to use, and multifunction printers come with special software that enables their extra features like faxing, scanning, and copying. If you allow Windows to auto-install the printer via Plug and Play, you may miss out on some of these features. Therefore, the instructions that come with some printers specify that you should run the setup software first, and then connect the printer only when specifically told to do so during the setup.

Some older printers use a *parallel printer* interface. A parallel printer cable connects to a 25-pin parallel connector, also called the *LPT port*, on the PC. (Most PCs made today don't have this connector.) At the other end of the parallel printer cable is a 36-pin Centronics connector that connects to the printer. (*Centronics* is a brand and type of connector that uses a plastic bar wrapped with metal tabs. Figure 3.1 shows a Centronics connector.) This type of connector isn't Plug and Play, and the computer must be off in order for it to be connected or disconnected.

FIGURE 3.1   Centronics connector on an old parallel printer interface

Sharing a Printer on a Network

After setting up a printer to print on your local PC, you may decide also to make it available to other users on your network. This is called *sharing* the printer. When a printer is shared, others can use it as long as the PC doing the sharing remains powered on. If you turn off that PC, nobody else will be able to use the shared printer. (If that's unacceptable, consider a network-enabled printer, which has its own address on the network independent of any PC.) To share a printer, open the Printer Properties for the printer and, on the Sharing tab, select the Share This Printer check box.

EXERCISE 3.1

Share a Printer on a Network

1. In Windows 7, click Start ➢ Printers And Devices.

2. Right-click the printer you want to share. This should be a local printer, not one that you access via the network.

3. Click Printer Properties.

4. Click the Sharing tab.

5. Select the Share This Printer check box.

6. Click OK. The dialog box closes, and the printer becomes shared.

Connecting to a Network Printer

If someone else has shared their printer on the network, or if the network contains one or more network-enabled printers, you can set up those printers on your own PC so that you can print to them via the network. To do so, start adding a new printer from Windows and, when prompted, specify that it's a network printer. Windows will then check the network and present you with a list of the available printers it finds. From that point you just follow the prompts to set up the printer on your PC.

EXERCISE 3.2

Connect to a Network Printer

1. In Windows 7, click Start ➤ Printers And Devices.

2. Click Add A Printer.

3. Click Add A Network, Wireless, Or Bluetooth Printer. A list of printers on your network appears.

    Notice in the following graphic that the same printer was found twice because it has two connections: it's locally connected to one of the PCs on the network—hence the network path \\XPS\HP Photosmart C4700 series. Because it also has its own network IP address, 192.168.2.4, it appears that way too. In this case, it would be better to share the printer via its IP address so that it will continue to be available even when the local computer isn't running.

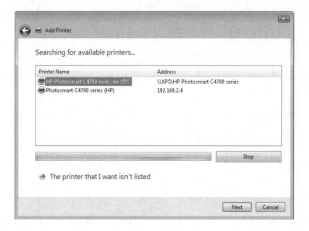

4. Click the printer to which you'd like to connect, and then click Next. The printer driver is installed. Windows may prompt you for a driver, on CD for example, if it can't find one.

5. Follow the prompts that appear (which may vary depending on the printer) to complete the installation.

Monitors

A *monitor* is a video display screen. On a notebook computer, the monitor is built in; on a desktop computer, it's a separate component attached to the main computer with a cable.

LCDs

Most monitors sold today are *liquid crystal display (LCD)*, the same type of flat-panel display found on modern TVs (see Figure 3.2).

FIGURE 3.2 LCD monitor

An LCD screen has two polarized filters, between which are liquid crystals. In order for light to appear on the display screen, it must pass through both filters and the crystals. The second filter, however, is at an angle to the first, so by default nothing passes through. By applying current to the crystal, you can cause it to twist, which also twists the light passing through it. If the light twists so that it matches the angle of the second filter, it can pass through the filter and light up an area of the display. On a color LCD, an additional filter splits the light into separate cells for red, green, and blue.

CRTs

You may occasionally also see an older type of monitor, the *cathode ray tube (CRT)*. This is a boxy monitor, like an old-style television.

A CRT is essentially a large vacuum tube. At the back of the CRT is a long, narrow neck containing a cathode, and at the front is a broad, rectangular surface with colored phosphors on it. When the cathode is heated, it emits negatively charged electrons. Those electrons are attracted to the positively charged front of the CRT where they strike the phosphors and cause them to light up. In a color CRT, there are three electron guns, one for each color: red, green, and blue. The actual colors are created by the phosphors on the screen. For each *pixel* (colored dot) on the screen, there are three phosphors—red, green, and blue—arranged in a triangle formation called a *triad*. Each electron gun works only on dots of a certain color. So, for example, if a certain pixel is supposed to be purple, the red and blue guns will fire at it, but the green gun won't.

The distance between one color in a triad and the same color in the adjacent triad is the *dot pitch* of the monitor. Dot pitch is the primary measurement of CRT quality. The lower the number, the closer the dots are together, which makes for a better quality picture.

Types of Monitor Connectors

A monitor can use either an analog or a digital connection to the computer. CRTs are analog only, by their nature. LCD monitors can use either an analog or digital connector, and they usually come with both types of plugs. (Some low-end LCD models are analog-interface only.)

Video Graphics Adapter (VGA) is the analog style of monitor connector (see Figure 3.3). For many years, VGA was the most popular monitor connector type available for personal computers. A VGA connector is a *D-sub connector* (that is, a connector with a D-shaped metal ring around a set of pins) with 15 pins arranged in three rows (4, 5, and 6 pins). When a VGA connector is used, the computer converts the data to an analog signal before sending it to the monitor; the monitor passively receives the signal and displays the information.

FIGURE 3.3 VGA connector

Digital Visual Interface (DVI) is the modern alternative (and successor) to VGA. It's a rectangular plug consisting of 24 pins (arranged in three rows of 8) for digital transmission plus an extra 4-pin block arranged around a plus-shaped spacer that sends analog signals (for backward compatibility). See Figure 3.4.

FIGURE 3.4 DVI connector

High-Definition Multimedia Interface (HDMI) is an even newer digital video interface. DVI and HDMI share some specifications, but HDMI doesn't have the four analog pins for VGA compatibility (see Figure 3.5). HDMI also carries digital audio as well as video. HDMI is used most often for television and home theatre components; it isn't commonly used on personal computers as of this writing.

FIGURE 3.5 HDMI connector

Photo by Alexey Goral

Adjusting a Monitor

When you change the monitor resolution (via the display driver properties in the Control Panel in Windows, for example), the onscreen image may shift in one direction or become slightly larger or smaller than it was before. Most monitors have onscreen controls that can be used to adjust the image size, image position (known as *phase* when referring to left-right positioning), contrast, brightness, and other factors. Check the monitor's manual to figure out how the controls work; they're different for each model.

Inexpensive or old CRTs may have just a couple of thumbwheels or knobs for monitor adjustment; newer and more sophisticated monitors will have a complete digital menu system of controls that pop up when you press a certain button. You then move through the menu system by pressing buttons on the monitor or moving a wheel or stick on the front or back of the monitor.

 On a CRT, there may be a *Degauss* button. You press this button to discharge a built-up magnetic field within the monitor that may be causing the picture to be distorted. LCDs don't have this problem, so they don't have a Degauss feature. It's named after Carl Friedrich Gauss, a researcher who studied magnetism.

On a notebook PC's built-in monitor, adjustment controls may be more basic. You're likely to find certain keys on the keyboard with extra symbols in a contrasting color. Pressing these keys in combination with the Fn key activates that special function. For example, there may be a key with a picture of the sun with an up arrow that increases the display brightness. Consult the notebook PC's manual to learn the various meanings of the Fn function keys.

EXERCISE 3.3

Adjust a Monitor

1. Locate the buttons on your monitor that control its image.

2. Experiment with the buttons to see if you can determine what they do. Or, look up the buttons in the monitor's documentation or on the manufacturer's website.

Sound Systems

A computer's sound subsystem consists of all the components involved in sound input and output. The brain of this operation is the *sound card*. On some systems, the sound card is a separate expansion board; on others, sound-card functionality is built into the motherboard. The other major components of the sound subsystem are the speakers (for output) and the microphone (for input). You can also optionally hook up other output and input sources as needed. For example, you may connect a home stereo system as an input device to record music from LPs onto audio CDs.

Sound cards and sound support on PCs rely almost exclusively on small round audio jacks that accommodate 3.5 mm plugs. If you need to connect something that doesn't have that kind of plug, you'll need to purchase an adapter.

The Strata objectives' Acronyms list includes MPEG, MP3, and MP4. MPEG stands for Moving Pictures Experts Group, which is an organization that governs the standards for some video and audio file formats. MP3 stands for Moving Picture Experts Group Layer 3, an audio standard. MP3 clips are usually music files. MP4 stands for Moving Picture Experts Group Layer 4, a video standard.

Speakers

Speakers enable you to hear the audio output from the PC. Speakers can be either internal (as in a notebook PC) or external (as on a desktop PC).

Depending on the quality of the sound support in the PC (either built in or an add-on expansion card), there may be one speaker jack or several. A system that supports surround sound or other advanced speaker sets may have color-coded jacks, as described in Table 3.1.

TABLE 3.1   Color coding for sound output plugs

Color	Role
Lime green	Main audio output for speakers or headphones
Dark brown	Audio output for special panning, right to left speaker
Black	Surround-sound speakers
Orange	Center speaker and subwoofer

Speakers differ from one another in the following ways:

Amplification   Most speakers provide some sort of *amplification*, which makes the sound louder as it comes out of the PC. Without amplification, the sound generated by the PC may not be loud enough to listen to comfortably. Amplification requires electrical power, either AC or battery, so any speakers that don't have either type of power are non-amplified. Amplification is power measured in watts. If there's a subwoofer, it will have its own watts (more is better), as will each of the satellite speakers. An average wattage for a subwoofer is around 18, and for each satellite speaker it may be around 6.

There are three ways of describing a speaker's maximum wattage. Make sure when you're comparing models that you're getting an apples-to-apples comparison. *Root mean square (RMS)* is the standard measurement of the wattage a speaker can reliably handle in a sustained manner. RMS maximum is the wattage the speaker can handle in short bursts. *Peak music power output (PMPO)* is the absolute maximum the speaker can handle for a split second, just before it dies from wattage overload.

Shielding   Speakers designed to be used on or near computers typically have shielding built in so the magnets in the speakers don't interfere with any of the computer's components. In contrast, speakers designed for home stereo systems usually don't have shielding.

Frequency Range   Speaker systems with a very wide frequency range will reproduce sounds much more accurately. Look for a frequency range of at least 50 to 10,000 Hz.

Analog vs. Digital   Most speakers are analog. The speaker connector on a sound card sends analog data to the speaker. However, digital speakers are also available, and hardcore audiophiles claim that they're better—less background noise and hiss at higher volumes. To use digital speakers, you have to have a digital out port on the sound card.

EXERCISE 3.4

Configure Speaker Options in Windows

1. Choose Start ➤ Control Panel ➤ Hardware And Sound ➤ Sound. The Sound dialog box opens with the Playback tab displayed. (Another way to get to this dialog box is to right-click the speaker icon in the notification area and click Playback devices.)

2. On the Playback tab, click Speakers/Headphones.

3. Click Properties. The Speakers/Headphones Properties dialog box opens.

4. Click through each of the tabs in the dialog box to see what options are available for your speakers.

5. Click Cancel, and then click Cancel again to close the open dialog boxes.

6. In the Control Panel window, under the Sound heading, click Adjust System Volume. A Volume Mixer dialog box opens.

7. Browse the available options for controlling the relative volumes of different types of sounds. Close the window when you're finished.

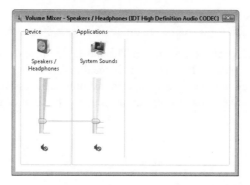

Microphones

Most computer systems have at least one built-in microphone input. A pink socket is for unpowered sound input such as a microphone, whereas a light blue line-in socket is used when the sound is expected to come from a powered source such as an MP3 player. Digital microphones plug into a USB port instead of a mic port.

Many laptops come with built-in microphones. For desktop systems, you can purchase standalone desktop microphones or combination headset microphones. If the PC supports Bluetooth devices, you can also use a Bluetooth headset as a microphone. Stereo headphones are also available that come with built-in microphones. These are popular among online gamers who use team-talk style technologies to communicate and interact during game play.

Here are the key factors involved in shopping for a microphone:

Frequency Response   This should be at least 100 to 8,000 Hz for the microphone.

Stereo vs. Mono   If you're choosing a headset/microphone combo, make sure the headphones are stereo.

Unidirectional   Make sure you get a microphone that is *unidirectional*, not omnidirectional. An *omnidirectional* microphone picks up sound in all directions, so in addition to capturing your voice, it also captures background sounds. That's usually undesirable.

Headset vs. Desktop   A desktop microphone has its own stand that holds it upright on your desk. It's hard to get your mouth close enough to it and keep it in the right position to ensure consistent recording level. Go for a headset microphone if possible.

Analog vs. Digital   An analog microphone plugs into the mic port on the sound card. The headset kind has two plugs: one for the mic jack and one for the headphones jack on the computer. A digital microphone plugs into a USB port. Digital microphones tend to have better frequency response. However, you have to have a free USB port in order to use one.

A microphone is technologically pretty simple. Just plug it into the computer, and it starts working. Any configuration you may need to do would be in the sound card's properties, not on the microphone itself.

EXERCISE 3.5

Configure Microphone Options in Windows

1. Right-click the speaker icon in the notification area (by the clock), and click Recording Devices. The Sound dialog box opens with the Recording tab displayed.

2. Click Microphone Array.

3. Click Properties. The Microphone Array Properties dialog box opens.

4. Click through each of the tabs in the dialog box to see what options are available for your microphone.

5. Click Cancel twice to close the open dialog boxes.

Scanners

A *scanner* digitizes a hard-copy page, converting it into a graphic file on the PC. Most scanners are flatbed, like a copier. Figure 3.6 shows an example of a flatbed scanner.

FIGURE 3.6   Flatbed scanner

You place the original face down on the glass and close the lid, and then either press a button on the scanner or issue a command in a scanning program to start the scan. Scanners can be purchased as stand-alone units or as part of a multifunction printer-scanner-copier. Scanners can use parallel, network, or USB interfaces, but most use USB.

Inside a scanner is a fixed linear array called a *charge-coupled device (CCD)*. It's composed of an array of photosensitive cells, similar to the eye of an insect, which converts light into an electrical charge. A light bar moves across the object being scanned. A system of mirrors reflects the light to a lens and then into the CCD. The mirrors are slightly curved to compact the image as it reflects. Each of the photosensitive cells produces an electrical signal proportional to the strength of the reflected light that hits it, and that signal is converted to a binary number and sent to the computer. Dark areas have lower numbers; light ones have higher numbers.

The CCD receives data for one line of the image at a time, sends it on to the computer, and then tells the stepper motor to advance the lamp to the next line. The CCD doesn't have to have a number of cells equivalent to the number of pixels in the entire page—only the number of pixels in a single row. On a scanner that can accept an 8.5 × 11-inch sheet, at 300 dpi, that's about 2,600 cells. Scanners with a higher dpi have more CCD cells—for example, about 10,400 in a 1,200 dpi scanner. This is the scanner's *horizontal dpi*, or *horizontal resolution* (also called the *x-direction sampling rate*). Some scanners also report a *vertical dpi*, or *vertical resolution*, also called the *y-direction sampling rate*. This is the number of separate lines per inch that are recorded as the light moves down the page.

Some scanners also have an *interpolated resolution*. Interpolation invents extra pixels between the actual scanned ones and uses a math formula to determine their value. For example, if one pixel has a value of 10 and the next one is 20, interpolation will insert a pixel between them with the value of 15.

In a color scanner, there are three separate evaluations of each pixel in the image: amount of red, amount of blue, and amount of green. The original scanners were 1-bit systems; they were black-and-white only and transmitted a single bit of data for each cell in the CCD. The number of bits is the number of binary digits required to represent each pixel's value. In a 1-bit system, each pixel is either 0 or 1, off or on. Then came 4-bit scanners (16 unique shades of gray) and 8-bit (256 shades of gray). Today, all scanners support at least 24-bit scanning (8 bits each for red, green, and blue). This is known as *true color*, and it uses a 24-digit binary code to represent each pixel.

Digital Cameras

A digital camera is like a scanner except that it works standing up. Rather than scan a flat, two-dimensional image, it projects its vision out into the 3D world and creates an image based on what it sees.

How Digital Cameras Work

Technologically, a digital camera has a lot in common with a traditional camera. They both have a lens that "sees" the image, and they both have focusing controls for that lens and usually a built-in flash. The main difference is that a traditional camera's lens sends its data to film, whereas a digital camera sends its data to a digital storage medium such as flash RAM, or directly to a computer if it's connected to one (as with a webcam).

The camera lens in a digital camera sends its data to a CCD like the one in a scanner, which measures the amount of light received in each cell and conveys an electrical charge to the camera's processor in proportion to the amount of light in a particular spot. As with a scanner, a color filter is applied to the CCD to enable color photography. This data passes through an analog-to-digital converter, which turns those electrical charges into binary computer data.

The data from the CCD passes through a digital signal processor that cleans it up and makes some corrections that improve the image quality. Then the data is stored inside the camera until it can be transferred to a computer.

Digital Camera Features

Some of the factors that differentiate one digital camera from another include the following:

Resolution   This is the number of pixels that form an image, measured in millions (megapixels). The more pixels, the better an image will look when printed at a large size. Multiply the camera's maximum picture height by the maximum picture width to determine the total number of pixels. Table 3.2 provides some examples. Some of the highest-quality digital cameras today exceed 24 megapixels in resolution.

TABLE 3.2 Megapixel to resolution comparison

Megapixels	Image Resolution
4	2272 × 1712
6	3072 × 2000
8	3264 × 2468
10	3872 × 2592

Camera Size   Some cameras are much more lightweight and portable than others.

Zoom   There are two types. An *optical zoom* camera uses a real multifocal length lens, and it's preferred. A *digital zoom* camera doesn't use a zoom lens; it simulates zooming by interpolating the picture. Digital zoom isn't as good because it's guessing at some of the pixels, rather than actually capturing them.

Storage Medium   Most digital cameras store pictures on flash memory cards like the ones you learned about in Chapter 2, "Input and Storage Devices." They vary in the types they support (CompactFlash, Secure Digital, memory stick, and so on).

PC Interface   Different cameras have different means of connecting to a computer. Most use either a USB or FireWire connection. (Not all PCs have a FireWire port, so a USB-interface camera is a safer bet for wide compatibility with the different computers you may use.)

Manual Adjustments   Most digital cameras are fully automatic, but experienced 35 mm camera users may want a model that has more manual options available such as aperture, exposure compensation, focus, and shutter speed.

Delay Between Pictures   Higher-end cameras can take multiple shots very quickly, with limited recovery time between pictures.

Video Capture   Some video cameras, although primarily used for still images, can also record short motion video clips, with or without sound.

Webcams

A web camera, or *webcam*, is a low-resolution video camera that feeds its images directly into a computer or network, most often using a USB or network connection. A webcam can also double as a digital camera, although you can't use it while it's disconnected from the computer. Many people use webcams for online video chatting and conferencing.

Webcams are now commonly built in to notebook computers, and they're available as low-cost add-ons to desktop systems. With the availability of Internet messaging services such as Skype, Google Talk, and Windows Live Messenger, as well as web conferencing systems such as Cisco's WebEx (see Figure 3.7), the webcam lets work-at-home professionals collaborate nationally and internationally by maintaining face-to-face contact with their colleagues.

FIGURE 3.7   Web conference in progress

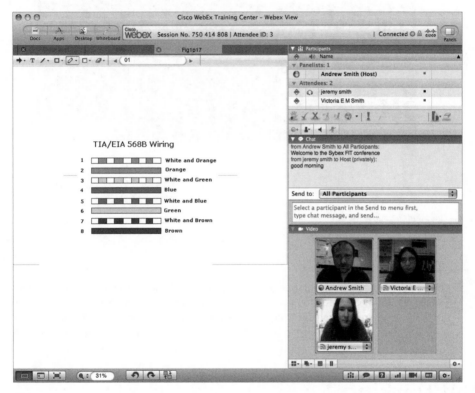

TV Tuners

TV tuners enable a PC to receive broadcast TV signals (with a compatible antenna) or to show TV programs from cable or satellite input. With a tuner, you can use your computer's monitor as a television and use your computer's hard disk as a digital video recorder. Tuners are available as internal expansion cards, as shown in Figure 3.8, or as external USB devices.

FIGURE 3.8   An expansion card TV tuner

Source: Wikipedia, © Darkone

WARNING   Although you may be able to capture TV shows with your TV tuner to watch later, you must be aware of the legal implications of doing so in the country where you're capturing the TV signal. Some countries place legal limitations on doing this, and in many nations, sharing such recordings may be illegal.

Networking

A *network* is a group of two or more computers that are connected in order to share data and resources. Networks can connect computers that are physically near to each other (a *local area network, or LAN*), or computers that are halfway around the world from one another (a *wide area network, or WAN*). The Internet is the biggest WAN of them all, connecting millions of LANs and individual PCs.

The most common resource shared on a network is hard-disk space. One PC can access a hard disk on another PC through the network. The Internet's main functionality also involves file sharing; whenever you access a website, you're reading a file from the remote server's hard drive. Another commonly shared network resource is printer access. One user can send print jobs to a printer attached to someone else's PC or attached directly to the network itself. A network can also serve as a conduit to other resources, such as Internet access.

In the following sections, you'll learn some basic terms and concepts related to home, business, and Internet networking.

 Network throughput is measured in *bits per second (bps)*, using the same multiplier words as with bytes (as in Chapter 2): 1,000 bits is a *kilobit (Kbps)*, 1,000 kilobits is a *megabit (Mbps),* and 1,000 megabits is a *gigabit (Gbps)*. Note that, when measuring bits per second, the multiplier is an even thousand, not 1,024 as it is with memory. When the *b* is lowercase, as in gigabits (Gb), it means *bits*; when it's uppercase, it means *bytes*, as in gigabytes (GB).

Clients and Servers

There are two basic models for network operation: client/server and peer-to-peer.

A *server* is a PC that exists only to route network traffic and provides access to shared files and printers. It manages the connections between the client PCs and serves as a storage repository for files that users want to make available to others. A *client* is an ordinary PC that an end-user employs. A server can be physically just an ordinary PC, but it has a special server operating system installed (such as Windows Server) that enables it to provide network services. Client/server (see Figure 3.9) is the network model used for almost all business networks because the presence of the server takes the networking burden off the clients. The main drawback to a client/server network is that there must be a PC dedicated to functioning as a server, and not every company or home can spare the extra PC.

FIGURE 3.9   A client/server network contains one or more servers that manage the network.

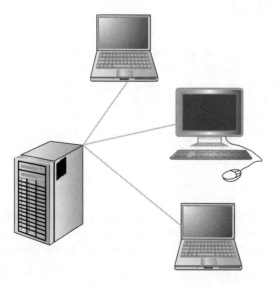

Small networks, such as those found in a home, are often set up as *peer-to-peer (P2P) networks* (see Figure 3.10). The HomeGroup networking feature in Windows 7 sets up P2P networks, for example. In a P2P network, there is no server; each of the client PCs takes on a portion of the burden of maintaining the network. Instead of a server managing the traffic, all the PCs in the network listen for traffic and grab any messages that are addressed to them. Instead of a server storing shared files, the shared files remain on the individual client hard disks. Another name for a P2P network is a *workgroup*.

FIGURE 3.10   A peer-to-peer network operates without a server.

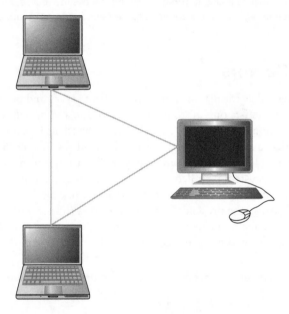

Large networks often have many servers, each with specific functions. For example, one might be a file server, one might be a print server, and one might provide Internet services. In large organizations, a server may be a much more powerful computer than an ordinary desktop PC, and may include many processors and a large amount of RAM.

Having a server doesn't preclude individual client PCs from sharing their available resources with other clients. For example, you might have a central file server, but users could also share folders on their own hard disks.

Ethernet

Ethernet is by far the most popular networking technology for both personal and business networks. As far back as two decades ago, there were several other competing network technologies, such as Token Ring. However, Ethernet has become the predominant technology in recent years to the point that you can assume almost all personal computer networks are Ethernet based.

When most people talk about Ethernet, they mean the physical components involved in wired networking (that is, networking that relies on cables or other physical conduits), and that's how the Strata objectives use the term. Technically, however, Ethernet is a logical network architecture that applies to both wired and wireless networking. Except for cables, all the hardware discussed in this section applies to both wired and wireless Ethernet.

The physical components involved in wired Ethernet networking include the following:

Network Adapters   Each computer must have a *network interface card (NIC)*, either an add-on card or an interface built in to the motherboard.

Switch, Router, or Other Connection Point   This is a box with multiple sockets into which cables plug. Each of the computers in the network connects to that central connection point. If it's a large network, there may be several connector boxes, chained together with more cables.

Network Cables   These cables carry data between the computers (or printers or other devices) and the switch or router.

The following sections discuss each of these pieces in more detail.

The Strata objectives' Acronyms list includes *PoE*, which stands for *Power over Ethernet*. It's a standard for using Ethernet cables to conduct electricity. For example, a webcam mounted on a roof wouldn't have an electrical outlet available to power it, so PoE could supply both network access and electrical power to it. This is a specialized technology, not common for consumer use.

Network Adapter

Many computers, especially notebook PCs, have network adapters (aka network interface cards, or NICs) built into them already, both wired and wireless. If your computer doesn't have a network adapter of the type you need to connect to the desired network (wired or wireless), you must install an expansion board or connect a USB adapter to add the needed capability.

If you aren't sure whether your computer already has wired network support, look for an RJ-45 jack on the back of the computer. (It looks like a wider-than-normal telephone outlet.) If you aren't sure about wireless support, look in the Device Manager in Windows. To open Device Manager, click Start, type **Device**, and click Device Manager when it appears at the top of the Start menu.

When you're selecting a network adapter, the most important shopping considerations are as follows:

Wired or Wireless   Choose according to the way you plan to connect to the router or switch.

Network Adapter Standard   You must determine the standard to which the network adapter conforms. For wired adapters, this is easy, because you'll probably find only one type for sale: 1 Gbps Ethernet. For wireless adapters, you'll need to choose between 802.11g (cheaper) and 802.11n (faster and with greater range). These standards are covered in more detail later in this chapter.

Interface Type   A desktop PC can accept an expansion board (provided the PC has an open slot for it); a notebook PC will probably require a USB adapter.

Most network adapters are Plug and Play, so Windows recognizes them and sets them up automatically when you install them. In some cases, you may need to run the Setup program that comes with the adapter to finalize its installation in Windows.

Each network adapter has a unique 48-bit *Media Access Control (MAC)* address. No two network adapters in the entire world have the same MAC address; it's assigned by the manufacturer of the device. Mac addresses are usually written as six groups of two hexadecimal digits, separated by hyphens or colons, like this: 01-23-45-67-89-AB. As an end user, you don't need to know the network adapter's MAC address; however, the internal workings of network transmission rely heavily on the MAC address in order to ensure that packets of data are intelligently routed to the right locations.

> Although originally intended to be permanent and globally unique hardware identifiers, MAC addresses can be faked and even changed, so they can't be used as 100 percent positive identifiers of the origin of a message.

EXERCISE 3.6

Explore Your Computer's Network Adapters

1. Look on the outside of your computer's case for a wired Ethernet jack. This will be an RJ-45 jack, like a wider-than-normal telephone jack. On a desktop PC, it'll be on the back; on a notebook PC, it may be on the back or on one side. Don't confuse the Ethernet jack with modem jacks, which look like two regular-width telephone jacks side-by-side.

2. In Windows, click Start ➢ Control Panel ➢ System And Security ➢ System ➢ Device Manager. The Device Manager window opens.

3. Double-click the Network Adapters category to open it. All the networking adapters on your system appear here. In the following graphic, there are four. The first is the wired adapter, and the second is the wireless adapter. The other two are special-purpose network adapters that are beyond the scope of this book.

4. Double-click the first network adapter you see on the list, and examine its properties. Note the Device Status on the General tab.

5. Close Device Manager. In the Control Panel window, in the address bar at the top, click Control Panel to return to the top level of the Control Panel.

6. Click Network And Internet.

7. Click Network And Sharing Center. Information about your currently connected networks appears.

8. Close the Network And Sharing Center window.

Routers and Switches

Routers and switches are connection boxes with multiple plugs into which you can attach cables. A *switch* takes in the incoming traffic from the various cables connected to it and directs the data to the appropriate outward-bound lane.

A *router* is a smarter version of a switch, able to direct traffic intelligently not only within your local network but also to other connected networks (including the Internet). A router attempts to find the best route from point A to point B, even if the points are halfway around the world.

The Internet is full of routers, and those routers direct the messages you send to the recipient's address. When you send email to a friend, you don't have to specify the names of all the servers to pass through on the way there—routers handle that task. You specify the end address, and the routers plan and execute the journey.

Routers can be wired, wireless, or both. A wireless router has an antenna that helps it communicate with wireless devices nearby, such as notebook computers, wireless printers, and entertainment devices like a TiVo (see Figure 3.11). To share an Internet connection with multiple computers in a home or office, you need a basic router. Larger and more sophisticated routers are used for high-traffic commercial applications.

FIGURE 3.11   Wireless router

EXERCISE 3.7

Explore Your Router or Switch Configuration

1.   Look in the documentation that came with your router, switch, or wireless access point to find out the IP address to use to access it. (Search the user documentation for the model number at the manufacturer's website if needed.)

2.   Open a web browser, and type **http://** followed by the IP address of the device. A page appears, showing the configuration information for the device. (You may need to enter a password if one has been set for the device.)

3.   Browse through the information and settings for the device. The graphic here shows an example.

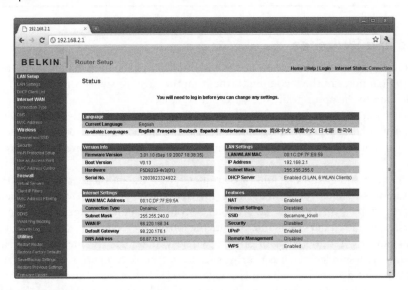

4.   Leave the browser window open for use in Exercise 3.9, or close it if you aren't planning to do Exercise 3.9 shortly.

Cables

The most common type of cabling used for Ethernet networks is an *unshielded twisted pair (UTP)* cable with an *RJ-45 connector* at each end. RJ stands for Registered Jack. Telephone systems also use RJ connectors, so you're probably familiar with that connector type already. An RJ-45 connector is slightly wider than a normal telephone plug (an RJ-11 or RJ-14), though, so it doesn't fit in telephone outlets. Figure 3-12 shows an RJ-45 connector.

FIGURE 3.12   Ethernet cable with RJ-45 connector

UTP cable carries data on pairs of wires. The types of UTP cables used for Ethernet have four pairs (eight wires total). The pairs of wires are twisted in order to minimize any magnetic interference that may be generated as the electrical signals pass through the wires. Each pair shares a color scheme. For example, the first pair is orange and orange-and-white. The other colors are green, blue, and brown, each pair with one solid wire and one striped with white.

The cables are considered *unshielded* because they don't have any special built-in protection from magnetic interference that may come from outside of the cable. Shielded twisted pair cables (STP) are also available for Ethernet use, but they're much more expensive and so are used only in situations where magnetic interference is a problem.

There are different categories of UTP cables. The higher the category number, the better the cable can conduct data at a high speed. For example, *Category 5 (Cat5) cable* can carry data at up to 100 Mbps. *Cat5e* cable can carry data at up to 1 Gbps, and *Cat6* cable can carry data at 10 Gbps. (Those are just the maximum transfer rates that the cables can support with an adequate level of accuracy; the cables are passive and don't control the data transmission rate.)

Standard and Crossover Cables

The way the individual wires in a cable are connected into the connectors on each end is known as the cable's *pin out*. On standard network cables, it's a straight-through pin out, so that the wire colors are in the same order at each end of the cable. If you look at any UTP Ethernet cable, for example, you'll see that the orange wires are in the same place on both ends. Standard cables like that are used to connect devices such as printers and computers to the switch or router.

A *crossover cable*, less common but still very important, connects two similar devices, such as the sockets on patch-panels (panels that connect networks). You may use one to connect two routers or switches, for example, or one laptop to another laptop. Another name for this cable type is *patch cable*. If you look at the ends of one of these cables, you'll notice that the order of the colored wires is reversed on one end.

EXERCISE 3.8

Compare Ethernet and Phone Cables

1. Locate an Ethernet cable and a telephone cable.

2. Looking at the plugs at the ends of the cable (which are usually translucent), count the number of wires in each cable. For an Ethernet cable, there are eight. For a telephone cable, there are either two (for a single-line cable, an RJ-11 plug) or four (for a dual-line cable, an RJ-14 plug).

Powerline Ethernet (HomePlug)

In a large home or office, where computers are spread out over multiple floors and rooms, running Ethernet cable often isn't practical. One solution is to use wireless networking, as discussed later in this chapter. If wireless networking isn't an option for some reason, though, *Powerline Ethernet*, aka *HomePlug*, may be an attractive alternative.

Powerline Ethernet uses the electrical wiring in your home or office to carry network traffic, sharing those existing wires with the electricity being delivered through them. You buy Powerline adapters (see Figure 3.13) that plug into any electrical outlet (avoiding those with surge suppression or filtering), and the adapters create a wired Ethernet connection between the device and other devices that are also similarly connected within the same location. Powerline Ethernet is most commonly used in homes to connect gaming devices, home computers, and home theatre systems.

FIGURE 3.13   These HomePlug adapters connect to power outlets

Wireless Networking

Wireless networking uses radio (sound) waves to transmit data, much like a cordless telephone. With wireless Ethernet, nearly everything is the same as with wired Ethernet from a user perspective, except that instead of cables, radio signals are used.

Wi-Fi: The 802.11 Standards

There are several wireless networking technologies, but the most popular of these is *Wireless Fidelity*, also known as *Wi-Fi*. Wi-Fi is a nickname for a collection of standards known as IEEE 802.11.

An organization called *Institute of Electrical and Electronics Engineers (IEEE)* controls, among other things, the various wireless networking standards. The standards governing networking are contained in the 802 range of numbering, and the standards governing wireless networking are in the 802.11 range. Table 3.3 lists the 802.11 standards you may encounter.

TABLE 3.3   IEE 802.11 wireless networking standards

Standard	Frequency	Top Speed	Range (Indoors/Outdoors) in Meters
802.11a	5 GHz	22 Mbps	15 / 34
802.11b	2.4 GHz	11 Mbps	46 / 92
802.11g	2.4 GHz	22 Mbps	46 / 92
802.11n	2.4 GHz and 5 GHz	600 Mbps	70 / 250

Most wireless networking devices you buy today are backward-compatible with the earlier standards. For example, if you buy an 802.11n router, a computer that has an 802.11b wireless adapter installed in it will be able to communicate with that router. However, the speed of the connection will be limited to the fastest speed the two devices can negotiate in common (11 Mbps, or possibly less, depending on environmental factors such as the distance between the two devices and any interference like walls or competition for bandwidth from cordless phones and other devices).

Although wireless is ideal for creating networks without the expense and complication of cabling, not every environment is ideal for it. You may find that wireless behaves poorly in the following environments:

- In metal-framed (and -covered) industrial units

- Where concrete is used for walls and floors. This will absorb the wireless signal (as well as other forms of radiation).

- If there is a large, active power supply in close proximity to the wireless network, such as a power generator or switch room.

- If your home wireless system is close to a microwave oven when it's operating.

- When electrical storms are in the area.

Wi-Fi Hardware

A wireless network uses hardware similar to that in a wired one. You must have a wireless network adapter in each computer that will connect to the network, and you must have a switch or router to join the computers into a cohesive network.

Wireless switches or routers look similar to wired ones, but they have antennas. A wireless switch is called a *wireless access point (WAP)*. Just like a wired switch, a WAP provides a central switching station for data to be sent and received between the devices on the network. Routers are still called routers and perform the same functions they do on a wired network.

The acronym WAP also has another meaning: *Wireless Application Protocol*. This is a standard for web applications, used mainly by small mobile devices such as cell phones.

When you're setting up a wireless network, it's important to find a good location for the router or WAP. A central location is best to ensure that its signal can reach as much of the home or office as possible. For example, if there are three floors in the house, place the router on the second floor. You may need to move it around if you find that locations where you want to use the Internet are inaccessible.

If you're using a wireless router to share Internet access, you may be limited by the place where the Internet service enters the building. For example, if you get Internet service via cable TV, you must place the router near a cable jack; if you get Internet service via phone lines, such as with DSL service (covered later in this chapter), you must place the router near a phone jack.

Auto-Negotiating Speed and Duplexing

Here's something you need to know about for the Strata exam, but you don't have to worry about much in real-life: network auto-negotiation.

Network transmission speed is measured in megabits per second (Mbps) or gigabits per second (Gbps). Both wired and wireless Ethernet components automatically negotiate the ideal speed to use by finding the maximum that both devices involved in the communication can support. For example, if you have an 802.11n router and it's talking to an 802.11b device, communication will be negotiated at no more than 11 Mbps because that's the maximum an 802.11b device can handle. The same goes for a wired network. Components of different ages and abilities negotiate a mutually agreeable transmission rate between them.

Similarly, the duplex setting is also auto-negotiated. Duplexing is the ability of devices to both talk and listen:

- *Simplex* means the communication is one-way only. For example, a car radio is a simplex device; it receives but doesn't send. It requires only one communication channel.

- *Half-duplex* means there is two-way communication, but only in one direction at a time. After a device is finished sending, it must send an "all clear" signal to indicate that it's done speaking; only then may the other device respond. This also requires only one communication channel.

- *Full duplex* means there is two-way simultaneous communication. When you talk on the telephone, for example, that's full duplex, because you can hear the other person speaking even when you're speaking too.

Configuring Wireless Networking and Encryption

A wireless router or access point is assigned a *service set identifier (SSID)*, which is a name by which it's known on the network. By entering its setup page with your browser (as in Exercise 3.7), you can name it anything you like. For a computer or other device to connect to the wireless network, its user must know the SSID. You can set the router or WAP to broadcast its SSID or not, making the network easier or harder for new users to find. For example, in Figure 3.14, a user is browsing for an available wireless network and some of the SSIDs are visible (like ouresearch and ouguest), whereas other networks show up as <hidden network>.

FIGURE 3.14   SSIDs can be broadcast or not.

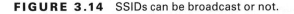

To prevent unauthorized users from accessing a wireless network further, you can set up security for it so that only users who enter the specified code or passphrase may connect. There are two popular means of encrypting a wireless connection:

Wired Equivalent Privacy (WEP)   An older but still used method of encryption that is controlled by entering a 128-bit or 256-bit key consisting of up to 26 hexadecimal digits. Two authentication methods are used with WEP: Open System authentication and Shared Key authentication. (You may need to know which one your router or WAP uses when setting up a secure encrypted connection on your PC.)

Wi-Fi Protected Access (WPA)   A newer type of encryption, more flexible and secure than WEP. There are two types: WPA-Personal, which is similar to WEP in terms of setup, and WPA-Enterprise, which requires an authentication server and is designed for large networks. There are two encryption protocols: Temporal Key Integrity Protocol (TKIP) and Computer Mode with Cipher Block Chaining Message Authentication Code Protocol (CCMP). On a typical home network, you would use WPA-PSK mode with TKIP encryption.

All those names and statistics may seem a little overwhelming, but don't worry too much about their details. The main thing is to make sure that, whatever security system you implement in the setup for your WAP or wireless router, you use those same settings when setting up a computer to connect to it.

Explore Wireless Security

1. If you have a wireless router or access point, open its configuration page in your web browser as you did in Exercise 3.7. It may already be open from that exercise.

2. Find the Security settings, where you choose the security mode (WEP, WPA, or Disabled/None). The exact arrangement of the settings depends on the make and model of the device. The following graphic shows one example. Don't change the current setting.

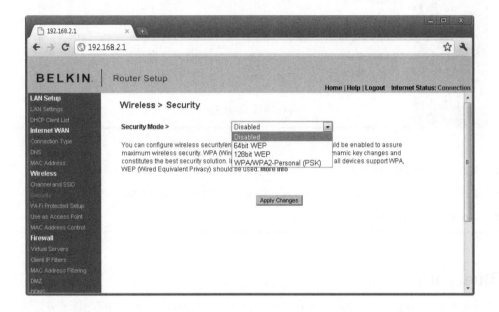

3. Find the Channel And SSID settings. Note the current wireless channel in use and the current SSID.

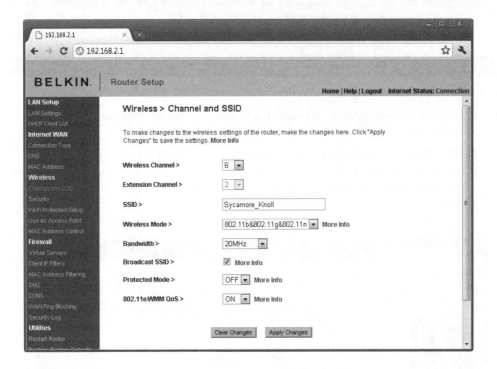

4.   If desired, change the SSID to a more meaningful name.

5.   Save the changes. (Look for an Apply Changes or Save Changes button or similar.)

6.   Close the web browser window.

Bluetooth

Bluetooth is a short-range wireless networking protocol, separate from Wi-Fi. It's also known as IEEE 802.15. Bluetooth is used for many types of connections, not just with computers, but also with cell phones, home theatre devices, and gaming consoles. For example, many cordless headsets for cell phones are Bluetooth-controlled. Bluetooth is also used for some cordless keyboards, mice, and other input devices, as well as some car stereo systems and GPS devices. A USB Bluetooth adapter looks very similar to a USB flash drive (see Figure 3.15).

FIGURE 3.15   USB Bluetooth adapter

Whereas Wi-Fi technology is designed to help devices participate in group networks, Bluetooth is a one-to-one connection. For example, one cell phone headset can communicate with exactly one cell phone at a time, and one Bluetooth-enabled notebook computer can connect with exactly one Bluetooth peripheral device per adapter.

For Bluetooth connectivity, both devices must support it and must have Bluetooth transmitter/receivers. Most notebook computers today come with Bluetooth adapters built in; most desktop computers don't. You can add Bluetooth support to almost any computer via a USB adapter. Bluetooth adapters, like other network adapters, have MAC addresses.

Bluetooth devices come in three classes. Each class has a different maximum range, from 1 meter to 100 meters, and a different data transmission rate, between 1 Mbps and 24 Mbps, as listed in Table 3.4.

TABLE 3.4   Bluetooth classes

Class	Maximum Data Rate	Maximum Distance (Meters)
1	1 Mbps	1
2	3 Mbps	10
3	24 Mbps	100

A decade or so ago, infrared (IR) connections were commonly used for very-short-distance wireless communication between devices, such as to exchange data between PDAs or notebook PCs. But IR is inferior to Bluetooth in terms of range and reliability, and it requires a clear line of sight between the two devices. Thus it's seldom used anymore.

Networking Protocols

A *protocol* is set of language rules used between two devices or two points in a process. Networking involves many different protocols operating at different levels of the transmission.

The *Open Systems Architecture (OSI) model* defines seven different layers of network communication, each with its own protocols. The levels, from lowest to highest, are 1: Physical, 2: Data Link, 3: Network, 4: Transport, 5: Session, 6: Presentation, and 7: Application. You don't have to know these for the Strata exam, but knowing at which levels the various protocols take place may help you in your overall understanding of network communication. The CompTIA A+ exam does require you to know these layers. Throughout the rest of this chapter, we'll mention at which OSI layer a particular protocol operates for your reference. For more information, see http://en.wikipedia.org/wiki/OSI_model.

TCP/IP

Transmission Control Protocol/Internet Protocol (TCP/IP) is the most widely used protocol in the world. It's actually an interconnected set of protocols, rather than a single one; the IP portion operates at the Network layer, and the TCP portion operates at the Transport layer. TCP/IP is important not only because most LANs use it internally as their primary means of communication, but because it's the protocol used on the Internet, so all Internet-capable devices also employ TCP/IP.

IP Addresses

Each device on a network has a unique *IP address*, which consists of four numbers (each between 0 and 255) separated by periods like this: 204.52.0.23. This is known as *IP version 4 (IPv4)*.

Even though the numbers are written as decimals, to make them easier to read, in reality an IPv4 address is a 32-bit binary number. Each of the four numbers is machine-translated into binary, so the previous example IP address looks like this to a computer: 11001100.00110100.00000000.00010111

IPv4 is the original type of IP addressing used on the Internet, and it's also widely used in local area networking. Each IP address is allocated to a particular company, organization, or individual, and there are complex rules as to who may own and use which IP addresses on the Internet. (Within a private network that isn't connected to the Internet, you may use whatever IP addresses you like.) About 4 billion possible IP addresses are available with IPv4, but many of those numbers are ineligible for use as Internet addresses because of the rules governing Internet addressing. For example, the entire block of 192.168.x.x numbers is reserved for internal addressing on private networks.

Because the Internet has grown so large, we as a global community are running out of available IP addresses. There are various translation systems in place that enable large groups of computers on an internal network to share one or two IP addresses on the Internet, but even those means aren't enough. Therefore *Internet Protocol version 6 (IPv6)* was invented, and it will at some point be implemented as the new means of identifying computers on the Internet at large. IPv6 numbers are 128-bit binary numbers but are written in hexadecimal to make them easier to comprehend. The number is broken into four-digit sections separated by colons. (Hexadecimal is used instead of decimal so that an IPv6 number is never confused with an IPv4 number, which uses decimal numbering.) Here's an example:

4FFE:190C:4545:0003:0200:F8FF:FA21:67CF

With this large a number, the number of available addresses is virtually limitless. (Well, not completely limitless. But 10 to the 36th power is a lot of addresses, and we'll probably never use them up on planet Earth, even if every person alive has dozens of addresses.)

Static vs. Dynamic IP Addressing

When you set up a network connection on a PC, there are two ways to handle IP addressing. One is to configure a *static IP address* on the device. Such an address is assigned by the network administrator or your Internet service provider. Network administrators at large companies spend a lot of time and energy developing complex systems of IP addressing, so you should never guess at an IP address—always ask.

The other way is to allow a *Dynamic Host Configuration Protocol (DHCP) server* to assign a *dynamic IP address* to a computer automatically. This is how large corporate networks generally do it. They set up a server with DHCP, and every time a computer logs on, the computer asks the DHCP server "What is my IP address?" The server assigns it one immediately or reconfirms that it's still okay to use the one it used last time. This system is advantageous because it eliminates the possibility of duplicate IP addresses on a network and saves the network administrator's time.

Automatic Private IP Addressing

Because a small peer-to-peer network doesn't have a DHCP server, small networks need an alternative way of assigning IP addresses to its computers. You can assign static IP addresses to computers if you like, but Windows networking is able to pass out IP addresses automatically without a DHCP server via a system called *automatic private IP addressing (APIPA)*. Windows automatically assigns IP addresses within a certain range of reserved addresses whenever it can't locate a DHCP server and no static address has been supplied. The addresses in this reserved block begin with 169.254, as in 169.254.2.1.

If you set up a static IP address, you also have the opportunity to enter a *subnet mask*. This usually involves 255s and 0s, as in 255.255.255.0. Subnet masks are used to indicate what portion of the IP address is being used as a prefix, like an area code, and what portion is being used as a unique identifier within that area, like a telephone number without the area code. Different networks divide up (that is, subnet) the IP addresses differently. Specifying a subnet mask is an issue mostly on large private networks, and not a concern if you acquire your IP address from a DHCP server. Just enter the subnet mask that you're instructed to use by your network administrator.

If you use a static IP address, you may also need to enter a *default gateway*. This is the address of the router through which your computer goes out to the Internet (or other larger network segment). Again, enter what you're instructed to do for this setting.

You don't have to worry about subnet masks and default gateways if you let DHCP or APIPA assign your IP addresses.

EXERCISE 3.10

Explore IP Addresses

1. In Windows, click Start ➤ Control Panel ➤ Network And Internet ➤ Network And Sharing Center.

2. Next to Connections, click the hyperlink for your network connection. A Wireless Network Connection Status dialog box opens if it's a wireless network, or an equivalent dialog box opens if it's a wired network.

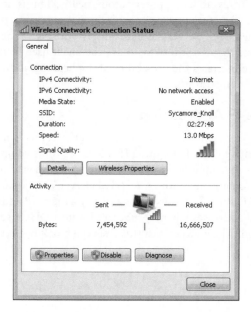

3. Click Details. The Network Connection Details dialog box opens. It lists, among other things, both the IPv4 and IPv6 addresses, subnet mask, and default gateway for your current network connection. It also lists the MAC address, under Physical Address.

4. Click Close twice to close both dialog boxes.

5. Choose Start ➢ All Programs ➢ Accessories ➢ Command Prompt. A command-line window opens.

6. Type **IPCONFIG**, and press Enter. Information about each of the network adapters installed on the computer appears, even the ones that aren't in use right now.

7. Close the command-line window.

TCP Ports

The TCP portion of TCP/IP governs transport of data. As part of this, different higher-level protocols are assigned port numbers, which are somewhat like radio or TV stations or channels. Having different ports assigned to different kinds of data makes it possible for the operating system to sort out the incoming data from the network, or from the Internet, and deliver it to the appropriate application. Table 3.5 summarizes some of the most common port numbers assigned to various Internet protocols. You've already learned about one of these: DHCP. The others you'll learn about later in this chapter.

TABLE 3.5 Common protocol TCP ports

Protocol	Port
FTP	20 and 21
HTTP	80
HTTPS	443
POP3	110
SMTP	25
IMAP	143
DHCP	546 and 547(IPv6); 67 and 68 (IPv4) (also BOOTP)
DNS	53

You usually don't have to worry about the port assignments. One situation where you may is if the network administrator in charge of some portion of your Internet experience (such as your mail server) has decided to use a nonstandard port for one of the services. In a case like that, you may need to go into the connection or account properties in the application in which you use that service and specify the port being used.

Internet Connections

Adding Internet to the mix of computer networking introduces new types of hardware and new sets of communication protocols to your computer literacy vocabulary. In this section, you'll learn about the hardware and software involved in Internet connectivity as well as some web browser features that employ other related protocols and technologies.

Hardware for Internet Connections

A decade or more ago, most people connected to their *Internet service provider (ISP)* via a dial-up modem. A *modem*, short for modulator-demodulator, is an analog-to-digital and digital-to-analog converter that translates digital computer data into sounds that can be sent on a regular telephone line. Then another modem at the other end converts the analog signal back to digital.

Not sure if you have a built-in dial-up modem in your computer? On a desktop PC, a built-in modem is indicated by two telephone jacks, side by side. On a notebook PC, there is typically just one telephone jack for a modem. Look closely, because a wider-than-normal jack that looks like it's for a telephone cord is actually for an RJ-45 connector for Ethernet.

Nowadays, most people use always-on broadband connections for Internet access. *Broadband* literally means a wide pathway, capable of carrying data at a high rate of speed. There are two major technologies in the broadband Internet service market:

Digital Subscriber Line (DSL)   Carries Internet signals through telephone lines.

Cable Internet   Carries Internet signals through the same cables that deliver cable TV service.

In addition, several other smaller players exist in the broadband Internet market, including satellite Internet, Wi-Max, and broadband over cell phones (3G, 4G, and so on).

Each of these technologies requires a terminal adapter (for example, a cable modem or a DSL modem). These boxes are loosely called modems in popular usage, but they don't modulate and demodulate between analog and digital in the way traditional modems did.

Broadband cable or DSL network technology can theoretically operate at very fast speeds—over 100 Mbps in some cases. However, the actual speed at which you experience Internet connectivity depends on many factors, including the service plan you've purchased (with faster plans being more expensive), how many other users in your area are using the connection at the same time as you (more an issue with cable than with DSL), what sites you're accessing, and the overall level of traffic on the Internet at the moment.

DSL

DSL relies on the presence of an existing telephone network where the local relay (normally a telephone exchange) has been upgraded to support DSL communication. The speeds available on a DSL service depend on the technology implemented in the telephone exchange as well as the quality and the distance of the telephone lines. The actual speeds you achieve from a DSL connection depend, among other things, on the distance your location is from the *central office*, a switching station for your phone company from which DSL is administered.

An old type of broadband called *Integrated Switched Digital Network (ISDN)* was available in the early days of the Internet, offering approximately twice the speed of dial-up service (56 Kbps, which is *really slow* by today's standards).

DSL service is either *asymmetric DSL (ADSL)* or *symmetric DSL (SDSL)*.

Symmetric, in the context of network traffic, means equal. A symmetric DSL connection transfers data at the same speed whether uploading or downloading. An SDSL connection of 2 Mbps transfers data both ways at that speed.

On the other hand, *asymmetric* means unequal. With an asymmetric DSL connection, the upload speed is slower than the download speed. An ADSL connection may download at 12 Mbps but upload at only 1.8 Mbps, for example. For most people this is acceptable because the volume of data is much higher coming to them than going from them.

ADSL service is typically much less expensive than SDSL, and it works fine for most users. People who need high-speed uploading, though, such as someone who is running an Internet file-sharing service, may find it worthwhile to pay extra for SDSL service.

DSL service requires a telephone line, of course. You also need a DSL terminal adapter (modem). Some service providers distribute a box that is a combination of a DSL modem and a router (wired or wireless) for sharing the DSL connection with multiple computers. Others provide just a basic DSL terminal adapter, and you must provide your own router if you want to share its connection. You may also need a splitter, or a micro filter, to separate the analog telephone signal from the digital Internet signal, both passing through the same lines.

Cable

Cable Internet service uses the unused bandwidth on the same cables that carry your TV signal. Cable service in many areas is faster than DSL, but it's a shared pipeline. So if your neighbors are also heavy Internet users, you may experience a slowing down of your service at peak usage times. Cable Internet service is symmetric, so upload and download speeds are approximately the same, unless your cable company intentionally throttles upload speeds (for example, to discourage users from running high-traffic servers from their homes).

To get Internet from your cable TV provider, you'll need a cable modem. The providers typically lease these to you, so you don't have to buy your own and worry about obsolescence a few years down the road. A cable modem accepts input from a coaxial cable from the wall, the same kind of cable that brings in your TV programming. It has an RJ-45 output jack, just like that for an Ethernet cable, which then can be connected to a broadband router (wired or wireless) to share the cable Internet connection with multiple computers in your home or office.

Satellite

Satellite Internet service isn't as fast or as efficient as cable or DSL, but it's more widely available. Whereas cable service requires you to be within the service area of your cable company, and DSL connections are limited to within a few miles of the telephone company's central office, satellite Internet can be picked up anywhere that has a clear view of the southern sky. Satellite service is asymmetric, like ADSL; you may have a download speed of 1.5 Mbps and an upload speed of 256 Kbps, for example.

Satellite Internet requires a special satellite dish, similar to the ones used for satellite TV, but with a transmitter on it. (Ordinary satellite dishes are receive-only.) Two cables run from the dish to your residence—one for input and one for output. These cables connect to a satellite terminal adapter (modem), which then connects either directly to a PC or to a broadband router to share the connection.

Satellite service is more susceptible to harsh weather conditions, and it may cut out during rain or snowstorms. It's also slower and more expensive per month than cable or DSL, and you usually have to buy all the equipment up front, rather than lease it.

Broadband Router

Nearly all of the various broadband Internet connection technologies can be shared on a LAN by using a broadband router. A *broadband router* is basically a regular consumer-level router, but it may come with software, instructions, or other extras that make it especially easy for an average person to set up to share a broadband Internet connection.

To share an Internet connection, connect an Ethernet cable from the Internet source (for example, the cable modem to the Internet or uplink or input jack on the back of the router). Then connect all the computers in your network to the router, either with Ethernet cables or wirelessly (if it's a wireless router). The router handles the *network address translation (NAT)* required for each of the computers to use that single Internet connection.

DNS Servers

Earlier in the chapter, you learned that IP addresses are 32-bit binary numbers expressed as sets of four decimal numbers like this: 208.215.179.220. All Internet servers must have an IP address in order to be able to communicate. For our purposes, though, domain names like Microsoft.com are used instead of the numbers, because they're easier to remember.

Domain Name System (DNS) servers translate between the numeric addresses and the friendlier domain names. These servers store and provide access to translation tables based on information they get from domain registrar companies.

 There is a misconception that all web addresses must start with www. This is only customary, not required. Large sites, such as Microsoft, divide the websites into multiple servers, each one having a different prefix, like support.microsoft.com and office.microsoft.com.

DNS works from right to left, with each part of the address separated by periods. To look up the IP address for a web address (a *uniform resource locator*, or *URL*) is known as *resolving* the address.

An organization called InterNIC controls the issuing of Internet addresses. It manages a group of registrars, who in turn manage a range of domains and ensure that DNS lookup information is available for them worldwide.

For example, to resolve www.biguniversity.ac.uk, the browser first consults a top-level DNS server, which contains only information about where other DNS servers are stored for the various top-level codes. This first DNS server, owned by InterNIC itself, directs the request to a DNS server, managed by Nominet, which handles only domain names that end in .uk. That server, in turn, sends the request to another DNS server, managed by JANET (Joint Academic Network), which manages .ac and .gov addresses. Finally, the request is sent to the university's own DNS server, which manages its own domain and any subordinate domains.

InterNIC controls all address naming conventions to the right of the domain name. (In this example, that's biguniversity and everything to its right). On the left side, however, the organization that owns and hosts the domain has control. For example, Big University's network administrators may set up the following servers, each with its own IP address:

- www.biguniversity.ac.uk for the web server
- mail.biguniversity.ac.uk for the mail server
- technology.biguniversity.ac.uk for the technology campus

Big University runs its own servers and maintains its own DNS server to provide information about them. For example:

- www.biguniversity.ac.uk could map to 80.10.55.1
- mail.biguniversity.ac.uk could map to 80.10.55.2
- technology.biguniversity.ac.uk could map to 80.10.55.3

If you host your website on someone else's server, that hosting company maintains its own DNS servers, and you share in their use. When you host a website somewhere, you enter a primary and secondary DNS address and that information is populated across the entire Internet, replicated from server to server until all the appropriate DNS servers have been notified and their databases updated to contain your information.

EXERCISE 3.11

DNS and IP Addresses

1. Open a command-line window as you did in Exercise 3.10.

2. Type `ping http://www.speedtest.net/` followed by the address of any website. For example, try `ping www.speedtest.net`.

   Notice that the IP address for that site appears as its status is checked.

3. Open a web browser window, and enter the IP address you got in step 2. Does the page load? Some servers will load the page correctly based on the IP address, and some won't. It depends on whether a default (index) page has been set to load when no particular page is specified, and other security settings.

4. Repeat steps 2–3 with several different websites, and compare the results. You may or may not find a site that will display using its IP address in raw form.

HTTP and HTTPS

Next let's look at Internet connectivity at a higher level. Now that you have a connection established, what can you *do* with it? One thing you can do is request and receive web pages. Several protocols are used to request and receive web pages on a computer. These protocols operate at Session layer (level 5) in the OSI model that was mentioned earlier in the chapter.

The basic unsecured protocol used for web traffic is *Hypertext Transport Protocol (HTTP)*. Addresses that begin with http:// produce results sent to your computer in an unsecured, unencrypted way that is easy to spy on with *packet-sniffing* software. Packet-sniffing software allows even not-very-technical users to view data that is being sent online.

Hypertext Transfer Protocol Secure (HTTPS) is a secure version of Hypertext Transport Protocol (HTTP) that combines regular HTTP with *Transport Layer Security (TLS)* or *Secure Sockets Layer (SSL)* security encryption to exchange data between a web browser and a web server in privacy. HTTPS connections are typically used when valuable information is involved, such as credit card numbers. Addresses that begin with https:// are secure HTTP addresses.

There are two parts to HTTPS security: ensuring that the website is what it seems, and ensuring that data sent to it won't be snooped on its way there.

For the first part, ensuring the identity of the website, HTTPS relies on *certificate authorities*: companies that issue and manage digital certificates for a fee. A certificate authority such as VeriSign or Microsoft issues a certificate to a website, and then the website sends information about its certificate to the requesting page. The web browser receiving the data checks with the certificate authority to make sure the certificate is valid.

For the second part, ensuring the data isn't snooped, TLS or SSL is used to encrypt the data being sent and then unencrypt it at the receiving end. TLS and SSL are two different versions of the same basic technology, with TLS being the newer version. You don't need to know the technical details of how it works for the Strata exam.

Companies that need web-based communications to be secure at all times can create a *virtual private network (VPN)*. A VPN is like a secure tunnel that runs from one point to another across the Internet. It uses the public Internet routes, but the transactions are shielded from snooping because they're in an encrypted secure pathway.

EXERCISE 3.12

Secure vs. Unsecure Web Transactions

1. Open a web browser window, and go to www.amazon.com. Notice the address in the address bar: http://www.amazon.com.

2. Add an item to your shopping cart. (It can be any item; you aren't actually going to buy it.) Then view the shopping cart. Notice that the address bar still starts with http:.

3. Click the Proceed To Checkout button. If prompted to log in, do so if you already have an account; otherwise create one.

4. At the Review Your Order page, look in the address bar. Notice that the address now begins with https://. This indicates that you've been moved to a secure server to complete the transaction.

5. Close the browser window without completing the transaction.

POP, SMTP, and IMAP

Mail handling involves its own set of protocols. These also operate at the Session layer (level 5 of the OSI model), but they use different applications: email handling programs. (Some webmail is delivered via HTTP, through a web browser, but that's not the kind of email we're talking about in this section.)

The most popular type of mail handling is a store-and-forward system that uses *Post Office Protocol 3* (POP3, or POP for short) to receive mail and *Simple Mail Transport Protocol (SMTP)* to send mail. With this type of mail system, your mail accumulates on the mail server (that's the *store* part) until you use an email client like Outlook or Windows Mail to log in and pick it up (that's the *forward* part), at which time the mail is deleted from the server. This type of system is usually referred to as POP3 or POP, even though technically that protocol is only half the equation—the receiving half.

POP3 mail is the most commonly offered type of mail system because it's the least cumbersome from the server's perspective and the cheapest for ISPs to offer. Once you retrieve your mail, the server no longer has any responsibility for it, so the server doesn't get bogged down storing months or even years of email.

POP3 works well when the user always (or nearly always) logs in from the same computer using the same mail program. That's because this type of system stores the incoming mail on whatever computer you're using at the moment, and if you use lots of different computers, your mail gets scattered over all those computers.

When the user logs in from several different locations, *Internet Mail Access Protocol (IMAP)* is sometimes used instead. An IMAP mail system uses the interface of a mail program like Outlook or Windows Mail, but the mail itself is stored on and accessed from the server; that each time you access your mail account, all your mail is there, regardless of where you log in from. The drawbacks of IMAP are that it requires more administrative overhead for the server, and the interface runs more slowly because each message must be retrieved from the server as you view it.

When you set up a mail account in a mail-handling program, you tell it what type of mail server you're connecting to: POP3 or IMAP. You also fill in the incoming and outgoing mail server names, your username, and your password. Depending on the service provider, you may also have to fine-tune some of the mail settings to match the server's requirements. Figure 3.16 shows a mail account configuration screen from Outlook 2010 that illustrates the choice of mail types.

FIGURE 3.16   Mail setup in Outlook 2010

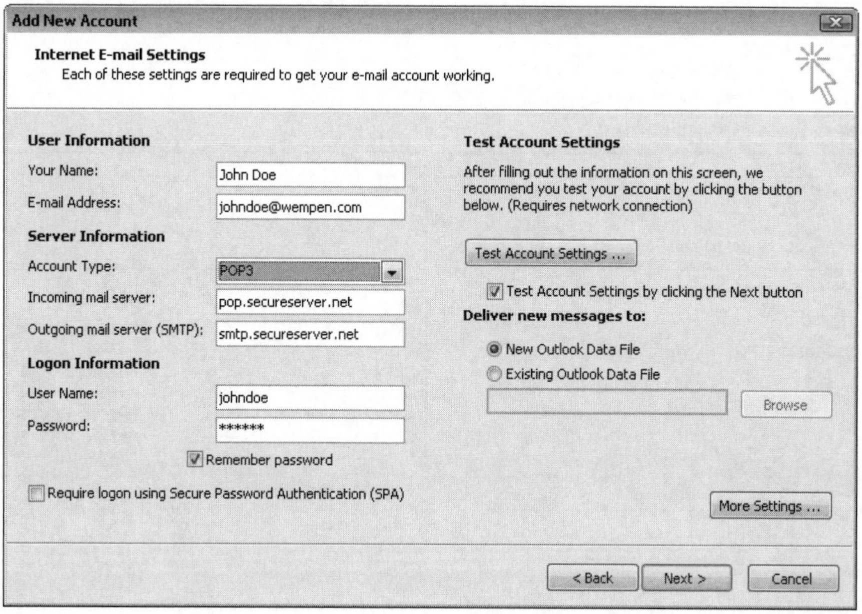

FTP

You can download files from a website, but to upload and download files in bulk, many individuals and companies prefer to use a different system designed specifically for file transfer: File Transfer Protocol (FTP).

FTP is a very old protocol, used in the early days of the Internet before web access was popular. An FTP server functions as a drop box from which you can pick up and to which you can deposit files. Some FTP servers are public; others are password-protected.

Most people use an FTP client application to do FTP transfers. However, you can also use a web browser for FTP downloads, and in some cases uploads (depending on the browser and the FTP server). One popular free FTP client is FileZilla (www.filezilla-project.org), shown in Figure 3.17.

FTP addresses begin with ftp://, just like web addresses begin with http://. This prefix tells the application what protocol to use. In an FTP client, the protocol is assumed. However, when using a web browser for FTP, you must make sure to add that prefix to an FTP address.

FIGURE 3.17   FileZilla is a popular FTP application

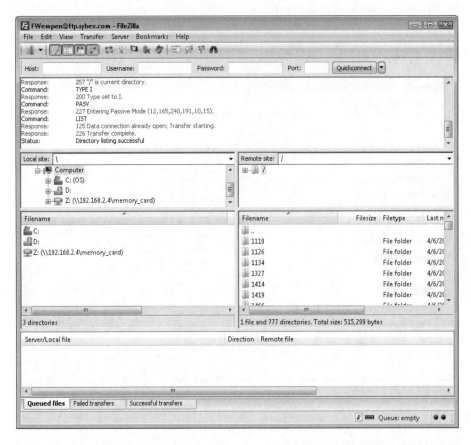

Like plain HTTP, the FTP protocol isn't secure. If you need secure file transfer, use a security-enabled transfer method instead of plain FTP, such as *Secure Shell (SSH) FTP*, sometimes called *Secure FTP (SFTP)*.

VoIP

Voice over Internet Protocol (VoIP) is a set of applications, technologies, and protocols to provide IP-based telephony services In other words, it lets you use the Internet to make and receive "telephone" calls. From the end-user's standpoint, it's just another form of the same telephone service they've always enjoyed, but the calls are all-digital. The analog data from the person's speech is digitized, sent as data across the Internet, and then re-created as an analog sound at the other end.

Many companies offer low-cost VoIP service to consumers, including Skype. In addition, cable companies like Comcast offer digital phone service through their cable lines in conjunction with Internet service.

Web Browser Features

At the top level of the networking model, applications run that manage and display Internet data. A web browser is one of the most important applications, enabling users to browse and search the Web.

The Strata objectives require that you become familiar with several specific features of a web browser. Understanding these features makes you better able not only to use a web browser, but also to customize and troubleshoot one.

Most web browsers have the same features and capabilities, but the exact steps involved in changing or activating them vary depending on the application and its version. Some of the most popular browsers available today include the following:

- Internet Explorer
- Firefox
- Chrome
- Safari
- Opera

On Windows-based PCs, Internet Explorer is the most widely used because it comes free with Windows; other browsers must be downloaded and installed from their respective websites. There are different versions of Internet Explorer; as of this writing, the newest version is Internet Explorer 9. Windows Update, if enabled, will automatically download and install new versions of Internet Explorer as they become available.

Firefox, one of the most popular alternatives to Internet Explorer, is available for free for almost every operating system at www.mozilla.org.

Browser Add-Ons (Plug-Ins)

Today's browsers are fairly adept at handling a range of content types, but they can't always do it alone. An *add-on* (also called a *plug-in*) is a helper program for a browser that increases its capabilities, such as the ability to play a certain type of video clip (like QuickTime) or to run a certain type of embedded application (such as Shockwave Flash).

When you visit a web page that requires a certain add-on, if you already have the add-on, it activates automatically to display the content. If you don't have that add-on installed, a prompt may appear to help you download it, or an error message may appear telling you that you don't have it.

Be cautious about clicking links to install add-ons. Some less reputable sites will try to trick you into clicking a link to install an add-on and then will use that add-on to display ads on your computer, spy on you, or take over your computer to send out spam or spread viruses.

You can view and manage the add-ons installed for your browser. The exact steps vary depending on the browser, but in most cases you can enable or disable an add-on or remove it entirely. This is important because it gives you the control to stop an add-on that may be malfunctioning or that may be harmful to your system, causing your browser to crash.

EXERCISE 3.13

Viewing the Installed Add-ons in Firefox

1. Download and install Firefox from www.mozilla.org if it isn't already installed on your computer.

2. Choose Tools ➢ Add-Ons. The Add-ons dialog box opens.

3. Click the Add-Ons icon. A list of installed add-ons appears.

4. Click any of the add-ons on the list. A Disable button appears next to it.

5. Click the Disable button. The button changes to Enable.

6. Click the Enable button to re-enable that add-on.

7. Click the Extensions icon. Other add-ons appear.

8. Click one of the add-ons, and note the buttons available for it. In addition to a Disable button, there are also Options and Uninstall buttons.

9. Click the Options button. Examine the options available, and then click Cancel to close the dialog box without making any changes.

10. Close the Add-ons window, and close the browser.

Browser Customization

Some web pages are written so that they use the same fonts and font sizes on every computer that displays them, regardless of the browser's settings. Other pages, though, allow the browser some control over the text sizes and text styles.

By increasing the default font size used for web pages, you can make the text easier to read for those with vision impairment. You can also choose different fonts and colors that may be easier to read than others. It's all up to your own preferences.

Another way to increase the readability of a web page is to change the Zoom setting in the browser. Zooming in on a page enlarges not just the text, but everything else on the page too, including graphics.

EXERCISE 3.14

Customizing Appearance Settings in Firefox

1. Download and install Firefox from www.mozilla.org if it isn't already installed on your computer.

2. In Firefox, display this website: http://news.google.com. If that site isn't available, view some other site that contains a lot of text, so you can see the effect on the text.

3. Choose Tools ➢ Options. The Options dialog box opens.

4. Click the Content icon at the top.

5. In the Fonts & Colors section, open the Size drop-down list and click one size larger than the current setting.

6. Open the Default Font drop-down list, and click Century Schoolbook (or any other font of your choice).

EXERCISE 3.14 *(continued)*

7. Click OK to close the dialog box. The font used to show the news stories doesn't change because this page specifies what font to use, but the font size does change because this page allows the browser to specify the size with its own settings.

8. Reset the font size to its earlier setting. (Repeat steps 3–6.)

9. Choose View ➢ Zoom ➢ Zoom In. The entire page gets larger in view, not just the fonts, when you zoom.

10. Choose View ➢ Zoom ➢ Reset to reset the zoom level to the default.

11. Close the browser window.

Anti-Phishing Features

One technique that online criminals use to steal people's personal information is to create a *phishing* site, which looks just like a legitimate site where people commonly enter financial and personal information. People unwittingly enter their usernames and passwords into the fake site, and then the criminals take that information and use it to log into the real site and steal identities or money.

Most web browsers have an anti-phishing feature that references a central database of known phishing sites and warns you if you display a page that is known to be fraudulent.

Internet Street-Smarts

Everyone would like to think that they aren't susceptible to fraud. Sometimes the best frauds seem so realistic that you may easily fall for them. Here are some common lures:

- An email purporting to be from a trusted service such as your bank

- A pop-up advertisement that appears to be from your favorite online retailer

- An address that is very similar to one you visit often, such that you don't notice it's slightly misspelled when you click the link

---

ActiveX and Java

ActiveX is a Microsoft technology that uses the Microsoft .NET programming framework. It enables a web browser to interact with the underlying operating system in order to run mini-applications called *ActiveX controls* that do more sophisticated things than a plain web page can do.

There are two parts to ActiveX: the browser plug-in, which is like a player for the ActiveX content, and the individual ActiveX controls that you encounter as you visit websites. For example, an ActiveX control may run an interactive game within a web page, or it may collect information from your system for diagnostic purposes.

ActiveX is a powerful web technology, but it can also be dangerous in the hands of criminals. Therefore, when your browser prompts you to download an ActiveX control in order to display a page's content, you should be very suspicious and make sure you trust the website. Some browsers don't support ActiveX controls at all because of the potential security risks.

Java is a programming language that works across multiple platforms (that is, multiple operating systems and types of computer hardware). Many web programmers use Java to write mini-applications for the Web as an alternative to using ActiveX. *JavaScript* is a variant of Java designed for inserting code (scripts) on web pages.

From a security standpoint, using Java for web applications is considered somewhat safer than ActiveX, because it doesn't interact with the underlying operating system. Instead, Java is part of an environment that contains all the interactions within a closed bubble, sometimes called a *virtual machine*, which exists only as long as that web page is displayed.

Cookies

In its raw form, HTTP is a *stateless* protocol. That means every exchange between a web server and your web browser is a clean slate, with no memory of any previous exchanges. Each time you visit a website, it's like you were never there before.

Have you ever noticed that, when you revisit some shopping sites, the page welcomes you back by name, and even makes product suggestions based on your previous purchases? This is possible because the site stores data about you and your previous activities in a plain-text file in a hidden area of your hard drive. This text file is called a *cookie*.

Cookies can originate either from the main site you're visiting (a first-party cookie) or from one of the companies that has an ad on the page (a third-party cookie). Most web browsers have separate settings for controlling and deleting first-party and third-party cookies.

Cookies can also be temporary (session cookies) or permanent (persistent cookies). A session cookie keeps track of your back-and-forth exchange with a website for as long as that page remains loaded: that is, for the current session. If you close the web browser, though, that cookie is deleted. A persistent cookie remains on your hard disk until you delete it. Websites use cookies differently. For example, one website may use a session cookie for a shopping cart, so that if you leave the site without making a purchase, the next time you return your shopping cart is empty. Other sites may use persistent cookies for a shopping cart, so that the next time you return to the site, the items you placed in the shopping cart are still there.

Like many other "innocent" technologies on the Internet, cookies have been exploited by aggressive advertisers. You can easily delete any (or all) of the cookies stored on your system, or you can ensure that they expire after a time limit or when the browser is closed.

Cached Web Data

A *browser cache* retains a copy of some of the files required to display the web pages you visit. When you revisit a page, your browser may be able to reload certain files, such as the page's graphics, from the stored cache rather than re-retrieving them from the Web. This makes your Internet connection seem faster.

Some people consider this data caching to be a privacy concern, because others can snoop on the hard drive to view cached copies of some of the web content previously viewed. Because of this, browsers have a feature that allows you to clear the cache and to elect not to cache pages in the future.

A browser's *history* also provides a record of the pages recently viewed, but for a different reason. The history is useful if you need to find and return to a site when you've forgotten its web address, for example. The history doesn't retain copies of any of the content—it only remembers the addresses of the pages visited. The history can also be cleared, and you can elect to prevent it from storing information in the future.

EXERCISE 3.15

Adjusting Security and Privacy Settings in Firefox

1. Download and install Firefox from www.mozilla.org if it isn't already installed on your computer.

2. In Firefox, choose Tools ➤ Options. The Options dialog box opens.

3. Click the Security icon at the top.

4. Make sure the Block Reported Web Forgeries check box is selected. (That's the phishing filter.)

5. Click the Content icon at the top.

6. Make sure the Enable JavaScript and Block Pop-Up Windows check boxes are selected.

7. Click the Privacy icon at the top.

8. Clear the Accept Third-Party Cookies check box.

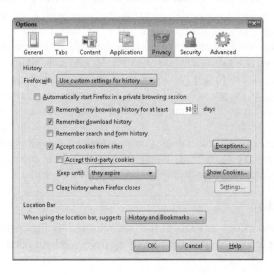

9. Click the Show Cookies button. The Cookies dialog box opens, and a comprehensive list of all cookies appears arranged by site.

10. Double-click one of the folders to open a list of its cookies, and click a cookie file. Its content appears in the gray-shaded pane below the list.

11. Click Remove Cookie. That cookie file is deleted.

12. Click Close to close the Cookies dialog box.

13. Click OK to close the Options dialog box.

14. Choose Tools ➢ Clear Recent History. The Clear Recent History dialog box opens.

15. Open the Time Range To Clear drop-down list, and click Today.

16. Click Clear Now.

17. Close the browser window.

Summary

In this chapter, you learned about several types of peripheral devices, including printers, monitors, sound systems, scanners, and digital cameras. These input and output devices may not be critical to a computer's operation, but they greatly add to its capabilities.

You also learned some basics about networking. You learned about wired and wireless Ethernet network hardware, standards, and protocols, and you learned how IP addressing works. You learned about several types of Internet connections too and Internet technologies and protocols including DNS, HTTP, FTP, POP3, and IMAP. Finally, you learned about some browser settings that enable you to customize and control your browsing experience online.

Exam Essentials

Identify common input and output peripherals. Printers, monitors, and speakers accept output from a computer; scanners and digital cameras provide input. You should know the technology basics of each of those devices.

Understand printer technologies. The two main printer technologies are inkjet and laser. Each has its own pros and cons in terms of initial cost, cost of operation, and print quality.

Understand how scanners and digital cameras capture images. Scanners and digital cameras bounce light off the image they're capturing and measure the amount that comes back to the sensor. Based on those values, they digitize the image.

Identify the hardware involved in networking. Each network device has a network interface card (NIC) and a way of connecting it to a central gathering point, which could be a switch, router, or wireless access point. For wired technologies, know about Cat5e and other cable types. For wireless, know the 802.11 standards.

Understand IP addresses and DNS servers. An IPv4 address consists of four numbers between 0 and 255, separated by periods. An IPv6 address consists of eight 4-digit hexadecimal numbers, separated by colons. On the Internet, domain names are translated to and from IP addresses by Domain Name System (DNS) servers.

Understand Internet connection technologies and protocols. Cable and DSL are the most popular types of broadband connections. To share a broadband connection within a location, use a router. Common protocols used on the Internet include HTTP, POP3, IMAP, and FTP.

Know how to customize a web browser. Web browsers have many options for controlling the web browsing experience, including enabling/disabling plug-ins, changing fonts/sizes, managing cookies, and allowing or disallowing certain technologies such as ActiveX and Java.

Review Questions

1. What type of printer uses liquid ink that it squirts out onto the paper?

   A. Laser

   B. Inkjet

   C. Daisywheel

   D. Dot matrix

2. Which type of printer includes a drum where the page image is written with electrical charges?

   A. Laser

   B. Inkjet

   C. Daisywheel

   D. Dot matrix

3. What type of interface do most modern printers use?

   A. Parallel

   B. LPT

   C. USB

   D. FireWire

4. A(n) _____ connector for a monitor is a 15-pin D-sub connector, used for analog output.

   A. VGA

   B. DVI

   C. HDMI

   D. HTTP

5. Scanners and digital cameras both pick up images using a(n) _____.

   A. DVI

   B. stylus

   C. OCD

   D. CCD

6. On a digital camera, which results in a better quality picture?

   A. Digital zoom

   B. Optical zoom

   C. Vertical zoom

   D. Horizontal zoom

7. What kind of network has computers that are all physically near each other?

    A. MAN

    B. WAN

    C. SAN

    D. LAN

8. What type of network requires no servers?

    A. P2P

    B. Client/server

    C. Internet

    D. Ethernet

9. A NIC is a(n) _____.

    A. Adapter in an individual computer that allows a network connection

    B. Switch or router

    C. Type of cable

    D. Wireless access point

10. To share an Internet connection in your home, you need a(n) _____.

    A. Switch

    B. Hub

    C. Router

    D. Subnet

11. Cat5e Ethernet cables are a type of _____.

    A. Fiber optic

    B. Coax

    C. SCSI

    D. UTP

12. Which type of connector is used for Ethernet cables such as Cat5e?

    A. RJ-11

    B. RJ-14

    C. RJ-45

    D. RJ-50

13. HomePlug technology enables you to use _____ as Ethernet cables in your home.

A. Radio signals

B. Power lines

C. Phone lines

D. Infrared light

14. Which is the newest and fastest wireless networking type?

A. 802.11n

B. 802.11g

C. 802.11a

D. 802.11b

15. In _____ communication, there is two-way communication, but communication in only one direction at a time.

A. Simplex

B. Complex

C. Half duplex

D. Full duplex

16. When you search for wireless networks, the name that appears for each network is its _____.

A. SSID

B. Channel

C. Encryption code

D. Frequency

17. WEP and WPA are two types of _____.

A. Ethernet adapters

B. Wireless network technologies

C. Routers

D. Wireless network security

18. 204.55.25.10 is an example of a(n) _____.

A. IPv6 address

B. IPv4 address

C. WEP encryption code

D. SSID

19. Domain names are translated to IP addresses on the Web via _____.

    A. DHCP

    B. APIPA

    C. DNS

    D. HTML

20. Which of these is a protocol for sending email?

    A. POP3

    B. SMTP

    C. FTP

    D. HTTPS

Answers to Review Questions

1. B. Inkjet printers use liquid ink. Laser printers use dry toner. Daisywheel and dot matrix printers, now long obsolete, used an inked ribbon.

2. A. A laser printer writes the page image to a drum and then transfers it onto paper.

3. C. Most printers employ a USB interface today. Parallel (which is the same as LPT) was an older technology for a printer interface and is now obsolete. FireWire could theoretically be used for a printer interface, but it is not traditionally used for one.

4. A. VGA is an analog connector, still used for some monitors. However, digital connectors such as DVI and HDMI are becoming more common. HTTP is an Internet protocol, not a connector.

5. D. A charge-coupled device (CCD) is the optical technology used in both digital cameras and scanners.

6. B. Optical zoom is "real" zoom, with a real lens. Digital zoom is a simulation of zooming by adding extra pixels (interpolating).

7. D. A local area network (LAN) is a network where the computers are co-located. A WAN is a wide area network. A MAN is a metropolitan area network. SAN is a storage technology, not a physical network type.

8. A. A peer to peer (P2P) network requires no servers. A client/server network requires at least one server. The Internet has many servers. Ethernet is a technology that supports both P2P and client/server networks.

9. A. A network interface card (NIC) is a network adapter in an individual computer or other device.

10. C. A router enables one Internet connection to be shared among multiple PCs.

11. D. Parallel Cat5e is an unshielded twisted pair (UTP) type of cable.

12. C. RJ-45 connectors are used for Ethernet. RJ-11 and RJ-14 cables are telephone cables.

13. B. HomePlug, also called Powerline Ethernet, uses the existing electrical wiring in a building to carry network signals.

14. A. 802.11n is the fastest and newest wireless standard. 802.11a, b, and g are all older standards.

15. C. Half-duplex communication is bidirectional, but only one direction at a time.

16. A. The service set identifier (SSID) appears as the network's name.

17. D. Wired Equivalent Privacy (WEP) and Wi-Fi Protected Access (WPA) are types of wireless security encryption.

18. B. An IPv4 address is four numbers between 0 and 255 separated by periods.

19. C. A Domain Name System (DNS) server translates between numeric addresses and domain names.

20. B. SMTP is a mail-sending protocol. POP3 is its counterpart, but for receiving mail, not sending it. FTP is a file transfer protocol. HTTPS is a secure version of HTTP, used for displaying secure web pages.

Installation, Maintenance, and Upgrades

Chapter

4

Setting Up a Computer

FUNDAMENTALS OF PC TECHNOLOGY OBJECTIVES COVERED IN THIS CHAPTER:

✓ **1.1 U.K. / 1.2 U.S. Demonstrate the proper use of the following devices:**

- Desktop
- Server
- Portable computer

FUNDAMENTALS OF PC FUNCTIONALITY OBJECTIVES COVERED IN THIS CHAPTER:

✓ **1.3 U.K. / 1.7 U.S. Demonstrate the ability to set up a basic PC workstation**

- Identify differences between connector types
- Computer (desktop, tower, laptop, custom cases)
- Voltage and power requirements
- Turn on and use the PC and peripherals

Selecting and setting up a computer system is a basic skill for a computer-literate person. This can include understanding the physical differences among available systems and knowing "what goes where" in terms of plugging in the various external components and peripherals.

Choosing a Computer Type

Different personal computer types are appropriate for different situations, and it's important to be able to identify the right computer for your—or someone else's—needs.

Computers vary according to the following:

Size and Portability   The smaller the computer, the easier it is to transport. However, small size may mean that you have to compromise on some other feature, such as ease of input or processing power.

Processing Speed and Multitasking   As you learned in Chapter 1, "Core Computer Hardware," the faster the CPU, the faster the computer operates overall. Lots of RAM, as well as a multitasking-capable operating system, gives a computer the ability to handle many tasks at once.

Ease of Input and Output   It's easier to put data into, and get data out of, a device with a full-size keyboard and mouse.

Multiple Capabilities   Some computers double as book readers, cell phones, Internet devices, global positioning systems (GPS), and so on. Others strictly function as personal computers.

Desktop PCs are the traditional rectangular-box models with separate keyboard, video monitor, and mouse (sometimes referred to as KVM). A desktop PC provides an optimal user experience because it has a full-size keyboard and mouse and a large monitor—no compromises are needed in any of those areas. Desktop PCs also provide more processing power for the money than other types of PCs. A desktop PC's main drawback is its lack of portability (see Figure 4.1).

FIGURE 4.1   Desktop PC

Courtesy of Lenovo

 Desktop PCs are widely used in SOHO environments. SOHO stands for *small office/home office.*

A *server* is like a desktop PC in terms of size and components. The main difference between a server and a desktop PC is the operating system: a server uses a server OS, such as Windows Server, which has special utilities built in for managing a network. A server may also have multiple CPUs and a large amount of RAM in order to process efficiently the heavy computing demands that a server's job entails. As you learned in Chapter 2, "Input and Storage Devices," home networks don't usually have servers; they're not needed for networks that consist of 10 or fewer computers.

Portable computers are characterized by a built-in LCD monitor and a built-in keyboard (or other data-entry mechanism, such as a touch screen). Some of the different types of portables include the following:

Notebook or Laptop   A notebook or laptop is a computer that's approximately the size of a paper notebook, with a screen ranging from about 12" to 16" in diagonal. Notebook PCs are usually full-featured computers, running a regular version of Windows and handling all the tasks that a desktop PC can handle. A notebook may be appropriate for business professionals who need to take their computer home from the office every night, for example, but who need the computer to be powerful enough to run standard business applications (see Figure 4.2).

FIGURE 4.2   Notebook PC

Courtesy of Dell, Inc.

Netbook, Mini, or Subnotebook   These are smaller versions of a notebook PC, with screens ranging from about 9" to 11" in diagonal. Because of its smaller size and lighter weight, a netbook may be less powerful and fast in completing tasks, and it may have a smaller keyboard that is less comfortable on which to type. Other than that, though, netbooks usually perform all the same tasks as a desktop or notebook. A netbook may be appropriate for someone who is on the go constantly, doesn't want to carry a computer that is very heavy, and doesn't mind trading a little usability for that freedom.

Tablet   There are two types of tablet PCs. The bigger, older type looks a lot like a notebook PC, but the screen rotates so that it's visible when the notebook is closed. You can use a stylus on the screen to "write" and interact with the operating system (see Figure 4.3). The other type has no keyboard and is basically a touch-sensitive LCD screen with a small computer behind it. (The Motorola Xoom, shown in Figure 4.4, and the Apple iPad are examples of this type of tablet computer.) Tablets are suitable for people who, like netbook users, are constantly on the go, but who spend more time viewing data on the computer than entering it. For example, a typical user of one of the newer tablets may spend a lot of time reading online magazines or surfing the Internet.

FIGURE 4.3   Tablet PC that converts from a notebook PC

FIGURE 4.4   The Motorola Xoom is an example of a tablet PC with no external keyboard.

Source: Courtesy of Motorola

Smartphone   A smartphone is a handheld device that not only serves as a cell phone but also functions as a basic computer, including running some applications (such as a contact manager and an email reader) and accessing the Internet via a web browser. Some smartphones have a keyboard, like the Blackberry; others, such as an iPhone, Droid (see Figure 4-5), or Windows phone, have a touch screen that can pop up a virtual keyboard as needed. Smartphones can substitute for computers for people who need frequent access to the Internet no matter where they are.

FIGURE 4.5   The Motorola Droid is an example of a smartphone

Photo credit: Courtesy of Motorola

Personal Digital Assistant (PDA)   Mostly obsolete now, PDAs used to be widely used by businesspeople to track appointments and contact information. Palm was one of the most popular makers of these devices in the 1990s and 2000s. PDAs fell out of fashion when smartphones began offering the same or better computing capabilities.

EXERCISE 4.1

Comparing Portable Computers

Visit the websites of several major manufacturers of portable computers, and compare the specifications of their tablet or subnotebook (netbook) line. Pick one or two models of each brand and note the following:

- Price

- Screen size

- Amount of RAM

- Processor type and model

- Ports

- Operating system

- Special features (if any)

Setting Up a Computer

As a Strata-certified computer user, you should be able to take a new computer out of its boxes and set it up. Doing so mainly consists of being able to plug the cables for the various components into the right sockets on the back of the computer. In the following sections, you'll learn about some of the basic connector types you may encounter, as well as how to evaluate voltage and power requirements and how to turn on and use the PC and its peripherals.

Desktop Computer Form Factors

The *case* of a desktop computer is the big rectangular box to which everything else connects. There are different sizes and shapes of cases. A case's size and orientation is called its *form factor.*

Almost all computer cases these days are *towers,* which means they're taller than they are wide or deep. A *full tower* is one that has lots of expansion bays for drives (like CD or DVD drives). There's no official standardization as to how many bays a case has to have to be considered a full tower, but four is a rough estimate. Most servers are in full-tower cases. A *mini-tower* is smaller and has fewer drive bays, perhaps only two or three.

All computers that consist of a big rectangular box with a separate monitor and keyboard are desktop PCs. But there is also a special style of case called a *desktop case*, which sits on the desk with its largest side down. Figure 4.6 shows a desktop case, and Figure 4.7 shows a full tower.

FIGURE 4.6 Desktop case

Courtesy of Lenovo

FIGURE 4.7 Full-tower case

Some PC manufacturers use custom cases for special purposes. For example, a PC that is designed primarily to serve as part of a home entertainment system may be smaller than a regular PC case and oriented flat like a desktop case so it can fit in an entertainment center. Another common custom case is a *slimline*, which is thinner than normal and can be oriented either flat like a desktop model or upright like a tower.

Some cases are designed to optimize the airflow inside them and thereby dissipate heat and keep things cool by the strategic positioning of air vents and fans. Such cases are called *thermally advantaged chassis*.

EXERCISE 4.2

Investigating Case Form Factors

1. Use a search engine to locate a company that makes computer cases.

2. At that company's site, locate examples of the following:

    -   A full-tower case

    -   A mid-tower case

    -   A mini-tower case

    -   A horizontally oriented desktop case

3. For each of the cases, determine how many drive bays it has, both internally and externally accessible.

4. Find two other sites that also sell cases, and repeat the exercise. Evaluate whether the sites are consistent regarding how many drive bays a case can have to be considered full tower, mid-tower, or mini-tower. Does there appear to be much standardization in the use of those terms?

Unpacking a New Computer

When you're unpacking a new computer, open the box carefully. If you're using a sharp knife to cut the tape holding the box closed, make sure you don't cut too deeply into the box and cut any components.

When you're removing components from the box, do so with an awareness of possibly having to repack them if the computer turns out to be defective. If there are Styrofoam supports, make sure they don't get broken. Save all the packing materials, including any plastic bags containing components, and save all the instructions and discs that come with the computer. Store the instructions and discs in a safe place, because you may need them tomorrow, next week, or next year.

Some components may have a protective plastic film over them, such as the monitor screen or the corners or logos on a case. Pull these off and discard them.

Set the case either on a solid desk (not a wobbly card table or TV tray) or on the floor, so there is no danger of the case being knocked off or falling. If the case will be in a cubbyhole, drawer, or cabinet where there is limited airflow, consider what you can do to increase airflow to that area so the computer doesn't overheat.

Don't plug in the computer's power until you've plugged in all the other components; power should be the last cable to be connected. (You'll learn about the plugs for other components in the next section.)

As you position the desk and the computer, think about where the cords will run. Set the keyboard, mouse, and monitor where you think you'll want them, and note whether the cables will reach to the case, and whether those cables will be draped across any areas where they may be in danger of getting yanked or dragged accidentally.

Verifying Voltage and Power Requirements

The power supply in a PC serves two purposes: first, it steps down the voltage from the AC wall outlet from its default to the much lower voltages required by the PC's components. Second, it converts the alternating current (AC) to direct current (DC), which is what the PC needs.

Personal computer power cords plug into standard household electrical outlets. Depending on where you live, this could be either 230v (such as in most of Europe) or 120v service (such as in the USA). When you buy a computer, the company that sells it to you configures your PC for the correct voltage based on your location. If you move to a country that uses different voltage, you must have your computer modified or use a power outlet voltage converter. Many desktop PCs have a voltage switch on the power supply box that you can flip to change between voltages. (You'll need a new power cord, of course, because your old one won't connect to the differently shaped AC outlet socket.) Laptop PCs typically require a power cord replacement when you change regions.

WARNING Look at http://electricaloutlet.org/, and compare the electrical voltages and outlets of your nation to that of others in your region or internationally.

In the United States and most other places that use 120v power, desktop PCs (well, at least the non-Macintosh ones) use the three-prong Type B power cord type shown in Figure 4.8. Figure 4.9 shows the connector on the back of a power supply for attaching such a power cord. Also note the voltage switch in this figure. In the United Kingdom, a three-prong Type G power connector is used. In most of the rest of Europe, a type C or F connector is used.

FIGURE 4.8   Power cord for a desktop PC

FIGURE 4.9   Power connector on a desktop PC

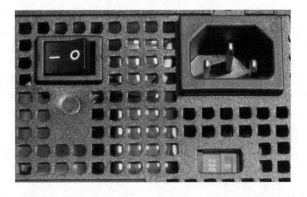

   The official standard for countries in the European Union is 230v, but some countries still use the older 220v standard. A power supply designed for 230v will work on a power grid that provides 220v power and vice versa. This small variation is well within acceptable tolerance.

A notebook PC typically has a power cord with an AC adapter built into it. The AC adapter is a black rectangular block (sometimes called a *power brick*) that performs the same functions as the power supply box in a desktop PC: it lowers the voltage to what the computer needs, and it converts the AC power to DC (see Figure 4.10). The plug that connects the notebook power cord to the computer is typically a small round plug.

FIGURE 4.10   The AC adapter is built into the power cord for a notebook PC

 The voltages supplied to the individual internal components vary. Inside the PC, connectors with various colored wires attach to the motherboard and to drives, and each wire color has a unique meaning. For example, black is a grounding wire, red is +5v, and yellow is +12v. You don't have to worry about these values when you're setting up a PC, though. A technician testing a possibly defective system may use a voltmeter or multimeter to see if each of those wires is delivering the right voltage to the system, but that's way beyond what you need to know.

Connecting Components to a PC's Ports

Look on the back of the computer, and examine the various connectors (aka *ports*) available. You may not use all these ports, but you should know what ports are there for future reference. Figure 4.11 shows the back of a typical desktop PC and points out some of the ports.

FIGURE 4.11   Ports on a typical desktop PC

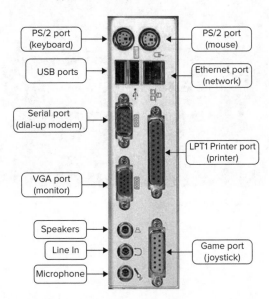

Some connectors have pins sticking out of them; these are called *male connectors*. Others have holes into which pins fit; these are called *female connectors*. They're often referred to by abbreviations of M and F.

Some connectors have D-shaped metal rings around the pins to keep them from getting hit and bent. These connectors are called *D-sub connectors*, abbreviated as DB, and are referred to by the number of pins and whether they're male or female. For example, the VGA port on the back of a computer is a 15-pin female D-sub connector and may be abbreviated DB15F.

Video Monitor

Every computer has at least one video port—that is, a port for connecting a monitor. This can be a VGA, DVI, or HDMI port, depending on the computer. (Most computers have VGA and/or DVI; HDMI is fairly rare for a consumer-level computer.) Look back to the "Monitors" section in Chapter 3, "Peripherals and Networking," for a discussion of each connector's pros and cons. HDMI is the highest quality, followed by DVI, with VGA being the lowest quality. If you have a choice, go with the highest-quality option available.

Figure 4.12 shows a DVI connector on the back of a computer, and Figure 4.13 shows a VGA type (DB15F). Notice that there are screw holes on either side of these connectors. These correspond to thumbscrews on the cable connector. To connect a DVI or VGA connector, plug it firmly into the socket, and then tighten the thumbscrews. The thumbscrews prevent the connector from being accidentally jerked out and damaged if someone trips over the cord or knocks over the case.

FIGURE 4.12   A DVI port on a computer

FIGURE 4.13   A VGA port on a computer

Universal Serial Bus (USB)

USB is the jack-of-all-trades port, used to connect many different types of input and output devices to a computer. Most keyboards and mice use this interface, as do flash RAM drives, digital cameras, printers, scanners, and almost any other type of device you may have. USB ports are denoted by the USB symbol, shown in Figure 4.14.

FIGURE 4.14   A USB port showing the USB symbol

Photo credit: Aidan C. Siegel

There are several different sizes and shapes of USB connectors. The most common type is a USB Standard A/B cable. The Standard A end connects to the computer and is wide and flat (see Figure 4.15). The Standard B end connects to the device, such as a printer, and is more square-shaped (see Figure 4.16).

FIGURE 4.15   A USB A connector, which connects to a computer

Photo credit: Andreas Frank

FIGURE 4.16   A USB B connector, which connects to a large peripheral, such as a printer

Photo credit: www.chotocheeta.com

There are also mini (small) and micro (even smaller) versions of USB connectors, used to connect smaller devices like phones and cameras. Figure 4.17 shows a USB Micro B connector, for example, which may be used to connect a cell phone.

FIGURE 4.17   A USB Micro B connector, which connects to a very small peripheral, such as a cell phone

Photo credit: Copyright 2002 coolgear.com

There are also different versions of the USB standard, each with its own maximum speed. (There's no direct relationship between the physical connectors and the USB standard being used.) Currently, most USB ports on computers are USB 2.0 compatible, but USB 3.0 has recently been introduced and will be offered on more PCs and devices soon. Table 4.1 summarizes the USB versions and their speeds. They all use the same connectors, so the higher versions are backward-compatible with devices designed for the lower versions; they just run at the lower speeds when not all components are higher-speed capable.

TABLE 4.1   USB versions

USB Version	Speed
1.0	1.5 Mbps
1.1 (Full Speed)	12 Mbps
2.0 (High Speed)	480 Mbps
3.0 (Super Speed)	4800 Mbps

EXERCISE 4.3

Getting USB Port Information

One of the benefits of USB devices is that a single USB controller can manage multiple devices with very little additional system resources required. Each controller manages one or more USB hubs. A hub can be a physical box outside a computer but is more commonly a built-in motherboard component that routes signals from multiple USB ports on your computer into one of the USB controllers. In the following exercise, you'll explore the USB devices on your Windows-based computer using Device Manager to see the relationships between the controllers and the hubs.

1. In Windows, click Start, type **Device**, and click Device Manager on the list of programs that appears at the top of the Start menu.

2. Double-click Universal Serial Bus Controllers to expand that category. A list of hubs and controllers appears. The hubs are internal and may not have a one-to-one relationship with the actual USB ports on your system.

3. Double-click one of the entries on the list that contains the word *controller*. Most systems have two controllers listed. A dialog box for the controller appears.

4. Click through each of the tabs in the dialog box to note what information is available for the USB controller. In particular, look on the Advanced tab and see what devices are consuming bandwidth. Each controller will show System Reserved 20%, even if there are no devices listed for that controller. Below that will appear any USB devices it's supporting.

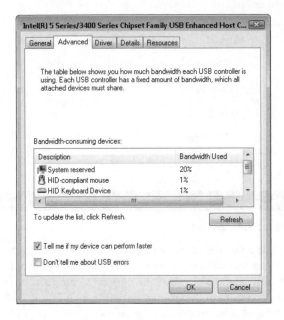

5. Click Cancel to close the dialog box.

6. Repeat steps 3–5 for any other entries that contain the word *controller*.

7. Using the same process, browse the properties of each of the USB items on the list that contain the word *hub*.

8. Close the Device Manager window.

FireWire

FireWire is a competitive technology to USB. Its official name is IEEE 1394, after the IEEE standard that defines it, but FireWire is the friendlier and more common moniker. However, it's typically labeled IEEE1394, as shown in Figure 4.18.

FIGURE 4.18   FireWire ports on a PC

Photo credit: Copyright ® 2001–2011 Cybernet Manufacturing, Inc. All Rights Reserved.

Figure 4.19 shows both ends of a FireWire cable; the smaller end plugs into a peripheral device. At the computer end, a FireWire port looks like a small rectangle with one end beveled, and it has six circuits (pins) inside. This is called a FireWire Alpha connector.

FIGURE 4.19   A FireWire cable. The plug on the right connects to the computer.

FireWire is commonly used with video-capture and -transfer devices, such as high-end video cameras, because of its speed and efficiency at moving data. The original FireWire specification, also called FireWire 400, is the most commonly used type (see Figure 4.18 and Figure 4.19). It transfers data at up to 400 Mbps. USB 2.0 is just as fast as the original FireWire, the most common type in use today, so there is no real necessity for devices that transfer a lot of data to use FireWire; it's simply a matter of product development and marketing decisions on the part of the peripheral manufacturers.

Two newer and faster FireWire specs have been released, but they use different cables and connectors and so aren't port-compatible with the standard FireWire Alpha ports unless you use an adapter plug. FireWire 800 uses a nine-pin FireWire Beta connector and transfers data at up to 786 Mbps. FireWire S800T uses Cat5e Ethernet cable and transfers data at up to 800 Mbps.

PS/2

PS/2 is an obsolete type of round connector that older systems used for keyboard and mouse connections. You may still see this port on the back of an older computer. These ports were typically color-coded, with purple being used for wired keyboard connections and green for wired mouse connections. Figure 4.20 shows a PS/2 port on a computer, and Figure 4.21 shows the corresponding connector on a cable.

FIGURE 4.20 A PS/2 port

FIGURE 4.21 A PS/2 cable connector

Legacy Serial Port

Serial ports aren't used for many consumer devices anymore, having mostly been replaced by USB. They're now referred to as *legacy serial*, with *legacy* being a polite word for outdated.

A legacy serial connector was a 9-pin (or, even older, 25-pin) connector, similar to a VGA connector but with only two rows of pins. It was an inexpensive connector used with devices that didn't require high data throughput, but it was replaced almost a decade ago by USB. Figure 4.22 shows a DB9M serial port on a computer. (Remember, DB means it has a D-shaped ring around it, 9 is the number of pins, and M means there are pins rather than holes.) Another name for this type of connection is RS232.

FIGURE 4.22 A serial connector

Legacy Parallel Port

Parallel ports, like serial ports, are mostly obsolete nowadays, and hence have the word *legacy* associated with them. They were used for connecting printers prior to the popularization of USB. Although technically they can be used for other device types, parallel ports became so closely associated with printing that alternative names for the parallel port include *printer port* and *LPT (line printer) port*. Figure 4.23 shows a DB25F parallel port. (Remember, DB refers to the D-shaped ring, 25 is the number of pins, and F means there are holes rather than pins.)

FIGURE 4.23   A parallel connector

Network and Modem Ports

Ethernet networks use the RJ-45 connector standard, as you learned in Chapter 3. The jacks on the PC look like wide telephone jacks. Figure 4.24 shows a modem jack (regular telephone connector, RJ-11 or RJ-14) and a network jack (RJ-45) for comparison.

FIGURE 4.24   Modem (left) vs. Ethernet (right)

As you learned in Chapter 2, there are always-on broadband modems available today for cable and DSL service. However, the modem jack in Figure 4.24 is for a dial-up modem via regular telephone service (the very slow kind of connection that nobody uses anymore for Internet service if they have any alternative available).

3.5 mm Audio Jack

A standard technology for all portable headphones and earpieces, the 3.5 mm audio jack is used for a variety of audio input and output devices, as you learned in Chapter 3. On some systems, the jacks are color-coded; on others, tiny writing or symbols next to a port identifies its purpose. Figure 4.25 shows a microphone with 3.5 mm connectors.

FIGURE 4.25   3.5 mm connectors on a microphone

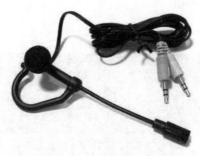

Photo credit: ©2010 Soundwise—Edinburgh, Scotland

ExpressCard and CardBus/PC Card

Some notebook computers have a multipurpose slot for add-on adapters that are approximately the height and width of a credit card (only thicker). Adapters that fit into one of these slots can add any of a wide range of capabilities to the system, including Ethernet, storage, add-on graphics cards, wireless networking, and TV tuners.

The original type of these slots was called PCMCIA, named for the association that created it (Personal Computer Memory Card International Association). This association lives on, and it continues to manage the current standard. Updated versions have been released over the years that come in different sizes and shapes, which hook into different buses inside the computer and transfer data at different rates.

ExpressCard is the current standard, which was first introduced around 2005. It fits into a 34 mm slot with a 26-pin connector. There are two types: ExpressCard|34 and ExpressCard|54. The latter is L-shaped so the connector portion is the same as on ExpressCard|34. It can use either the PCI Express or the USB bus inside the computer. ExpressCard devices have a throughput of up to 2.5 Gbps via the PCI Express bus or 480 Mbps through the USB 2.0 bus.

PCI stands for *peripheral component interconnect*. It's a rather fast bus on the motherboard that carries data between expansion cards and the system bus. The original version was just called PCI, but updated versions called *PCI-Extended* (PCI-X) and *PCI Express* (PCIe) have been released that are even faster. Make sure you know those acronyms for the Strata exam. PCI-X is a double-wide version of PCI, used primarily in servers in the early 2000s. PCIe is the current standard, and it's faster, smaller, and more efficient than its predecessors.

Before that, CardBus was the standard, from the late 1990s to around 2005. It was 54 mm wide with a 68-pin connector. CardBus slots communicated with a 32-bit PCI bus on the motherboard, with all CardBus cards sharing a 1.06 Gbps bandwidth. Figure 4.26 compares the physical dimensions of the two ExpressCard sizes with that of CardBus. PC Card was a 16-bit type card prior to the advent of CardBus. The term *PC Card* is often used generically to refer to both the older 16-bit type and the 32-bit CardBus type.

FIGURE 4.26   ExpressCard vs. CardBus sizes

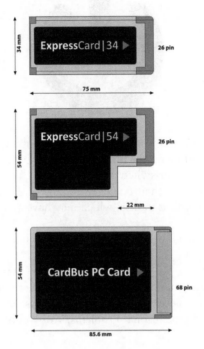

PC Cards were available in three thicknesses: Type I, Type II, and Type III. Type I cards (3.3 mm thick) were rare; they were used primarily for adding memory and were 16-bit only. Type II cards (5.0 mm thick) were the most popular type and were widely used for purposes such as modems and network cards.

PC Card and CardBus were at their height of popularity back in the days before USB, when the only other way of connecting peripherals to a notebook computer was through the very slow parallel and serial ports. Now that USB 2.0 is the dominant standard for peripherals, fewer devices use these card types, and many notebook computers don't have any card slots at all.

Turn On and Use the PC and Peripherals

When all the components are connected, using whatever combination of the ports and connectors you just learned about is appropriate for your system, it's time for the big moment: turning it all on. (Maybe you've already turned yours on; if so, play along for now.)

On each device, look for a button with a power symbol on it, like the symbol shown in Figure 4.27. This is the standard symbol you'll find on most of the power buttons on various peripherals, as well as on the PC itself.

FIGURE 4.27 Power symbol

Start with the monitor, so you'll be able to see any startup messages that may appear. Next, turn on the PC. Depending on the model, there may be a power button on the front of the case (most likely) or a rocker switch on the back.

The keyboard and mouse draw their power from the PC, so you don't need to turn them on. An exception may be a cordless mouse, which may have an on-off switch to save its battery.

Finally, turn on any peripheral devices, such as external hard drives, printers, or scanners.

If this is the first time anyone has started up this PC, you may be guided through a one-time setup process where you're prompted to enter a username, register your copy of Windows, and/or connect to a network. Follow the prompts as they appear, and refer to Chapter 8, "Troubleshooting Operational Problems," for troubleshooting help if needed.

Summary

In this chapter, you learned about the various types of computers, including desktops, notebooks, netbooks, tablets, and even smartphones. You learned about the ports for connecting peripherals that are found on these devices, and you learned how to turn on a PC and its peripherals and begin using it.

Exam Essentials

Demonstrate the proper use of various computer types. Desktop PCs are the most comfortable to use, but they take up the most space and are the least portable. Notebooks are more portable but can still be cumbersome to carry around. Netbooks are even more portable, but the small keyboard and screen size may be uncomfortable to use for extended sessions. Tablets and smartphones provide the ultimate in portability but at the expense of visibility and ease of use.

Understand the differences between cases. Nonportable (desktop) PC cases vary in terms of their size and orientation. A case that sits tall on its smallest side is called a tower. A case that sits flat on its largest side is called a desktop. (Note that the term *desktop* has two different meanings here.)

Verify voltage and power requirements. A PC is designed to run on AC current, either 110v or 230v, depending on the country and region. Desktop PCs sometimes have a switch on the power supply that determines which voltage it accepts. Laptop PCs typically have different power cords for one voltage or the other. It's important to verify the voltage a system needs against the voltage your wall outlet provides.

Understand the common ports. Look on the back of a desktop PC, or along the sides of a notebook, and peruse the ports available there. You should be able to identify what each of these ports is used for. Some of the most common ones include USB, VGA, FireWire (IEEE1394), Ethernet (RJ-45), and 3.5 mm (audio).

Review Questions

1. Which of these is the most portable computer type?

   A. Netbook

   B. Notebook

   C. Server

   D. Desktop

2. What's the difference between a desktop PC and a server?

   A. The desktop PC has more RAM.

   B. The server has a server-based OS.

   C. The server does not have a monitor.

   D. The server does not use a mouse.

3. What type of computing device would be best for someone who travels a lot and needs constant Internet access?

   A. Server

   B. Notebook

   C. Smartphone

   D. Desktop

4. What case form factor would be best for someone who needed to have five disk drives in a computer?

   A. Mini-tower

   B. Full tower

   C. Slimline

   D. Desktop

5. What does a thermally advantaged chassis do better than a regular computer case?

   A. Keeps the system cool without using any fans

   B. Adjusts to the room temperature, heating or cooling the inside of the PC as needed

   C. Keeps heat in, ensuring that the processor stays warm enough

   D. Expels heat, keeping the processor cool

6. If you are setting up a PC in the UK, how do you set the voltage switch on the back of a desktop PC?

   A. 120v

   B. 230v

   C. 150v

   D. 350v

7. Which type of connector might you use to connect a monitor?

    A. DVI

    B. PCI

    C. CPU

    D. ATA

8. When connecting a computer to a printer, what type of plug is most likely to be used to plug into the printer?

    A. USB Standard A

    B. USB Standard B

    C. USB Mini A

    D. USB Micro B

9. Which type of USB, also known as High Speed, transfers data at 480 Mbps?

    A. 1.0

    B. 1.1

    C. 2.0

    D. 3.0

10. What type of device would be most likely to use a FireWire connection?

    A. Printer

    B. Mouse

    C. Keyboard

    D. Video camera

11. What type of device should be connected to a purple PS/2 connector on the back of an older desktop PC?

    A. Printer

    B. Mouse

    C. Keyboard

    D. Video camera

12. If a device requires a DB9M connector, what type of connector would you look for?

    A. Serial 9-pin male

    B. Parallel 9-pin male

    C. PS/2

    D. IEEE1394

13. If you see a DB25F port on the back of a computer, what could you connect to it?

    A. Mouse

    B. Keyboard

    C. Printer

    D. Monitor

14. If you see a DB15F port on the back of a computer, what could you connect to it?

  A. Mouse

  B. Keyboard

  C. Printer

  D. Monitor

15. Which type of port is used for a dial-up modem?

  A. DB15F

  B. RJ-11

  C. RJ-45

  D. PS/2

16. Which of these is the newest and most modern card-based expansion slot in a notebook PC?

  A. CardBus

  B. PC Card Type I

  C. ExpressCard

  D. PC Card Type III

17. What does a circle symbol with a vertical line cutting halfway through it mean?

  A. USB

  B. Microphone

  C. Ethernet

  D. Power

18. Can an ExpressCard|54 and an ExpressCard|34 use the same card slot on a notebook PC?

  A. Yes

  B. No

19. What kind of port does a Bluetooth connection use?

  A. USB

  B. RJ-45

  C. FireWire

  D. None of the above

20. Another name for FireWire is _____.

  A. IEEE1394

  B. Bluetooth

  C. LPT

  D. RS232

Answers to Review Questions

1. A. A netbook is a mini-notebook, and it is the most portable. Servers and desktop PCs are not very portable, requiring disconnecting and moving several separate components including monitor, keyboard, and mouse.

2. B. A server is very much like a desktop PC and has both a monitor and a mouse; the main difference is that it runs a server version of the operating system. Servers tend to have more RAM than desktop PCs, but this is not a hard-and-fast rule.

3. C. A smartphone combines the easy portability of a cell phone with Internet capabilities. Servers and desktops are not easily portable. A notebook is portable but may not always have Internet access available to it.

4. B. A full-tower case provides the largest number of drive bays of any case type.

5. D. A thermally advantaged chassis is a case designed to keep the system cool by efficiently flowing air through the case through a system of air vents and fans.

6. B. 230v is the standard for countries in the European Union (EU). 120v is appropriate for the USA. There are no countries that use 150v or 350v.

7. A. Digital Video Interface (DVI) is a monitor connector. PCI is a type of motherboard bus. CPU is the central processing unit (the processor). ATA is a standard for hard disks.

8. B. The USB Standard B connector is the one that plugs into a printer. USB Standard A plugs into a computer. Mini and micro connectors are used for smaller devices, such as cell phones and digital cameras.

9. C. USB 2.0 is also known as High Speed, and it transfers data at up to 480 Mbps. Refer to Table 4.1 for the other types of USB connectors and their speeds.

10. D. FireWire is a very fast connection, so it is often employed by devices that need to move a lot of data, like a video camera. Printers, mice, and keyboards most often use a USB connection.

11. C. Purple PS/2 connectors are for keyboards. Green ones are for mice. Printers and video cameras do not use PS/2 connectors.

12. A. A DB9 connector is a 9-pin serial connector. The M stands for male, meaning it has pins rather than holes.

13. C. A DB25 female connector on a computer is designed for an older-style printer connection. A mouse and keyboard would use a USB or PS/2 connection. A monitor would use a VGA, a DVI, or an HDMI connection.

14. D. A DB15 female connector on a computer is for a VGA monitor connection. A VGA connector has three rows of holes in a D-shaped connector.

15. B. An RJ-11 jack, which is an ordinary phone jack connector, is used for a dial-up modem. A DB15F connector is a VGA connector for a monitor. RJ-45 is for Ethernet networking. PS/2 is used for an older keyboard or mouse.

16. C. ExpressCard is the modern standard for notebook expansion cards. PC Card was an earlier standard that supported 16-bit or 32-bit connections. CardBus came after PC Card but before ExpressCard.

17. D. That symbol is found on most power buttons. The USB symbol looks like a branching tree of arrows. Ethernet is often symbolized by three connected boxes. A microphone port may have a picture of a microphone on it.

18. A. Both of those cards fit in a 34 mm slot with a 26-pin connector. The ExpressCard|54's back end is wider, but the end that connects to the PC is the same. See Figure 4.26.

19. D. Bluetooth, being a wireless technology, does not use a cable, so it does not require a port to plug into. It does require a Bluetooth adapter in the computer, but it communicates with the adapter wirelessly.

20. A. IEEE1394 is the FireWire standard. RS232 is a legacy serial port. LPT is a legacy parallel port.

Chapter

5

Maintaining a Computer

FUNDAMENTALS OF PC FUNCTIONALITY OBJECTIVES COVERED IN THIS CHAPTER:

✓ **2.2 U.K. / 3.2 U.S. Identify issues related to folder and file management**

- Create, delete, rename, and move folders
- Assign folder structure during installation
- Create, delete, rename, move, and print files
- Importance of following back-up guidelines and procedures

✓ **2.3 U.K. / 3.3 U.S. Explain the function and purpose of software tools**

- Performance and error correction tools
- Activity or event logging
- Back-up tools
- Disk cleanup tools
- File compression tools

FUNDAMENTALS OF PC TECHNOLOGY OBJECTIVES COVERED IN THIS CHAPTER:

✓ **2.3 Demonstrate the ability to minimize risks**

- Data loss
- Loss of service
- Damage to equipment

✓ **3.2 U.K. / 5.3 U.S. Identify preventative maintenance products, procedures, and how to use them**

- Liquid cleaning compounds
- Types of materials used to clean contacts and connections

- Compressed air
- Cleaning monitors
- Cleaning removable media devices
- Ventilation, dust, and moisture control on PC hardware interior
- Surge suppressors
- Replacing printer consumables (U.K. only)
- Use of ESD equipment (U.S. only)
- Wire placement and safety (U.S. only)

✓ **3.1 U.K (only) Recognize safety hazards and identify corresponding guidelines**

- Hazards
- Fire
- Flood
- Electrical surges
- Extreme storms
- Environmental hazards
- Guidelines
- Use of ESD equipment
- Use of tools and equipment
- Electricity and safety
- Wire placement and safety

Preventive maintenance is an important part of computer usage. This can include cleaning the computer, backing up files, and preventing damage from electrical surges and static electricity. This chapter covers all those skills and several other important maintenance tasks.

Managing files and folders is also a daily or near-daily process. Part of keeping a computer's contents orderly is moving, copying, renaming, and deleting files. In this chapter, you'll learn all those skills, as well as how to print files.

Cleaning a Computer

Computers that are cleaned regularly are not only more pleasant to use, but also can last longer. Dirt, clumps of debris, and other accumulation can make components run hotter, shortening their lives.

In the following sections, you'll learn about some of the cleaning products available for cleaning a computer inside and out. You'll also study some techniques for cleaning various areas without damaging them.

Cleaning Supplies

Expensive cleaning supplies aren't required to clean a PC, but neither should you use whatever products happen to be lying around. Here is a list of basic supplies to have on hand:

- A spray cleaning product designed for plastics, preferably one designed for computers. The ones designed for computers often have antistatic properties that regular cleaners lack.

- A monitor cleaner, either spray or towelette, designed specifically for cleaning monitors or other electronics screens (like televisions). Don't use a glass-cleaning product that contains ammonia because ammonia can destroy the antiglare coating on some monitors.

- A can of compressed air for blowing dust out of crevices.

- Cotton swabs.

- Denatured isopropyl alcohol (not rubbing alcohol, because that has too much water in it).

- An antistatic spray designed for computer work areas.

- (Optional) A small handheld vacuum cleaner designed for electronics. (Don't use a regular vacuum cleaner because the filter isn't fine enough and because a regular vacuum can generate static electricity that can harm equipment.)

Cleaning a Monitor

Always turn a monitor off before cleaning it. If any liquid gets inside, the monitor can air dry without worries of short-circuiting. It's also much easier to see dirt and spots on the screen when it's dark.

First, clean the outer casing with a spray computer-cleaning solution. Spray the cleaner on the cloth, not directly on the casing, to avoid spraying into vent holes.

Next, clean the glass using a cleaner designed specifically for monitors. This can be in the form of a spray or a towelette. Don't use ordinary cleaning products on monitors because they can leave streaks and sometimes harm the antiglare coating. Don't use regular glass cleaner either, because it contains ammonia, which can also harm the surface. Don't spray the screen directly, because the liquid may drip down below the bottom bezel; spray on a cloth and then wipe the screen.

Cleaning External Surfaces

As with monitors, clean the outside casing of PCs, printers, scanners, and similar equipment with a computer-cleaning spray product. Mild general-purpose spray cleaners also work. You can also use mild soapy water and a damp cloth (not soaking wet) to clean external surfaces only—nothing internal or with a vent or crack that leads inside.

Cleaning a Keyboard

Because it's always at the forefront of activity, the keyboard can get very dirty. Although technicians may remind end users to keep their computing areas clean, more often than not people neglect to do so. They may type with unwashed hands, or eat, drink, or even play with their pets while they work. All this activity leaves dirt, oil, and other residue on the keyboard.

To clean a keyboard, first turn off the PC. The keyboard need not be unplugged from the PC. Then, turn the keyboard upside down and shake it to remove any loose debris, or hold it over a trashcan and spray beneath the keys with compressed air (see Figure 5.1). What falls out—and the amount of it—is often surprising!

FIGURE 5.1 Clean the debris out from under the keys with compressed air.

Photo credit: CNET

Use a cloth dampened with a spray cleaning solution designed for PCs, or a towelette containing a PC cleaning product, to clean all visible surfaces. Get down between the cracks with a cotton swab or a bit of folded paper towel. Removing the keys isn't recommended because it can be difficult to get them back on again. If you have access to one, a small handheld vacuum cleaner designed specifically for working with electronics can be useful in sucking debris out from under the keys.

If liquid is spilled onto a keyboard, turn the keyboard upside down and unplug it immediately from the PC (if possible), or turn off the PC. Turn the keyboard upside-down to release as much of the liquid as possible, and then let it dry for at least 48 hours. If the liquid was plain water, the keyboard will probably be fine after it dries; just clean the outside as well as possible. But if the liquid contained sugar, the keyboard may never be completely clean again. Some people have successfully cleaned sticky keyboards (the separate kind, not those found on a notebook PC) in a dishwasher. To try this (there is little to lose with a keyboard that is otherwise on its way to the trash can), place the keyboard on the upper rack, wash it without using the heat-dry feature and with very little or no detergent, remove it after the wash, rinse it, and set it in a dish drainer for several days to dry out.

Cleaning a Mouse

A mouse, like a keyboard, gets very dirty because it's constantly being handled. In addition, a mechanical mouse has the added feature of the ball on the bottom, which rolls across the desk picking up dirt and lint and moving it inside the mouse. As a result, the rollers and sensors on a mechanical mouse can become encrusted with dirt rather quickly, causing the mouse to malfunction. An optical mouse has fewer problems with dirt inside, but dust and hair can still accumulate at the opening where the light shines through.

When a mouse is dirty, the pointer on-screen may jump or stutter, or moving the mouse in one direction may result in no action at all. In addition, the mouse may become more difficult to roll.

To clean a mouse, first wipe off the outside with mild soapy water or cleaning product designed for computers. Then turn the mouse on its back. If it's an optical mouse, use a cotton swab dipped in denatured alcohol to clean out the hollow area where the light shines through if there is any debris inside. (Alcohol dries quickly, so it's used instead of water anytime you clean internal areas of electronics.)

If it's a mechanical mouse, rotate the plastic plate that holds the ball in place. Then turn the mouse over again, and the ball and plate should fall into your hand. Clean inside the ball's chamber with alcohol on a cotton swab. Clean the ball itself with mild soapy water, and dry it thoroughly (see Figure 5.2). (Don't use alcohol on a rubber ball because it dries the rubber and makes it brittle.)

FIGURE 5.2   To clean a mechanical mouse, remove the ball, and clean inside the mouse's chamber.

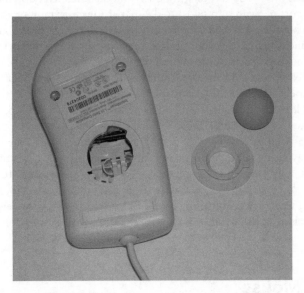

Cleaning the Inside of a PC

A desktop PC should be cleaned out regularly—at least once a year. Its cooling and ventilation fans suck in a lot of air, and with that air come pollutants that can build up over time. Even a thin layer of dust on a circuit board can make it run hotter, shortening its life; and clumps of dirt and hair can prevent the free flow of air through the case.

Remove the cover from the case (following the directions that came with it on how to do so). Inside a desktop PC there may be big clumps of hair and dirt; fish these out by hand and throw them away. Then check the motherboard and expansion boards for dust accumulation, and blow it out with compressed air. If it's been a long time since the PC has been cleaned, you may want to take it outside or to an open area so you don't blow dust all over someone's work area. The motherboard doesn't have to be sparkling clean; it just needs to have the major clumps of visible debris removed. A handheld vacuum cleaner designed for electronics can come in handy if available.

WARNING   Hold your breath as you blast out the dust with compressed air, or you'll be coughing from the dust flying around. It's best to do it outdoors if weather permits. Keep in mind, too, that canned air generates a blast of cold, so don't blow it on yourself or others. Some technicians use this side effect as a tool for cooling off overheated chips on a circuit board when troubleshooting.

To clean anything that involves circuit boards or chips, stay away from liquids, especially water, because of the danger of short-circuiting if the board isn't completely dry when the PC powers up. If some kind of moisture is absolutely necessary, use alcohol on a cotton swab.

Old circuit boards can build up deposits on the metal pins (contacts) along the edge; you can remove these deposits with a pencil eraser or with alcohol and a cotton swab. Avoid touching any of the circuitry, chips, or transistors on a circuit board; it's easy to damage them. Handle circuit boards only by the edges.

Other parts that tend to accumulate dust include the fan on the power supply, the fan on the processor, and the air vents in the case. Wipe off the case's air vents with a damp paper towel. For the power supply, point the compressed air nozzle at an angle to the fan opening rather than blowing straight down into it to avoid driving the dirt even deeper into the power supply box instead of blowing it out.

Notebook PCs and all-in-ones also need to be cleaned out periodically, although not as often as desktops because there is less airflow in them and the vents are smaller, so less debris tends to accumulate. Non-desktop models are often harder to get into; you may need to obtain instructions from a service manual to know which screws to remove to open one and access its inner spaces where dust and dirt may have accumulated.

Moisture inside a PC can be a problem in humid environments because water conducts electricity, which can create short-circuiting. Many server rooms have environmental dehumidifiers to control moisture in the atmosphere. You may wish to use a room-based dehumidifier if your region is prone to high summer humidity.

EXERCISE 5.1

Cleaning a Desktop Computer

1. Turn off the PC, and unplug it.

2. Clean all the externally accessible plastic surfaces with a spray cleaner designed for electronics and paper towels or a soft cloth.

3. Clean the mouse, using whatever techniques are most appropriate for the model.

4. Clean the keyboard, including turning it upside down and shaking it to remove debris under the keys. Clean the individual keys with the spray cleaner and paper towels or cloth.

5. Clean the monitor screen with a spray or towelette cleaner designed for monitors. Don't spray the cleaner directly onto the monitor surface.

6. Remove the cover from the case. Remove any clumps of hair or dirt with your fingers.

7. If there is additional dust inside, vacuum it out with a vacuum designed for electronics, or blow it out with compressed air.

8. Wait for all damp areas to dry, and then plug the computer back in and restart it.

Cleaning a Printer and Replacing Consumables

All types of printers can be cleaned on the outside with a cloth dampened with a spray cleaner for PCs. This won't make the printer perform any better, but it will make for a nicer office environment.

The only parts inside an inkjet printer that need cleaning are the inkjets, and these aren't cleaned by hand—a utility built into the printer cleans them. The ink in an inkjet printer is liquid; if the printer isn't in frequent use, the ink dries out and bits of dried ink remain in the nozzles. The cleaning procedure flushes out any dried-up ink. It uses some ink to do so, so don't clean the inkjets unless the print quality has declined.

On most inkjet printers, there are two ways to activate the cleaning utility: pressing a sequence of buttons on the printer itself, or using the cleaning utility in the printer's software. For example, Figure 5.3 shows the Toolbox utility for an HP printer; there are commands for cleaning and aligning print cartridges and printing test pages.

FIGURE 5.3   Software utilities for cleaning print heads for an inkjet printer

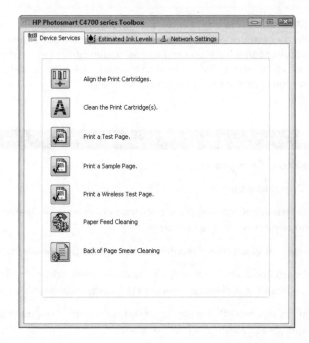

Laser printers use toner rather than ink. Because toner is a dry substance (a mixture of plastic resin and iron oxide), it doesn't clog things the way liquid ink does. However, toner is a loose powder that can scatter over clothing and the work area if the cartridges aren't handled with care. Clean up any spilled toner with a vacuum designed for electronics or with a damp paper towel. If it gets on clothing, you can get it out with a magnet, because toner is half iron. Don't use a regular vacuum cleaner: general-use vacuums don't have fine enough filters, so the toner particles can pass through them and get into the air where they become a health hazard to breathe.

Several specific parts of a laser printer can accumulate toner, making them less effective over time. Depending on the age and model of the printer, though, these parts may or may not reachable. Consult the manual that came with the printer to find out what you can do to clean your laser printer.

Consumables is another name for the ink or toner cartridges in a printer, the paper, and any other parts that regularly must be replaced, such as a felt cleaning pad on some models of laser printers.

When considering what printer to buy, it is prudent to look at the *TCO*, or *total cost of ownership*. This includes not only the initial cost of the printer, but the cost of the consumables.

Each printer has a specific procedure for replacing consumables; follow the instructions for your model. Here are some general tips, though:

Inkjet Tips

- On an inkjet printer, the printer will tell you when it's low on ink or completely out. You may also notice degradation in image quality or a missing, faded, or striped color on some printouts.

- The printer may have a sequence of buttons you have to press to bring the ink cartridge into view where it's accessible, or the cartridge may move into an accessible position when you open the lid.

- There is usually a lever or button you press to release the old cartridge. Then it slides out of a groove or socket.

- Unwrap the new cartridge, and remove the piece of tape that is covering the metal contacts on the bottom of the cartridge. Insert it firmly into the socket in the same orientation as the one you removed. Then close the printer.

- The printer may ask you to print a test page, or to clean or align the print heads. Do whatever it suggests. Check the manual as needed.

Laser Tips

- On a laser printer, the printer will indicate when it's getting low on toner. At this point, you may be able to get a bit of extra life out of the cartridge by taking it out and shaking it gently from side to side. Don't turn it upside down or tilt it, or toner may fall out. Handle it very gently.

- A new toner cartridge may have multiple pieces of tape or plastic guards on it to prevent toner leakage. Make sure you remove them all before inserting the cartridge.

- The printer may recognize the new toner cartridge immediately, or you may have to use the printer's menu system to let it know that it has new toner.

Both ink and toner cartridges can be recycled. Recycling companies often offer free shipping bags that you can use to send in your used cartridges. Some companies even pay you (a small amount) for empty toner cartridges.

WARNING

Using refilled ink or toner cartridges can void your printer's warranty. Don't attempt to refill cartridges yourself, as tempting as that may seem. It's messy, and if you do it wrong, you can damage your printer. In addition, some cartridges have print heads or drums built into them, and those parts need replacing as often as you replace the ink or toner. Reusing them results in degraded print quality.

Cleaning Removable Media

Disc drives that read removable media like CDs and DVDs don't usually require any cleaning. The discs themselves, however, can sometimes become dirty or damaged such that they won't play properly without some rehab. To remove fingerprints, buff them off gently with a soft cloth. If the surface is grimy or sticky, use an alcohol-dampened towelette or cloth, and air-dry the disc thoroughly before use.

Is the problem more than just a few fingerprints? Some scratches on a disc can be minimized by using a scratch-remover kit, to the point that the disc is made readable. These kits are available for home use, and most disc rental stores have a better-quality kit that you may be able to use for a fee.

EXERCISE 5.2

Cleaning a CD or DVD

1. Locate a CD or DVD that has fingerprints on it.

2. Buff out the fingerprints using a soft dry cloth.

Preventing Damage to Equipment

Some beginning computer users are terrified of damaging their computers, having paid so much for them, but computers are actually fairly sturdy. They do have a few Achilles heels, such as water and electrical shock, but some basic common sense can go a long way toward mitigating any risks. In the following sections, you'll learn some of the ways you can keep a computer physically safe and healthy.

Preventing Electrical Damage

Computers run on electricity, but they're pretty specific about the amount and type they need. The wrong type of electricity can weaken and even destroy a circuit board or processor chip. Here are some electrical threats about which you should be aware.

Electrostatic Discharge

Electrostatic discharge (*ESD*) is the most common culprit for ruined PC parts, although many people have never heard of it. ESD is really just static electricity, the same thing that can shock a person on a low-humidity day.

ESD occurs when two items of unequal voltage potential come into contact with one another. The item with the higher charge passes electricity to the one with the lower charge to even out the voltage. As an analogy, picture two bodies of water meeting; if one has a higher level, water will flow quickly into the other one until they're the same. In the case of electricity, the equalization happens so fast that the item of lower charge receives a rush of electricity that feels like a shock. You've experienced ESD firsthand if you've ever scuffed your socks on the carpet and then touched someone, giving the person a shock. You were not shocked yourself because, in that case, *you* were the item of higher charge.

Whereas voltage (measured in volts) is the difference in electrical charge, *current* is the rate at which electrical charge flows and is measure in *amps*. ESD is a high-voltage shock (3,000 volts or so), but it doesn't harm a person because it has very low current. The human body doesn't draw electricity very strongly; it merely draws enough to equalize the charge and then stops. To damage a human body, there must be sufficient amps as well as volts. That is why a 110-volt wall outlet can hurt a person more than a 3,000-volt static electricity shock.

Electronic equipment, though, is extremely sensitive to damage by high voltage, even when the amperage is very low. Humans notice ESD only when it reaches 3,000 volts or so, but ESD can damage a circuit board with less than 1 percent of that. (Some experts say as little as one volt is enough to do some damage.) This means that a person could touch a circuit board and destroy it with static electricity without even noticing. The next time they tried to use that circuit board it would be dead, and they would have no idea why. Furthermore, ESD damage doesn't always show up immediately. It may cause the device to malfunction, or it may weaken the device to the point that it fails a week or a month later.

Generally speaking, any exposed circuit boards are targets for ESD damage, especially motherboards. Also at risk are microchips both on and off those boards, particularly RAM and ROM. Devices *not* very susceptible to ESD damage include those in which circuit boards are never exposed, such as keyboards, mice, speakers, monitors, and printers, and those that don't contain circuit boards.

If you never open your computer's case, the risks of harming it via ESD are very low. If you have to work inside a computer for some reason, such as to install a new circuit board or more RAM, here are some tips:

- Be aware of the clothing you wear when working inside a PC. Synthetic materials such as nylon generate much more ESD than natural fibers like cotton and wool, so dress in natural fabrics. Avoid working in stocking feet—wear rubber-soled shoes. Keeping the humidity high in the work area can also help considerably. The ideal humidity for working on PC hardware is 50 to 80 percent.

- The work surface can also make a difference. Try not to work in a carpeted area; tile or linoleum is preferred. Carpet, especially nylon carpet, tends to generate ESD the same way that nylon clothing does.

- Grounding both the person and equipment can eliminate ESD risk, because any ESD that builds up can bleed off to the ground harmlessly. To ground yourself, wear an *antistatic wrist strap* as you work (see Figure 5.4). At your end of the strap is a Velcro bracelet containing a diode that fits against your skin. At the other end is an alligator clip that you attach to the grounding pin on an electrical outlet (the round, third hole) or to some other grounding source. If no grounding source is available, attach the clip to the PC's metal frame. For maximum ESD prevention, wear an antistatic wrist strap whenever you're working on a PC with the cover off, especially when handling circuit boards.

FIGURE 5.4   An antistatic wrist strap can help prevent ESD damage.

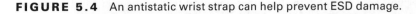

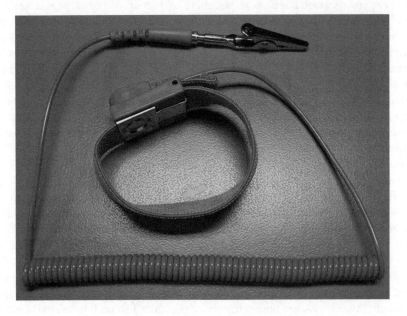

Photo credit: Kms

Another way to minimize ESD risks is to touch the metal frame or power supply of the PC frequently as you work. Doing so doesn't ground you, but it does equalize the electrical charge between you and the PC so there is no difference in potential between you and the components you touch. Do this every few minutes to make sure no built-up occurs.

Antistatic mats are also available. These sit on the work surface and perform the same function for the parts on which you're working as the wrist strap does; the mat has a cord that attaches to the ground pin on an outlet.

Most new circuit boards, like a replacement video card or sound card, come in an antistatic plastic bag. These bags have a coating that collects static charge on the outside of the bag, keeping it away from what's inside the bag. Expensive circuit boards should always be stored in an antistatic bag when not in use. Computer stores sell extra bags, but most people accumulate a collection of them simply from buying and installing new hardware.

Finally, you can buy antistatic spray that minimizes static charge in your environment. This is usually a colorless, odorless liquid in a pump bottle that you spray on the carpet and on your clothing.

Electromagnetic Interference

Electromagnetic interference (EMI) is caused when electricity passing nearby generates a magnetic field that interferes with the operation of a cable or device. Another name for this is *crosstalk*. It occurs only when the PC is on, and it goes away when the PC is off. It causes no permanent damage (usually), but can cause data loss if the affected cable is transporting data.

The Strata objectives include the acronym EMP, which stands for electromagnetic pulse, in the Acronyms list. The most common usage of this term pertains to electromagnetic interference caused by nuclear blasts, which doesn't have much to do with computers. Make sure you know what EMP stands for, but you shouldn't need to know much more about it than that.

EMI can come from unshielded cables, high-voltage power lines, radio transmitters, or other sources. Electricity passing through a wire generates a magnetic field, and magnetic fields generate electricity. Most computer cables move data via electrical pulses, so a changing magnetic field builds up around the cable. When one cable runs next to another, each cable's changing magnetic field can interfere with the data being sent along the other cable. Why? Because changing magnetic fields generate electricity, and the pattern of electricity through the cable is what forms the data being sent. When that pattern is altered, the data can become corrupted.

EMI may be a problem when a data cable isn't carrying its data reliably to its destination. For example, perhaps a printer is printing garbage characters interspersed with the normal characters, or perhaps a network connection keeps timing out due to transmission errors. Power cables can also be susceptible to EMI; this can manifest itself as a power fluctuation. Power fluctuations, in turn, can cause lasting damage to equipment, so in that sense EMI is capable of causing permanent damage.

One way to avoid EMI problems from unshielded cables is simply not to run any cables next to one another, and not to allow a cable to be placed near any other cable. This isn't often practical, though, because most computer users have a tangle of cables behind their PCs going in many directions. The best thing you can do is to troubleshoot EMI problems as they occur by selectively moving cables that are causing problems.

Another way to minimize EMI is to select the proper cables to begin with. Shorter cables are less prone to EMI than longer ones, so use the shortest cable that will do the job.

Many cables sold these days are shielded, which means they have a special wrapping that minimizes EMI interference. Buying shielded cables, although more expensive, can help greatly with EMI problems.

EMI problems caused by external sources, such as power lines, can be difficult to solve; sometimes moving the devices to a different area in the room or building can help.

Surge Suppressors

Electrical devices rely on the power coming from the wall outlet to maintain a certain well-defined voltage range. However, the actual range may differ because of problems with the local electricity provider, wiring in the home or office, or environmental conditions. Sometimes there are outages, power surges or spikes, or sags, any of which can inflict major damage to a PC's power supply.

A *surge* and a *spike* are basically the same thing: too much voltage. The term *spike* is used to describe a more dramatic surge. A *sag,* sometimes called a *brownout,* is insufficient voltage. An occasional power surge can be the result of poor electrical service, but the really damaging power spikes almost always come from lightning strikes during extreme storms.

External devices can help compensate for the various failings of household and office electricity. The most basic of these is a surge suppressor. A *surge suppressor*, also called a *surge protector*, is basically an extension cord, but inside it is a metal oxide variable resistor (*varistor*), sometimes abbreviated MOV, which can absorb any excess power during a surge or spike, preventing it from reaching the plugged-in devices. The varistor works by depleting its own ability to resist, so over time a surge suppressor loses its effectiveness in protecting the PC from power overage. With an inexpensive model, there is no way of gauging the hits the suppressor has taken or the remaining effectiveness. Some of the better models have lights that indicate the surge suppressor's "ready" status, like the one shown in Figure 5.5.

FIGURE 5.5 Surge suppressor

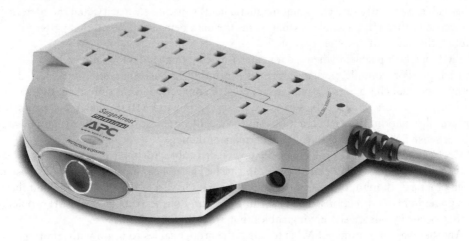

Courtesy of APC

Some surge suppressors also include a pass-through for a telephone line, adding surge protection to it as well. This is valuable if you're using a DSL modem, because a lightning strike can come through a phone line and destroy a modem. Modems are one of the components most often damaged by power surges, because phone lines are frequently left unprotected.

Uninterruptible Power Supplies

A surge suppressor does nothing to help with power sags or outages. For that you need an *uninterruptible power supply (UPS)*: a combination of a surge suppressor and a battery backup. It handles power surges in the same way as a surge suppressor, but it has the added bonus of being able to power the PC for a few minutes when a power outage occurs. This is very useful because it helps avoid problems that crop up when a PC is shut down incorrectly, such as disk errors.

In some cases, a UPS also includes *power conditioning*, so it protects against under-voltage situations (brownouts) as well as complete power failures. (Not every UPS has this feature.)

Most UPS devices have a cable that connects to a PC that allows the operating system to interact with the UPS. With this feature enabled, the UPS can signal the OS when the battery is being used, and Windows can shut itself down automatically. This is useful for people who leave a PC running when away from home or overnight at the office.

There are two types of UPS devices. An *online UPS* runs the PC off the battery at all times. The power comes into the battery and charges it continuously, and the PC draws its power from the battery. If power stops coming from the wall outlet, the PC continues running on the battery as long as it can. This type of UPS is rather expensive. Some call it a "true UPS."

The other type is a standby UPS. It works as a surge suppressor most of the time, passing the wall outlet current straight through to the devices plugged into it. The battery stays charged but isn't in the main loop. If the wall outlet stops providing power, the UPS quickly switches the devices over to the battery. There is a momentary skip when the power changes over, but it's so brief that most devices will continue working without interruption. This type of UPS is the model that local computer stores typically carry for sale and is much more affordable. However, some people argue that it isn't a real UPS, but rather a *standby power source* (or *standby power supply) (SPS)*.

A UPS is much larger and heavier than a surge suppressor, mainly because of its big battery. The battery will last for many years, but it's replaceable if it ever goes bad. The UPS has self-testing routines and lights that show the battery's status, and it will let you know when it's time to replace the battery. Figure 5.6 shows the back of a typical consumer-level UPS. Notice that there are outlets for surge protection only for both power and modems, and also three outlets that provide both battery backup and surge protection.

FIGURE 5.6   UPS (back view)

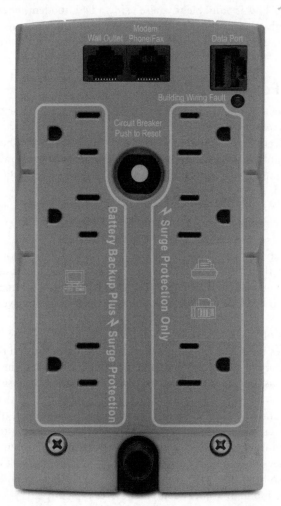

Courtesy of APC

Preventing Other Types of Damage

Besides electricity, there are several other threats to a PC's health and safety. The following sections summarize the most common ones about which you should be aware.

Liquids

Water and electronics don't mix. Do whatever you can to keep water away from your computer. This includes not setting beverages near the computer where they can be knocked over into it, not setting cold items on an air vent that may drip water from condensation into the PC, and not spraying liquid cleaning products directly onto the PC, especially anywhere near its air vents.

A computer damaged by flooding or submersion in water may be beyond repair, but to maximize the chances of recovering some of the data, you should disassemble the computer and dry the pieces out thoroughly, and then reassemble it before attempting to turn it on. Any water left in crevices can cause a short-circuit, ruining whatever is left of the computer's functionality.

Temperature

As a PC operates, certain components become hot; cooling fans and heat sinks help channel the heat away, as you learned in Chapter 1, "Understanding Computer Hardware." The cooler the room in which the PC sits, the easier it is for those components to stay cool. Don't make the room too cool, though, because at very low temperatures (below freezing), frost build-up can become an issue. The heat from the PC melts the frost, which creates water, and with water comes the possibility of short-circuiting.

In the past, computers were more sensitive to temperature than they are today. At one time it was common to find a computer room at a corporate headquarters where a raised floor kept cool air circulating, where the air conditioning was on high, and where employees dressed warmly all year round. Today these huge computers have mostly been replaced by ordinary-looking PCs that don't require any special temperature treatment. The main reason PC cooling requirements are now less stringent is that today's CPUs run at much lower voltages. Still, it pays to remember that PCs like the cold more than people do. If the people are cold, the PC is probably comfortable. If the people are hot, the PC is probably very hot. Storage temperature for PC components is less of an issue than operating temperature, but extremes still must be avoided. Don't store your PC in an unheated shed in a cold climate all winter, and don't leave it baking in the back seat of a car in the summer months.

When you bring a PC inside after it has been very cold or very hot, let it sit until its temperature is the same as that of the room before turning it on. This is especially important when bringing it in from the cold, because condensation can create dampness inside the PC.

Computers subjected to ultra-hot temperatures, such as in building fires, will probably not work anymore because plastic parts will have melted. However, the hard disk might still have recoverable data. Try connecting the hard disk to another computer to see if it is readable. If it contains very important data, and can't be read normally, a data recovery service may be able to help (although not cheaply).

Physical Trauma

Computers aren't highly susceptible to physical trauma, but it's always best to handle them with reasonable care. Everyday bumps like inadvertently kicking a PC that is sitting on the floor probably won't cause any problems, but knocking a PC off a table while it's running can cause some damage.

There are two reasons why physical trauma is bad for a PC. One is that it causes parts to come loose. If someone drops a bare circuit board and it hits the floor just right, a wire connecting a chip or resistor to the board can come undone, or some solder can be knocked off. Most people don't have the skill to repair a circuit board, so a board with a broken connection is basically ruined. Connectors inside a PC can come loose as well. For example, the cables that connect drives to the motherboard can work loose, as can power-supply plugs to drives. Circuit boards can also pop out of expansion slots, and chips can pop out of their sockets.

The other reason to avoid physical trauma pertains specifically to magnetic hard disks. A hard disk has read/write heads that skim just above the surface of the drive. When the drive is subjected to physical trauma, those heads can bounce, scratching the surface of the drive and causing disk errors. The risk of this type of damage is less when the computer is off because the read/write heads move into a parked position away from any data when the drive powers down.

"Be careful" is the best advice to follow for avoiding physical trauma. Examine your work area for hazards such as cords running across a path where people walk or devices sitting too near the edge of a table. Make any corrections you can to ensure a safer work area. If you accidentally jar a PC so that it stops working, remove the cover and check that all the connections are snug.

For a notebook computer, invest in a well-padded carrying case for use whenever you transport it.

Magnets

Magnets and computers don't mix. You learned in the discussion of EMI that changing magnetic fields generate electricity. A magnet can create an electrical charge in a component just by being near it, and that charge can harm the component or cause data corruption in magnetic storage devices such as hard disks. For this reason, you shouldn't use magnetic screwdrivers or other magnetized tools inside a PC. Toolkits designed for use with electronics are non-magnetized.

EXERCISE 5.3

Checking a PC Workstation for Risks

1. Check to make sure there are no cables stretching across areas where people walk.

2. Check to see where the PC is plugged in. Is there a surge suppressor or UPS? If so, does it have a light on it that indicates whether it's in good operating condition?

3. Check to see whether the PC is near the edge of the desk, or whether it's in any danger of being accidentally knocked off the desk.

4. Evaluate the temperature and humidity in the room. Could the room temperature be cooler without making people uncomfortable? The ideal humidity for a computing environment is around 50%; would a humidifier or dehumidifier be useful?

5. Check what you're wearing. Are you wearing artificial-fiber clothing that generates static electricity?

6. Look for any food or drink hazards at the workstation. Are any food or liquids in danger of coming into contact with any part of the computer?

Preventing Data or Service Loss

Often the data stored on the computer, or the ability to use the computer in the moment (for example, to access Internet services to send and receive important messages) is more valuable than the computer hardware itself. In this section, you'll learn about some ways to minimize the risk of data loss and service outage.

Battery Conservation

On a notebook computer, nothing can kill a productive work session like a dead battery. For people who frequently travel where no electrical outlet is available, lack of battery power is a big risk of service loss.

One guard against loss of service via battery power is to carry one or more extra batteries with you. Batteries for notebook computers are available as replacement parts from a variety of vendors and are usually specific to a certain model or narrow range of models. (Some notebooks, mostly Macs, don't have user-replaceable batteries, so you must have the battery replaced by a service center if it fails.)

You can also adjust the power settings on your notebook PC to extend the battery life. Windows has a Power Options group in the Control Panel that lets you make some adjustments. On a Mac, these settings are found in the Energy Saver preference pane in System Preferences. You can further extend your battery's life by using some of these tips:

- Turn off your wireless network adapter unless you're actively using it.
- Set the screen display to be less bright.
- Set the computer to Sleep mode when you aren't actively using it.
- Set the screen saver to blank the screen after a certain amount of idle time.
- Mute the sound.
- Minimize the use of external devices that draw power from the notebook, such as external keyboards and pointing devices.
- Remove any unused ExpressCards or other peripheral cards.

EXERCISE 5.4

Adjusting Power Options in Windows

1. Choose Start ➢ Control Panel ➢ System And Security ➢ Power Options.

2. Click the Balanced power plan. If you don't see it, click the down-pointing arrow next to Show Additional Plans.

3. Click Change Plan Settings next to Balanced.

EXERCISE 5.4 *(continued)*

4. Next to Dim the Display, open the drop-down list and choose 10 minutes. If you're working on a notebook PC, there are two separate settings: one for On Battery and one for Plugged In. Adjust the setting for Plugged In. On a desktop PC, there is only one setting.

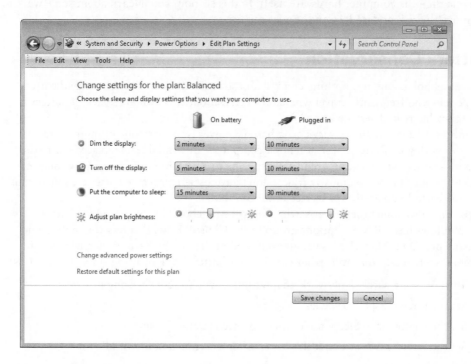

5. Click Save Changes.

6. Close the Control Panel window.

Backup Solutions

Computer users often take their data for granted, forgetting the large quantity of important and irreplaceable documents, images, and music files they collect over the years. A hard disk failure or virus can wipe out years of stored memories, not to mention files of significant value to a business.

There are many ways to ensure that a system failure doesn't result in data loss. In Chapter 2 ("Core Computer Hardware"), for example, you learned how a multidisk RAID system protects against data loss caused by a physical hard disk failure by mirroring a drive (RAID 1) or striping data across multiple drives (RAID 5).

You don't need anything as complex as a RAID system to keep your data safe. Here are some other methods:

Use a Local Backup Application   Backup programs, such as the Backup and Restore utilities that come with Windows 7, enable you to select the files to back up, the media on which to back them up, and the interval at which to do it.

Use an Online Backup Service   There are many economically priced services available online that will automatically back up the files you choose at the interval you specify. Such a service works much like a local backup application except that the files are stored safely off site.

Copy Files Manually to Another Drive   You can copy files to a secondary hard disk or to any removable disk, such as a writeable CD or DVD or a flash drive. The drawback is that you have to remember to do it.

Make a System Image   Some backup utilities, including the one that comes with Windows 7, can make a *system image*, an exact copy of an entire hard disk. You can do that to create a snapshot in time of your system, and then restore that copy if something ever happens to the original. The drawback is that a whole-drive image takes a long time to make, so you won't want to do it very often.

Table 5.1 summarizes the backup solutions available and their characteristics.

TABLE 5.1   Comparison of backup solutions

	Local Backup	**Online Backup**	**Manual Copy**	**System Image**
Automated?	Yes	Yes	No	No
Quick?	Yes	Yes	Yes	No
Recoverable after a virus infection?	Only if backup drive isn't also infected	Yes	Only if backup drive isn't also infected	Yes
Recoverable after a hard-disk crash?	Yes	Yes	Yes	Yes
Secure from theft or natural disaster?	Only if backup is stored off site	Yes	Only if backup is stored off site	Only if backup is stored off site
Free?	Yes, if Windows Backup is used	No	Yes	Yes, if Windows Backup is used

Windows includes a System Restore feature that backs up important system files, such as the files that make up the Windows Registry. These files are essential for Windows operation, but they don't include your data. Therefore, saving a System Restore point isn't a substitute for backing up data.

When considering a backup solution, the following questions are pertinent:

- How often do you plan to back up? For business-critical data, every day is appropriate. For casual home users and their personal files, once a week or even once a month may be enough.

- How large are the files? Backing up a large amount of data takes more time and takes up more disk space. You may choose to back up large files like videos and music less often than other files for this reason.

- What backup software is available? Many different applications will do local and online backups and system images. Some have more features and higher price tags than others.

- Should each backup recopy all files, or should there be incremental backups done that copy only files that have changed? Some backup programs enable you to choose among the following settings:

Full   Backs up everything, regardless of its backup status.

Differential   Backs up only what's changed since the last full backup.

Incremental   Backs up only what's changed since the last backup of any kind (not just full).

Whatever backup guidelines and procedures your company or school implements, it's important that you follow them. In many cases, backups will be automatic and invisible to the end user; but if you're asked to run a backup utility on a certain schedule, make sure you do so.

Drive Recovery

In the event of a system failure, you may be able to recover some data even if you haven't diligently made backups as you should have.

When a computer fails to boot, it isn't always the hard disk's fault. A variety of other components can fail, resulting in a nonworking system. If the problem turns out to be anything other than the hard disk, your data is safe—it's just temporarily inaccessible. You can put the hard disk in a different PC, or hook it up as an external drive with an inexpensive internal-to-USB drive conversion kit to retrieve its data. You may also be able to boot from a Linux boot CD or DVD to access the data from a drive that won't boot its own OS.

If the problem occurred because of a logical error on the hard disk, or a virus or other software problem that caused the drive's *master file table (MFT)* or partition table to be damaged, you may be able to recover some of the files off it by using a special disk-recovery program. Such programs aren't cheap; plan on spending $100 or more. If the files are worth more than that to you, though, it may be your best bet.

If doing the recovery yourself doesn't work, the next step up is to use a professional data-recovery service. Such services can easily run into thousands of dollars because not only do they use professional-quality disk-recovery software, but they can also remove the platters from a physically damaged hard disk and put them in another mechanical drive unit.

Managing Files and Folders

Working with files and folders in your OS of choice is an important basic skill to have, both for Strata certification and for everyday use. In the following sections, you'll learn (or review) how to create, delete, rename, move, and copy files and folders, and how to print files. Most of the examples focus on Windows, but other OSs are covered too.

Opening a File-Management Interface

In a graphical OS like Windows, Mac OS, or Linux, you manage files via a window-based system where each file and folder is represented by an icon. In Windows, this interface is called *Windows Explorer*; in Mac OS, it's called *Finder*.

There are many potential entry points into the file-management interface, depending on which location (drive and folder) you want to start in. For example, in Windows, you can click the Start button and then choose Computer to start with a list of drives, or choose Documents to start with your Documents folder, or choose Pictures to start with your Pictures folder. You can also place folder shortcuts on the desktop or Start menu that open to a folder of your choice. After you open the file-management interface, you can navigate to other folders as desired.

A command-line OS like Unix uses text commands for file management. Windows, Mac OS, and Linux all have optional command-line interfaces you can open to manage files via text commands too.

Table 5.2 summarizes the methods of opening a file-management interface in Windows, Mac OS, and Linux. In Unix, it's not an issue because the command line is the default interface.

TABLE 5.2   Opening a file-management interface

	Graphical Interface	**Command Prompt**
Windows Vista and Windows 7	Start ➢ Computer	Click Start, type cmd, and press Enter.
Windows XP	Start ➢ My Computer	Choose Start ➢ Run, type cmd, and press Enter.
Mac OS	Finder	Choose Applications ➢ Utilities ➢ Terminal.
Linux	Varies	Varies; in Ubuntu, choose Applications ➢ Accessories ➢ Terminal.

Viewing and Changing Locations

The folder structure on a drive is hierarchically based. At the top level is the *root folder* (or *root directory*). Very little is stored there; it's like the lobby of a building. Within the root folder are the first-level folders, such as Windows, Program Files, and Users. Within each of those folders are other folders (subordinate to them, therefore sometimes referred to as *subfolders*). Within each of those folders can be other folders, and so on. See Figure 5.7 for an extremely simplified example. An actual hard disk may have hundreds or even thousands of folders.

FIGURE 5.7   Folder hierarchy on a disk drive

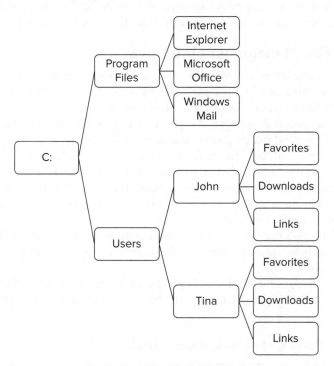

The *path* to a file is the list of folders you travel through to get there, starting with the drive letter. The names are separated by backslashes (\) on a Windows system or forward slashes (/) on Mac OS or Linux systems. For example, on a Windows 7 PC, the Internet Explorer favorites for John may be stored in C:\Users\John\Favorites.

In each file-management interface, only one location is active at a time. The active location's content is displayed in the main pane of the file-management interface. In a graphical interface, the list of files and folders in that location appears automatically when you navigate to that location. At a command prompt, you must issue a command to display the listing. Table 5.3 summarizes the commands needed for each OS to display a file listing at a command prompt.

TABLE 5.3   Viewing the contents of a location at a command prompt

Operating System	Command (Typed at Command Prompt)
Windows	dir
Mac OS and Linux	ls

You change to a particular location by navigating through the interface. This process is somewhat different for each OS.

In Windows Vista and Windows 7, an address bar appears across the top of the file-management window, with triangle arrows separating each level in the path. You can click the triangles to open lists of folders at different levels and then click the folder to switch to it. You can also use shortcuts to common locations in the Favorites bar along the left side. There is also a hierarchical tree view of all the folders at the bottom left (see Figure 5.8).

FIGURE 5.8   A Windows 7 folder-management window

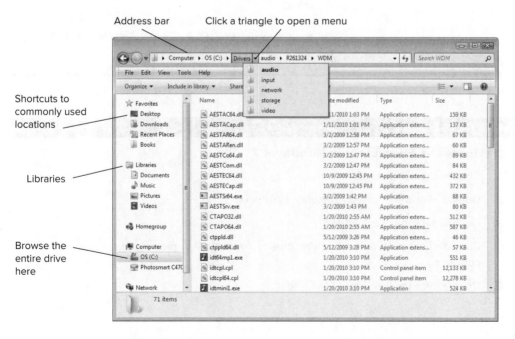

In a command-line interface, you type a command to change to a different location. For example, at a Windows command line, type a drive letter followed by a colon to change to that drive (C: for example). Table 5.4 summarizes the commands for changing to a different location.

TABLE 5.4 Changing locations

Operating System	Command/Procedure	Example
Windows, Mac OS, or Linux (graphical interface)	Click a different folder or drive.	
Windows (command prompt)	Drives: Type the drive letter followed by a colon, and press Enter.	C:
	Folders: Type **cd** followed by a space, backslash, and the folder name. Then press Enter. Separate multiple levels with backslashes.	**cd** \Books **cd** \Books\MyRecentBook
Mac OS and Linux (command prompt)	Drives: Type **cd** followed by a space, **/Volumes/**, and then the drive name.	**cd** /Volumes/Macintosh HD
	Folders: Type **cd** followed by a space, and then the path to the folder.	**cd** /Joe/Applications

EXERCISE 5.5

Navigate the Filesystem in Windows 7

1. Choose Start ➢ Computer.

2. Double-click the C: drive to display its folders.

3. Double-click the Users folder.

4. Click the Back button (left-pointing blue arrow button) to return to the C: drive's contents.

5. Double-click the Program Files folder.

6. In the Address bar, click the triangle to the right of the C: drive. A list of all the folders at the top level of the C: drive appears.

7. Choose Users on that menu (scrolling down if necessary to find it), returning to the Users folder.

8. In the Favorites list at the left, click Desktop. Icons for everything that's on the desktop appear.

9. In the Libraries list, choose Documents. The folders and files that are in your Documents library appear.

10. Scroll down in the left pane if needed, and locate the Computer section. Under Computer, click the C: drive to return to it.

11. Point to C: in the left pane so that a triangle appears to its left. Click the triangle to expand a list of the folders, and then scroll that pane down to browse the folders.

12. Click the triangle again next to C: to re-collapse the list of folders.

13. Click in the address bar, type `C:\Program Files\Internet Explorer`, and press Enter. The listing jumps to that folder.

14. Close the window.

Creating Folders

Folders hold files, so they're important organizing units in a filesystem. Without folders, you'd have to browse through thousands of files on your hard disk every time you needed to find a certain one. Windows creates many folders when you install it, and each application you install creates its own folder(s) too.

You can also create your own folders. The most common reason to do so is to create a separate storage space for data files of a certain type. For example, you could create a folder called Brown to hold all the files for a client named Brown. In most graphical OSs, including Windows, you can right-click in a file-management window and choose New Folder (or some such similar command) to create a new folder. Then type a name for the new folder, and press Enter to accept the name. Table 5.5 summarizes the commands and procedures for creating folders.

TABLE 5.5 Creating folders

Operating System	Command/Procedure	Example
Windows (graphical interface)	Right-click an empty area and choose New ➢ Folder, or click the New Folder button. Then type the new folder's name and press Enter.	
Mac OS (graphical interface)	Right-click an empty area, and choose New Folder. Then type the new folder's name and press Enter.	
Linux (graphical interface)	Right-click an empty area, and choose Create Folder. Then type the new folder's name and press Enter.	
Windows (command prompt)	md or mkdir	`md newfolder`
Mac OS or Linux (command prompt)	mkdir	`mkdir newfolder`

Deleting Files and Folders

When you no longer need a file or folder, you can delete it. Deleting a folder also deletes all the files within it, so be careful not to delete folders that contain files you want to keep. You can select the file or folder and press Delete on the keyboard, or drag the file or folder to the Recycle Bin (Windows) or Trash (Mac).

At a command prompt, you can use rmdir (Windows, Mac, or Linux) or rd (Windows). In Windows, the rd or rmdir command works only if the folder is empty. If it's not, use the deltree command instead (or del, in some Windows versions), to avoid having to delete all the files and subfolders first. Table 5.6 summarizes the commands and procedures for deleting files and folders.

TABLE 5.6 Deleting folders or files

Operating System	Command/Procedure	Example
Windows (graphical interface)	Select the file or folder and press the Delete key, or drag it to the Recycle Bin.	
Mac OS (graphical interface)	Ctrl+click (or right-click) the file or folder and select Move To Trash, or drag it to the Trash.	
Linux (graphical interface)	Select the file or folder and press the Delete key, or drag it to the Trash.	

TABLE 5.6   Deleting folders or files   (*continued*)

Operating System	Command/Procedure	Example
Windows (command prompt)	For folders: rd, rmdir, or deltree	**rd \myfolder**
	Deltree also deletes any files and subfolders; rd doesn't work unless the folder is empty.	**rmdir \myfolder**
		deltree \myfolder
	Precede the folder name with a backslash if it isn't an immediate subordinate of the active location.	
	For files: del	**del myoldfile.txt**
	Precede the filename with a path to it if it isn't contained in the active location.	**del C:\Books\ myoldfile.txt**
Mac OS or Linux (command prompt)	For folders: rmdir	**rmdir \myfolder**
	For files: rm	**rm myoldfile. txt**

Renaming Files and Folders

In most OSs, the commands and procedures for renaming files and folders are identical; no distinction is made between them.

There is one major thing to watch out for, though, when renaming files: file extensions. An extension is a code (usually three letters, but not always) that follows the filename, indicating the type of file. The name and the extension are typically separated by a period, like this: myfile.txt. When you rename a file, you should make sure you keep the same file extension. Otherwise, the file may be rendered unusable.

Here's where it gets tricky in Windows: by default, Windows hides the file extensions for known file types. That means the file myfile.txt is likely to appear in a file-management window as myfile. When you rename it, if you type the extension as part of the new name, you end up with a double extension, like this: myfile.txt.txt. You won't notice it immediately, though, because the final extension is hidden, as specified by the OS.

That leads us to a general rule of thumb: if the file doesn't show an extension on its name, don't type one when renaming it. If it does show an extension, make sure you keep that same extension. If you want to change the display/hide status for known file types in Windows, from any file-management window, choose Tools ➢ Folder Options and, on the View tab, clear the Hide Extensions For Known File Types check box. You'll have a chance to practice this in Exercise 5.13, later in the chapter.

Table 5.7 summarizes the methods of renaming files and folders.

TABLE 5.7 Renaming folders or files

Operating System	Command/Procedure	Example
Windows, Mac OS, or Linux (graphical interface)	Click in the name to move the insertion point there, and type the new name.	
Windows (command prompt)	ren Type the old name first, a space, and the new name.	`ren myoldfile.txt newname.txt`
Mac OS or Linux (command prompt)	mv Type the old name first, a space, and the new name.	`mv myoldfile.txt newname.txt`

EXERCISE 5.6

Create, Rename, and Delete a Folder in Windows

1. Choose Start ➤ Computer.

2. Double-click the C: drive to display its contents.

3. Click New Folder. A new folder appears.

4. Type **Strata**, and press Enter. The folder appears with the name you typed.

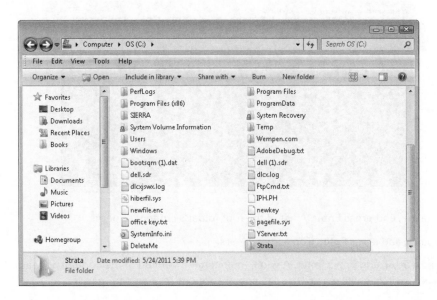

5. Double-click the Strata folder. Its content appears. (It's empty.)

6. Click the Back button to return to the C: drive's content.

7. Click once on the Strata folder, pause, and then click it again to move the insertion point into its name. (If the second click comes too quickly, Windows interprets it as a double-click.) If you have trouble with this method, select the folder and press F2 to make it editable.

8. Edit the folder name to DeleteMe. Press Enter to accept the new name.

9. Select the DeleteMe folder, and press Delete on the keyboard. The folder is moved to the Recycle Bin.

10. Close the window.

Create, Rename, and Delete a Folder at a Command Prompt

1. Click Start, type **cmd**, and press Enter. A command prompt window opens.

2. Type **cd **, and press Enter. The prompt changes to C:\>, indicating you're in the top-level (root) folder.

3. Type **dir**, and press Enter. A list of the root folder's content appears.

4. Type **cl**, and press Enter. The screen clears.

5. Type **dir /w**, and press Enter. A wide, multicolumn version of the content appears. The /w is a *switch*; switches are used to specify options for text commands.

```
Administrator: C:\Windows\system32\cmd.exe

C:\>dir /w
 Volume in drive C is OS
 Volume Serial Number is E04B-F4C8

 Directory of C:\

[A86]                 AdobeDebug.txt        [assembly]
[Books]               bootsqm (1).dat       [DeleteMe]
[dell]                [Desktop]             dlcx.log
dlcxjswx.log          [Downloads]           [Drivers]
FtpCmd.txt            [Games]               [Uware Online]
newfile.enc           newkey                office key.txt
[PerfLogs]            [Program Files]       [Program Files (x86)]
[SIERRA]              SystemInfo.ini        [Temp]
[Users]               [Wempen.com]          [Windows]
YServer.txt           [_AcroTemp]
               10 File(s)         72,675 bytes
               19 Dir(s)  384,605,278,208 bytes free

C:\>_
```

6. Type **md Strata**, and press Enter.

7. Type **dir /w**, and press Enter. The listing reappears, this time including [Strata]. The square brackets indicate that it's a folder.

8. Type **ren Strata Deleteme**, and press Enter. The folder is renamed.

9. Type **rd Deleteme**, and press Enter. The folder is deleted.

10. Close the command prompt window.

Printing Files

In most cases, you'll print a file by opening it in its native application and using the Print command there. (The native application for a file is the one associated with its file extension, and it's usually the application in which the file was created.) The Print command is usually on the File menu in the application, as shown in Figure 5.9. This method has the advantage that you can review and edit the file before you print it.

FIGURE 5.9 Printing from within an application

If you need to make a quick printout of a data file and don't want to take the time to open it in its application, you may be able to print it directly from the OS. In Windows, you can right-click the data file, and if there is a Print command on the shortcut menu that appears, as seen in Figure 5.10, click Print to print the file without opening it. When you print using this method, you don't get to choose any print options, such as number of copies or page range.

FIGURE 5.10 Printing from a file listing without opening the file

Print a File Without Opening It

1. In Windows, choose Start ➢ Documents, and locate a document file.

2. Right-click the document file, and click Print. The document prints on your default printer.

3. Close the Documents window.

Moving and Copying Files and Folders

Moving and copying are very similar operations. With a move, the original is deleted from its original location, and it's copied to the new location. With a copy, the original stays put, and it's copied to the new location. When you move or copy a folder, everything in it moves or is copied too.

In Windows, when you drag an item from one location to another, it's either moved or copied, depending on the relationship between the two locations:

- If both locations are on the same drive, is the item is moved.

- If the locations are on different drives, is the item is copied.

If you want to alter that default behavior, you can force a copy by holding down Ctrl as you drag, or you can right-drag (that is, drag with the right mouse button). When you drop after right-dragging, a menu appears, asking whether you want to move, copy, or create a shortcut.

WARNING   Be careful not to move a folder that contains a Windows application, because that application may not work anymore after you move it; Windows relies on an application staying where it was originally placed.

Table 5.8 summarizes the commands for moving and copying files and folders.

TABLE 5.8   Moving and copying files and folders

Operating System	Command/Procedure	Example
Windows (graphical interface)	To move or copy: Right-drag to the new location, and then choose Move Here or Copy Here on the menu that appears.	
	Alternate method: Select the file, and press Ctrl+C to copy or Ctrl+X to cut. Then navigate to the new location and press Ctrl+V to paste.	
Mac OS (graphical interface)	Drag and drop (moves original to new location) or cut or copy and paste both work.	
Linux (graphical interface)	Varies	
Windows (command prompt)	To copy: copy You don't need to specify the path for a file in the current location. Specify the path of the destination following the filename.	`copy myfile.txt c:\newlocation`

	To move: copy and then del
	There is no move command in Windows, so you have to use two separate commands.
		`copy myfile.txt c:\newlocation`
		
		`del myfile.txt`

Mac OS and Linux (command prompt)	To copy: cp Notice that Mac OS and Linux use a slash that is reversed from the one used by Windows.	`cp myfile.txt /newlocation`
	To move: mv	`mv myfile.txt /newlocation`

Wildcards and Multifile Selection

In a graphical interface, you can select multiple files and/or folders before acting on them, so you don't have to act on each one individually.

Items can either be *contiguous* (next to each other in the file listing) or *noncontiguous* (not next to each other). To make a contiguous selection, click the first file or folder in the group and then hold down Shift as you click the last one. To make a noncontiguous selection, hold down Ctrl (on a PC) or Command (on a Mac) as you click individually on each item to include.

At a command prompt, you can use *wildcards* to specify a group of files or folders based on their names. Use a question mark ? for individual characters and an asterisk * for multiple characters. For example, to select all documents that begin with *W* and have a .doc extension, use W*.doc. To select all documents that are five characters in length where the first two characters are *Wi*, use Wi???.doc.

Shortcuts

A *shortcut* is a pointer to a file. Shortcut is the Windows term. In Mac OS, they're called aliases, whereas in Linux they're known as links, or symbolic links. You can place a shortcut anywhere that you want quick access to a file, a folder, or an application, such as on the desktop. The original remains in its original location. The shortcut isn't a copy of the actual file; it's just a pointer on a map that tells the OS how to get to the file. Most shortcuts can be distinguished from regular files because they have an arrow in their lower-left corner, as shown in Figure 5.11.

FIGURE 5.11   Shortcut icon

You can create a shortcut in Windows by holding down the Alt key as you drag a file or folder, or by right-dragging and then choosing Create Shortcut(s) Here from the menu that appears. In Mac OS X, right-click or Ctrl-click a file or folder, and then choose Make Alias.

EXERCISE 5.9

Copy a File in Windows

1.   Choose Start ➢ Documents, and locate a document file.

2.   Select the file, and press Ctrl+C to copy it.

3. In the Favorites list at the left, click Desktop.

4. Click Ctrl+V to paste the copy onto the desktop.

5. Select the copy, and press Delete to delete it.

EXERCISE 5.10

Copy a File at a Command Prompt

1. Click Start. Type **cmd**, and press Enter. A command prompt window opens.

2. Type **cd documents**, and press Enter. A list of all the files in your Documents folder appears.

3. Pick one of the files. (For this example, I'll use chart.ppt, but you can use any file.)

4. At the command prompt, type **copy *chart.ppt* backup.ppt**, substituting the file you chose for *chart.ppt*. Press Enter. A backup copy of the file is created in the same folder.

5. Type **del backup.ppt** to delete the file.

6. Type **copy** *chart.ppt* **C:\Users\backup.ppt**, substituting the file you chose earlier for chart.ppt. Press Enter. A backup copy of the file is created in the C:\Users folder.

7. Type **cd \Users**, and press Enter.

8. Type **dir backup.*****, and press Enter. All the files named backup in this folder appear. The wildcard * includes all file extensions.

9. Type **del backup.ppt**, and press Enter. The file you placed here earlier is now deleted.

10. Close the command prompt window.

Assigning a Folder Structure During Installation

When you install a new application, there is usually an option to specify into what folder the application's files will be placed. You may need to click a Custom or Options link or button during setup to access that screen. It's a one-time offer to get to specify the location; you can't usually rename or move application files after you do the install, or they won't work anymore. In most cases, the default location that the setup program suggests is fine, if you have no other preference.

On a Windows PC, most applications place their files in a subfolder within the C:\ Program Files folder. This centralizes the locations of application files. It would be less desirable to create a separate folder at the top level of the folder structure for each application because it doing so clutters up the root folder.

Many Windows applications are 32-bit, so they run on either 32-bit or 64-bit versions of Windows. If you're running a 64-bit version of Windows, there may be two separate folders: Program Files for 64-bit applications and Program Files (x86) for 32-bit applications.

Using Software Tools for PC Maintenance

Your OS includes many applications and utilities that help you manage and maintain your computer. You may find that you don't need to download/install any additional applications, because the OS has everything you need.

In the following sections, you'll learn about several types of maintenance utilities that come with Windows, the most popular OS. In most cases, similar utilities are also available in Mac OS X. and Linux. Some of these tools are covered in greater detail in later chapters.

Tools for Managing Disks and Data Storage

Having quick and reliable access to the data and applications stored on your hard disk is critical, as anyone who has run into a situation where they *didn't* have this access can attest. Table 5.9 summarizes the tools available in Windows 7 for working with disks. Earlier versions of Windows have similar (but not identical) tools. Mac OS X has a utility called Disk Utility that performs some of these functions too.

TABLE 5.9   Disk- and data-management tools

Utility	Description	Accessed From
Disk Defragmenter	Relocates the pieces of fragmented files to contiguous locations on the hard disk so that files can be retrieved more quickly when they're needed, modestly improving disk performance.	Start ≻ Computer, then right-click a drive and choose Properties. In the Properties dialog box, click the Tools tab, and click Defragment Now.
Check Disk (chkdsk)	Identifies and fixes logical problems with the hard disk's filesystem and optionally finds physical errors on the hard disk, relocating the data away from the damaged area if possible.	Start ≻ Computer, then right-click a drive and choose Properties. In the Properties dialog box, click the Tools tab, and click Check Now.
Disk Management	Enables you to partition and format disk drives, as well as view the status of drives.	Start ≻ Control Panel ≻ System And Security ≻ Administrative Tools ≻ Computer Management, and then click Disk Management in the navigation panel at the left.
Backup	Saves backup sets that contain the important files you chose to back up, and then restores them from the backup in the event they're needed.	Start ≻ Control Panel ≻ System And Security ≻ Backup And Restore

Utility	Description	Accessed From
Disk Cleanup	Deletes files that are potentially unwanted, including temporary files, Recycle Bin contents, and cached Internet pages, freeing up hard-disk space.	Start ➤ Computer. Right-click a drive, and click Properties. On the General tab, click Disk Cleanup.
Folder/Disk Compression	Compresses the files stored in a certain location to save a small amount of disk space	Start ➤ Computer. Right-click a drive or folder, and choose Properties. On the General tab, select the Compress This Drive To Save Disk Space check box.
Compressed Archive (Zipping)	Combines and compresses multiple files into a single file with a `.zip` extension (a Zip file), suitable for archiving or transferring to others.	Select and then right-click the file(s) or folder(s), and choose Send To ➤ Compressed (Zipped) Folder.

EXERCISE 5.11

Use Disk- and File-Maintenance Tools

1. Choose Start ➤ Computer. Right-click the C: drive, and choose Properties.

2. On the Tools tab, click Check Now. The Check Disk dialog box opens.

3. Click Start. A message appears that Windows can't check the disk while it's in use.

4. Click Schedule Disk Check.

5. Reboot the computer, and allow the disk to be checked.

6. After Windows restarts, choose Start ➤ Computer. Right-click the C: drive, and choose Properties.

7. On the Tools tab, click Defragment Now. The Disk Defragmenter dialog box opens.

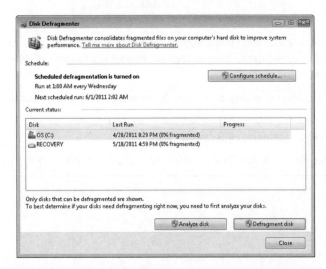

8. Click Analyze Disk. Wait for the disk's fragmentation to be assessed. While you're waiting, click Configure Schedule and examine the current settings for automatic defragmentation. Click Cancel to close the Modify Schedule dialog box without making any changes.

9. When the analysis is complete, if the disk is more than 5 percent fragmented, click Defragment Disk and wait for that process to complete. Otherwise, click Close to close the Disk Defragmenter, because the drive doesn't need to be defragmented now.

10. Back in the C: drive's Properties box, on the General tab, click Disk Cleanup. Wait for Disk Cleanup to analyze the drive.

11. When the results of the analysis appear, examine the list of Files To Delete.

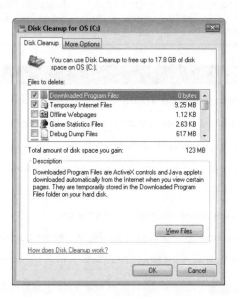

12. Click the Temporary Internet Files category, and click View Files. A file-management window appears, showing the temporary files stored. Close this window when you're finished looking at them.

13. Back in the Disk Cleanup dialog box, click OK to delete the files that were recommended for deletion.

14. A confirmation box appears; click Delete Files.

15. Wait for the deletion to finish. Then click OK to close the C: drive's Properties box.

Tools for Optimizing Performance and Fixing Problems

Several software tools are available that make a PC run better and faster by fine-tuning settings, eliminating bottleneck-causing errors, or providing information about trouble spots that may be creating problems behind the scenes. Table 5.9 summarizes some of these tools that come with Windows 7. (Utilities that improve disk performance specifically were covered in Table 5.10 and so aren't included here.)

TABLE 5.10 Troubleshooting and performance-monitoring/enhancing tools

Utility	Description	Accessed From
Windows Experience Index	Evaluates the performance of key components, and tells you which one is the bottleneck in performance	Start ➢ Control Panel ➢ System And Security and, under the System heading, click Check The Windows Experience Index.
Resource Monitor	Provides moment-by-moment information about CPU, disk, network, and memory usage	Start ➢ All Programs ➢ Accessories ➢ System Tools ➢ Resource Monitor.
Windows Update	Finds and downloads the latest updates for Windows and for some applications and hardware devices to add new features and/or correct problems or security holes	Start ➢ Control Panel ➢ System And Security ➢ Windows Update.
Action Center	Provides information about any problems the system has encountered, and suggests fixes	Start ➢ Control Panel ➢ System And Security ➢ Action Center.
Event Viewer	Lists information and error messages generated by the OS for advanced troubleshooting use	Start ➢ Control Panel ➢ System And Security ➢ Administrative Tools ➢ Event Viewer.
Task Manager	Lists the currently running applications and processes, and enables you to shut down any that have stopped responding	Right-click the taskbar or press Ctrl+Alt+Delete, and then click Start Task Manager.
Troubleshooting	Walks you step by step through troubleshooting procedures with yes/no questions	Start ➢ Control Panel ➢ System And Security ➢ Action Center, and then scroll down to the bottom of the page and click Troubleshooting.
System Restore	Enables you to return your system files to an earlier backed-up copy to correct recently developed system errors	Start ➢ Control Panel ➢ System And Security ➢ Action Center, and then scroll down to the bottom of the page and click Recovery.

EXERCISE 5.12

Evaluate and Troubleshoot Windows Performance

1. Choose Start ➢ Control Panel ➢ System And Security and, under the System heading, click Check The Windows Experience Index. Examine the scores for each subsystem. Identify which score is the lowest. This is the bottleneck to better performance on your system.

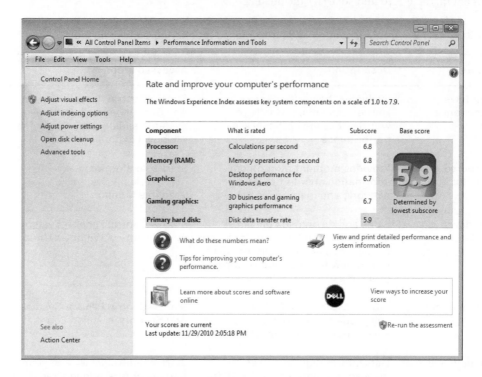

2. Click the Back button (left-pointing blue arrow button) to go back to the System And Security page of the Control Panel, and click Action Center.

3. Review any problems that the Action Center identifies. A button next to each problem recommends what to do.

4. If Check For Solutions To Unreported Problems appears, click the Check For Solutions button next to it. Wait for the Problem Reporting tool to check for solutions, and follow the recommendations to resolve any problems for which solutions are found.

5. Click back to the Control Panel window. Click the Back button to return to the System And Security page. Choose Administrative Tools ➢ Event Viewer.

6. In the Event Viewer window, examine the Overview And Summary information. Click each of the categories at the left, and review their information. Then close the Event Viewer.

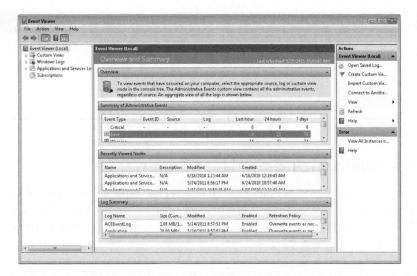

7. In the Control Panel window, in the Address bar, click System And Security to return to that page. (That's an alternate method to using the Back button.)

8. Click Windows Update.

9. Click the hyperlink for the available updates, if there are any. The wording varies depending on how many updates are available; for example, it may read "2 important updates are available." If there are no pending updates, a green bar appears to the left (as opposed to a yellow one when updates are available), and you can skip to step 13.

10. Examine the list of available updates. If any aren't marked that you want, select their check boxes. If any are marked and you don't want them, clear their check boxes.

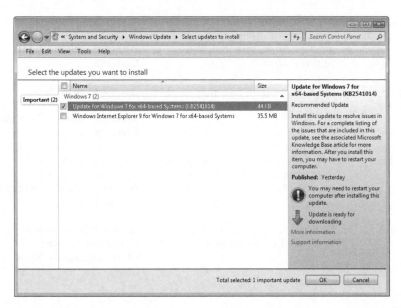

EXERCISE 5.12 *(continued)*

11. Click OK to return to the main Windows Update page.

12. Click Install Updates.

13. Close the Control Panel.

Tools for Customizing the User Experience

Nearly every aspect of the Windows user experience is customizable, from the colors used onscreen to the way the mouse moves. Most of these settings can be adjusted from the Control Panel in the Appearance And Personalization area. Table 5.11 summarizes these settings and tools in Windows 7.

TABLE 5.11   Appearance and personalization utilities in Windows 7

Utility	Description	Accessed From
Personalization	Changes the appearance theme, colors, background, and sound effects	Start ➢ Control Panel ➢ Appearance And Personalization ➢ Personalization
Display	Makes text larger or smaller, adjusts screen resolution, and connects to an external display	Start ➢ Control Panel ➢ Appearance And Personalization ➢ Display
Desktop Gadgets	Adds or removes mini-applications on the desktop, such as clock, calendar, and photo viewer	Start	Control Panel ➢ Appearance And Personalization ➢ Desktop Gadgets
Taskbar and Start Menu	Customizes the Start menu and taskbar	Start ➢ Control Panel ➢ Appearance And Personalization ➢ Taskbar and Start Menu
Ease of Access Center	Applies settings that help people who have limited vision, hearing, or mobility	Start ➢ Control Panel ➢ Appearance And Personalization ➢ Ease of Access Center
Folder Options	Changes settings that affect folder and file management	Start ➢ Control Panel ➢ Appearance And Personalization ➢ Folder Options

Utility	Description	Accessed From
Fonts	Displays the installed fonts, and provides an interface for adding and removing fonts	Start ➢ Control Panel ➢ Appearance And Personalization ➢ Fonts
Mouse	Adjusts the pointer appearance, pointer speed, and double-click speed	Start ➢ Control Panel ➢ Hardware And Sound; under the Devices And Printers heading, click Mouse
Sound	Adjusts the system volume and system sounds, and manages audio devices	Start ➢ Control Panel ➢ Hardware And Sound ➢ Sound
Power Options	Changes the battery settings, and controls what happens when you press the Power button or shut the lid of a notebook PC	Start ➢ Control Panel ➢ Hardware And Sound ➢ Power Options

Summary

In this chapter, you learned how to clean a computer inside and out, and how to prevent damage to computer equipment by avoiding electrical, temperature, magnetic, and physical damage. We discussed methods of preventing data or service loss, including battery conservation, backup solutions, and drive recovery.

Next, you reviewed the procedures for managing files and folders, both at a command prompt and in a graphical environment, using a variety of OSs, including Windows, Mac OS, and Linux. Finally, you learned about many of the maintenance utilities that come with Windows, the purpose of each one, and how to find them in Windows.

Exam Essentials

Be able to work with files and folders.   You can create, delete, rename, and move folders and files from either a graphical interface, such as Windows Explorer, or from a command prompt. Make sure you know the basics of both methods, as well as the key differences between OSs.

Understand the function and purpose of software tools.   Most OSs, including Windows, include various utility programs for maintaining the system. Make sure you can name and use performance and error-correction tools, backup tools, and disk tools. You should also be able to look up event logs and set a folder or drive to compress its contents to save space.

Identify techniques for minimizing risk.   When using a computer, the risks include damaging yourself, damaging the computer hardware, losing data, and losing access to services. You should be able to identify ways to minimize all of those risk types, using techniques such as battery conservation, backups, data recovery, and physical safety precautions.

Be able to clean all parts of a computer.   Key cleaning equipment for a PC includes spray cleaners for plastic parts and monitors, compressed air, and soft cloths. Make sure you know the proper procedures for cleaning monitors, keyboards, mice, and removable media (such as CDs). You should also understand how ink and toner consumables are stored and replaced in a printer.

Review Questions

1. Do not use cleaning solutions that contains _____ on a monitor.
   A. Water
   B. Alcohol
   C. Ammonia
   D. All of the above

2. A side effect of using compressed air is generation of _____.
   A. Static electricity
   B. Cold
   C. Heat
   D. Fire

3. How do you get debris out from under the keys of a keyboard?
   A. Dig it out with a screwdriver
   B. Blow it out with compressed air
   C. Heat it until the debris burns up
   D. Use a magnet

4. When cleaning around the LED in an optical mouse, what's the best liquid to use?
   A. Oil
   B. Alcohol
   C. Water
   D. Vinegar

5. How do you clean the inkjets on an inkjet printer?
   A. Utility program
   B. Soft cloth
   C. Compressed air
   D. Sandpaper

6. How do you clean fingerprints off a DVD?
   A. Utility program
   B. Soft cloth
   C. Compressed air
   D. Sandpaper

7. A more common name for ESD is _____.
   A. Static electricity
   B. Radio frequency interference
   C. Magnetic interference
   D. Melting

8. Why does static electricity not kill you, given that it is a high-voltage shock?

   A. Short duration

   B. Low amps

   C. It's DC volts, not AC

   D. Low resistance

9. _____ can eliminate the risk of equipment being harmed by ESD.

   A. Water

   B. Electrodes

   C. Metal

   D. Grounding

10. _____ can cause data loss via crosstalk between adjacent cables.

   A. ESD

   B. RFD

   C. EMI

   D. VGA

11. A varistor inside a surge suppressor helps prevent damage due to _____.

   A. Brownouts

   B. Surges

   C. Sags

   D. Outages

12. Another name for a battery backup system for a PC is _____.

   A. API

   B. RFI

   C. UPS

   D. CGI

13. Desktop computer systems operate best at what temperature range?

   A. Warmer than is comfortable for humans

   B. The same as is comfortable for humans

   C. Colder than is comfortable for humans, but not freezing

   D. Below freezing

14. What is the primary drawback of creating a system image as a means of data backup?

   A. It takes a long time

   B. It is very expensive

   C. It must be constantly monitored

   D. It does not back up data files

15. In Windows, the file-management interface is called Windows Explorer; on a Mac, it's called _____.

    A. Chooser

    B. Finder

    C. Browser

    D. Legacy

16. The top level of the folder structure is called the _____.

    A. Windows folder

    B. System folder

    C. Root folder

    D. Lobby

17. What's the command-line command for renaming a folder at a Windows command prompt?

    A. ren

    B. mv

    C. mov

    D. name

18. When you drag-and-drop a file in Windows between two locations on the same drive, it is moved. If you would prefer to make a copy, hold down _____ as you drag.

    A. Shift

    B. Alt

    C. Tab

    D. Ctrl

19. Which utility lists the currently running applications and processes in Windows and enables you to shut down any that have stopped responding?

    A. Resource Monitor

    B. Task Manager

    C. Windows Explorer

    D. Disk Management

20. In the Control Panel, where do you adjust the screen resolution?

    A. Taskbar And Start Menu

    B. Folder Options

    C. Personalization

    D. Display

Answers to Review Questions

1. C. Ammonia can destroy the antiglare coating on a monitor.

2. B. Compressed air generates cold as it is expelled from the can. For this reason, it is sometimes used to cool overheated chips.

3. B. Compressed air is the best of these solutions because it is least likely to damage the keyboard.

4. B. Alcohol dries quickly and leaves no residue.

5. A. Use the utility program built into the printer itself, or the printer's driver in the operating system, to clean the ink jets.

6. B. Use a soft cloth to buff the fingerprints off a DVD.

7. A. ESD stands for electrostatic discharge—in other words, static electricity.

8. B. Static electricity is a low-amperage shock, so it does not harm people. However, it does harm sensitive electronics.

9. D. Grounding yourself before you touch electronics can prevent you from accidentally damaging them due to static electricity (ESD).

10. C. Electromagnetic interference, or EMI, is data interference caused by the magnetic fields that build up around adjacent cables that are carrying data.

11. B. A varistor absorbs excess voltage, preventing it from reaching the devices plugged into the surge suppressor in the event of a power surge or spike.

12. C. An uninterruptible power supply (UPS) is a battery backup system for a PC, usually combined with surge-suppression capabilities.

13. C. Cold temperatures help a computer by making it easier for it to keep the chips cool that heat up as it operates. Below freezing, though, frost and condensation may develop, which can cause short-circuits.

14. A. A system image is a complete copy of the entire hard disk. It is very effective as a backup, but it takes a long time to make. Therefore most people make a system image infrequently.

15. B. Finder is the file-management tool in the Mac OS.

16. C. The root folder, or root directory, is the top level in the file structure on a disk.

17. A. Ren, which is short for rename, is the command for renaming a folder or file at a Windows command prompt. The syntax is ren *oldname newname*.

18. D. Hold down Ctrl to force a drag-and-drop operation to make a copy.

19. B. Task Manager displays running tasks and enables you to shut them down if needed. To access it, right-click the taskbar and choose Start Task Manager.

20. D. The Display options make text larger or smaller, adjust screen resolution, and can help you connect to an external display.

Chapter 6

Installing and Configuring Software

FUNDAMENTALS OF PC FUNCTIONALITY OBJECTIVES COVERED IN THIS CHAPTER:

✓ **1.2 U.K. / 1.6 U.S. Identify the risks associated with upgrading the following technologies and equipment:**

- Operating systems (open source and commercial)
- Applications
- Automatic applications and operating system updates

✓ **2.1 U.K. / 3.1 U.S. Conduct basic software installation, removal, and/or upgrading:**

- Follow basic installation/upgrade procedures
- Configure the OS
- Documentation
- Digital rights management
- Software removal
- Re-installation

Most of the productive activities you can perform with a computer involve installing some kind of software other than the operating system. In this chapter, you'll learn how to configure the OS, how to install new software, how to upgrade an existing application, and how to remove unwanted software. You'll learn how to access software documentation and how to register and activate applications that require it. You'll also learn some basic skills for configuring the OS including creating user accounts, adjusting power settings, and changing the display resolution.

Configuring the Operating System

Whatever OS you use, you'll probably want to adjust its configuration settings to make it your own. This can include creating separate user profiles for the different people who use the PC, customizing the interface, adjusting security levels, and more.

Working with User Accounts

A *user account* is an identity by which you're known when using the OS. Most OSs allow (or require) you to log in, identifying yourself by your user account, and then adjust the system and user environment settings appropriately to match your user level and preferences.

Most OSs allow you to create multiple levels of users, with each level having different permissions. This enables you to grant access to the system to someone that you perhaps don't trust to have full access to it. For example, you might give a child permission to run applications on the system but not to make changes that affect other users (like changing system settings).

To configure a user in Windows 7, you can either make them a standard user or an administrator. People who don't have a user account on the computer can use the generic Guest account if it's turned on. The Guest account has very limited permissions, and it can't make system changes. In Figure 6.1, for example, there are three accounts: one administrator, one standard user, and a generic Guest account (which is built in with Windows). It's turned off (so it isn't visible at the Login screen).

FIGURE 6.1   Managing user accounts in Windows 7

On a Mac, you also have Standard and Administrator accounts available, plus a Managed with Parental Controls account and a Sharing Only account. As shown in Figure 6.2, you can make a user an administrator by selecting the Allow User To Administer This Computer check box, and you can impose parental controls with the Enable Parental Controls check box.

FIGURE 6.2   User permissions in Mac OS X

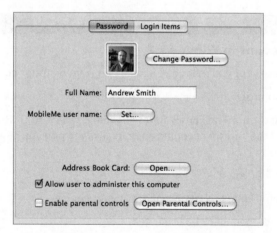

For Linux, the options available depend on the version you're using. For example, Ubuntu offers Administrator, Desktop User, and Unprivileged. Ubuntu also allows you to fine-tune the user's properties and privileges, as shown in Figure 6.3.

FIGURE 6.3   Linux (Ubuntu) enables you to fine-tune user settings.

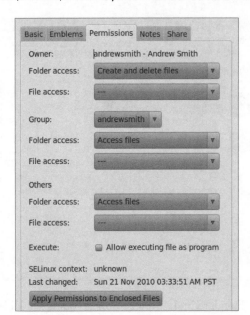

No matter which account type and OS you choose, it's a good idea to password-protect it. (An exception to that is the Guest account on a Windows system, which has no password because it's by its nature accessible to the public.) Chapter 9, "Security and Access Control," discusses how to choose an effective password.

EXERCISE 6.1

Create a User Account in Windows 7

1. In Windows 7, make sure you're logged in using an Administrator account type.

2. Choose Start ➤ Control Panel.

3. Under the User Accounts And Family Safety heading, click Add Or Remove User Accounts. A list of the current accounts appears, like the one you saw earlier in Figure 6.1.

4. Click Create A New Account.

5. In the New Account Name box, type a name of your choice.

6. Leave the Standard User check box selected.

7. Click Create Account. The account appears on the list of accounts.

8. Click the new account's icon. A list of options appears that you can use to make changes.

9. Click Create A Password.

10. Type a password of your choice in the New Password and Confirm New Password boxes.

11. (Optional) Enter a password hint in the Type A Password Hint box.

12. Click Create Password. The account is now password-protected.

13. Click Remove The Password. Confirmation information appears.

14. Click Remove Password. The account no longer has a password.

15. Click Delete The Account. Confirmation information appears.

16. Click Delete Files. (This deletes any files for that user, but there are none.)

17. Click Delete Account. The list of accounts appears, without that account.

18. Close all open windows.

Adjusting the Sound Volume

Some keyboards have volume-control buttons on them that adjust sound up or down or mute it completely. You can also adjust the volume within the OS. In Windows, click the speaker icon in the notification area (in the bottom-right corner of the screen, down by the clock), and then drag the slider up or down or click the Mute button below the slider to mute or unmute (see Figure 6.4). You can also right-click the Volume icon and choose Open Volume Mixer to control the volume for different types of sound individually.

FIGURE 6.4   Adjusting the sound volume in Windows

On a Mac, the process is similar. On the right side of the Finder menu bar at the top of the screen, click the sound volume icon (which looks like a speaker). Then drag the slider up or down. Many keyboards for both PCs and Macs also have volume-adjustment buttons.

Changing the Date and Time

The computer keeps track of the current date and time so that it can accurately display a clock and calendar. This clock/calendar is kept up to date by a chip on the motherboard. You can manually change the date and time, either in the OS or in BIOS Setup, or you can allow the OS to check the date and time periodically and update them as needed, using an Internet time server.

On a PC, the current date and time are part of the BIOS data stored by the motherboard. In addition to the ROM BIOS information (that is, the part of the BIOS that never changes), there are also settings you can change via the BIOS Setup program. Any nondefault settings you specify in that program are stored on a chip on the motherboard. In earlier years, it was common for this data to be stored on a CMOS chip. *CMOS* stands for complementary metal oxide semiconductor, a type of dynamic memory that requires very little power to remain active. The motherboard's battery would keep that information alive on the CMOS chip when the computer's power was off. If the battery died, one way to tell was that the computer's date and time would reset back to January 1, 1900. Nowadays, with the ready availability of static RAM, the BIOS settings are stored on a flash RAM chip on the motherboard.

On a Windows PC, click the clock in the lower-right corner of the screen, opening a window that displays the calendar and clock, and click Change Date And Time Settings. Then use the Date And Time dialog box to change the date and/or time, change the time zone, and select a time server from which to update them automatically.

On a Mac, click the System Preferences icon on the Dock, and then click the Date & Time icon. Adjust the date, time, and time zone from the System Preferences window (see Figure 6.5).

FIGURE 6.5   Adjusting the date and time in Mac OS X

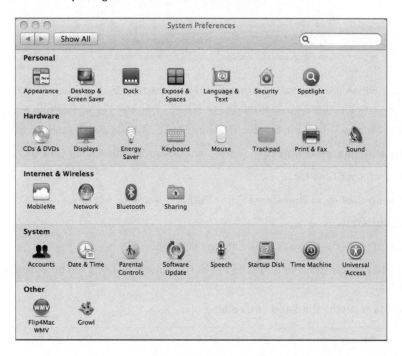

EXERCISE 6.2

Change the Time in Windows 7

1. In Windows 7, click the digital clock in the lower-right corner of the screen.

2. Click Change Date And Time Settings. The Date And Time dialog box opens.

3. Click Change Date And Time. The Date And Time Settings dialog box opens.

4. Click in the minutes to move the insertion point there. (For example, if the time is 6:44:01 PM, click in the 44.)

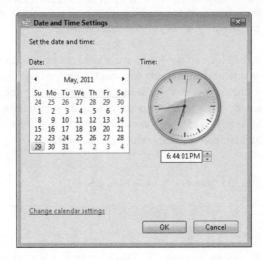

5. Click the up increment arrow five times to advance the time by 5 minutes. Click OK. Look at the clock in the lower-right corner of the screen; it shows the updated time.

6. Click the Change Time Zone button. The Time Zone Settings dialog box opens.

7. Confirm that the correct time zone is selected for your location; then click OK.

8. Click the Internet Time tab.

9. Click Change Settings. The Internet Time Settings dialog box opens.

10. Click Update Now.

11. Click OK to close the Internet Time Settings dialog box.

12. Look at the clock in the lower-right corner of the screen; it shows the time reset to the actual time.

13. Click OK to close the Date And Time dialog box.

Changing the Screen Resolution

A *pixel* (picture element) is the smallest point of a display that can be individually controlled in terms of color and brightness. The *screen resolution* is the number of pixels that form the display. For example, 1600 × 900 is a common resolution for a wide-screen notebook computer display. The first number is the width, measured in number of pixels, and the second number is the height in pixels. Figure 6.6 shows the same Windows desktop in two different resolutions—one widescreen and one with a standard 4:3 width-height ratio. The higher the resolution, the smaller everything appears onscreen (icons, text, and so on).

FIGURE 6.6   Two different Windows screen resolutions: 1600 × 900 (top) and 1024 × 768 (bottom)

 On a CRT monitor, there isn't much visible difference in sharpness among the various resolutions. On an LCD monitor, however, the sharpest image results from using the monitor's highest available resolution.

The highest resolution available is the one that both the monitor and the display adapter can support. The display adapter's maximum resolution is limited mainly by the amount of memory on the adapter (or allocated to it, in a system where the display adapter shares the motherboard's RAM). Most display adapters have more RAM than needed to support most consumer-level monitors. Therefore, on most systems, it's the monitor's maximum resolution, and not the display adapter's, that is the limiting factor.

The display adapter's maximum resolution also depends on the color depth you're using. The color depth is the number of bits used to describe the color of each pixel. In the last several versions of Windows, and in most other OSs, 32-bit color (True Color) is the standard assumed. The alternative is 16-bit (High Color). If you need a higher display resolution than your display adapter can support at 32-bit color depth, you might try switching to 16-bit color depth to see if higher display resolutions become available. In the next exercise, you'll see where color depth is controlled in Windows 7.

On a Mac, you can control screen resolution by choosing System Preferences from the Dock and clicking Displays (see Figure 6.7).

FIGURE 6.7   Adjusting the resolution in Mac OS X

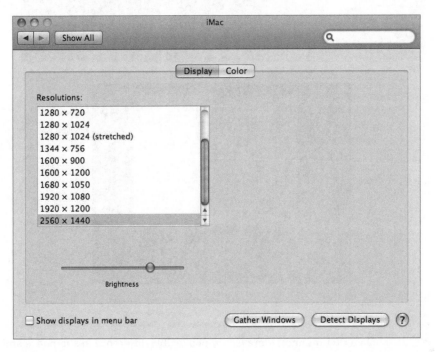

To control the screen resolution in Windows 7, right-click the desktop and choose Screen Resolution. This opens the Screen Resolution section of the Control Panel. You'll get a chance to practice this in more detail in the following exercise.

In earlier Windows versions, right-click the desktop, choose Properties, and set the resolution in the Display dialog box.

EXERCISE 6.3

Change the Screen Resolution in Windows 7

1. In Windows 7, right-click the desktop and choose Screen Resolution.

2. Open the Resolution drop-down list, and drag the slider to the next-to-highest setting.

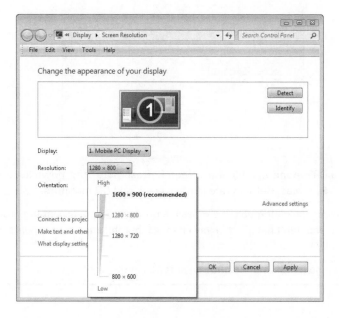

3. Click OK. The resolution changes, and a message asks if you want to keep the changes.

4. Click Revert. The resolution returns to its previous setting.

5. Click Advanced Settings. A dialog box for the display adapter appears.

6. Click the Monitor tab.

EXERCISE 6.3 (continued)

7. Open the Colors list, and check the available color depths. Don't make a change.

8. If you have a CRT monitor, open the Screen Refresh Rate drop-down list and check the available refresh rates. Refresh rate isn't an issue on LCD monitors.

9. Click OK to close the dialog box. If a message prompts you to accept the new settings, click No. (You shouldn't have made any changes, but this message appears if you did accidentally.)

10. Click OK to close the Screen Resolution settings in the Control Panel.

Other Ways to Customize the User Experience

Nearly every aspect of the user experience is customizable on both the Mac and the PC, from the colors onscreen to the way the mouse moves.

In Windows, most of these settings can be adjusted from the Control Panel in the Appearance And Personalization area. Table 6.1 summarizes these settings and tools in Windows 7, and Table 6.2 provides the same for Mac OS X.

TABLE 6.1 Appearance and personalization utilities in Windows 7

Utility	Description	Accessed From
Personalization	Changes the appearance theme, colors, background, and sound effects	Start ➢ Control Panel ➢ Appearance And Personalization ➢ Personalization
Display	Makes text larger or smaller, adjusts screen resolution, and connects to an external display	Start ➢ Control Panel ➢ Appearance And Personalization ➢ Display
Desktop Gadgets	Adds or removes mini-applications on the desktop, such as clock, calendar, and photo viewer	Start ➢ Control Panel ➢ Appearance And Personalization ➢ Desktop Gadgets
Taskbar and Start Menu	Customizes the Start menu and taskbar	Start ➢ Control Panel ➢ Appearance And Personalization ➢ Taskbar And Start Menu
Ease of Access Center	Applies settings that help people who have limited vision, hearing, or mobility	Start ➢ Control Panel ➢ Appearance And Personalization ➢ Ease Of Access Center
Folder Options	Changes settings that affect folder and file management	Start ➢ Control Panel ➢ Appearance And Personalization ➢ Folder Options
Fonts	Displays the installed fonts, and provides an interface for adding and removing fonts	Start ➢ Control Panel ➢ Appearance And Personalization ➢ Fonts
Mouse	Adjusts the pointer appearance, pointer speed, and double-click speed	Start ➢ Control Panel ➢ Hardware And Sound; under the Devices And Printers heading, click Mouse
Sound	Adjusts the system volume and system sounds, and manages audio devices	Start ➢ Control Panel ➢ Hardware And Sound ➢ Sound
Power Options	Changes the battery settings; controls what happens when you press the Power button or shut the lid of a notebook PC	Start ➢ Control Panel ➢ Hardware And Sound ➢ Power Options

TABLE 6.2 Appearance and personalization utilities in Mac OS X

Utility	Description	Accessed From
Appearance	Changes the color of buttons and highlighting, whether scroll arrows appear at the top or bottom of scrollbars, the number of items that appear in "recent items" menus, and minimum sizes for font smoothing.	System Preferences ➢ Appearance.
Desktop & Screen Saver	Selects the image for the desktop background and sets the screen saver.	System Preferences ➢ Desktop & Screen Saver; or right-click the desktop and choose Change Desktop Background.
Language & Text	Selects the language used by the OS; how symbols, smart quotes, and fractions are displayed; formats for dates and numbers; and formats for international keyboards.	System Preferences ➢ Language & Text.
Dock	Sets where the Dock appears on the screen (top, side, or bottom); controls the size of the Dock and whether icons magnify on mouseover; what effects windows use when they minimize; and whether the Dock hides when not in use.	System Preferences ➢ Dock; or right-click the Dock separator and choose Dock Preferences.
Displays	Controls screen resolution; manages all displays, including external monitors and projectors; controls brightness; and lets you calibrate the monitor's color.	System Preferences ➢ Displays
Universal Access	Applies settings that help people who have limited vision, hearing, or mobility.	System Preferences ➢ Universal Access.
Mouse and Trackpad	Both items control tracking, scrolling, double-click speed, button assignments and, on wireless input devices, battery levels. The Mouse pane controls multitouch gestures on the Magic Mouse. The Trackpad pane controls more multitouch gestures and only appears on notebooks or on iMacs and Mac Pros with a Magic Trackpad.	System Preferences ➢ Mouse; System Preferences ➢ Trackpad.

Utility	Description	Accessed From
Energy Saver	Controls when the computer's display blanks, how soon it sleeps when inactive, whether the screen dims before sleep or blanking, whether it dims on battery power, and whether the battery status shows in the menu bar.	System Preferences ➢ Energy Saver.
Sound	Adjusts the system volume and system sounds and manages audio devices.	System Preferences ➢ Sound.
Finder Preferences	Controls what objects appear on the desktop, such as drives and servers; controls what items appear in the left pane of the Finder window; and enables the use of color labels for files.	Click the Finder icon in the Dock, then choose Finder ➢ Preferences.
Fonts	Provides a Finder-like interface for adding, removing, and managing fonts.	Applications ➢ Font Book.
Dashboard	Provides access to a screen of widgets offering specialized information such as weather, time, a flight tracker, Yellow Pages, stocks, news headlines, and more.	Click the Dashboard icon on the Dock. On newer Macintosh keyboards, press the F4 key. Look for a fuel gauge icon on older Mac keyboards.

EXERCISE 6.4

Customize Windows

1. Choose Start ➢ Control Panel ➢ Appearance And Personalization ➢ Personalization.

2. In the Aero Themes section, click Landscapes. Wait for the theme to be changed.

3. Click Desktop Background at the bottom of the dialog box. Scroll through the available pictures, click one you like, and click Save Changes.

4. Click Window Color. Click one of the colors you like. Clear the Enable Transparency check box. Drag the Color Intensity slider to the left or right to create a look you like. Then click Save Changes.

5. In the lower-left corner of the Personalization page, click Taskbar And Start Menu. The Taskbar And Start Menu Properties dialog box opens.

6. Clear the Lock The Taskbar check box if it's selected. Select the Auto-Hide The Taskbar check box if it isn't already selected.

7. Under Notification Area, click Customize. A list of notification tray icons appears. Each one has a status under Behaviors. Change the behavior for any of them as desired. The ones set to Show Icon And Notifications always appear; the ones set to Only Show Notifications appear only when the application has something to report. The Hide Icon And Notifications option always hides the icon.

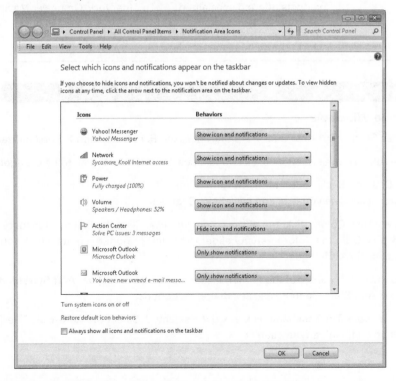

8. Click OK to return to the Taskbar And Start Menu Properties box.

9. Click the Start Menu tab, and click Customize. The Customize Start Menu dialog box opens. Here you can control what appears on the Start menu and how.

10. Under the Games heading, click Don't Display This Item.

11. In the Start Menu Size section, set Number Of Recent Programs To Display to 7, and set Number Of Recent Items To Display In Jump Lists to 8.

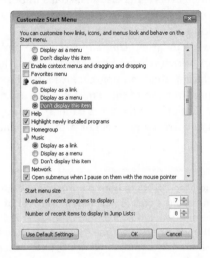

12. Click OK to close the Customize Start Menu dialog box, and click OK to close the Taskbar And Start Menu Properties dialog box.

13. Click Back to return to the Appearance And Personalization page of the Control Panel.

14. Click Folder Options. The Folder Options dialog box opens.

15. On the View tab, clear the Hide Extensions For Known File types check box.

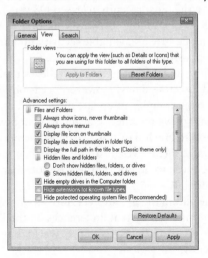

16. Click OK.

17. Close the Control Panel.

Updating and Upgrading the Operating System

The OS is the platform on which everything else sits, so it's important that it be a stable and reliable platform. (By the way, *platform* isn't just a metaphor we're making up here; it's a common industry convention.)

Don't confuse upgrading with updating. *Upgrading* refers to replacing your current OS with a newer or more feature-rich release. For example, if you have Windows XP and you install Windows 7 to replace it, that's an upgrade. It's also an upgrade if you go from a more basic to a more advanced version of the same OS, such as from Windows 7 Home Basic to Windows 7 Ultimate Edition. On the other hand, if you apply a free patch from the Microsoft that's designed to correct a problem or provide a minor enhancement, that's an *update*.

> Windows and Mac OS X are both *commercial OSs*, which means you pay for the OS initially (its cost is included in the cost of a new PC), and you pay for each upgrade. Linux is a free, *open-source* OS. No one may charge for it, and all updates are also free. However, Linux itself is a somewhat cryptic and unfriendly command-line OS, like Unix, and most people use a graphical *shell* on top of it to provide a graphical user interface. A shell comes packaged with the free OS in a *distribution package*, or *distro*, and distribution packages can either be free or commercial.

Updating the Operating System

You don't always have to have the most recently released OS version, but you do need a version that's current enough so that all the software you want to use runs on it. Whatever version you use, you should make sure all available security updates are applied to it to avoid problems due to viruses, worms, and other exploits.

Most OSs have an automatic update feature, which relieves users of the burden of remembering to look for and install updates. However, occasionally an update may cause a problem on some systems. For example, an update may have an incompatibility with a certain piece of hardware that you've installed, causing it to stop working; or an update may cause an older application to crash. For this reason, some network administrators prefer to keep control of updates themselves on all the PCs they support rather than enabling individual users to choose to download them or not; therefore, they may disable automatic updates on individual PCs.

On a Mac, you control the automatic updates via the Software Update dialog box, shown in Figure 6.8. (Access this from System Preferences on the Dock.) You can specify an interval at which to check for updates (for example, Weekly) and choose whether to download updates automatically.

FIGURE 6.8   Automatic updates for a Mac

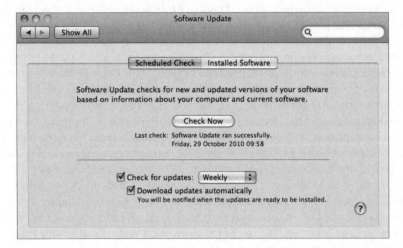

In Windows, you control automatic updates via the Windows Update section of the Control Panel. (It's in the System And Security area.) You can turn updating on/off, manually check for updates, review update history, and more. If updates are available, you can choose to install them or hide the notification of them without installing them (see Figure 6.9).

FIGURE 6.9   Windows Update in Windows 7

When you're installing updates, be aware that some updates require you to reboot the computer when they're finished installing. This can be an inconvenience if you're in the middle of an important project or have many open windows and applications. When an update requires a reboot, you can decline to restart until a more convenient time. If it's an update where a reboot is very important, the OS will remind you until you do it, letting you postpone the next reminder for a certain amount of time, from a few minutes to a few hours.

Although it may seem more convenient to avoid automatic updates because of that pesky restarting directive, there are risks associated with ignoring an available update. Some updates address critical security flaws. If you don't install updates promptly that are designed to protect your system, your PC may be vulnerable to security attacks from the Internet.

Windows Update (or Software Update on the Mac) can also recommend and install updates for certain applications, especially those made by the same company as the OS itself. Also, depending on your hardware, it may be able to make updates for your hardware drivers available, such as a new version of a display-adapter driver or network-adapter driver.

A major update to the OS is typically rolled out to consumers as a *service pack*. A service pack is like any other update except for its scope; it typically alters the inner workings of the OS in a deeper way than a regular update.

EXERCISE 6.5

Configure Windows Update

1. Choose Start ≻ Control Panel ≻ System And Security ≻ Windows Update. Review whether there are any updates to be installed. (Back in Figure 6.9, for example, there was one important update shown.)

2. Click Change Settings. Options appear for configuring Windows Update.

3. In the Important Updates section, open the drop-down list and choose Check For Updates But Let Me Choose Whether To Download And Install Them.

4. Make sure all the other check boxes are selected except the last one (Show Me Detailed Notifications When New Microsoft Software Is Available).

5. Click OK to return to the main Windows Update window.

6. Click View Update History. A list of the previously installed updates appears. Review this information, noting whether they were successful, their importance, and their dates installed.

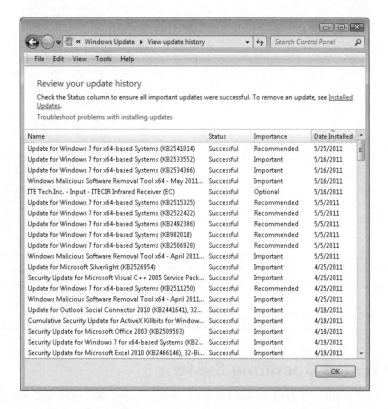

7. Click the Installed Updates hyperlink near the top of the window. A list of updates appears. From this screen, you could remove an installed update.

8. Click one of the updates. An Uninstall button appears at the top of the list. If you wanted to remove this update, you would click Uninstall to begin that process.

9. Click the back button (blue left-pointing arrow) to return to the View Update History list, and then click back again to return to Windows Update.

10. If there are any updates available that haven't yet been installed, click the hyperlink to view them. The exact wording of the hyperlink depends on the number of updates available; if there is one, it will say *1 important update is available*. Review the information about the update. If you decide you want it, select its check box and click OK.

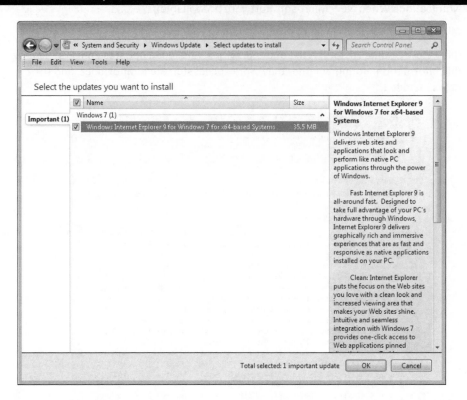

11. Close the Control Panel window.

Upgrading the Operating System

As we mentioned earlier, upgrading is different from updating. Whereas updating simply maintains what you already have, upgrading improves on what you have by either installing a newer version or installing a version with better capabilities.

You may think that newer would always be better when it comes to OSs, but that's not the case. The latest OS versions are designed to run on the latest hardware. If you have an older PC (more than a year or two old), you may find that installing a new OS can actually make the PC perform worse than before.

Looking at the Available Versions and Editions

It's important to understand what OS versions are available when you're thinking about upgrading, and what new features and capabilities you'll get when upgrading.

A *version* is a major release of the OS, such as Windows 7. An *edition* is one of the available packages of that OS, such as Windows 7 Home Premium Edition.

Microsoft Windows versions come out every two to three years, generally with a big splash of publicity. Each version comes in several editions, each with a different subset of features at a different price and designed for a different type of user. Both 32-bit and 64-bit editions have been available since Windows XP. The 32-bit editions can run on either 32-bit or 64-bit systems; the 64-bit editions run only on 64-bit systems. Table 6.3 summarizes the Windows versions and editions from the past decade and their system requirements.

TABLE 6.3 Windows versions (Windows XP and higher)

Version	Year Released	Editions Available	System Requirements
XP	2001	Home Edition Professional Media Center Edition Tablet PC Edition Starter Edition (not available in the USA)	Processor: 233 MHz or higher (300 MHz or higher recommended) RAM: 64 MB (128 MB recommended) Display: 800 × 600 or higher resolution Hard drive space: 1.5 GB CD or DVD drive (for installation)
Vista	2007	Home Basic Home Premium Business Enterprise Ultimate Home and Business Starter Edition (not available in the USA)	Processor: 800 MHz or higher (1 GHz or higher recommended) RAM: 512 MB (1 GB recommended) Graphics card: DirectX 9.0 capable, with 32 MB of video RAM (128 MB video RAM recommended) Hard drive space: 15 GB DVD drive (for installation)
7	2009	Home Premium Professional Ultimate Starter Edition (not available in the USA)	Processor: 1 GHz RAM: 1 GB for 32-bit, 2 GB for 64-bit Graphics card: DirectX 9.0 capable Hard drive space: 16 GB for 32-bit, 20 GB for 64-bit DVD drive (for installation)

For the last decade or so, the Mac OS has been Mac OS X, where X is the Roman numeral 10. That's its overall version number (10), but new sub-versions have been introduced through the years, each with an animal name. Table 6.4 summarizes these.

TABLE 6.4   Mac OS X versions

Version	Name	Year Released	System Requirements
10.0	Cheetah	2001	Supported computers: Power Mac G3, G3 B&W, G4, G4 Cube, iMac, PowerBook G3, PowerBook G4, iBook RAM: 128 MB Hard drive space: 1.5 GB
10.1	Puma	2001	Same as previous
10.2	Jaguar	2002	Supported computers: PowerMac G3, G4, early PowerMac G5, iMac, eMac, PowerBook G3 or G4, iBook RAM: 128 MB (256–512 MB recommended) Processor type: PowerPC, G3, G4, G5 at 233 MHz or higher Hard drive space: 1.5 GB
10.3	Panther	2003	Processor type: PowerPC G, G4, or G5 at 233 MHz or higher Built-in USB RAM: 128 MB (256–512 MB recommended) Hard drive space: 1.5 GB CD drive
10.4	Tiger	2005	Processor type: PowerPC G3, G4, or G5 at 300 MHz or higher Built-in FireWire RAM: 256 MB (512 MB to 1 GB recommended) Hard drive space: 3 GB DVD-R drive There was also a version available for Intel processors, which were just starting to be used in Macs.

Version	Name	Year Released	System Requirements
10.5	Leopard	2007	Processor type: PowerPC G4 or G5, or any Intel, 867 MHz or higher
			DVD drive (for installation)
			RAM: 512 MB (1 GB recommended)
			Hard drive space: 9 GB
			Some applications work only with an Intel processor.
10.6	Snow Leopard	2009	Processor type: Intel (IA-32)
			RAM: 1 GB
			Hard drive space: 5 GB
			DVD drive or external USB or FireWire DVD drive (for installation)
10.7	Lion	2011	Processor: Intel Core 2 Duo or later CPU
			RAM: 1 GB
			Video RAM: At least 64 MB (128 MB recommended)
			Hard drive space: 5 GB
			DVD drive or external USB or FireWire DVD drive (for installation)

Assessing Compatibility

When considering an OS upgrade, you must look not only at the minimum system requirements (from the preceding tables), but also at compatibility for individual pieces of hardware and software. For example, not only should you ensure that you have enough display adapter RAM to meet the system requirements, but you should also check to make sure your make and model of display adapter are supported under the new version. If the OS version is very new, not all hardware manufacturers may have released a driver yet for it. If the piece of hardware is very old, the manufacturer may not ever release a driver for it for that OS version. Sometimes drivers designed for older OS versions will work fine, but you can't rely on that.

Compatibility checking prior to upgrading is particularly important if you're upgrading from a 32-bit version to a 64-bit version of the OS, because you'll need 64-bit versions of the hardware drivers. Windows comes with a basic set of drivers for generic use, and it will try to use one of these if it can't find the exact driver, but it's better if you have the specific drivers from the hardware manufacturers.

Some of the components for which you should research compatibility before upgrading include the following:

- Dial-up modem
- Network adapter
- Display adapter
- Sound card (or built-in sound support)

Be particularly sure you have a usable driver for your network adapter before upgrading, because you'll need that to connect to the Internet to find any other drivers you may be missing. It's a real pickle when you need the Internet to find a network driver, but you need a network driver to get to the Internet.

Components like the hard drive, processor, and RAM can generally be assumed to be compatible as long as they meet the minimum system requirements. The keyboard and mouse can also generally be assumed to be functional when you upgrade, although if you have a special model of either of those with extra features and buttons, you may need a driver update to continue to use those extras.

One good way to investigate hardware and software compatibility for Windows 7 is via Microsoft's Windows 7 Compatibility Center, located at www.microsoft.com/windows/compatibility/windows-7/en-us/ default.aspx.

If you aren't able to locate a driver for a device from the official channels of either the hardware manufacturer or the OS manufacturer, it may be tempting to turn to a third-party driver website. In some cases, you may be able to find a driver at one of these sites that will serve your needs; but be very cautious, because there are many third-party sites that try to steal your personal information or download harmful malware to your computer.

Assessing Upgrade Paths

An *upgrade path* is a means of getting from one OS version or edition to another. Depending on the versions involved, you may be able to do an *upgrade install*, which installs the new version over the top of the old one, retaining all applications and data files; or you may have to do a *clean install*, which wipes everything out and starts fresh.

Microsoft has offered less-expensive upgrade versions of some OS versions for sale; these are exactly the same as the non-upgrade versions except that as part of the setup process, they check to make sure you have an eligible previous version installed. One common misconception people have is that you can't upgrade your OS unless you have an upgrade version, but that's not true. Both the upgrade and the non-upgrade versions will work to upgrade the OS, provided there is a valid upgrade path between the old and new OSs.

Here are some of the web pages that provide upgrade path information for Windows systems:

- From Windows XP to Windows Vista:

`http://windows.microsoft.com/en-US/windows-vista/Upgrading-from-Windows-XP-to-Windows-Vista`

- From Windows XP or Vista to Windows 7:

`http://windows.microsoft.com/en-us/windows7/products/upgrade`

You can also upgrade from one edition of the same version to another. Windows 7 makes that particularly easy with its Anytime Upgrade feature. Choose Start ➢ All Programs ➢ Windows Anytime Upgrade, and follow the prompts to upgrade. With Windows Vista, you have to buy a different edition and install it as if you were installing an upgrade. This isn't an issue on Macs, because Apple doesn't offer different editions of the Mac OS X.

Securing Administrative Rights and Firewall Access

To make system-level changes to the OS (and upgrading certainly qualifies!), you must make sure you have administrative rights to the PC. That means making sure the user ID with which you log in is an administrator. If you need to contact a network administrator to get the security level on your user ID increased, do so before you get started.

There are two kinds of firewalls: hardware-based (used in large companies) and software-based (built into the OS, as with Windows Firewall, or available as third-party software). Both types of firewalls prevent unauthorized incoming and outgoing network traffic as a security measure. If the PC you're upgrading is part of a corporate network where a hardware firewall is in use, check with a network administrator to make sure there won't be any problems with accessing the Internet during and after the upgrade.

Preventing Data Loss When Installing a New OS

When you do an upgrade install, you get to keep all your data and installed applications. There's a small risk of data loss with any installation of a different OS, so back up your important files beforehand as a precaution. However, chances are good that everything will come through just fine.

When you do a clean install, however, everything on the hard disk gets wiped away (in most cases). Before doing a clean install, therefore, you must make very certain that you have good backups of everything you want to keep.

With a clean install, you can't back up and restore your installed applications the way you do your data files. Applications must be reinstalled after installing the new OS. That's because an installed application isn't simply copied to the hard drive; it also has configuration entries in the system files for the OS. When you do a clean install, all those system files are replaced with new clean versions of them that don't include any application data. That's why it's desirable to do an upgrade install of the OS if possible.

When you're doing a clean install, the Setup program may ask whether you want to repartition and reformat. As you learned in Chapter 2, "Input and Storage Devices," repartitioning isn't necessary unless you want to change the distribution of hard-disk space among the partitions and logical drives you already have. Reformatting isn't necessary either, unless you want to ensure that everything on the drive is wiped away. (You may want to do this if the system has been plagued by viruses, for example, and you want to make sure no traces of them remain.)

If you're doing a clean install of an OS on a system that has a hidden partition where the previous version stored recovery files, you probably won't need that partition or those recovery files anymore after the new OS has been installed because they will no longer be appropriate for recovering your system. Therefore, you may choose to delete the current partitions and create a new, single partition that includes all the available space.

Installing a New OS Version

After all the preparations that happen beforehand, installing a new OS version is surprisingly simple and straightforward.

To do an upgrade install, start up the computer in its current OS, and then pop the CD or DVD in the drive. The Setup program will start automatically, prompting you through each step. During the setup process, you may be asked about some of the following:

Product Key   As an antipiracy measure, Windows comes with a product key, which is a string of letters and numbers that is unique to that copy. You must enter a valid product key to complete the setup. The product key is usually on the sleeve in which the disc came, or possibly on the box or on a card inserted in the box. Mac OS X doesn't use product keys, so this isn't an issue.

Username   You can set up more users later, but you may be prompted for a username to start with.

Network to Connect To   If the Setup program finds available wireless networks, it may ask to which one you want to connect. Setup usually identifies and uses a wired network without a prompt.

If you do a clean install, boot the PC from the Setup CD/DVD. To do this, insert the setup disc and then reboot the computer. If it boots from the disc—great. If it doesn't, you'll need to go into the BIOS Setup program for the PC and change the preferred boot order so that the CD/DVD drive is preferred over the hard disk. To do so, watch the screen as the PC boots for a message that tells you what key to press to enter BIOS Setup. It may be a function key, like F12, or it may be Esc or Delete or some other key, depending on the BIOS version and brand.

During the process of a clean install, you may be asked about some of the following:

Partitioning and Formatting   If you're prompted to redo the partitions or formatting, think hard about this. Redo the partitions only if the current ones are unacceptable. Reformat a drive only if you want to wipe out everything on it.

System Folder   You may be asked into what folder you want to put the system files. Accept the default (for example, `Windows`) unless you have a specific reason for wanting them somewhere else, because if someone else is troubleshooting your computer later, they will expect the system files to be in the default location.

Drive on Which to Install the OS   If you have more than one hard disk, you can put the OS on any of them. However, it's a good idea to put your primary OS on your primary internal hard disk. Don't put your primary OS on an external drive, such as a USB drive, because the interface is slower and system performance will suffer. If you install the new OS on a different drive than your current one, you'll be able to *dual-boot*. A menu will appear each time you start the PC, asking which OS you would like to boot.

Administrator Password   Windows has a special hidden user account with the username Administrator; it's used for troubleshooting. (This is different from a named user account with administrator permissions set for it.) You can put a password on that account if you like. It's more secure to do so, but if you forget the password, you won't be able to get into troubleshooting tools like the Windows Recovery Console.

Installing Applications

PCs don't exist to run OSs, of course—they exist to run applications that enable users to perform useful tasks like writing letters, calculating budgets, and creating artwork.

In this section, you'll learn about installing applications. The actual process of installing an app can be pretty simple, but there are often other things to consider in preparation beforehand.

Assessing Compatibility and Minimum Requirements

On the box for each retail application you buy, and in the documentation for each application available for download, you'll find a Minimum System Requirements section. This usually includes a list of compatible OS versions, a minimum processor speed, a minimum amount of RAM, and a minimum amount of hard disk space available. There may also be additional requirements, such as a particular display adapter or amount of display adapter RAM.

Besides the generic minimum requirements, you would also be wise to research compatibility issues before spending a lot of money on an application. For example, some applications (particularly games) have known problems with certain display adapters.

 When judging whether you have enough hard-disk space, keep in mind that at least 15 to 20 percent of the hard-disk space should be left empty to ensure best performance. Don't assume that if your hard disk has 1 GB of space left on it, you can install an application that requires 1 GB of space.

If your system barely meets the requirements in one or more aspects, the application may install but performance may suffer. For example, the application may crash frequently, run slowly, or have poor graphic or sound performance.

If you want to run an older application that is designed for a previous version of Windows, you may find the Compatibility Mode feature in Windows to be useful. This feature enables a newer version of Windows to mimic an older version selectively when it deals with an individual application. For example, an application may require a lower display resolution than Windows 7 or Windows Vista provides; the Compatibility Mode feature can temporarily permit that lower resolution.

Securing Administrative Rights and Firewall Access

If you use the OS under a standard user account rather than an administrator account, you may not have the right to install new software. Standard users don't usually have permission to make changes that will affect other users, and installing or removing software is such an activity.

As a remedy, you can choose to upgrade your user account temporarily to administrator status (if you're able to do so, given your network administrator's restrictions), or you can log in as a different user with administrative permission. A third option is to right-click the setup file for the application and choose Run as Administrator. Doing so enables you to use an administrator account to grant permission to install, without having to log out of the account under which you're currently logged in.

> *Administrator* is a Windows and Macintosh term; in other OSs, accounts with full administrative privileges may be called *supervisor* or *superuser*.

Some applications require an Internet or network address in order to install them. Depending on the settings of your firewall software (such as Windows Firewall), a warning may appear when the Setup program tries to access the Internet. In most cases, you can click a button to let the firewall know that it's okay to proceed.

You may sometimes have to unblock certain port numbers manually in your firewall software in order to permit an application to access the Internet. As you learned in Chapter 3, "Peripherals and Networking," ports are numbered pathways that help the OS keep Internet traffic routed to the right applications. The exact steps for blocking and unblocking ports and allowing applications vary depending on the OS and the firewall software. The following exercise shows you how to do it in Windows 7. (Note that you would go through this process *after* installing the new software; otherwise the new software would not appear on the list.)

EXERCISE 6.6

Configure the Windows Firewall

1. Choose Start ➢ Control Panel ➢ System and Security and, under the Windows Firewall heading, click Allow A Program Through Windows Firewall.

2. Scroll down to the bottom of the list, and click Windows Remote Management. Select the check box to its left. The Home/Work (Private) check box is automatically selected for that entry. This is the basic way to enable a program.

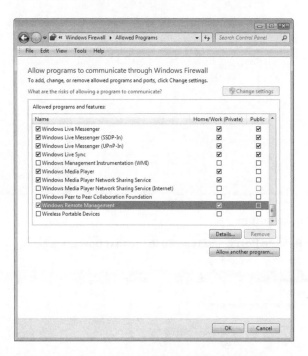

3. Clear the check box for Windows Remote Management, and click OK.

   Next, you'll learn how to open a particular port number by creating a new rule.

4. Back in the Control Panel's System And Security page, click the Windows Firewall heading.

5. In the pane at the left, click Advanced Settings. Advanced information for the firewall appears in the Windows Firewall With Advanced Security window.

6. Scroll down to the View And Create Firewall Rules section, and click Outbound Rules.

7. Choose Action ➢ New Rule. The New Outbound Rule Wizard dialog box opens.

8. Select the Port radio button, and click Next.

EXERCISE 6.6 *(continued)*

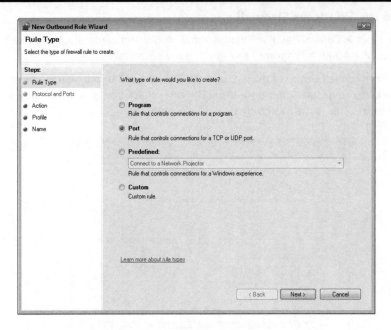

9. Select the TCP radio button.

10. Select Specific Remote Ports, and type **80** in the text box. Click Next.

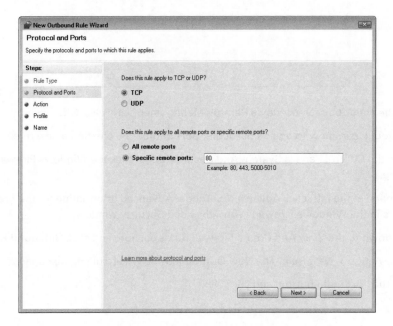

11. Select Allow The Connection, and click Next.

12. Leave all three of the check boxes selected (Domain, Private, and Public) and click Next.

13. In the Name box, type **Open Port 80**.

14. Click Finish. The rule is created.

15. Scroll through the Outbound Rules list, and select the new rule.

16. Choose Action ➤ Delete. In the confirmation dialog box, click Yes.

17. Close the Windows Firewall With Advanced Security window.

Internet Access Issues

When you're installing an application that requires Internet access as an integral part of its functionality, you have some additional considerations to evaluate.

First and foremost, does your Internet connection have the bandwidth to handle this application's demands? *Bandwidth*, in this context, refers to the connection's ability to send data swiftly and in large quantities. For example, if you want to play an online game, such as World of Warcraft, the life and death of your game character could depend on your Internet connection sending your instructions to swing your sword instantaneously; a two-second delay because of slow or unreliable Internet service can mean the difference between winning and losing a battle.

Contention is also an issue—that is, competition with other Internet users for the bandwidth. Perhaps your Internet connection is fast enough in theory, but because several other users with whom you share a connection are also trying to use the Internet at the same time, traffic gets bogged down. If you have cable Internet service, you share the bandwidth with everyone else in your neighborhood, not just those in your own building. Therefore, during periods of peak usage, you may not have nearly the same Internet bandwidth available that you do in off hours.

The raw speed of a broadband Internet connection is seldom the root cause of Internet delays. Therefore, upgrading to a level of Internet service with a faster maximum speed isn't the magic-bullet solution that it may seem on the surface. The advertised speed of your connection is the speed you would theoretically achieve if there were no other traffic, and if your connection always operated at that speed all the time, things would be great. But during high-traffic times, contention can cause major delays, just like a rush-hour traffic jam does on a highway.

Some of the applications that rely heavily on a fast and reliable Internet connection include the following.

Voice over Internet Protocol (VoIP)   Applications that enable you to use telephone or video-phone capabilities over the Internet, like Skype, are very bandwidth-hungry, demanding the best service at all times. Delays in transmission and reception can result in frustrating communication experiences. These delays can be caused not only by your Internet connection, but also by your computer's ability to process voice data, converting it between analog and digital.

Music and Video Streaming   To receive music and video content over the Internet, your connection must have enough bandwidth to accommodate a steady stream without pauses or breaks. Otherwise, you're in for a frustrating experience when the music or video starts and stops.

 Streamed services are often buffered to overcome minor service drops during transmission. In other words, the system pre-downloads the upcoming portion of the clip and stores it temporarily on your hard disk or in memory, anticipating the moment when it will be called. That way, if there is a minor delay in the Internet transmission, the clip can continue to play without interruption.

Web-Delivered Applications   Instead of buying an application and installing it on your own PC, you can in some cases buy permission to use an application online. For example, rather than buy a fully featured word-processing system, you can sign up for a service that gives you unlimited access to an online word-processing program. Such services are becoming more popular, especially with budget-conscious consumers, and they have many advantages. The main disadvantage, of course, is that if you don't have a fast and reliable Internet connection, your access to the service may suffer.

Remote Desktop Services   With remote desktop services, you can remotely connect to a computer that's not physically near you and access its desktop, applications, files, and other resources just as if you were there. Some versions of Windows include a free Remote Desktop application, and third-party services such as pcAnywhere also offer this capability. In Mac OS X, the Screen Sharing utility that's built into Finder offers equivalent capability. Unless the network/Internet connection is robust, though, service can be unsatisfactory.

Installing a New Application

Installing an application from a disc is simple. Just pop the disc into the drive, and the Setup program will generally start automatically. If it doesn't, double-click the drive icon for the drive. If that doesn't start the Setup program, it will open a list of files on that disc; locate and double-click the one named Setup (or something similar).

You can also download and install applications. If you download an executable Setup file (a file with an .exe or .com extension), you can double-click that file to start the setup routine.

Occasionally, an application you download may come in a compressed archive, such as a Zip file (that is, a file with a .zip extension). In such a case, you must extract the contents of the archive to a new folder on your hard disk and then run the setup from that new folder.

Applications are installed in variety of ways on a Mac. Some come with an installer, similar to Windows. In other cases, you drag the program into the `Applications` folder. In either case, applications are often delivered in either a `.zip` file or a disk image, designated with a `.dmg` file extension. Double-click either of these file types to access the program or installer.

Install an Application

1. Go to www.download.com, and locate a freeware or shareware program that interests you.

2. Download the Setup file for the program.

3. Run the Setup file to install the application. If any problems come up, such as system permission or firewall issues, troubleshoot and solve them.

Understanding Licenses and Usage Permissions

It's rare these days for an application to come with a thick printed manual, but that doesn't mean there isn't documentation. Each application typically has a help system built into it, as well as a number of special-purpose documents for granting licensing rights to users and encouraging users to register.

Understanding Licensing Agreements

When you buy an application, you aren't actually buying the application. Instead, you're buying the right to use the application in a limited way as prescribed by the licensing agreement that comes with it. Most people don't read these licensing agreements closely, but suffice it to say that they're pretty slanted in favor of the software manufacturer. Don't like the terms? Too bad. No negotiation is allowed. If you don't accept the license agreement, your only recourse is to return the software for a refund. (And good luck finding a vendor that will take back an opened box. Still, the software manufacturer is required to take it back and refund your money if you reject the licensing.)

Although the majority of the applications you acquire will probably be commercial products, there are a number of alternatives to commercial software sales. Here are some of the license types you may encounter:

Freeware   Freeware is software that is completely free. On the small scale, you can get such software from download sites such as www.download.com, or from the creator's personal website. Large companies like Google and Microsoft also sometimes offer products for free, because it serves the company's interests to have lots of people using that software. Examples include Google Chrome and Microsoft Internet Explorer. Freeware doesn't include source code, and users aren't allowed to modify the application.

Open Source   This software is freer than free: not only is the application free, but the source code (code used by programmers) is also shared to encourage others to contribute to the future development and improvement of the application. OSs such as Linux and applications like OpenOffice.org fit this category. Open source software can't be sold, although it can be bundled with commercial products that are sold.

Shareware   This is software that provides a free trial, with the expectation that you'll pay for it if you like it and decide to keep it. In some cases, a shareware version isn't the full product; in other cases, it expires after a certain amount of time. Some shareware provides a full and unlimited version, with payment requested on the honor system.

Multiuser   This is commercial software that you're allowed to install on more than one computer. For example, some versions of Microsoft Office allow you to install the same copy on two or three PCs.

Single User   This is commercial software for which the license restricts installation to a single PC. A common misconception is that a single-user license allows you to install the software on more than one computer as long as you use only one instance at a time, but that's not accurate. Commercial products sometimes have activation systems that lock the software to a specific PC once installed, so you can't install it elsewhere.

Concurrent   This is a license that allows the software to be installed on many PCs but used concurrently by a smaller number. For example, you may have 1,000 computers with the application installed, but only 100 users can use it simultaneously. This is useful in situations where everyone needs to have an application available, but the application gets very little actual use.

Corporate, Campus, or Site   This is a license that permits an organization to install the application on an agreed-upon number of PCs. For example, a school may buy a site license of an antivirus program and allow all students to download and install it freely to ensure that the school's network remains virus-free.

Registering Software

Registering software—that is, providing your contact information to the software maker—isn't usually required, but software makers try to make you believe it's in your best interest to do so. In actuality, it's a trade-off. Yes, companies want to collect your personal information for marketing purposes, and yes, they may sell it to a third party. However, if you register, you may be eligible for discounts on new versions, free updates, and other goodies.

Activating Software

Some products, especially expensive ones that are frequently pirated, include activation features that lock the installed copy (by installation key code) to a particular PC, so you can't use it on multiple PCs.

In a nutshell, here's how it works. The software company maintains an online database of all the installation key codes. When you install the software, you're prompted to activate it. (Usually you have 30 days to do so, or a certain number of uses, before it stops working.) The activation program examines the hardware on your system (processor, motherboard model, and so on) and generates a code that describes the general state of the hardware. It then sends that code to the activation server online. If you try to activate the software on a different PC, the activation server compares the hardware code it has on file to the new one coming in, and if they're too different, it assumes you're installing on a different PC and refuses to let you activate the software.

How is this code generated? Manufacturers are very cagey about that, because releasing too much information may give hackers what they need to thwart the system. Generally, a small hardware change on a PC, such as a different network card or display adapter, won't be a problem. However, if you replace the motherboard, the software probably won't reactivate through the automated system.

Most of the manufacturers that use activation allow you to phone in to request an activation reset, and they will give you no grief over it the first few times. But if you repeatedly call to request additional activation chances, they'll probably think you're trying to get around the license agreement and won't let you reset the activation anymore.

Digital Rights Management

Digital content is pirated even more frequently than applications, so over the years suppliers of digital content (books, music, videos, and so on) have developed various schemes of preventing unauthorized sharing of content. Generically, these schemes are known as *digital rights management* (*DRM*).

DRM is nothing new. Cable TV scrambling has been using this for years: your service provider issues a card with a recognized identifier that can be activated remotely to enable you to access an array of copyrighted content.

For music files, DRM has proved controversial, because people paying for music they have downloaded haven't always been able to transfer the files to other media they legitimately use (such as a CD for their automobile).

Applications are available that will crack the encryption on DRM-protected files (especially music and video). The makers maintain that the software is strictly to allow legitimate owners of the clips to make backup copies for their own use, which is legal; but in practice most of the "backup copies" end up being illegally shared with others.

Repairing or Reinstalling an Application

If an application doesn't work, you may be able to repair it. Some applications have a built-in repair feature that compares the installed files to a list of originals and fixes anything that has been improperly modified. For example, it may check the filenames and sizes of all the helper files, and if it finds a file that is a different size than expected, it assumes that file has been corrupted and recopies an original version from the setup files to overwrite it. The repair process can also include checking the Windows Registry (or equivalent in other OSs) to make sure the proper entries are present that will allow the application to function correctly.

To repair an application, view the list of installed applications; when a particular application is selected on the list, look for a Repair button or option. Alternately, re-run the Setup program for the application; instead of the regular Setup dialog box, you may see a box offering to repair or uninstall the application.

In some applications, you also may find a Repair option on the Help menu.

EXERCISE 6.8

Repair an Application in Windows

1. In Windows, choose Start ≻ Control Panel ≻ Programs ≻ Programs And Features. A list of installed applications appears.

2. Click the first application on the list, and see what options appear in the blue bar above the list, such as Uninstall, Change, Repair, and so on. Find an application that has a Repair option, and select it.

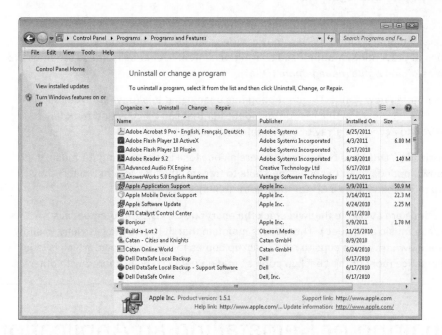

3. Click the Repair button, and follow the prompts to repair the application. (It doesn't matter that it was working correctly already. Repairing it won't hurt it. You may lose some custom settings, though.)

If an application won't work even after repairing it, the next step is to reinstall it. You can reinstall over the top of the old installation, which saves time but is less likely to take care of the problem; and some applications won't let you do this. It's better to uninstall the application (see the next section), reboot, and then do a clean install.

Removing an Application

Removing an application that you no longer want can free up disk space. In addition, if that application has a component that runs constantly in the background, removing the application can free up the memory that was previously occupied by that function.

> You usually don't have to remove an application completely in order to prevent it from running in the background. Most such programs have an option that will turn off the auto-running portion. Try right-clicking the application's icon in the notification area and looking for a command such as Options or Properties that may lead you to a dialog box where you can control the auto-start or background setting.

For Mac users, unless the application specifically has a Remove folder/application, you can delete the application by dragging it to the trash. Also delete any ancillary folders or files associated with that application that may be stored in other locations, such as in the Library/Application Support folder. Doing so removes all application files and associated system resources.

With Windows systems, uninstallation is a bit more complicated. The best and cleanest way to uninstall an application is via the Uninstall command for the application, in the Programs section of the Control Panel. (If there's an Uninstall command or icon in the folder where the application is stored, that will lead you to the same place.) Locate and select the application in the Control Panel, and then look for an Uninstall button or option. Figure 6.10 shows an example. Click Uninstall, and follow the prompts. Using this method is known as a *clean uninstallation*.

FIGURE 6.10 Uninstalling Windows applications from the Control Panel

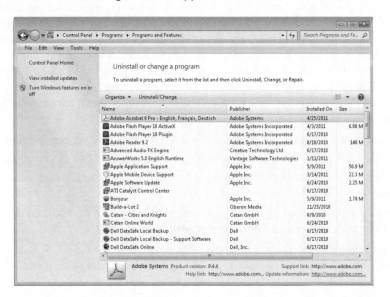

During the uninstall process, you may be asked whether you want to keep certain data or configuration files. That's up to you. If you plan to reinstall the same application later (for example, if you're uninstalling to try to correct a problem, rather than to get rid of the program entirely), you may want to save the configuration files. That's a double-edged sword, though, because if you're uninstalling to try to correct a problem, that problem could possibly be caused by one of those configuration files.

If you're using Linux, then depending on the version, you may find different resources. Common versions such as Ubuntu have a Software Center window, as shown in Figure 6.11, where you can view and remove installed applications.

FIGURE 6.11 You can uninstall programs in Ubuntu Linux from the Software Center window.

If for some reason you can't uninstall an application using the preferred clean method, you can remove it using a brute-force method that involves manually deleting the program's files and folders, and perhaps manually editing the Windows Registry to remove the references to it. This is known as an *unclean uninstallation*.

An unclean uninstall isn't a good idea, because the potential is great for accidentally deleting a file that is essential to some other application or making a change to the Registry that results in other problems. However, sometimes unclean uninstallations happen by accident. For example, you may accidentally delete the folder containing an application, or you may abort the standard Uninstall utility accidentally, resulting in a half-removed, unusable application that won't allow itself to be removed using the utility.

If you need to perform an unclean uninstallation for some reason, here are the basic steps for doing it:

1. Make sure the application isn't running. If it has a background component, turn that off.

2. Delete the folder containing the program files. It's probably in the C:\Program Files folder. If it's a 32-bit application on a 64-bit version of Windows, it may be in the C:\Program Files (x86) folder.

3. Delete the program's icons or folders from the Start menu. To do so, open the Start menu, right-click the icon or folder, and choose Delete.

4. If you have enough information to know what to delete in the Registry, start the Registry Editor (click Start, type **regedit**, and press Enter) and make the needed changes.

Beware of this step, though. It's better to leave the unused references to the application in the Registry if you're not absolutely sure what to delete. You may find such information at the software maker's website or on a support forum online.

Often it's possible to reinstall the application over a corrupt uninstall; the installation software will do the necessary work for you to repair it. Then, after the installation has been repaired, you can try again with the Uninstall utility.

EXERCISE 6.9

Remove an Application in Windows

1. In Windows, choose Start ➤ Control Panel ➤ Programs ➤ Programs And Features. A list of installed applications appears, as shown earlier in Figure 6.10.

2. Locate the application you installed in Exercise 6.7, or some other application that you don't need, and select it.

3. Click Uninstall.

4. Follow the prompts to uninstall the application.

Summary

In this chapter, you learned some OS configuration basics, including how to manage user accounts, control the date and time, and change the screen resolution. Your OS has many other configuration options that you may want to explore on your own if time permits.

Next, you learned how to update and upgrade the OS. You learned about the risks and rewards of installing manufacturer-provided updates and how to choose a new OS version and edition.

Finally, we looked at application installation, repair, and removal. You learned how to assess whether an application is likely to work well on your system, and you learned about important preinstallation activities like securing administrative rights and checking for Internet access issues. You also learned how application software is typically licensed.

Exam Essentials

Know how to make basic changes to the OS settings. In Windows, you can change most settings via the Control Panel. On a Mac, most commands for changing system settings are found in the System Preferences pane.

Be able to create and manage user accounts. You can create new user accounts and set their permissions to control who has access to the system and at what level. In Windows and Mac OS, you can create standard or administrator accounts.

Understand the risks and rewards of OS updates. OS updates, such as those delivered via Windows Update, can keep your system safer from outside attacks via Internet exploits. However, there is a chance that an update may cause a problem with your system.

Understand OS upgrade options. Make sure you understand the difference between a service pack, a new OS version, and an OS edition (applicable only for Windows). You should be able to explain what constitutes an upgrade path and find information about it online or in the OS's documentation.

Assess upgrade compatibility. Not all new OS versions are beneficial for all PCs; a new OS version for a system that doesn't meet the minimum requirements can actually result in a loss of performance. You should know how to compare the system requirements of a new OS to the current system's specs and how to get information about driver compatibility for your hardware.

Be able to install and remove applications. To install most applications, insert the CD or DVD and follow the prompts. Before you do that, though, make sure your system meets the application's minimum requirements. In Mac OS X, you can drag an application's folder to the Trash to remove it; in Windows, you should go through the Control Panel to ensure that an application is removed cleanly.

Review Questions

1. A(n) _____ is an identity by which you log into a PC in order to use it.
  A. Theme
  B. Scheme
  C. Persona
  D. User account

2. In Windows and the Mac OS, the basic levels of users are standard and _____.
  A. Limited
  B. Public
  C. Administrator
  D. Elevated

3. The _____ is the number of pixels that make up the display.
  A. Color depth
  B. Screen resolution
  C. Refresh rate
  D. DOS mode

4. When a free error fix is automatically downloaded and installed on your PC, that's an example of a(n) _____.
  A. Update
  B. Upgrade
  C. Edition change
  D. Version change

5. Which of these operating systems is open source?
  A. MS-DOS
  B. Windows
  C. Mac OS
  D. Linux

6. What is the minimum amount of RAM required for 64-bit Windows 7?
  A. 256 MB
  B. 512 MB
  C. 1 GB
  D. 2 GB

7. Which of these is *not* a version of Mac OS X?

    A. Tiger

    B. Snow Leopard

    C. Lion

    D. Drake

8. Which of these devices is most likely to require you to find a driver for it after upgrading from 32-bit to 64-bit Windows?

    A. Dial-up modem

    B. Keyboard

    C. Mouse

    D. Processor

9. Before upgrading the OS, make sure you are logged in as a(n) _____.

    A. Guest user

    B. Standard user

    C. Administrator

    D. Limited user

10. During a(n) _____ install, you may be asked whether you want to repartition and reformat your drive(s).

    A. Upgrade

    B. Clean

    C. Dirty

    D. Update

11. To prevent software piracy, each copy of Windows comes with a unique _____.

    A. Activator

    B. Registrar

    C. Product key

    D. Password

12. To assess whether your computer can run a new application, look for the _____ on the software's box.

    A. Product key

    B. System requirements

    C. Activation code

    D. Expiration date

13. A system's _____ may prevent an application from accessing the Internet without your permission.

   A. Virus checker

   B. Display adapter

   C. Cable modem

   D. Firewall

14. If you are experiencing stuttering or frequent delays when viewing an online video, your system may not have sufficient Internet _____.

   A. Contention

   B. Bandwidth

   C. VoIP

   D. Video memory

15. _____ is software that is free, but users are not permitted to modify it.

   A. Open source

   B. Freeware

   C. Shareware

   D. Site license

16. _____ is try-before-you-buy software; you can try it for a limited period of time before you are expected to pay.

   A. Open source

   B. Freeware

   C. Shareware

   D. Site license

17. Software that allows a certain number of simultaneous users of an application is _____.

   A. Concurrent license

   B. Multiuser

   C. Single user

   D. Site license

18. A(n) _____ enables an organization to supply an application to all its employees for a fixed fee.

   A. Concurrent license

   B. Multiuser

   C. Single user

   D. Site license

19. _____ is a common antipiracy measure in which a copy of an application is locked to a particular PC by a generated code that represents its hardware configuration.

    A. Registration

    B. Licensing

    C. Concurrency

    D. Activation

20. When you remove an application via the Control Panel's Programs section in Windows, it's a(n) _____ uninstall.

    A. Dirty

    B. Clean

    C. Partial

    D. Limited

Answers to Review Questions

1. D. User accounts differentiate one user from another on a PC, allowing each user to maintain separate preferences and files.

2. C. Standard and administrator are the two levels of user accounts. An administrator has the right to make system changes that affect other users; a standard user does not.

3. B. Screen resolution is the number of pixels, such as 1600×900. Color depth refers to the number of bits used to describe each pixel's color. Refresh rate is a setting mostly for CRT monitors that controls how often the display is repainted.

4. A. A free, automatically installed fix is a minor update. An upgrade would involve changing the version or edition of the OS.

5. D. Linux is an open-source operating system. The others listed are commercial products.

6. D. As listed in Table 6.3, the 64-bit version of Windows 7 requires 2 GB of RAM.

7. D. Mac OS X versions are all named for large cats.

8. A. Add-on devices such as a dial-up modem are most likely to require a third-party driver after changing OS versions. Most built-in components like the processor do not, and basic keyboard and mouse functionality are built into Windows.

9. C. Making changes that affect the entire system require that you be logged in as an administrator.

10. B. A clean install is one in which a new copy of the OS is installed, abandoning all old copies. With this comes the option of repartitioning and reformatting.

11. C. The product key, usually printed on the jacket in which the setup disc comes, is the unique identifier for that copy of Windows.

12. B. System requirements for each application are printed on its box or in its specifications when you buy or download it online.

13. D. Firewall software monitors the incoming and outgoing network traffic, and it queries the user when it sees activity from a new application.

14. B. Bandwidth is the connection's ability to send data swiftly and in large quantities. Interruptions in video playback online are usually a result of Internet delays caused by inadequate bandwidth.

15. B. Freeware is free, but users are not authorized to modify it. In contrast, open source software not only is free, but also may be freely modified by anyone, with source code provided.

16. C. Shareware is free for a limited-time trial or with limited features. Users who want to continue to use it are expected to pay for it.

17. A. A concurrent license specifies a maximum number of simultaneous users, rather than a maximum number of installs.

18. D. A site license allows organizations to distribute software to all their employees for a single price.

19. D. Activation, which is a separate process from either installation or registration, locks the copy of the software to the PC on which it is installed.

20. B. A clean install is one in which all the installed pieces of the application are removed, including files, Start menu shortcuts, folders, and Registry entries.

Chapter

7

Updating and Upgrading Hardware

OBJECTIVES COVERED IN THIS CHAPTER:

FUNDAMENTALS OF PC FUNCTIONALITY

✓ **1.2 U.K. / 1.6 U.S. Identify the risks associated with upgrading the following technologies and equipment:**

- PC Speed/Storage capability
- Compatibility issues
- Upgrade issues
- Bus differences
- Hardware failure

FUNDAMENTALS OF TECHNOLOGY

✓ **2.1 U.K. / 2.1 U.S. Identify basic compatibility issues between:**

- Processor performance
- RAM memory
- USB (1.1, 2.0)
- FireWire
- PS/2

As times goes by, you may find that your computer's hardware isn't adequate for the jobs you want it to do. Depending on the type and age of the system, you may be able to upgrade one or more components to bring the computer up to the level you need, so you don't have to replace the computer completely. In this chapter, you'll learn how to evaluate a system for possible upgrades, how to select a compatible upgrade component, and how to install the component safely.

Evaluating a Computer for Upgrades

The first step in upgrading is to understand what you already have:

- What components are fine as is?
- Which components are obsolete, failing, or weaker in capability than the rest?
- What components may benefit from a new driver?
- What components can't be replaced at all?

Answering these questions before you get out your wallet at the computer store can save you a lot of time and money.

Updating Device Drivers

Sometimes you can improve a device's performance, add new features to it, and/or fix problems with it by applying a free driver update from the manufacturer. If you're thinking of replacing a device because it isn't working very well for some reason, try updating its driver and see if that doesn't straighten things out.

To check a device's driver, use the operating system to find out the driver's current version number and date. (The exact steps depend on the OS; in Windows, you can use Device Manager as shown in Exercise 7-1.) Then visit the device manufacturer's website and search for the latest driver for your OS. If you find one that's newer than the one you have, install it. Some devices also have their own BIOS, which can be updated via downloadable executable file.

EXERCISE 7.1

Update a Device Driver

1. In Windows, display the Device Manager. In Windows 7, you can do so by following these steps:

    a.   Choose Start, right-click Computer, and choose Manage. The Computer Management window opens.

    b.   In the list of tools at left, click Device Manager.

2.   Choose a nonessential device, such as a modem, network adapter, or sound card, and display its properties. To do so:

    a.   Double-click a category to expand a list of devices within it.

    b.   Double-click a device to open its Properties box.

3.   Click the Driver tab, and make a note of the manufacturer and model number, the driver date, and the driver version.

4.   Click the Update Driver button.

5.   Click Search Automatically For Updated Driver Software, and wait for Windows to search for a newer driver. If it finds one, follow the prompts to install it. If a message appears that the best driver is already installed, click Close and continue to step 6.

6.   Open a web browser, and display the website of the device manufacturer. Search through the Support section to see if a newer driver is available. If it is, download and install it.

7.   Close all open windows.

Analyzing Current System Performance

What's the holdup? It's sometimes hard to know what is holding a system back from peak performance. In Windows Vista and Windows 7, though, you can use the Windows Experience Index, which is part of the Control Panel, to check out the key components, each of which is assigned a numeric score. (Higher is better.)The Base Score is the lowest score. The component with the lowest score is the one that is most likely to benefit the system by upgrading.

There's no built-in program for checking performance on the Mac, but there are a few freeware titles you can download. The most user-friendly of these right now is iBench (`www.sourceforge.net/projects/ibench/`), which runs a series of tests and generates a score for your Mac's performance. For detailed results, try Xbench (`www.xbench.com`), which lets you upload your tests to a central server so you can compare your Mac to other models.

There are also other ways you can assess your system's performance. Here are some ideas:

- If your system doesn't meet the minimum requirements for an application you want to install, consider upgrading the component(s) that aren't adequate. This option quickly loses its benefit, though, if more than one component needs to be upgraded; it may be cheaper to buy a new computer.

- If the screen seems to repaint itself slowly when running a graphics-intensive program such as a photo editor, or if video playback is choppy, you may benefit from a better display adapter (aka video card) or a more up-to-date driver for the current display adapter.

- If you get messages that the hard disk is becoming full, you may want to add another hard drive, replace your current drive with one with a larger capacity, or uninstall any unneeded applications on your system. You can also run Disk Cleanup on the hard disk (from the Tools tab of the drive's Properties box).

- If the computer seems to slow down when you run multiple programs simultaneously, or you hear the hard disk doing a lot of reading and writing even though you aren't opening or saving large files, you may benefit from installing more RAM.

- If you're using Windows as your OS, look in the Task Manager in Windows and, on the Performance tab, determine how much RAM is available and how much is installed in the total system. Exercise 7.2 shows how this process works and helps you interpret the information.

- If you're using Mac OS X, use the Activity Monitor to check performance; it's in the Applications/Utilities folder.

EXERCISE 7.2

Evaluate System Performance in Windows 7

1. In Windows 7, choose Start ➤ Control Panel ➤ System and Security. Under the System heading, click Check The Windows Experience Index.

2. Examine the information presented. The base score is the lowest score. The component with the lowest score is the one holding back the rest of the system. However, scores 4.0 or higher are considered adequate for most uses, so an upgrade may not be worthwhile if all scores are higher than that.

3. Click What Do These Numbers Mean? to open the Windows Help and Support page that explains the scores. Close it when you're finished reading the information.

4. Close the Control Panel.

5. Right-click the taskbar, and choose Start Task Manager.

6. Click the Performance tab.

7. Check the Total amount of memory under the Physical Memory (MB) heading. Check the Available amount of memory there too. Divide the Available memory by the Total memory to determine what percentage of the total memory is being used. For example, in the following illustration, 57% is free (3513/6132). If a much smaller amount were free, such as only 20–30%, the system might benefit from having more RAM installed.

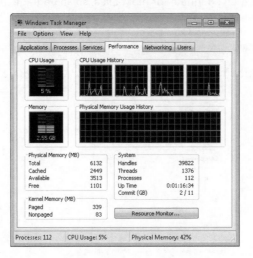

8. Click the Processes tab, and click the Memory column heading to sort by the amount of memory used. Examine the top two memory-using processes. The Description column tells you which program each process is from. If you have several memory-intensive programs running simultaneously, this can artificially inflate memory usage. Exit from those programs, and then check the memory usage again on the Performance tab.

9. Close the Task Manager window.

Selecting Upgrade Parts

Now that you have an idea about which components you may want to upgrade, it's time to get practical. Can those components be upgraded at all? If so, what type of parts will you need, and do those upgrades make economic sense when compared to buying a new computer?

Processor

Upgrading a processor is seldom a good idea. Most motherboards accept only a narrow range of processor types and speeds, so any processor you get that would be compatible with your motherboard probably won't offer a dramatic improvement in performance over the one you already have. In addition, especially on portable computers, the processor is often difficult to access to remove and replace.

If you do decide to upgrade the processor, consult the PC's documentation very carefully to make sure the processor you get is compatible. If the PC's documentation is no help, try contacting the PC manufacturer's tech support to see if they can give you any information. As a last resort, find the make and model of the motherboard (usually stamped on it somewhere) and try the tech support site for the motherboard manufacturer.

RAM

RAM is a fairly easy upgrade. The main concern is whether you have the available slots in which to place it. In some systems, all the RAM slots already filled. That means if you want to increase the amount of RAM, you must remove any lower-capacity RAM that you already have installed and replace it with new, higher-capacity RAM.

Thirty-two bit versions of OSs can support no more than 4 GB of RAM, so don't waste your money on upgrading RAM past 4 GB unless you're using a 64-bit OS. Windows XP and higher comes in both 32-bit and 64-bit editions. Mac OS X doesn't have separate editions like that; the latest versions are 64-bit.

In a desktop PC, check the documentation that came with the PC before buying RAM to make sure there are no special requirements. For example, if the motherboard uses dual-channel RAM, RAM must be installed in matched pairs and in certain RAM slots. For example, in Figure 7.1, there are two full RAM slots (white clips on the ends) and two empty RAM slots (black clips on the ends). The different colored clips are significant; the RAM slots with the same color clips must be populated with identical DIMMs. On some motherboards, the slots are different colors.

FIGURE 7.1   RAM slots on a desktop PC motherboard

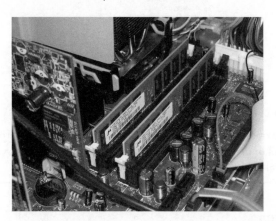

Some notebook computers have some of their RAM permanently built into the motherboard, so you can't replace it (or at least not easily). For example, you may have a notebook PC that has 4 GB of RAM in total—2 GB built in and 2 GB on a SODIMM in an expansion slot. If you want to upgrade this PC's RAM to 6 GB, for example, you can't do anything with the 2 GB on the motherboard, and the single RAM expansion slot is already full, so you need to remove the 2 GB in the expansion slot and replace it with a 4 GB SODIMM. You can open the computer's case and check the RAM slots, or you can use a software utility that tells you the status of each slot.

It's also very important to buy the right type of RAM. As you learned in Chapter 1, "Core Computer Hardware," there are many differentiating factors for RAM including speed, physical size, capacity, and error-correction features. Your motherboard probably supports only one or two different types, so consult your PC's manual or a reliable reference, such as the Crucial utility used in the following exercise, to determine what to buy.

EXERCISE 7.3

Checking the RAM

1. Open a web browser, and go to www.crucial.com/store/drammemory.aspx. Click Scan My System. Then click Download The Scanner, and follow the prompts to install the scanning tool. The website automatically detects your OS and offers the appropriate version; if you're installing the Mac version, drag it into the Applications folder after the download.

2. Run the scanning tool. It reports what memory you have installed and what slots are available. Here's an example of the results. On this system, one slot holds 4 GB, one holds 2 GB, and there are no empty slots. The report also tells what type(s) of RAM would be compatible with this system—DDR3 PC3-8500 or DD$3 PC3-10600.

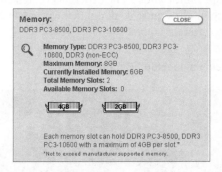

3. Close the web browser.

4. (Optional) If you don't want to keep this scanning tool, remove it from the Control Panel (Windows) or drag it out of the Applications folder (Mac) as you learned to do in Chapter 6, "Installing and Configuring Software."

Hard Disk Drives

Replacing the main hard disk drive in a notebook or other portable computer isn't easy, but it may be the only available option if there is room for only one hard drive. Replacing a hard drive means backing up all its data, installing the new drive, partitioning and formatting the drive, and then restoring the data to it.

Adding another hard drive and keeping your old one too is easier, but installing an internal drive requires an available *drive bay* (that is, a cavity where a drive can be mounted). In a desktop PC, there is almost always room for at least one more hard drive. (It doesn't hurt to peek inside the case and make sure before you buy, though.) In a notebook PC, there almost never is an open bay. If you don't have an open bay, you can use an external USB or FireWire drive instead to increase your storage capacity.

In addition to a drive bay for an additional drive, you'll also need an available power plug for it. Parallel ATA (PATA) drives use a standard 4-pin *Molex connector* like the one shown in Figure 7.2. Most Serial ATA (SATA) drives use a special power connector designed specifically for them, like the one shown in Figure 7.3. (Some use a traditional Molex connector, so that's another shopping factor to consider.) Make sure you have an available power connector inside the PC for the drive type you want.

FIGURE 7.2   Molex power connector for a PATA drive

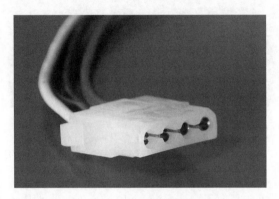

FIGURE 7.3   SATA power connector for a SATA drive

You'll also need to connect the drive to the motherboard. If you're replacing an existing drive, you can use the same connector the old one used. However, if you're adding a new hard drive, you'll need an available PATA or SATA connector.

If you're adding a PATA drive, your system probably has two PATA connectors on the motherboard (see Figure 7.4), and each one can support a cable that can have up to two drives on it. Therefore, you'll need to count the number of PATA devices you already have and make sure it's fewer than four. Otherwise, you need to remove one of the existing drives, install an expansion card that supports more PATA drives, or choose a SATA drive instead.

FIGURE 7.4   Parallel ATA motherboard connectors

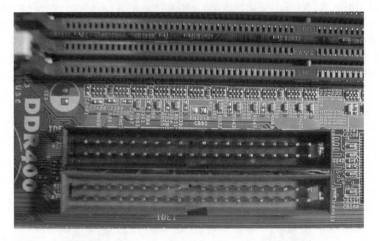

Photo credit: Wikimedia Commons

If you're adding a SATA drive, look for an available SATA connector on the motherboard (see Figure 7.5). With SATA, each drive has its own separate cable and connection to the motherboard. On some motherboards, there may be different speeds of SATA connectors, such as SATA 6.0 Gb/s and SATA 3.0 Gb/s. If so, they will be colored differently so you can easily tell them apart. Assign the fastest interface to the primary hard drive, or to the drive that is new and fast enough to benefit from its higher speed.

FIGURE 7.5   Serial ATA motherboard connectors

Copyright 2011, Bestofmedia, LLC

Regardless of the hard-drive interface you choose, you'll have choices to make in these other areas:

Capacity   How much data does the drive hold? More is better but also more expensive.

Rotational Speed   This applies to mechanical hard disks only, not solid state.

Revolutions Per Minute (RPM)   More RPM means faster data storage and retrieval. So, for example, 7200 RPM is better than 5400 RPM.

Mechanical vs. Solid State   As you learned in Chapter 2 ("Input and Storage Devices"), solid-state drives are quiet, fast, and reliable, but more expensive.

Display Adapters

On a notebook/portable computer, you're usually stuck with the display adapter that came with it. That is, display adapters are usually built into the motherboard.

On a desktop PC, the display adapter may be built into the motherboard or may be found on a separate circuit board (expansion card). Either way, you can choose to install another display adapter instead, or in addition to the one(s) installed already. If you don't want to use the one built into the motherboard anymore, you can disable it in the BIOS Setup program. You can add as many display adapters to the system as it has compatible expansion slots available. You can then hook up a different monitor to each one.

Most display adapters sold today use a PCI Express (PCIe) 16x slot (for the higher-end cards) or 4x slot (for the cheaper ones). Either will work fine for most uses; high-end gamers and graphics professionals prefer the 16x versions because they provide that extra oomph in graphics performance that most of us don't need.

Does your motherboard have the right slot for the display adapter you want to install? Entry-level motherboards may have only one 16x PCIe slot and one or two 1x slots (and perhaps no 4x slot), but higher-end motherboards may have multiples of one or more types. If you have a desktop PC, open the case and see what slots are available and in what slot your current display adapter resides. Figure 7.6 shows some PCIe slots, plus one older-type PCI slot at the bottom. One additional consideration is that there are different versions of PCIe; look for PCIe 2.0 or higher, and whether your motherboard's PCIe slots will support it.

FIGURE 7.6   PCIe and PCI slots (from top to bottom: PCIe 4x, PCIe 16x, PCIe 1x, PCIe 16X, and PCI)

Photo credit: Wikimedia Commons

Besides choosing the interface to use, you should also consider these factors when shopping for a display adapter (additional or replacement):

Amount of RAM   The more RAM a display adapter has available to it, the higher the resolutions it can display and the better its 3D support.

Cooling   Higher-powered display adapters typically have either an active or a passive cooling device on one or more of the chips. As you learned in Chapter 1, active cooling is more effective but requires more power to operate.

Output Ports   Some display adapters support only VGA or DVI output, but most cards have at least one of each of those port types, or two DVI ports.

Maximum Resolution   As you learned in Chapter 3 ("Peripherals and Networking"), monitor resolution is expressed in number of pixels horizontally × vertically, like this: 1920 × 1200. Higher is better, but only to the extent that your monitor can keep up.

Core Clock   A display adapter has its own processor, which has a clock speed measured in MHz. Higher is better.

Memory Speed   A display adapter that has its own RAM also has a RAM clock speed (in MHz) and a memory bandwidth (in GB/sec).

Devices That Use External Ports

If you're adding or upgrading an external device, what port will you plug it into? Does your computer have the right port? We looked at ports pretty extensively in Chapter 4 ("Setting Up a Computer"), so look back there now if you need a refresher on the various ports and their standards (USB, FireWire, and so on).

Most external devices use the USB port. Depending on the age of the system, this could be a USB 1.1, 2.0, or 3.0 port. Each of those has a different maximum speed, but they're backward compatible with earlier versions. So, for example, if the computer has a USB 2.0 port and you're using a device that requires a USB 1.1 port, you're good to go. The device will operate at its maximum speed. However, if the situation is reversed and the computer's USB port is of a lower standard than the device, you may have a problem if the device requires a high-speed connection. (An external hard disk is the most common example.)

With FireWire, the original spec is FireWire 400, the most commonly used type. A FireWire Alpha port is shown in Chapter 4, Figure 4.19. There are also two newer FireWire standards called FireWire 800 and FireWire S800T that are data-compatible with FireWire 400 but require a special adapter to make the ports physically compatible.

When you're replacing devices on an old PC, keep in mind that the type of port used in the original device may not be widely available anymore. For example, you may have an old parallel printer that you're replacing, but parallel-interface printers are no longer sold today; instead you'll need to get a USB model. Most PCs have at least one USB port, even those that are old enough to support parallel printers, but it doesn't hurt to check before you buy.

Keyboards and mice that use a PS/2 connection can easily be replaced by USB models; just leave the PS/2 ports on the system empty and connect the new devices to USB ports. If the system is so old that it doesn't have a USB port, or you don't have one free, you can buy

PS/2-to-USB adapters (and also the reverse) to swap keyboards and mice between those two interfaces.

 Newer Mac computers, including the MacBook Pro and iMac, have a new type of high-performance multiuse connector called Thunderbolt. It can be used for everything from hard drives to input devices to displays.

Assessing the Risks Involved in Hardware Upgrades

Any time you buy and attempt to install hardware, there are risks involved. Most of these are minor compared to the benefits you stand to achieve by upgrading. Such risks can be minimized with proper diligence.

One of the biggest risks in buying an upgrade component is that it won't be compatible with your system, and that you'll be stuck with a part that doesn't work and unable to return it for some reason. Buying from a retailer with a liberal return policy is one way to hedge your bet, but it's better to consider compatibility carefully before you reach for your wallet.

As we've outlined in greater detail in the preceding sections, compatibility involves the following:

Physical Compatibility   Will the component physically fit into your system or its ports? For example, if you're buying a FireWire external hard disk, make sure you have a FireWire port.

System Compatibility   Will your system recognize and accept the component? For example, when buying RAM, make sure you buy the right speed.

Operating System Compatibility   Is a driver available for this device for your OS? For example, if you buy a device designed for the Mac, it may not work on a PC and vice versa.

These compatibility concerns and more are usually addressed on the box in which the device is packaged, so you can read about its requirements before you leave the store.

When you upgrade to a new version of a device, the OS may get confused if you're replacing it with an only slightly different model. Therefore, it's best to uninstall the driver of the old device you're removing before you install a new one to replace it. To uninstall the software for an old device in Windows, first check the Programs list in the Control Panel as you learned in Chapter 6, and remove any software associated with that device. Then unplug the device, or remove it from the system. (Remember to shut down the PC first unless it's a USB or FireWire device you're removing.)

Upgrading a piece of hardware may also cause glitches with applications. For example, you may have webcam software that works only with certain models, and your new camera may be incompatible with it. Check with the software maker to see if an updated version is available that supports newer models.

Earlier in the chapter, you learned about the importance of an available PATA or SATA connector when selecting hard drives and expansion cards (such as display adapters). Data bus differences can also be the source of hardware incompatibilities, such as trying to use a

USB 2.0 device in a USB 1.1 port or a PCIe 16x display adapter in a system that doesn't have an available PCIe 16x slot. Power-connection incompatibilities can also occur, such as when you need to connect a SATA device but your power supply has no free SATA power-supply connectors.

Incompatible or insufficient hardware can result in failures of various types. Here are some examples:

- A USB hub, in theory, can support dozens of devices. However, if many of those devices are unpowered (that is, they rely on drawing the power they need from the USB port without a separate power supply), a USB hub can reach its maximum power output quickly, and some of the devices may not receive enough power. Your OS may warn you that that's what's going on or some of the devices may simply stop working.

- Your PC's power supply can also become overloaded if you have many devices installed that draw lots of power. For example, if you have three full-size mechanical hard drives in a system with a cheap power supply, installing a fourth drive may cause problems at startup because there isn't enough power to allow all four drives to spin up at once.

- A new device may not show up in the OS until you install the device driver for it. Further, when you install a new device driver, that driver may be incompatible with some other driver already installed, or it may overwrite system files that some other application or device needs.

- Although this rarely occurs anymore, on some older versions of Windows device-resource conflicts may still occur where Windows assigns the same resources to multiple devices. System resources include things like I/O addresses, memory addresses, and Interrupt Request lines (IRQs). You can troubleshoot such problems in the Device Manager by manually assigning resources to a device so that it no longer conflicts with other devices. That type of configuration is beyond the scope of this book.

Installing Upgrades

Next, let's get down to the nitty-gritty and talk about the procedures for physically installing upgrade components.

Safety Considerations

Computers aren't very dangerous; you generally have to work pretty hard to hurt yourself while working on one. Here are some safety tips:

- Wear short sleeves, or roll up your sleeves, so you don't get a sleeve caught on a sharp corner and rip it.

- Remove jewelry, especially dangling earrings and neck chains, so you don't catch them on anything that may be sticking out.

- Don't open a computer's power supply or poke around inside it through the vent holes, because its capacitor stores electricity and could shock you.

On the other hand, the innards of computers are quite susceptible to being damaged, so the more urgent safety concern is for the computer itself.

In Chapter 5 ("Maintaining a Computer"), you learned about electrostatic discharge (ESD) and how it can easily damage a sensitive component such as a circuit board or a DIMM. Reread the section "Electrostatic Discharge" in Chapter 5 now, before you get started inside a PC, paying special attention to the precautions recommended such as wearing natural-fiber clothing, not working in a carpeted area, and using an antistatic wrist strap (and antistatic mat, if available) to ground yourself. Figure 7.7 shows a wrist strap and mat.

FIGURE 7.7   An antistatic wrist strap and a grounded antistatic mat can help prevent electrostatic discharge damage.

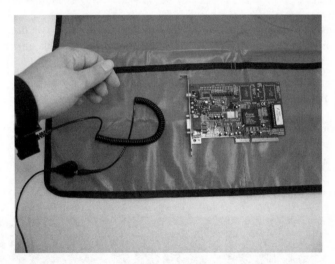

Disconnect the power to the PC before you open its case. The risk of shocking yourself is fairly low, but the risk of electrical damage to the PC itself is higher when it's plugged in.

It's also important to handle components carefully. Handle circuit boards by their edges, avoiding touching anything on the surfaces of the boards. Leave circuit boards and DIMMs in their antistatic bags until you're ready to install them, and ground yourself (by touching the metal frame of the PC) before you touch them. Figure 7.8 shows a circuit board in an antistatic bag. Notice the lines on the bag; they're part of the antistatic "cage" that the bag creates for the component.

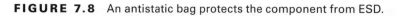

FIGURE 7.8 An antistatic bag protects the component from ESD.

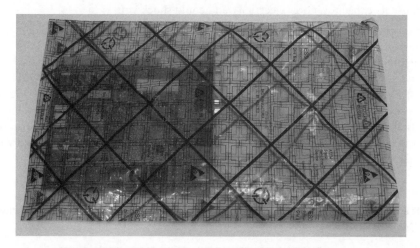

Be as gentle as possible with the cables you handle, making sure you don't loosen the wires' connection to the connector plugs. Don't bend or crimp a cable unnecessarily as doing so could cause a wire inside to break.

Installing Memory

To install memory, first determine where the memory should be placed. If it's a notebook/portable computer, there may be a panel that you remove from the bottom of the computer, perhaps with a small screwdriver (see Figure 7.9).

FIGURE 7.9 RAM on a notebook PC is often behind a removable panel.

If it's a desktop PC, you open the case and find the RAM slots on the motherboard.

Next, determine whether you need to remove any of the existing RAM. As mentioned earlier in this chapter, you may need to remove some lower-capacity RAM so that higher-capacity RAM can be inserted into its slot. To remove RAM, release any clips that are holding it in place, and then grasp the RAM firmly by its edge and pull it straight out.

To insert RAM, orient it so that it's going straight into the slot, and make sure any ridges or cutouts on the edge align with the corresponding tabs on the RAM slot. Then press firmly with the RAM perpendicular to the motherboard, pushing only on the edge of the RAM, until it snaps into place (see Figure 7.10).

FIGURE 7.10   Insert RAM firmly into a slot by pushing on the edge.

After you insert the RAM, push on it again to double-check that it's seated firmly and that the clips are holding it in place; then close the case and try booting the computer. If all goes well, the new RAM will be automatically recognized. If the PC boots OK but the RAM isn't recognized, you may have installed the wrong type, or it may not be firmly seated or may be in the wrong slot. If the PC beeps and doesn't boot, the new RAM may be defective.

EXERCISE 7.4

Remove and Install RAM

1. Unplug the PC, and open the case. If it's a notebook PC, open the panel where the RAM is contained.

2. Remove the RAM from the system.

3. Reinstall the RAM.

4. Restart the computer, and confirm that everything still works.

Installing an Internal Disk Drive

Installing an internal disk drive in a notebook computer can be a difficult process because the parts are so small; in addition, on most notebooks you must remove many layers to get to the hard disk. For example, you may need to remove the keyboard to access the chamber where the hard disk is stored. The difficulty is compounded by the fact that there are so many different notebook computer case designs, and each one comes apart differently. Therefore, it's a good idea to go online and get the service manual for your model of notebook if it's available. The service manual will provide step-by-step instructions about what screws and components need to be removed and in what order. If no service manual is available, you may want to have a professional do the upgrade for you in a computer repair shop. Figure 7.11 shows a PATA hard disk drive in a notebook computer, located under the touchpad. Notice that the cable is a thin plastic ribbon with very tiny wires, and there is a plastic loop you can pull to remove the connector from the drive.

FIGURE 7.11   Hard disk in a notebook computer

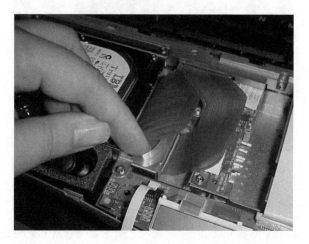

On the other hand, most users can easily install a new hard disk drive in a desktop PC with minimal effort. The following sections cover the basic information you need.

Setting Jumpers on a PATA Drive

If you're installing a parallel ATA drive, you have to set a jumper on the drive to tell it if it's the master, slave, or only drive on that cable, or to tell it that you're using Cable Select to determine the drive's master/slave status. As you learned in Chapter 2, PATA drives can be installed two per cable, but only one of them can be in charge. The drive in charge is the master. It receives all the data from the motherboard, and it passes on any messages to the other drive—the slave drive—as needed. Jumpers aren't present on a SATA drive because there is only one SATA drive per cable.

There should be a chart on the drive's label, or lettering above the jumpers, to tell you what the settings represent (see Figure 7.12). If you don't get the jumper setting right, the drive may not work and the other drive on that cable may stop working until you get the settings straightened out.

FIGURE 7.12   Setting the jumper on a PATA drive

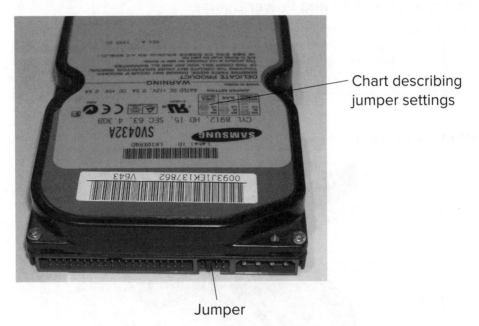

Chart describing jumper settings

Jumper

Selecting a Drive Bay and Installing the Drive

Open the case, and find an available drive bay. A *drive bay* is a chamber inside the PC that is designed to hold a disk drive. Hard drives don't need to be accessed externally, so you don't need one of the externally accessible drive bays for it; look for one of the smaller bays, sized to fit a hard drive. If there is an existing hard drive, notice how it's held in place in the case. It may be installed in a metal cage that can be removed from the rest of the case. You may need to remove the cage in order to attach the screws on the far side of the new drive. The cage is usually held in place by one or two screws.

All other drives are externally accessible, including DVD and CD drives. If installing an externally accessible drive, pop off the plastic faceplate in front of an available drive bay. (It's usually easiest to push it out from the back if you can reach your hand inside that far.) If there is a metal plate behind the plastic one, pop that out with a screwdriver.

Next, slide the drive into the bay. If you're working with a removable cage for a hard drive, attach the drive to the cage with screws and then replace the cage in the main case. If you're installing the drive in a bay that is part of the main case, simply set the drive loosely into the bay for the moment; you can attach it with screws after you've run the cables. It's easier to fit your hand into the tight spaces where the cables connect if the drive isn't already secured.

Some cases don't use screws to hold the drives in place; instead they use plastic rails that snap onto the sides of the drive and then slide into grooves in the drive bays. Check the existing drives to see how they're secured, and follow that lead.

Connecting the Data and Power Cables

Next, connect the cables to the drive. Each drive requires two cables: one to connect to the motherboard, and one to connect to the power supply. PATA drives use a 40-pin ribbon cable to connect to the motherboard and a four-pin Molex connector to the power supply. SATA drives use a small SATA connector and cable to connect to the motherboard and a SATA power connector to connect to the power supply (see Figure 7.13).

FIGURE 7.13 Connect the power and data cables.

If you're connecting a PATA ribbon cable, you need to make sure the red stripe on the cable, which signifies pin 1, is at the end closest to where the power connector plugs into the disk drive. Some cables are keyed to prevent you from putting them on backward.

 If your motherboard and/or power supply don't have the appropriate connectors to attach the drive you want to use, adapters are available at your local computer store that will change the plugs to the right size (and voltage).

Powering Up and Partitioning/Formatting

After the drive has been physically installed, start up the computer and try it out. If it's a CD or DVD drive, it should work automatically with no special setup. Optical drives use the standard drivers that come with the OS and don't require proprietary drivers in most cases.

If you fire up a new hard disk drive and it doesn't appear to be accessible, don't panic. That's normal. A new hard disk will need to be partitioned and formatted before you use it (unless it happens to be partitioned and formatted already). See Chapter 2, which explained the partitioning and formatting procedures. You can use the Disk Management utility, which is part of the Computer Management utility in Windows, to partition and format a drive.

If you're given a choice of filesystems with which to format a drive in Windows, choose NTFS. That's the most efficient and effective filesystem. Choose FAT32 only if you require backward-compatibility with a very old version of Windows (Windows 98/Millennium Edition, for example).

If Disk Management doesn't see the drive either, you may need to go into BIOS Setup and change a setting or two in order for the drive to be recognized. Some BIOS Setup programs enable certain PATA or SATA controllers to be turned off to save system resources, and if this drive is using a motherboard connector that has not been previously used, it may need to be turned on.

EXERCISE 7.5

Remove and Install a Disk Drive

1. Unplug a desktop PC, and open the case.

2. Remove one of the disk drives from the system. If it's a PATA drive, examine its jumper settings. Don't change them.

3. Reinstall the drive.

4. Restart the computer, and confirm that everything still works.

Installing a Circuit Board

Some upgrades for desktop PCs come in the form of circuit boards that fit into slots in the motherboard. Such upgrades can include display adapters, network adapters, modems, sound cards, and so on.

Before you bought the circuit board, presumably you checked to make sure you had the right slot available on the motherboard, so the actual process of installing the circuit board should be fairly simple.

First, open the case and identify how the circuit boards are held in place. On some systems, a clamp or bar holds them all down, as shown in Figure 7.14. On others, each board is held in place by its own screw that attaches to the metal back plate of the case.

Next, if you're replacing an old board, remove it. Release the clip or screw that holds it in place, and then pull it straight up out of the slot, holding the card by its edges.

FIGURE 7.14   Some cases use a single retaining bar for all circuit boards.

If you're installing the circuit board in a slot that wasn't previously in use, you may need to remove a metal spacer plate that exposes that slot to the outside. After doing so, press the circuit board firmly straight down into the slot, pressing only by the edges. You may need to "see-saw" it a bit lengthwise if it's a tight fit. After seating the card firmly in the slot, secure it with a clip or screw as appropriate.

Next, close the case, reconnect the power to the PC, and boot up. If the device is automatically detected—great. You can optionally install the software that came with it, or use it as is. If the device isn't automatically detected, run the Setup program that came with the device.

EXERCISE 7.6

Remove and Install a Circuit Board

1.   Unplug a desktop PC, and open the case.

2.   Remove one of the circuit boards from the motherboard.

3.   Reinstall the circuit board.

4.   Restart the computer, and confirm that everything still works.

Summary

In this chapter, you learned how to evaluate a system to see if a hardware upgrade would be advantageous. You learned how to select compatible components of several types including RAM, disk drives, and display adapters. You also studied how to install them safely.

Exam Essentials

Understand how to evaluate a system for possible upgrades.   You can examine the components physically to find out their specifications, but it's often easier to use a utility program such as System Information or the Windows Experience Index to determine what components may be holding back optimal performance.

Identify the risks associated with upgrading components.   When upgrading a working system, there is always a chance that the system will no longer function after the upgrade has been completed. This can be due to hardware, BIOS, or software incompatibilities; malfunctioning hardware; or improper installation.

Identify basic compatibility issues.   You must select upgrade components carefully with compatibility in mind, considering physical bus differences, bus speeds, and driver availability. It's especially important to understand the challenges of finding compatible components in the areas of processors and RAM, as well as external ports such as USB, FireWire, and PS/2.

Review Questions

1. A device that doesn't work well in a system can sometimes be improved by updating its _____.

   A. IRQ

   B. Driver

   C. CPU

   D. Registers

2. Where in Windows do you check a device-driver version and install a newer one?

   A. Device Manager

   B. System Configuration Utility

   C. System Information

   D. System Restore

3. How is the Windows Experience Index base score determined for a system?

   A. Lowest value of the key component scores

   B. Highest value of the key component scores

   C. Median value of the key component scores

   D. Average value of the key component scores

4. If video playback is choppy or the screen repaints itself slowly when loading a large graphic, which component may need an upgrade?

   A. CPU

   B. RAM

   C. Display adapter

   D. Hard disk

5. If the computer slows down when you run many programs at once, or you hear the hard disk doing a lot of reading and writing even though you aren't opening or saving large files, your system may need more _____.

   A. CPU speed

   B. RAM

   C. Display adapter memory

   D. Hard disk space

6. Which Windows utility can show you what processes are consuming the most RAM?

   A. System Information

   B. System Configuration Utility

   C. Disk Defragmenter

   D. Task Manager

7. Why is upgrading the processor seldom done?

   A. It is very difficult and time-consuming to do.

   B. Most motherboards accept only a narrow range of processors.

   C. Processors are so fragile that they often break as you install them.

   D. An operating system is locked to a specific processor.

8. To what type of component would a Molex power connector attach?

   A. SATA

   B. PATA

   C. Display adapter

   D. RAM

9. How many SATA drives can you have per cable?

   A. 1

   B. 2

   C. 4

   D. Unlimited

10. If your desktop system has a built-in display adapter and you want to replace it, what can you do?

   A. Nothing; you are stuck with it.

   B. Install a PCIe display adapter, and disable the old adapter in BIOS Setup.

   C. Install a new VGA display adapter. The old one will be disabled automatically.

   D. Install a new ExpressCard display adapter, and disable the old adapter in BIOS Setup.

11. Which type of PCIe slot would be most appropriate for a display adapter?

   A. 1x

   B. 2x

   C. 16x

   D. 32x

12. What will happen if you connect a USB 1.1 device to a USB 2.0 port on a PC?

    A. The device will work fine.

    B. The device will work, but in reduced functionality mode.

    C. The device will work, but at a lower speed than it is capable of.

    D. The device won't work at all.

13. Can you use a FireWire 400 device in a FireWire 800 port?

    A. Yes, with no adaptation needed.

    B. Yes, but the device will not operate at maximum speed.

    C. Yes, but you need an adapter to make the plug physically compatible.

    D. No, they are different technologies that are not compatible.

14. Handle circuit boards by touching only the _____.

    A. Flat part of the board

    B. Edges

    C. Transistors

    D. Chips

15. Circuit boards should be stored in an antistatic bag until you are ready to install them, to avoid _____ damage.

    A. DVI

    B. VGA

    C. ESI

    D. ESD

16. When installing a DIMM in a motherboard, which of the following should you do?

    A. Push the DIMM straight down into the slot, perpendicular to the motherboard.

    B. Push in the DIMM at a 45-degree angle.

    C. Push in the DIMM at a 30-degree angle, and then rotate it up to a 90-degree angle to lock it in place.

    D. Lay the DIMM into the motherboard flat, parallel to the motherboard.

17. What kind of drives require you to set master/slave jumpers?

    A. SATA

    B. PATA

    C. SCSI

    D. Solid state

18. To install a new hard disk in a desktop computer, you need an open _____.

    A. PCIe slot

    B. Drive bay

    C. Chipset

    D. DVI connector

19. If Windows doesn't see your new hard disk drive in the computer window, what may you need to do?

    A. Delete its previous contents.

    B. Copy files to it.

    C. Attach a USB device.

    D. Partition it.

20. If asked to choose a filesystem on a Windows 7 computer when formatting a new disk drive, what should you choose?

    A. CDFS

    B. NTFS

    C. FAT16

    D. FAT12

Answers to Review Questions

1. **B.** Installing a new device driver can sometimes fix problems or introduce minor feature upgrades.

2. **A.** Device Manager shows each device and its driver version. You can access it as a standalone tool or as part of Computer Management, as demonstrated in Exercise 7.1.

3. **A.** The lowest score among the key components determines the base score, because that component creates a bottleneck in performance.

4. **C.** Video playback problems and graphic delays may indicate that a better display adapter is needed.

5. **B.** More RAM can help run more programs at once without a performance slowdown.

6. **D.** In Task Manager, the Processes tab shows the amount of RAM used by each process.

7. **B.** Although processors are not particularly difficult to install, most motherboards accept only a few similar processors, so dramatic system improvement cannot usually be obtained by upgrading the processor.

8. **B.** A parallel ATA drive would use a Molex power connector from the power supply.

9. **A.** Serial ATA (SATA) drives can have only one drive per cable. That's why they don't require any jumpers, unlike PATA, which supports up to two drives per cable.

10. **B.** Add-on display adapters sold today use the PCIe bus. You can then disable the old adapter in BIOS Setup or leave it enabled for connecting additional monitors.

11. **C.** A 16x slot is most often used for a display adapter. 1x slots are used for devices requiring less bandwidth, such as modems. There is no such slot as 2x or 32x on PC motherboards.

12. **A.** Because a USB 1.1 device has a slower maximum speed than a USB 2.0 port, the device will be able to function at its full maximum speed, unhindered by the limitations of the port.

13. **C.** FireWire 400 and FireWire 800 are logically compatible (except for the speed, which is limited to the lower of the two's capabilities), but physically an adapter is required.

14. **B.** Circuit boards, including DIMMs, should be handled by the edges only whenever possible.

15. **D.** Electrostatic discharge, or static electricity, can ruin a circuit board. An antistatic bag protects against ESD.

16. **A.** DIMMS are inserted perpendicular to the motherboard.

17. **B.** Parallel ATA drives have a master/slave cable select setting that you control with a jumper.

18. **B.** A new hard disk needs a drive bay in which to mount it. A PCIe slot would hold a circuit board, not a drive.

19. **D.** Except in the Disk Management utility, Windows cannot see new hard drives until they have been partitioned.

20. **B.** NTFS is the best filesystem to use in most cases. FAT16 is a very old filesystem that is now obsolete. CDFS is the filesystem on CD-ROMs. FAT12 is the filesystem used on floppy disks, now obsolete.

Troubleshooting and Security

Chapter

8

Troubleshooting Operational Problems

OBJECTIVES COVERED IN THIS CHAPTER:

✓ **Fundamentals of Technology (U.K.)**

✓ **IT Fundamentals (U.S.)**

✓ **2.2 Recognize common operational problems caused by hardware**

- Critical error message or crash

- System lockup (freeze)

- Application will not start or load

- Cannot logon to network

- Driver/hardware compatibility

- Input device will not function

When computers don't work properly, they can create big headaches for the users who rely on them. In this chapter, you'll learn how to troubleshoot some common operational problems with personal computers, including crashes, error message, lockups, and hardware failures.

Startup Failure

The operating system provides the platform from which you launch all the activities you do with a computer, so when it won't start, nothing productive can happen until you fix it. Depending on the OS and version, the steps involved for troubleshooting will vary. The following sections present some general guidance and introduce some troubleshooting tools that may be useful.

Nothing on the Monitor

If you turn on the computer and nothing happens—no fan spinning, no nothing—you probably have some type of power problem. Check that the computer is plugged in. A bad motherboard or CPU can also cause the computer to appear dead. Those failures, however, are less likely if the computer has been working in the past than if you're assembling a new one from scratch.

If you hear fans spinning but nothing shows up onscreen, there's probably an issue with the monitor, display adapter, memory, or motherboard. It can be difficult to figure out which of these may be faulty without an error message to guide you. If you have a spare display adapter or DIMM, you can try swapping it out, but it's often easier to take the computer to a repair shop at this point.

If you're determined to troubleshoot on your own, a device called a *POST card* may be useful. POST stands for power-on Self test. A POST card is a circuit board you insert into an open slot in the motherboard. The card displays a two-digit numeric code on its LED to tell you where the system is in the booting process. A book that accompanies the POST card tells what each number represents. When the boot process stalls, read the code on the POST card and look it up to figure out where the boot process has broken down, and that may tell you which component has failed.

Black-Screen or Blue-Screen Error Message

A plain-text error message (gray text on a black screen) is usually a message from the BIOS prior to the OS load. A failed or soon-to-be-failed hard disk most often triggers such a message. The exact wording of the BIOS-thrown error messages varies depending on the BIOS company and version; you may see a message like "Disk Drive Failure" or "No Boot Disk Found."

Although hard-disk errors are the most common errors that appear before the OS load, they aren't the only possible errors at this point. You may see a message that the keyboard has a key stuck, for example, or that there is an error involving RAM.

If the error message appears as grey or white text on a bright blue background, that's a *STOP error*. It's called a STOP because the first word on the screen is usually STOP, and the PC freezes up when it appears, requiring you to power the PC off and back on again to continue. Some techie types call this error a *Blue Screen of Death (BSOD)*. This type of error often means that a piece of hardware (usually something like a network adapter, sound card, or modem) is defective or incompatible with your Windows version, but there are also other reasons for STOP errors, specific to the error code that displays.

To diagnose a STOP error, look up the error code on a website that provides a directory of such errors. Here are a few good sources to get you started:

http://www.aumha.org/a/stop.php

http://win-experts.com/windows-xp/xp-stop-errors/

http://pcsupport.about.com/od/findbyerrormessage/tp/stop_error_list.htm

Based on what you discover, you may need to remove or replace a hardware component or reinstall or repair the OS.

Windows Won't Load

Windows requires certain files to be present, usable, and in the expected location in order to start up. These files are mostly stored in the C:\Windows\System32 or C:\Windows SysWOW64 folder, and they include WinLoad.exe, Ntoskrnl.exe, Hal.dll, WinLogon.exe, and others. If any of these files are unavailable, Windows won't load and an error message will tell you what's missing. You may need to reinstall or repair Windows in order to fix the problem. If you have the setup CD available for your version of Windows, you may be able to boot into the Recovery Environment (Windows Vista or 7) or the Recovery Console (Windows XP) to repair Windows. (See the section "Using the Recovery Environment" later in this chapter for details.)

Assuming Windows has all the critical files it needs to load, it reads information from the Registry as it boots up. The Registry informs it of the settings to use, what device drivers to load, and what programs should start up automatically in the background. If any of the files called for during this process are unavailable, an error message appears or the boot process simply hangs, usually after the Windows logo has briefly appeared onscreen. You may be able to boot the PC using Safe Mode, which bypasses all noncritical startup options; if the problem is with one of the noncritical files, that problem will be temporarily disabled enough to start the system. After starting up Windows (in Safe Mode if necessary), if the problem was caused by a recently installed item of hardware or software, you may be able to use System Restore to return the system configuration to its earlier state, undoing whatever action caused the problem to occur.

Using Safe Mode

When Windows won't start normally, you can often boot into Safe Mode for access to your Windows Desktop. *Safe Mode* is a low-functionality mode that bypasses all optional components, both hardware and software, loading only the minimum required to display the Desktop. You shouldn't use the computer for normal tasks in Safe Mode because of its limited functionality; stay in Safe Mode only long enough to implement whatever fixes are needed to allow Windows to boot normally again.

To enter Safe Mode, restart the computer and, as soon as you see any text on the screen, begin pressing the F8 key. Doing so displays the Advanced Options menu, a text-based menu system. Using the arrow keys, select Safe Mode (or Safe Mode With Networking) from the menu, and press Enter to start the computer in Safe Mode.

In Safe Mode, the display adapter uses a generic driver, so the screen resolution is very low and uses only a limited color set. Nonessential hardware doesn't work, such as sound cards and modems; and unless you chose Safe Mode With Networking at the Advanced Options menu, the network doesn't work either (and that includes the Internet).

If the computer starts OK in Safe Mode but doesn't start normally, you can assume that the startup problem lies in one of the nonessential hardware drivers or software applications that Safe Mode blocks from starting. From here it's just a matter of elimination.

Here are some things to try once you're in Safe Mode:

- Disconnect all nonessential external hardware devices, such as modems, external hard disks, webcams, and so on. Try to boot normally. If you can, then plug the devices back in one at a time, rebooting after each one, until you find the one with the problem.

- If you've recently installed new internal hardware, remove it and see if the problem goes away.

- If you've recently installed a new application, remove it using the Control Panel (see Chapter 6, "Installing and Configuring Software") and reboot to see if the problem goes away.

- Use System Restore, as described in the next section, to return your computer to an earlier configuration point before the problem started.

- Run the System Configuration Utility (MSCONFIG), as described later in this chapter, to prevent all noncritical applications from loading at startup. Then re-enable them one by one, rebooting each time, until you find the problem.

EXERCISE 8.1

Boot into Safe Mode

1. Restart your PC, and as soon as you hear the single beep and see text on the screen, start pressing the F8 key. The Advanced Options menu opens.

2. Press the down arrow key to highlight Safe Mode With Networking, and press Enter. The system starts up in Safe Mode.

3. Explore Safe Mode, looking for differences from normal operation.

4. Restart the computer normally.

Using System Restore

The *System Restore* feature in Windows makes a backup copy of the important system configuration files once a day (by default). You can also make additional copies at any time, such as immediately before you install new and untried hardware or software. Then, if the system doesn't work anymore after you install the new item, you can revert the system files back to the earlier versions, removing all traces of anything the new item may have brought with it.

If Windows won't start normally, or if it runs poorly all of a sudden after previously running fairly well, it's often easier to revert to a System Restore point than to spend a lot of time trying to pinpoint what happened. Start System Restore from the Start menu (Accessories ➢ System Tools folder). Then follow the prompts to select a previously saved restore point and restore that copy. Exercise 8.2 provides an opportunity to try this.

EXERCISE 8.2

Use System Restore

1. In Windows 7, open the Control Panel and choose System And Security ➢ System.

2. In the navigation pane at the left, click System Protection. The System Properties dialog box opens with the System Protection tab displayed.

EXERCISE 8.2 *(continued)*

3. Click the Create button. A System Protection dialog box opens.

4. Type **Test 1** in the text box.

5. Click Create to create the restore point, and wait for the restore point to be created.

6. Click Close to close the message box that tells you the restore point was created.

7. Close all open windows and dialog boxes.

8. Right-click the Desktop, and click Personalize.

9. Choose a different Desktop background, and then close the Control Panel.

10. Choose Start ➢ All Programs ➢ Accessories ➢ System Tools ➢ System Restore. The System Restore application opens.

11. Click Next to continue.

12. In the list of restore points, click Test 1.

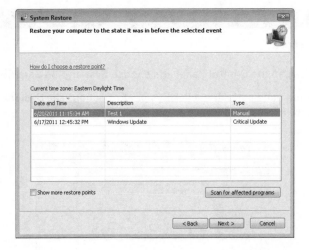

13. Click Next, and then click Finish. A warning appears that once started, System Restore can't be interrupted. Click Yes.

14. Wait for your system to restart. After it restarts, click Close to dismiss the dialog box that tells you the System Restore operation completed successfully.

15. Choose Start ➢ All Programs ➢ Accessories ➢ System Tools ➢ System Restore. The System Restore application opens.

16. Click Next to continue.

17. In the list of restore points, click Restore Operation. Notice that its type is Undo; you're going to undo the System Restore you just did.

18. Click Next, and then click Finish. A warning appears that, once started, System Restore can't be interrupted. Click Yes.

19. Wait for your system to restart. After it restarts, click Close to dismiss the confirmation box.

Using the System Configuration Utility

The *System Configuration Utility*, also known by its executable filename of *MSCONFIG*, allows Windows users to selectively disable certain applications and services that automatically load at startup. This can be a great benefit when you're trying to troubleshoot a startup problem that you're fairly sure involves one of your startup applications, but you have no idea which one.

This utility isn't found in the Windows menu system, so you have to run it using its name. Click the Start button, type **MSCONFIG**, and press Enter to open the System Configuration window shown in Figure 8.1. It's available in Safe Mode too.

FIGURE 8.1:   The System Configuration utility

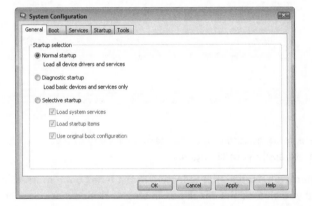

Notice that by default, Normal Startup is selected. That means everything that the Registry specifies should be loaded is loaded. The alternatives are Diagnostic Startup (which turns off everything nonessential and is useful in determining, in general, whether something loading at startup is causing the problem) and Selective Startup (which starts up using only the specific items you haven't excluded).

The Startup tab is the main feature of this utility. Click Startup to see a list of all the programs that load at startup. The length of the list may surprise you. You can drag the column widths to widen them so that you can see the text in them more clearly. The names, manufacturers, and commands can give you clues as to each program's origin and purpose. You can also use an online resource, such as the Task List reference found at www.answersthatwork.com.

EXERCISE 8.3

Use the System Configuration Utility

1. In Windows 7, click Start, type **MSCONFIG**, and press Enter. The System Configuration window opens.

2. Click the Startup tab.

3. Widen the Startup Item column by dragging the divider between the column headings until you can see all the names in that column.

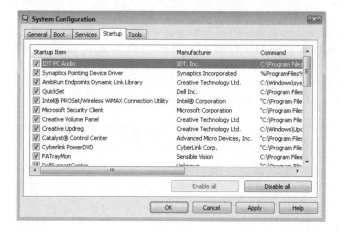

4. Clear the check mark next to one of the items. Pick any one you like, because you aren't actually going to apply your changes.

5. Click the General tab. Notice that Selective Startup has been marked. It became marked when you cleared the check box in step 4. Notice that Load System Services is still checked, and the Load Startup Items check box is solid blue, indicating that some but not all startup items are marked.

6. Click the Services tab, and clear one of the check boxes there.

7. Click back to the General tab. Notice that now the Load System Services check box is solid blue too, indicating that some but not all services are marked.

8. Click the Normal Startup option button to clear the changes you made.

9. Click the Tools tab. Notice that many of the troubleshooting tools available in Windows 7 are also available here from the central point, including Action Center, Windows Troubleshooting, and Event Viewer.

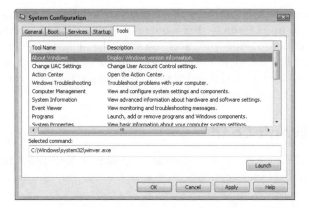

10. Click Cancel to close the System Configuration utility without making any changes.

This utility not only provides easy access to your startup options, but also offers links to many of the most commonly used troubleshooting utilities in Windows. Therefore you may want to create a shortcut for it on your Desktop. Exercise 8.4 shows you how.

EXERCISE 8.4

Create a Desktop Shortcut for MSCONFIG

1. Right-click the Desktop, and choose New ➢ Shortcut. The Create Shortcut dialog box opens.

2. In the Type The Location Of The Item text box, type **MSCONFIG**. Click Next.

3. In the Type A Name For This Shortcut text box, type **System Configuration Utility**, replacing the default name that's there.

4. Click Finish. A shortcut appears on the Desktop.

5. Double-click the shortcut to confirm that it opens the System Configuration Utility. Then close the utility window.

Using the Recovery Environment

Windows XP came with a rather difficult-to-use command-line interface called the *Recovery Console*, which you could use to access the hard disk and run a limited set of troubleshooting and recovery commands when Windows wouldn't start. The Recovery Console has been replaced in Windows Vista and Windows 7 with a friendlier interface called the *Windows Recovery Environment* (*Windows RE*).

To access Windows RE, boot from the Windows setup DVD. (You may need to change the boot sequence in BIOS Setup so that it boots from the DVD drive rather than the hard disk.) The Windows Setup utility runs as if you were installing a new copy of Windows. When prompted, click the Repair Your Computer option. Follow the prompts until you get to System Recovery Options, and then click Startup Repair. Follow the advice that Startup Repair gives to repair your Windows installation.

Mac OS X Won't Load

Macs go through the same basic process for startup as PCs. If there's a disk error, such as the ones on the black screen that a PC's BIOS may display, you'll see a flashing question-mark icon.

Here's a flowchart that can help you diagnose Mac startup problems:

http://web.whittier.edu/comp/macguide/flowchart.cfm

SOURCE: Whittier College, copyright ©2011

The flashing question mark icon means the startup process it can't find a hard disk or can't find a system folder on the hard disk. The hard disk may be disconnected, its driver may be bad, or its cable may be loose; or if it's an old enough system to still have a floppy disk drive, there may be a disk in that drive that the OS is trying to boot from instead of the hard disk.

On a Mac, the hard drive must have a System Folder that contains such items as accessories, fonts, and system utilities, plus the System file and Finder. Without these, the computer won't boot. The question-mark icon appears if this folder is missing or corrupted or doesn't contain the needed files.

Any other OS problems on a Mac result in a red circle with a diagonal line through it, called a *prohibition icon*. (Earlier versions of the Mac OS used a "sad Mac" icon in these cases.) Along with this icon, you'll see an error code that you can look up in an error-code listing, such as this one: http://support.apple.com/kb/HT1618.

Operating System Error Messages

Each OS has its own error messages that it displays in various circumstances. In most cases, you can look up these error messages online at the OS maker's website or third-party sites to determine what they mean.

To troubleshoot issues with Mac OS X, see the article "Isolating Issues in Mac OS X" on Apple's support knowledge base: http://support.apple.com/kb/TS1388.

To troubleshoot issues with Windows 7, see the article "Support for Windows 7 Technical Problems and Troubleshooting" at: http://support.microsoft.com/ph/14019.

Here are a few common Windows error messages you may encounter and what they mean:

Windows Has Recovered from a Serious Error   This message means something major has crashed, and Windows has restarted itself as a result. If you see this error once, it's probably a fluke; but if you see it frequently, you may need to repair Windows or take a critical look at what programs are loading at startup that may be causing the error.

The System Is Low on Virtual Memory. Windows Is Increasing the Size of Your Virtual Memory Paging File   This message describes what is happening when your system has run out of memory. Do you have too many applications running for the amount of memory installed? As a result, Windows increases the paging file size so that it won't happen again (presumably). If the PC is running slowly, try rebooting.

Data Error Reading/Writing Drive   This message means Windows is having trouble reading from or writing to whatever drive letter it lists in the error message. Run CHKDSK (from the drive's Properties dialog box on the Tools tab), and select the Scan For And Attempt Recovery Of Bad Sectors check box to assess the drive.

A Runtime Error Has Occurred. Do You Wish to Debug?   This is an Internet Explorer error message, normally caused by badly written code being delivered from the website. It isn't your PC's fault. If you find this message annoying, you can change a setting in Internet Explorer to prevent it from appearing. From the Control Panel, choose Network And Internet, and then Internet Options. On the Advanced tab, in the Browsing section, select the Disable Script Debugging (Internet Explorer) check box.

The Event Viewer utility in Windows can sometimes provide information about an error event that has occurred, helping you to narrow down what may have caused it. You can access the Event Viewer from the Control Panel in the Administrative Tools section.

OS Slowdown or Lockup

Sometimes you may be working along in your OS when, all of a sudden, everything slows to a crawl. Simple things like opening an application and closing a window take much longer than usual.

There are two basic reasons why slowdowns happen. One is that the physical memory is mostly used up, so the system is relying more on its paging file than usual. Because the paging file is on the hard disk, and the hard disk is slower than real RAM, operations involving heavy use of the paging file take longer. The other reason is that the CPU is being heavily used, so each operation that needs the CPU's attention has to wait its turn.

That begs the question: what causes the RAM and/or the CPU to be used heavily? They can be legitimately used by applications if you run a lot of applications at once, especially those that require a lot of processing power. Big graphics-editing programs like Photoshop qualify, for example. The RAM and CPU can also be improperly hijacked by a malfunctioning program or by a virus or other malware application.

> When you first start up the OS, it's normal for application-related activities to take longer than normal, because the OS continues to finish loading behind the scenes for up to several minutes after the OS interface becomes usable. If you try to start up several applications immediately after starting the PC, and they don't start up quickly enough to suit you, be patient. Within a few minutes, your computer should be running normally again.

To check the memory and CPU usage in Windows, use the Task Manager. You practiced doing this in Exercise 7.2. Right-click the taskbar, and choose Start Task Manager. Then, on the Processes tab, sort by the Memory column and look for a process that is using an inordinate amount of memory. Terminate it if necessary to get back normal control of your computer. You can also look on the Performance tab to see the RAM and CPU usage statistics.

If the OS locks up completely, usually including the mouse pointer, the most common cause is overheating. If the CPU or another chip on the motherboard overheats, the system locks up. The OS can lock up like that for other reasons than overheating, such as a corrupted system file (repair the OS to fix that), but that's less likely. By halting rather than continuing to operate in an overheated state, the motherboard preserves the valuable CPU chip, which may be damaged if it continued to run. The monitor may go blank, or it may keep displaying the last information it was sent, so the image on the screen appears frozen in time.

If your OS has locked up, shut off the PC if it didn't shut itself down. Open the case, and let the PC sit for 10 to 15 minutes so everything cools off. Then, with the case open, turn on the computer again and see whether any fans aren't spinning. The problem may be as simple as a faulty fan. There should be a fan inside the power supply, a fan on (or very near) the CPU, and possibly other fans that circulate air through the case. No faulty fans? Let the PC boot up the OS again, and let it sit. Don't run any applications. If it boots up just fine but then locks up after a few minutes without you doing anything to it, something is definitely overheating; consult a PC technician at your local repair shop for help.

Application Failures

Applications are more likely to cause problems than OSs, because there are so many different applications, all made by different manufacturers, and all expected to "play nicely" with each other, with your hardware, and with different versions of the OS.

Application Fails to Install or Fails to Run

Usually, when an application fails to install or fails to run, it's because it's somehow incompatible with your system. It could be that your OS version isn't supported or the application doesn't like a piece of hardware you've installed (most likely the sound or display adapter). The hardware may be inadequate (check the minimum requirements for the application) or simply incompatible.

Check the application's specs to make sure your system meets the minimum requirements in every way. If your system meets the requirements but the application still won't install, check out the Support section of the application manufacturer's website. There may be a patch you can download that will fix the problem, or there may be suggestions regarding workarounds. For example, in some cases, installing an updated driver for your display adapter or sound card can make an application work that previously didn't.

If the program meets all the hardware requirements but not the OS, you can try running the Setup program in *Compatibility Mode* (in Windows). Compatibility Mode tricks the application into thinking you have a different version of the OS than you actually have, bypassing any version requirements that may be built into the software. It doesn't always work, because different applications implement version requirements in various ways, and some of those ways have nothing to do with the version-specific bits and pieces that Compatibility Mode offers the application.

Another possible source of trouble when installing applications is over-zealous security. The OS itself may prevent you from installing an application, for example. If you're logged in as a standard user, you may need to log out and then log in again as an administrator. If the application being installed requires Internet access to complete the installation, you may need to tell your firewall that it's OK to let that application through. And finally, the application may make a system change that your antivirus program or security suite detects a as a threat (falsely), causing the security program to prevent the change from being made.

EXERCISE 8.5

Run an Application in Compatibility Mode

1. In Windows, choose Start ➢ All Programs, and then right-click any of the applications and choose Properties. The Properties box opens for that shortcut.

2. Click the Compatibility tab.

3. Select the Run This Program In Compatibility Mode For check box.

4. Open the drop-down list below the check box, and examine the available OSs. Click Windows 98 / Windows Me.

5. In the Settings area, select the Run In 256 Colors check box.

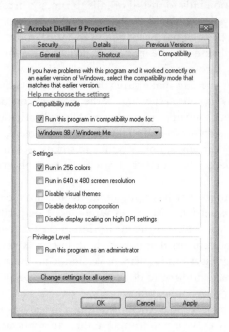

6. Click OK.

7. Select Start ➢ All Programs again, and click the program to run it. It may run, or it may not. It doesn't matter; you're just testing.

8. Close the application (if it ran).

9. Choose Start ➢ All Programs, and then right-click the same application and choose Properties again.

10. Click the Compatibility tab, and clear the Run This Program In Compatibility Mode For check box.

11. Clear the Run In 256 Colors check box.

12. Click OK to close the Properties box.

A Previously Working Application Won't Work Anymore

If an application stops working that previously worked, something has changed on your system—obviously. But what was it?

If any of the files belonging to the application have been deleted, you may need to reinstall the application. To save yourself some time, though, look in the Recycle Bin first and see if you may be able to restore the deleted files from there. If you put all the files back where they belong, the application may start working again.

A virus infection can cause programs to run slowly, poorly, or not at all. Many viruses affect the entire system, though, not just one program. Thus if you're having troubles with only one application, a virus isn't likely to be the cause. There's one exception to that: viruses sometimes target antivirus software specifically, so if everything's working other than your antivirus software, you're probably infected. See Chapter 9, "Security and Access Control," for more details about viruses and how to remove them.

Some programs have limited-time licenses, so it's possible that an application that previously worked may stop working due to a license expiration. In such cases, though, a helpful dialog box will usually appear to let you know how to pay the software maker, so there's not much doubt what's happening.

If you've recently installed an OS or application update, and then suddenly an old familiar application won't work anymore, it's probably the update's fault. You can try removing the update (if possible), or contact the application manufacturer's Support department for help.

Application Crashes

Crash is the term used to describe a situation when an application stops working. It may stop working due to a programming error in its own code or due to a conflict or compatibility issue with a device driver, with the OS, or with another application.

When an application stops working, it may terminate all by itself, or you may have to terminate it manually. To do so in Windows, right-click the taskbar and choose Start Task Manager. Then, in the Task Manager window, on the Applications tab, click the application. The task may have Not Responding in the Status column. Click End Task.

On a Mac, to force-quit an application, choose Force Quit from the Apple menu (or press Command+Option+Esc) and then select the unresponsive application in the Force Quit window and click Force Quit.

If an application crashes only once, it may be a fluke. However, if the same application keeps crashing repeatedly, it's time to do a little detective work to try to figure out what may be the problem. If an error message appears, make a note of it. Try closing all other applications, including any background applications you don't need, and running the application again to see if that helps. If it does, the problem stems from a conflict with some other program. You may need to uninstall and reinstall the crashing application, or check the manufacturer's website for troubleshooting tips.

Device Failures

Any hardware component can fail, and the longer you keep your computer, the more likely it is that you'll experience at least one hardware failure. Hardware troubleshooting can be complex, but the Strata exam confines itself to a few topics related to hardware troubleshooting. The following sections target the Strata-specified topics.

Hardware/Driver Compatibility

A *driver* is a file (or set of files) that contains information needed for the OS to communicate with a hardware device. One way to think of a driver is as a language translator between the OS, which speaks one language, and the hardware, which speaks an entirely different one.

The skill of the interpreter makes all the difference in any communication, and a driver that can accurately translate between the OS and the hardware is essential for satisfactory hardware functionality. Therefore, it's important to pick the best driver available. If an unsatisfactory driver is installed (perhaps one that's not designed specifically for the OS or device being used, or one that has been corrupted), the device may behave strangely or not work at all.

The best driver is one that is (1) specifically for that device (most important), (2) specifically for that OS (moderately important), and (3) the most recent version available (least important). When you install a hardware device, you have a choice of drivers, and your challenge is to figure out which of them fits the criteria the best. Your choices may include the following:

- The OS may supply a driver for the device and install it automatically via Plug and Play.

- The device may come with a setup CD or DVD that contains an appropriate driver.

- A driver may be available on the device manufacturer's website that is even more current than the one that came with the device.

See the section "Updating Device Drivers" in Chapter 7 ("Upgrading and Updating Hardware"), and Exercise 7.1, for information about replacing the driver a device is using.

Malfunctioning Input Devices

An input device, such as a keyboard or mouse, may malfunction for a variety of reasons. For example, the wrong driver may be installed for it (see the previous section), or it may be incompatible with your OS. For example, some mice and trackballs are specifically designed for Macintosh computers, and they won't work if you plug them into a Windows-based PC.

After you've eliminated incompatibility and bad drivers as the cause of an input device malfunction, next look at the device itself. Is there anything physically wrong with it? If it's a mouse with a ball, will the ball turn freely? If it's a keyboard, will all the keys press? Is the cord or connector damaged? Has something spilled on the device? Has it been dropped or hit?

If there's nothing physically wrong with the device, try plugging it into a different computer if possible. If it works there, then the problem is the relationship between the device and the original computer, and not the device itself. Investigate things like driver issues, incompatibility, and the connector on the PC into which the device connects. If it doesn't work on the other computer, the device is probably defective.

An input device that gradually stops working well over time, or that malfunctions only in a specific way (such as a certain key not working on a keyboard, or a mouse that moves in only one direction) may be dirty. Try cleaning the device, as you learned to do in the section "Cleaning a Computer" in Chapter 5 ("Maintaining a Computer").

Troubleshooting Network Connectivity

Hardware is often, but not always, to blame when a user can't log on to the local network or can't connect to the Internet. Here are some general troubleshooting tips:

1. If you can't browse network resources:

   a. Confirm that the computer's network adapter is installed and working. In Windows, look in Device Manager to make sure it's there and doesn't report any errors.

   b. Confirm that a cable or wireless connection is established between the network adapter and the router, switch, or wireless access point. If it's a wired connection, trace the cable from the PC to the router or switch. If wireless, check to make sure the OS recognizes the wireless connection.

   c. Make sure the right networking protocols are in place (TCP/IP being the most common). Exercise 8.6 shows you how to do this in Windows and how to use TCP/IP to troubleshoot an Internet connection problem.

2. If your network login keeps getting rejected on a corporate network:

   a. Check that Caps Lock isn't on and that you're typing your username and password accurately.

   b. Check with your network administrator to make sure there are no known problems with the network that may be preventing everyone from logging on (not just you).

3. If the problem is lack of Internet connectivity:

   a. You may need to reset or power-cycle your cable or DSL modem.

   b. Your Internet service provider (ISP) may be temporarily unavailable. Sometimes there are brief outages with even the most reliable services. Wait it out for a few hours before contacting your ISP.

   c. The Internet itself may be experiencing temporary delays or outages. This is likely the case if you can get to some but not all websites, or you can get email but not web access, or vice versa.

EXERCISE 8.6

Check TCP/IP Connectivity

1. In Windows, open a command prompt window. To do so, click Start, type **cmd**, and press Enter.

   You can also do this exercise on Linux or Mac systems by opening a command prompt as you learned in Chapter 5.

2. At the command prompt, type `ping 127.0.0.1` and press Enter.

   127.0.0.1 is the loopback address: that is, the IP address that refers to the machine that is issuing the command. If you get a reply from this command, you know your network adapter is working. This eliminates all problems within the PC from the troubleshooting process.

3. At the command prompt, type **ipconfig** and press Enter. The IP addresses for all the network adapters in your system appear. Some of them may show Media Disconnected, meaning that adapter isn't in use.

4. Find the network adapter you use to connect to the network, and look at the IPv4 address for it. For example, in the following figure, it's 192.168.2.2. IP addresses that begin with 192.168 are common on small home networks.

```
Administrator: C:\Windows\system32\cmd.exe

C:\>ipconfig

Windows IP Configuration

Ethernet adapter Local Area Connection 2:

   Media State . . . . . . . . . . . : Media disconnected
   Connection-specific DNS Suffix  . :

Wireless LAN adapter Wireless Network Connection 3:

   Media State . . . . . . . . . . . : Media disconnected
   Connection-specific DNS Suffix  . :

Wireless LAN adapter Wireless Network Connection:

   Connection-specific DNS Suffix  . : Belkin
   Link-local IPv6 Address . . . . . : fe80::7cd7:a6fe:1279:451x11
   IPv4 Address. . . . . . . . . . . : 192.168.2.2
   Subnet Mask . . . . . . . . . . . : 255.255.255.0
   Default Gateway . . . . . . . . . : 192.168.2.1

Ethernet adapter Local Area Connection:

   Media State . . . . . . . . . . . : Media disconnected
   Connection-specific DNS Suffix  . : NB1-DL

Tunnel adapter Local Area Connection* 13:

   Connection-specific DNS Suffix  . :
   IPv6 Address. . . . . . . . . . . : 2001:0:4137:9e76:38c1:36ff:9d20:1c02
   Link-local IPv6 Address . . . . . : fe80::38c1:36ff:9d20:1c02x22
   Default Gateway . . . . . . . . . : ::

Tunnel adapter isatap.Belkin:

   Media State . . . . . . . . . . . : Media disconnected
   Connection-specific DNS Suffix  . : Belkin

Tunnel adapter 6TO4 Adapter:

   Media State . . . . . . . . . . . : Media disconnected
   Connection-specific DNS Suffix  . :

C:\>ping 192.168.2.2
```

5. For that same network adapter, make a note of the Default Gateway. That's the address of the router that provides the exit point from the local network and connects you to the larger network (for example, the Internet). In the previous figure, it's 192.168.2.1.

6. Ping the default gateway to make sure it's reachable. To do this, type **ping**, a space, and then the address of the default gateway that you noted in step 5—for example, **ping 192.168.2.1**. If the default gateway is reachable, you should get back multiple Reply lines. If not, you'll get back multiple Timed Out lines.

7. Ping a website to see if you have Web connectivity. To do so, type **ping**, a space, and then either an IP address or a URL of a website. For example, type **ping www.google.com** and press Enter.

If you don't get a reply from the first site you try, try some other addresses. Some websites block ping inquiries as a matter of company policy.

8. If you can't get through to a particular website, you can use another command, tracert (short for "trace route"), to see the hops the message takes from router to router across the Internet. This can help you see where the transmission is breaking down.

Type **tracert google.com**, and press Enter. Information comes back about each of the routers the message passes through on the way, up to a maximum of 30 hops. Yours will have different addresses than those shown here.

9. Close the command prompt window.

Summary

In this chapter, you learned about many types of computer operational problems and how to fix them, including startup failures, error messages, lockups, application crashes, and hardware malfunctions. You also learned how to troubleshoot network connectivity issues using a command-line interface.

Exam Essentials

Understand why applications crash and how to recover.   Applications crash because of errors in their programming, conflicts with other applications, conflicts with the OS, and device-driver problems. You can terminate a nonresponsive program in Windows from the Task Manager window.

Identify the common reasons why the OS may lock up.   Programming errors and incompatibilities can sometimes make an OS lock up, but the most common reason for a complete system lockup is overheating.

Determine why an application won't start.   Applications that won't start may contain a programming error or may be incompatible with your OS version or a piece of hardware you've installed. It could also be that the minimum system requirements for the program aren't satisfied, or that the application's installation has been corrupted. Try removing and reinstalling the application and checking the manufacturer's website for help. You can also try updating your display adapter driver.

Troubleshoot network connection problems.   Network connection problems may be related to disconnected or malfunctioning hardware or software. Try using the `ipconfig`, `ping`, and `tracert` commands to get information about the network connection.

Understand hardware and driver incompatibility and its solutions.   For hardware to work, it must have a driver that is appropriate for both the hardware make/model and the OS version. Drivers that don't exactly match in one of those two areas may result in compatibility problems.

Troubleshoot malfunctioning input devices.   A keyboard or mouse that isn't working may be unplugged, physically defective, or dirty. It could also be that the OS doesn't have an appropriate driver for it, although this is unlikely because most keyboards and mice can use the generic drivers that come with the OS.

Review Questions

1. If you turn on a PC and you don't see anything onscreen or hear any fans spinning, what is the most likely reason?

   A. Defective monitor

   B. Bad power supply

   C. Wrong type of network adapter

   D. Broken fan

2. What does a POST card help diagnose?

   A. Startup problems where nothing is displayed onscreen

   B. Startup problems resulting in a BIOS error message

   C. Overheating problems

   D. Application problems

3. If you see a text error message onscreen as the computer boots up, with gray text on a black background, the message is most likely coming from _____.

   A. Windows

   B. An application

   C. BIOS

   D. The Internet

4. A BSOD, or Blue Screen of Death, is a(n) _____ message from Windows indicating that a serious error has occurred, possibly involving hardware.

   A. EXIT

   B. HALT

   C. QUIT

   D. STOP

5. The _____ is a graphical interface you can access by booting from the Windows Setup CD when you need to repair Windows.

   A. Recovery Console

   B. Recovery Environment

   C. Restore Mode

   D. Directory Service

6. On a Windows system, what key do you press at startup to display the Advanced Options menu?

    A. F1

    B. F5

    C. F8

    D. Depends on the BIOS

7. What does the Windows utility System Restore do?

    A. Restores data files

    B. Returns the system configuration files to a previous version

    C. Removes all third-party drivers

    D. Resets the RAM

8. What is the filename for the System Configuration Utility?

    A. CHKDSK

    B. DEFRAG

    C. MSCONFIG

    D. SYSINFO

9. In the System Configuration Utility, on which tab do you clear check boxes to prevent certain programs from loading automatically when Windows starts?

    A. Boot

    B. General

    C. Services

    D. Startup

10. On a Mac, a(n) _____ icon at startup may indicate that the hard disk is disconnected.

    A. Prohibition, or sad Mac

    B. Question mark

    C. Exclamation point

    D. Angry Mac

11. If Windows won't boot normally because of a bad startup application or driver, you may be able to boot into _____ Mode to fix the problem.

    A. Minimal

    B. Directory

    C. Network

    D. Safe

12. If the OS slows down dramatically, which components are probably being overtaxed?

  A. Hard disk or RAM

  B. RAM or display adapter

  C. RAM or CPU

  D. CPU or network adapter

13. If the OS locks up and the mouse won't work, what is the most common cause?

  A. Display adapter malfunction

  B. Corrupt mouse driver

  C. Overheating

  D. Corrupt hard disk

14. In Windows, you can sometimes use _____ Mode to run an application that is designed for an earlier Windows version.

  A. Function

  B. Compatibility

  C. Advanced

  D. Administrator

15. If you are logged in as a(n) _____ user and the OS won't let you install an application, try logging in as a(n) _____ user.

  A. Standard, administrator

  B. Administrator, standard

  C. Standard, guest

  D. Power, standard

16. A(n) _____ is a situation where an application stops working.

  A. BSOD

  B. Crash

  C. Timeout

  D. Configuration error

17. A device _____ communicates between a device and the OS.

  A. Header

  B. Manager

  C. Driver

  D. Query

18. Which of these is *not* a reason why a mouse may malfunction?

    A. It's dirty.

    B. The mouse is damaged.

    C. The wrong driver is installed for it.

    D. Electrostatic discharge.

19. If the network is rejecting your login password, check to make sure that
_____.

    A. The mouse is functioning

    B. Caps Lock is not on

    C. The display adapter is working

    D. The network interface is connected

20. To determine your network adapter's IP address, what command-line utility should you use?

    A. `ping`

    B. `cmd`

    C. `tracert`

    D. `ipconfig`

Answers to Review Questions

1. B. A bad power supply would cause both lack of onscreen display and no fan. A bad monitor would not cause the fans not to spin. A broken fan would not cause the screen to be blank. The wrong type of network adapter would not cause either of those symptoms.

2. A. A POST card is a circuit board you insert into an open slot on the motherboard. It displays a two-digit code to tell you where the system is in the booting process. This is useful when nothing is displayed onscreen.

3. C. A black-screen error usually comes from the BIOS, such as a message indicating that the hard disk is not bootable.

4. D. A blue-screen STOP error indicates a serious unrecoverable error in Windows. The system must be rebooted to continue.

5. B. The Recovery Environment is accessed from the Windows Setup CD for Windows Vista and higher. The Recovery Console is a command-line interface for system recovery used in Windows XP.

6. C. Press F8 to display the Advanced Options menu. The key you press to enter BIOS Setup depends on the BIOS, but the key you press to access Windows' Advanced Options menu does not vary.

7. B. System Restore replaces the current system configuration files, including Registry files, with a recent backup of them.

8. C. Run MSCONFIG to access the System Configuration Utility.

9. D. Applications set to load at startup appear on the Startup tab.

10. B. The question-mark icon appears at startup if the Mac can't find a hard disk or can't find a system folder on the hard disk.

11. D. Safe Mode loads a minimal set of drivers, so it can sometimes start a computer that will not start normally. To access it, press F8 while booting, and select it from the Advanced Options menu.

12. C. Dramatic slowdown of the computer's operation usually means either RAM or the CPU is being heavily used.

13. C. Overheating is the most common cause of complete system lockup, including unresponsive input devices (keyboard and mouse).

14. B. Compatibility Mode enables you to select an earlier version of Windows for the system to emulate when communicating with a certain application.

15. A. An administrator account can install new applications; a standard user may not be able to do so. A guest account cannot install applications.

16. B. An application crashes when it stops responding to your commands.

17. C. Device drivers translate instructions and status messages between the OS and the device.

18. D. Electrostatic discharge, or ESD, is static electricity. Mice are not particularly susceptible to that. The other three items listed are all common causes of mouse problems.

19. B. Caps Lock being on makes a case-sensitive password invalid. The mouse functionality has nothing to do with network login. The display adapter can be assumed to be working if you see the network login at all. If you had no connection to the network, it would not be asking for your login in the first place.

20. D. The `ipconfig` command reports the IP addresses and other information for each network adapter in your system.

Chapter
9

Security and Access Control

OBJECTIVES COVERED IN THIS CHAPTER:

FUNDAMENTALS OF PC FUNCTIONALITY

✓ **3.1 U.K. / 4.1 U.S. Recognize basic security risks and procedures to prevent them**

- Identify risks
- Identify prevention methods
- Identify access control methods
- Identify security threats related to: media used for backup; screen visibility; cookies; pop-ups; and accidental misconfiguration

✓ **3.2 U.K. / 4.2 U.S. Recognize security breaches and ways to resolve them**

- Recognize the proper diagnostic procedures when infected with a virus
- Recognize the proper procedures to maintain a secure environment

Computer security, in an ideal world, lets in the right people and applications without any hassle, and keeps out the wrong people and applications. Of course, in the real world, security systems don't always work that way. Effective computer security is a constant balance between safety and convenience. In this chapter, you'll learn about the many types of threats to safety, security, and privacy, both of the physical computer and of its data, and how to guard against threats and attacks without placing unnecessary obstacles in the way of legitimate users.

Understanding Hacking

Hacking refers to a variety of computer crimes that involve gaining unauthorized access to a computer system or its data, usually with the intent of stealing private information from, or causing harm or embarrassment to, the rightful owner.

The word *hacker* also has a benign meaning, referring to a computer expert who is thoroughly familiar with, and enthusiastic about, the inner workings of a computer system. This meaning is older, but the newer meaning, which associates the term *hacker* with criminal activities, is now more prevalent.

Some examples of hacking are as follows:

- Gaining remote access to a server
- Gaining control of an operating system
- Logging in locally and stealing data
- Changing a website's content
- Gaining access to the contents of a database
- Surreptitiously analyzing network traffic
- Introducing software designed to cause harm or steal data
- Creating a condition in which a computer or network no longer works well
- Modifying existing software so that it no longer performs as it should, or so that it secretly does harmful things in addition to its usual activity
- Stealing passwords
- Stealing personal details

Much of this chapter is devoted to helping you understand how hackers target a system and how you can defend yourself. Some of the ways that hackers gain access to a system that we'll explore in this chapter include the following:

- Booting the System from a Disk that Contains a Utility that can Read the Files from the Hard Disk Without Going Through the Existing Operating System (and its security)

If hackers can gain access to certain system files, for example, they may be able to retrieve the Administrator password for the system. To prevent this type of attack, you might use BIOS-level security to prevent a PC from booting from a disk other than the hard disk.

- Connecting to Wireless Networks and Looking for Computers or Data that isn't Protected

To prevent this type of attack, you can employ some of the wireless networking security techniques discussed in Chapter 3, "Peripherals and Networking," and also later in this chapter, such as not broadcasting the service set identifier (SSID) and using Wi-Fi Protected Access (WPA) encryption on the network connection.

- Taking Advantage of Open Network Ports to Access a Computer Remotely

To help prevent this type of attack, you can use a firewall, which blocks unauthorized network traffic.

- Introducing Software on a PC that Causes it to be Harmed, or Causes its Security to be Breached

There are many forms of such programs. You'll learn about their details later in the chapter. To prevent infection, you can use antivirus and antimalware utilities.

Physical Security

Organizations lose millions of dollars of equipment every year through thefts and multiple millions of dollars through the data that goes along with them. Therefore, it's important to secure your computer hardware physically in whatever environment you place it.

Preventing Hardware Theft

The risk of hardware theft varies with the environment, of course. Leaving a laptop unattended at an airport is a very different matter from leaving it unattended in your own office when you go to lunch.

When travelling with a notebook PC or other portable technology device, the emphasis should be placed on the physical security of the individual device. Here are some pointers:

- Know where the device is at all times—preferably within your sight.
- Don't leave the device unattended, even for a minute.
- Carry the device in an unconventional bag, rather than an expensive-looking laptop bag.

- Install an alarm that beeps if your device gets more than a certain distance away from a transponder that you keep close to you (such as on your keychain or belt).

Within your own company's offices, solutions for securing computers and peripherals focus mainly on securing the environment overall, rather than securing an individual piece of hardware. For example, some possible measures include:

- Requiring a security keycard for access to the office area
- Having a professional security presence in large organizations
- Keeping doors and windows locked
- Being prepared to challenge anyone who isn't normally a part of your work environment

If it isn't possible to secure the area physically, it may be appropriate to use locks and other devices that physically attach the hardware to a desk or other fixed object in order to prevent it from "walking away." There are various types of locks, cages, and racks designed to make it difficult for someone to remove a computer from its location.

Many notebook computers have a K-slot, which is short for Kensington security slot. Kensington is a company that makes a type of lock that fits into that slot. The lock is then attached to a security cable, and the other end of is bolted to the wall or furniture. The locks are secured with either a key or a combination. Figure 9.1 shows an example of a security cable attached to a K-slot on a notebook PC.

Services are available, such as LoJack, that can track stolen hardware via a small radio installed inside the device and disable a stolen computer remotely so the data that resides on it won't be compromised. LoJack functionality comes preinstalled in the BIOS of many major brand-name notebook computers, including Dell, Lenovo, HP, Toshiba, and Fujitsu. The radio-tracking unit comes free with the computer, but you must pay to install and use the software that enables it. You can learn more about this software at: http://store.lojackforlaptops.com.

FIGURE 9.1   Lock on a computer case

Photo credit: Yetzt. Wikimedia Commons

Preventing Data Theft

Although physical theft is everyone's first thought, there is also the issue of data theft, which can cost a company even more than hardware theft in the long run. For any organization, the loss of data can equate to the following:

- Loss of trust from your customers/clients when they discover that someone else has their personal information

- Serious embarrassment if there are public media reports that your company has lost control of its data

- Legal liabilities from either regulatory authorities or angry customers whose data you've compromised

- Loss of competitive advantage when commercially sensitive data falls into the hands of rivals

A thief doesn't need to steal a computer to steal data; someone can sit down at your computer, plug in a USB memory stick, and be gone with important data files in a couple of minutes. For this reason, some organizations have OS security policies that disable the USB ports on PCs that contain sensitive data.

One way to prevent others from booting from a device other than the hard disk is to modify the BIOS Setup settings so that a password is required to save changes to BIOS Setup. That way, nobody can change the system's boot order to prefer a USB port over the main hard disk.

Locking your computer as you leave your desk (via the OS's lock command), as well as having your screensaver set to resume on password after a short period of time, will help reduce the risk of someone using your computer while you're away.

EXERCISE 9.1

Secure a Windows PC from Unauthorized Local Use

1. In Windows 7, right-click the desktop and choose Personalize.

2. Click Screen Saver. The Screen Saver dialog box opens.

3. Open the Screen Saver drop-down list, and pick any of the screensavers (for example, Bubbles).

4. Select the On Resume, Display Logon Screen check box.

5. In the Wait box, change the value to 2 minutes.

6. Click OK.

7. Wait 2 minutes for the screensaver to start.

8. Move the mouse to awaken the computer. The logon screen appears.

9. Click your user account, and retype your password to resume.

10. Repeat steps 1–7, returning to your previous screensaver settings.

11. Choose Start ➢ Lock. The logon screen appears.

12. Click your user account, and retype your password to resume.

Securing Backup Media

Large companies typically back up their data using their network, with the backups stored on the same type of secure servers on which the data itself resides. However, smaller companies sometimes rely on data backups to external hard disks, optical media, and even memory sticks and tape drives. The data is no safer than the physical safety of these backup devices.

Keep in mind that data can be stolen from backup devices just as easily as from the original storage locations. Physically secure all backup devices and media, both from theft and from accidents and disasters, such as fires and flooding. Data should be stored off-site, in a fireproof safe.

Access Control

Access control describes the technologies used to control who or what has access to your system(s). Access control can take many forms, from the key to the door on the room that houses your computer system to the username and password with which you log in, and the permissions you receive as a result of that login. Examples of access control measures include passwords, fingerprint readers, and smart cards.

User IDs and Passwords

User IDs and passwords are the bedrock of most computer access-control systems. You use an ID and password combination to log into everything from the OS to your bank's website. User IDs and passwords identify you as you log onto the local area network at your workplace, as you access wireless hotspots, and just about everywhere that you have to be authorized in order to participate.

Access control at an OS level is usually local to that PC (that is, with the database of authorized users and passwords stored locally). No matter where that PC goes, or what networks it is or isn't connected to, the authorized users remain the same. The security risk in such a system is that someone could hack the file where the passwords are stored and gain access to everything on the PC.

As an alternative, some companies that have client/server networks choose to manage user logon via an independent directory service stored on a separate server. For Windows servers, this service is called *Active Directory*. When logins are managed on the network, users can potentially sit down at any PC anywhere in the building and log in with their own credentials. The Active Directory service then retrieves the user's preferences, data folders, and other settings and makes them available.

Creating Effective Passwords

A *strong password* is one that is difficult for someone to guess. Strong passwords have these characteristics:

- Long   The longer, the better. At least eight characters is optimal.
- Varied   The password contains at least one capital letter and at least one number and/or symbol.
- Unusual   The password doesn't appear in a dictionary and isn't a proper noun.

Passwords that are easy to guess are considered *weak passwords*. Some of the worst passwords of all are things like *qwerty*, *12345*, the user ID, and the word *password*. Only slightly better are the names of people, pets, and places.

Even though a password should be difficult for others to guess, it's OK to make it easy for you to remember. To do this, try combining numbers and letters that make sense to you but won't make sense to other people. For example, suppose you have a cousin Albert who grew up in Indianapolis, and you used to call him a lot, so you remember that his phone number was 555-1192. An effective password might be *Albert-Indy#1192*. Notice that this password is long (15 characters), varied (uppercase, lowercase, numeric, and symbol characters), and unusual, yet it's fairly easy for you to remember just by thinking about your cousin.

Here are some other techniques for creating passwords that are easy to remember but difficult to guess:

Substitute zero for the letter O in words   For example, `St0rageR00m`.

Substitute numbers for letters   To make it easier to remember, use the numeral that represents the letter of the alphabet (for example, *b*=2) or use the numeral that represents the position in the word (for example, take the word *teacher* and substitute numerals for the second and fourth digits, like this: `t2a4her`.

Combine two or more unrelated but memorable words   For example, `GroceryCandleAshtray`.

Substitute a symbol for a letter that it resembles   For example, $ looks like an *S*, as in `$ubstitution$alary`; and ! looks like a capital *I*, as in `!temized`.

As tempting as it may be to use the same password for multiple systems or sites, you're safer using a different password for every site you access. That way, if one site is hacked, it won't affect your security on another site.

If you can't remember all the passwords in your head, one possible solution is to store them in a password-protected file on your hard drive. Yes, someone could steal that file from your hard disk and possibly even unencrypt it, but the chances of that happening are slim compared to the chances of a server being hacked where your password for a certain site is stored.

Another possible solution is to reuse the same password for sites that don't store any financial information. For example, you might use the same password for logging into message boards and chat rooms at various sites, because if your password is discovered at those sites the consequences are generally mild. Someone might log in and impersonate you, causing you some temporary embarrassment, but you haven't lost any money. On the other hand, you should use a different password for each of your important banking or stock-trading accounts, because a thief could cause you significant financial problems on these sites.

Password Changes

Some companies' IT policies require that you change your password at regular intervals, such as every 90 days. The rationale is that the longer you keep a password, the more likely that someone has surreptitiously seen you type it, or you've written it down somewhere, or some other security breach has occurred.

Even if a system doesn't require you to change your password on a certain timetable, you may want to take the initiative to change it yourself, especially on sites where you manage your financial affairs.

To help you remember your password in a frequently changing environment, you may want to develop a structured system of changes. For example, suppose your password is video%Furrier. When you change it, you might add the two-digit number of the month in which you changed it. For example, if you change it in February, you can make it video$02Furrier. Then, when you change it again in May, you can change it to video$05Furrier.

One-Time Passwords

Some systems issue temporary passwords to users. These passwords are either time-limited (for example, you must use it within 24 hours) or instance-limited (for example, you can use it to log in only once, at which point you're forced to create a new password).

Some systems have a time-based token on which the user can press a button and get a randomly generated password. This token uses an algorithm (a mathematical method) recognized by the server and uses the current time as a part of the key to the password, knowing that the server will be running to the same time.

A one-time password prevents theft from a key-logging system or from someone watching you type the password and remembering it. By the time someone has stolen it, it's already out of date. One-time passwords can also be used to help verify a user's identity when resetting a forgotten password. For example, if you're locked out of logging into your cell-phone provider's website, the provider may send a temporary password to your phone, ensuring that you possess that phone before resetting the password for the website.

Smart Cards

A *smart card* is a plastic card, similar in dimensions to a credit card, that contains a microchip that a card-reader can scan, such as on a security system. Smart cards often double as employee badges, enabling employees to access employee-only areas of a building or to use elevators that go to restricted areas, or as credit cards. Smart cards are also used in some countries, such as France, to store and transfer health insurance information.

Smart cards can also be used to allow or prevent computer access. For example, a PC may have a card reader on it through which the employee has to swipe the card, or that reads the card's chip automatically when the card comes into its vicinity.

Smart cards are sometimes used as a substitute for user IDs and passwords. In other applications, they're combined with PIN numbers or used as an add-on to a standard login system, to give an additional layer of security verification. For someone to gain unauthorized access, they have to not only know a user's ID and password (or PIN), but also steal their smart card. That makes it much more difficult to be a thief!

Biometric Devices

Biometric devices identify users by scanning for one or more physical traits. Some common types include fingerprint recognition, facial recognition, and retina scanning.

Law enforcement agencies have been using *fingerprint recognition* for over 100 years, and no two prints have yet been found to be identical, even in genetically identical twins. That's because fingerprints develop in the womb, and they aren't preprogrammed at conception. More recently, computerized fingerprint scanners have taken the place of manual ink prints, and the technology for reading fingerprints has become so affordable that it's built into many computer systems, including consumer-level notebook PCs.

Some fingerprint scanners use a rapid laser to detect the ridges in a person's fingers; others have an electrostatically sensitive pad that detects the current formed by the small quantities of water in a fingerprint.

Facial recognition software works in conjunction with a camera (like the webcams built into some notebook computers) to scan the face of the person who is logging in. The facial scan is matched with existing previous scans of that same person stored on the computer. Some consumer-level notebook PCs now come with an option of logging into the OS via facial recognition as an alternative to typing a login password.

Data and Usage Permission

Next we'll look at security measures that allow authorized users to view certain data or use certain applications while preventing unauthorized users from doing so.

Controlling Screen Visibility

Unauthorized people can gain access to confidential information not only by actively stealing the data, but by viewing the screen casually, as a passer-by or as a nonchalant snoop in an adjacent workstation.

One way to prevent others from looking at your screen while you're away from your desk is to set up a screensaver, as you did in Exercise 9.1. The screen becomes obscured after a certain period of inactivity. Not all the screensaver choices provide the same level of screen-hiding, so choose a screensaver with an eye toward finding one that provides as much privacy as possible.

To prevent others from looking at your screen as you're working, you might consider orienting your monitor in such a way that it's difficult for others to read. For example, you can sit with your back to a wall or window, with the monitor's back side facing out.

If it's impossible to hide the monitor from unauthorized lookers adequately, and if the data on the screen is highly confidential, you may find a screen filter useful. A *screen filter* (also called a *privacy screen*) directs the light from the display at a restricted angle so that anyone who isn't viewing it straight on won't be able to read it clearly.

Managing User Types

As you learned in "Working with User Accounts" in Chapter 6 ("Installing and Configuring Software"), you can set up different user accounts in the OS with different levels of permission. In Windows and Mac OS X, a standard user account can't make changes that will affect other users, whereas an administrator account can make all types of changes. This prevents people from uninstalling applications that they personally don't need but others do.

To prevent unauthorized changes to a computer, it's a good practice to have everyone use a standard account for daily operations and have an administrator account available that is used only when performing activities that require it, such as installing or removing software or updating a device driver.

Controlling File and Folder Sharing

In addition to using shared files on a file server, computer users can also use shared files on other individuals' computers and can share their own files. In principle, sharing your files and folders on the network can make your life easier. However, file sharing is a security risk as well. To mitigate this risk, be very judicious about the permissions you assign, using only the ones that are necessary. For example, if a group of users needs only to read a folder, don't assign Read-Write permission to it. And if only one or two people in a group need that access, assign permission to their user accounts and not to their entire group.

File/folder sharing differs according to OS, based on how the relevant permissions are allocated. A file or folder permission is a marker (called a *flag*) placed on the file or folder to declare who can view, change, create, and delete files, as well as run executable files and assign permissions to others.

 You can assign sharing permissions to individual files, but in most cases it's better to assign permissions to a folder and then put into that folder whatever files require those permissions. Folder sharing is more efficient because you need to set the permissions only once. It also avoids thorny, difficult-to-troubleshoot problems with file permissions that occur when each file has its own unique permission settings.

Mac OS X Sharing

By default, file sharing is turned off on a Mac. To enable it, open the Apple menu and choose System Preferences ➤ Internet & Wireless ➤ Sharing. Click the + (plus) icon below the Shared Folders field, and a sheet appears where you can navigate to the folders you wish to share (see Figure 9.2).

FIGURE 9.2 Choosing folders to share in Mac OS X

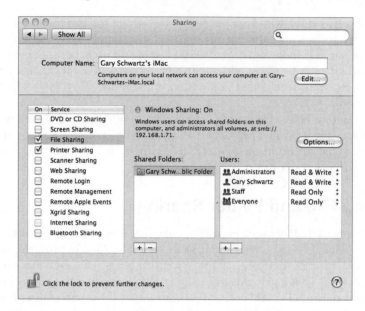

Next, configure the user and group accounts with appropriate access privileges:

1. In Sharing Preferences, select the folder that's being shared.

2. To add to the default user accounts and groups that were selected when you shared the folder, click the + (plus) icon below the Users field.

3. In the sheet that appears, select an existing user account or group. (User accounts are created in Accounts preferences, in System Preferences.)

4. The default privilege for a user account or group you add is Read Only. If you want to change this, choose one of the following privilege options from the Read Only pop-up menu:

   Read & Write   The user can read, copy, edit, and delete the contents of the folder.

   Read Only   The user can only read and copy (to another location) the contents of the folder.

   Write Only (Drop Box)   The user can only copy content into the folder. The user can't see the contents of the folder.

   No Access (Groups Only)   User accounts in the assigned group have no access to the folder. However, if their user account is added, the privileges assigned to the user account will override the group restrictions.

5. Repeat the process for each folder being shared.

   You can also select a folder directly in the Finder to share. Select the folder, choose File ➢ Get Info, and select the Shared Folder check box (see Figure 9.3). You can also manage user or group access to the shared folder via Finder; select the folder, choose File ➢ Get Info, and then choose Sharing & Permissions.

FIGURE 9.3   Sharing a specific folder in Mac OS X

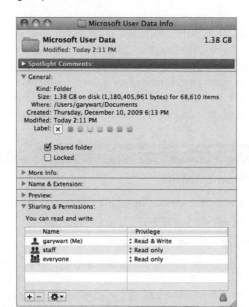

Configuring a Mac to Share with Other Computer Types

The default sharing protocol is Apple Filing Protocol (AFP), which is used to share files with other Macs. If other computers need access too, click the Options button at right side of the Sharing window (see Figure 9.2), and then enable one or both of the other protocols too:

Share Files and Folders Using FTP Apple Filing Protocol   For sharing with Unix and Linux systems. FTP stands for File Transfer Protocol.

Share Files and Folders using SMB   For sharing with Windows-based PCs. SMB stands for Server Message Block.

If you're sharing files with a Windows-based PC, you'll need to join the appropriate Windows workgroup:

1. Choose System Preferences ➢ Network Preferences, and ensure that the padlock is unlocked. If it's locked, click it and, when prompted, enter an administrator name and password. Click OK.

2. Click Network, select an interface, click Advanced, and click WINS.

3. Enter a name for your Mac in the NetBIOS Name field, and enter the name of the workgroup you want to join in the Workgroup field.

4. Click OK, and then click Apply.

Windows 7 Sharing

In Windows 7, there are two ways to manage file and folder sharing. One is to create a HomeGroup, which is a small, tightly controlled workgroup, and set permissions for sharing within that group. That's the ideal solution for most home networks and small offices. The main drawbacks are that all the computers have to be running Windows 7, and each computer must be configured individually (so the prospect of setting this up for a large network can be daunting). Exercise 9.2 walks you through the steps for creating a HomeGroup on a network of at least two PCs that are running Windows 7.

EXERCISE 9.2

Create a Windows 7 HomeGroup

1. On any of the PCs you wish to connect, open the Control Panel and go to Network And Internet ➤ Network And Sharing Center.

2. Click Choose Homegroup And Sharing Options.

3. Click Create A Homegroup. The Create A Homegroup dialog box opens.

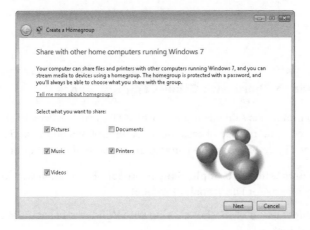

4. Select or clear the check boxes for the file types you want to share with other members of the HomeGroup.

5. Click Next. A network password appears. It's a string of random numbers and letters, something like this: 6dH2EB7kK4. Write down the password, and click Finish.

6. Go to each of the other PCs you want to connect, open the Control Panel, and go to Network And Internet ➤ Network and Sharing Center.

7. Click Choose Homegroup And Sharing Options.

8. Click Join Now.

9. Select or clear the check boxes for the file types you want to share with other members of the HomeGroup.

10. Click Next.

11. Type the password that you wrote down earlier, and click Next.

12. Click Finish. The PCs are now configured to share files with one another of the types you specified when you set up each PC.

After creating the HomeGroup and connecting to it, you can share other files and folders as needed; you aren't stuck with just the set that the HomeGroup Wizard chooses for you with the check boxes.

To share any file or folder, right-click it, choose Share With, and then select one of these options:

- Homegroup (Read)
- Homegroup (Read/Write)
- Specific People

If you choose Specific People, you get the same advanced sharing options that you do without a HomeGroup. (You'll see those in Exercise 9.3.)

The other sharing method uses the standard Windows networking tools without going through the HomeGroup. This type of sharing works among different Windows versions as well as non-Windows computers. A system administrator can also administer this type of connection remotely, so each PC doesn't have to be touched individually. Exercise 9.3 shows how to configure non-HomeGroup sharing settings and how to share a folder.

You don't have to choose between HomeGroup and non-HomeGroup network sharing; you can have both. When you have a HomeGroup enabled, you can use the HomeGroup sharing options with those computers participating in it, and standard folder sharing with every other computer participating in your network.

EXERCISE 9.3

Share Folders in Windows 7

1. Choose Start ➤ Control Panel ➤ Network And Internet ➤ Network And Sharing Center.

2. In the left pane, click Change Advanced Sharing Settings.

3. In the File And Printer Sharing section, make sure Turn On File And Printer Sharing is selected.

4. In the Public Folder Sharing section, make sure Turn On Sharing So That Anyone With Network Access Can Read And Write Files In The Public Folders is selected.

5. In the Password Protected Sharing section, make sure Turn Off Password Protected Sharing is selected.

6. If you made any changes, click Save Changes. Then close the Control Panel.

7. Choose Start ➢ Documents.

8. Click New Folder. Type `Class Sharing`, and press Enter to name the new folder.

9. Right-click the `Class Sharing` folder, point to Share With, and choose Specific People.

10. In the File Sharing dialog box, type **Everyone** and click Add. (The Everyone group is predefined in Windows 7, and all users are included in it.)

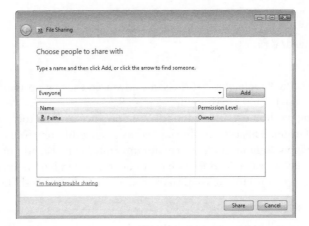

11. Click Share.

12. Click Done.

13. Copy a document file into the `Class Sharing` folder.

14. On another computer, confirm that you can access that file in the shared folder.

Another way to share a folder is via its Properties dialog box. Right-click the folder and choose Properties. Then, on the Sharing tab, click the Share button to open the same dialog box you saw in Exercise 9.3.

Locally Securing and Encrypting Files and Folders

The file sharing you learned about in the previous section applies only when people are connecting to the computer via the network. When different users log into the same computer locally, though, you need to employ other methods to keep their private data separate.

One way is to set certain folders to be inaccessible to other local users. To do this in Windows, use the Security tab in the folder's Properties box. It contains file-sharing permission settings that apply to local access. You can also *encrypt* certain folders so their content is scrambled if someone tries to browse the file contents, such as with a disk-editor utility. To encrypt a folder, in the folder's Properties box, click the Advanced button, and select the Encrypt Contents To Secure Data check box. You'll practice these skills in Exercise 9.4. Only the Professional, Enterprise, and Ultimate versions of Windows 7 support encryption; in other versions, the check box for encrypting files is unavailable.

When you encrypt folders, as long as you're logged in as the user who did the encrypting, the files are available normally and the encryption is invisible to you. However, if you log in as some other user, the files are inaccessible. Encryption is based on security certificates stored on the hard disk for each user. There's a risk involved, though, because if the security certificate becomes corrupted or deleted, you won't be able to access files that are legitimately yours. It's therefore important to back up your certificate before you start relying on encryption to protect your files locally. A lost or damaged certificate can be recovered, but not easily. Exercise 9.4 practices encrypting files and setting security permissions, and Exercise 9.5 provides practice in backing up a security certificate.

EXERCISE 9.4

Secure and Encrypt Local Folders in Windows 7

1. If you don't already have at least two user accounts on your PC, create one. To do so:

    a. Choose Start ➢ Control Panel ➢ User Accounts (or User Accounts And Family Safety, depending on your Windows version) ➢ Add Or Remove User Accounts.

    b. Click Create New Account.

    c. Type the new account name.

    d. Click Create Account.

2. Open the Documents folder. Click New Folder, type **Private** as its name, and press Enter to accept the new name.

3. Right-click the Private folder, and choose Properties.

4. On the Security tab, click Edit. The Permissions For Private dialog box opens.

5. Click Add. The Select Users Or Groups dialog box opens.

6. In the Enter The Object Names To Select box, type the username for the other user on this PC that you want to use for the exercise.

7. Click Check Names. The username appears, preceded by the computer name.

EXERCISE 9.4 *(continued)*

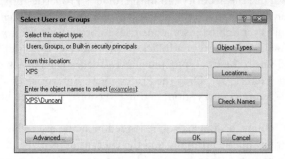

8. Click OK. Now that user appears on the Group Or User Name list in the Permissions dialog box.

9. With the user's name selected, notice the permissions in the lower pane. The Full Control and Modify check boxes aren't selected.

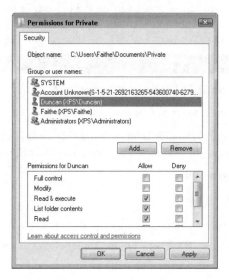

10. Click OK.

11. Click OK to close the Private Properties dialog box.

12. Copy a document file into the Private folder.

13. Log off your current user account, and log in as the other user.

14. Attempt to open the document. Note what happens.

15. Attempt to save changes to the document. Note what happens.

16. Log off, and log in again using the original username.

17. Open the Documents folder. Right-click the Private folder, and choose Properties.

18. On the General tab, click Advanced.

19. In the Advanced Attributes dialog box, select the Encrypt Contents To Secure Data check box if it's available.

Note: You must have the Professional, Ultimate, or Enterprise edition of Windows 7 to encrypt a folder's contents as detailed in step 19. On any other Windows 7 version, the check box will be grayed out.

20. Click OK.

21. Click OK to close the Private Properties dialog box.

22. Log off your current user account, and log in as the other user.

23. Attempt to access the Private folder, and note what happens. If you chose to encrypt the contents in step 19, it isn't accessible.

24. Log off, and log in again using the original username. Delete the Private folder.

EXERCISE 9.5

Back Up a Windows Security Certificate

1. In Windows, click Start, type **certmgr.msc**, and press Enter. The Certificate Manager utility opens.

2. Click the Personal folder to expand it.

3. Click Certificates.

4. Click the certificate that shows Encrypting File System in the Intended Purposes column.

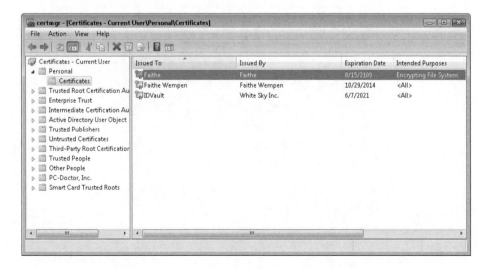

5. Choose Action ➢ All Tasks ➢ Export. The Certificate Export Wizard runs.

6. Click Next.

7. Click Yes, export the private key, and then click Next.

8. Make sure Personal Information Exchange is selected, and click Next.

9. In the Password box, type a password of your choice. Type it again in the Type And Confirm Password box. Then click Next.

10. In the File Name box, type the name you want to use to save the backup file. For example, if your username is jsmith, you might use jsmith-certbackup.

11. The default storage location for the backup is your Documents folder. If you want to place it somewhere else, click Browse, change locations, and then click Save.

12. Click Next. The Completing The Certificate Export Wizard screen appears.

13. Click Finish.

14. In the confirmation box, click OK.

15. Close the Certificate Manager window.

On a Mac, local encryption can't be applied to individual folders and files; you must encrypt the entire disk. You can do this via the Disk Utility, as shown in Figure 9.4, or encrypt the home folder using FileVault as shown in Figure 9.5.

FIGURE 9.4   Encrypting a disk in Mac OS X

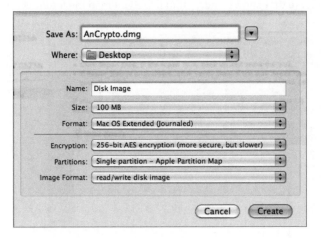

FIGURE 9.5 The Mac FileVault

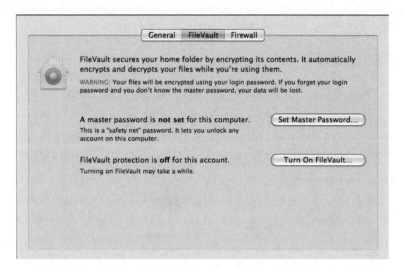

The easiest way to encrypt files and folders on a Linux system is via the command-line interface like this:

```
openssl des3 -salt -in originalfile.txt -out encryptedfile.txt
```

To decrypt, use a command like this:

```
openssl des3 -d -salt -in encryptedfile.txt -out unencryptedfile.txt
```

Parental Controls

Parental controls restrict certain activities or prevent the display of certain web content. Adults who are responsible for children's computer usage typically use these restrictions to prevent children from being exposed to adult content.

Each OS has its own version of parental controls, and you can also buy third-party add-on programs that have parental control features.

With Windows 7 parental controls, you can work with the following:

Time Limits You can control when children are allowed to log on to the computer. You can set when children can and can't log in, and you can set different logon hours for every day of the week. If they're logged on when their allotted time ends, they'll automatically be logged off.

Games You can control access to games, choose an age-rating level, choose the types of content you want to block, and decide whether you want to allow or block unrated or specific games.

Allow or Block Specific Programs You can prevent children from running programs that you don't want them to run.

To access Parental Controls, open the Control Panel, choose User Accounts And Family Safety, and click Parental Controls (see Figure 9.6). (Not all versions of Windows have the Family Safety designation; if yours doesn't, choose User Accounts.)

FIGURE 9.6 Windows 7 parental controls

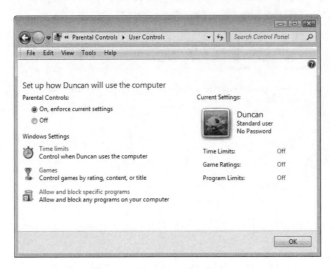

On a Mac, the parental controls are found under System Preferences (see Figure 9.7). You can do the following:

- Set controls on how children browse the filesystem
- Control which applications they can or can't use
- Control administration rights to printers
- Control whether children can change the dock (the lower graphical menu bar)
- Restrict children's ability to burn CDs/DVDs
- Restrict website access
- Restrict profanity (rude words) in the dictionary
- Limit email and chat to specific users and email addresses, with an additional option for the child to request approval to connect to a new email address (this can be sent to a parental email)
- Set time limits, based on the number of hours/minutes, with variations for weekdays and weekends
- Invoke a bedtime rule
- Show the activity of the child and what they have been doing

FIGURE 9.7   Mac OS X parental controls

Linux, by default, doesn't have parental controls; it's an optional add-on package that can be downloaded with Ubuntu and other Linux distributions.

In the Internet Explorer browser, you can also turn on the Content Advisor feature, which limits the websites that can be displayed using Internet Explorer.

Network Control

Next we'll look at security risks and controls associated with connecting to a network.

Open Wireless Networks

As you learned in Chapter 3, wireless (Wi-Fi) networks can be either open (no encryption) or secured (using encryption). Encryption is set at the router, so whether or not a network has encryption on it is determined by the router settings. The router, in turn, connects its users to the Internet.

If a network is secured, you must type its encryption key (password) when connecting to it. If it's not, anyone may connect to it. However, connecting to a network may not be sufficient to gain access to all its services (such as Internet access). Additional login information may be required. When you open a web browser window, a redirect operation displays a login page in which you may need to accept a user agreement, enter a username and password (or create one), and/or provide credit-card information to buy Internet access.

There are security risks associated with connecting to any network, but especially a free public network. Although most of your fellow users who share that network just want to use the Internet, as you do, hackers occasionally lurk about who may try to browse or even steal files from your computer via your shared network connection.

To minimize the risk associated with connecting to a specific network, you can change your file-sharing settings to more restrictive ones while you're connected to that network. In Windows, when you connect to a new network, you're prompted to select whether it's a Home, Work, or Public network. If you choose Public, file- and printer-sharing features are disabled on that network connection. This makes it more difficult for someone to snoop or harm your computer (see Figure 9.8).

FIGURE 9.8 Specify the security level desired when making a new wireless network connection

Wireless Encryption

Wireless networking encryption enables the owners of routers to prevent anyone from connecting to them who doesn't know the encryption key (password). Many wireless networks employ encryption, especially those in home or secure work environments.

In Chapter 3, you learned how to configure wireless networking, including setting a Service Set ID (SSID) and a type of encryption, which may include Wired Equivalent Privacy (WEP) or the more modern and advanced Wi-Fi Protected Access (WPA). Review "Configuring Wireless Networking and Encryption" in Chapter 3 for details.

Be aware that an encrypted network connection can still pose hazards. Hackers and snoops who also have access to the network key can be a threat, so make sure you don't have file and printer sharing turned on while connected to any network if you aren't sure who the other users are.

Firewalls

Firewalls prevent unauthorized activity on particular ports. A *port* is a TCP channel used to transport network traffic. There are many TCP ports, with some reserved for common services such as FTP, HTTP, email, and so on. Most firewalls filter traffic based on rules, which are based on ports and trusted zones. These can be open pathways for a hacker to abuse. Most OSs have a software-based firewall that is enabled by default. Hardware-based firewall devices are also available, but they're usually used on servers and not on individual user PCs.

When you're connected to a network that you may be sharing with others whom you don't know, you should make sure a firewall is running. A firewall is also important whenever you're connected to the Internet, which is essentially just a big public network.

Some firewalls block all incoming traffic on any port, unless your system has initiated a network connection with an outside service (such as a website you've visited). You can configure a firewall to let certain applications in and to keep others out. See Exercise 6.6, "Configure the Windows Firewall," in Chapter 6 for practice configuring a firewall.

Internet Privacy and Security

After you've established an Internet connection, a whole new set of security and privacy concerns come into play. There are threats from many directions, including from pop-ups, cookies, phishing, and so on, as well as more human threats such as con artists who try to get you to reveal information you shouldn't.

Identity Fraud and Social Engineering

Online, it's easy to impersonate someone. You don't even have to look or sound similar. All you need is enough personal information about them to trick a website or service provider into thinking you're that person. That's how millions of consumers are ripped off each year. Identity fraud is a very real and present danger online.

The most important thing you can do to prevent someone from stealing your online identity is to use strong passwords, as described earlier in this chapter, and change them frequently. Gaining access to someone's username and password for a site is one of the most common ways that criminals operate. If you keep your passwords written down somewhere, guard that piece of paper (or electronic file) as closely as you would guard a valuable possession.

Ironically, many people freely give away the information that thieves need to impersonate them, out of naivety. Tricking someone into sharing personal information or letting their guard down so a criminal can exploit them is called *social engineering*. This isn't new—people have been ripping off others through deception since the beginning of history. Here are some examples:

- Someone (in person) trying to gain your trust, in order to get you to reveal personal information

- An email or pop-up message designed to trick you into revealing personal information
- A phone call or instant message, again designed to trick you into revealing personal information

The personal touch is often the hardest to resist, because the individuals concerned are normally very good at encouraging you to reveal personal information. It's more difficult when you're unsure if they're genuine—it's unpleasant to mistrust everyone.

This book can't teach you good judgment and provide you with the life experience to discern who is honest and who is dishonest. However, you may wish to consider with care anyone who asks questions about the following:

- Your preferred email address
- Where you were born
- Your maiden name (if you have one)
- Your mother's maiden name
- The school(s) you went to
- Where you currently live
- Your date of birth
- Your favorite sports team
- The type of music you listen to

As you can see, such questioning could give someone enough information to work out the answers to forgotten-password security questions as well as commit identity fraud.

Unexpected phone calls that include subtle questioning can also be an issue. It's possible to make you believe that the call may be genuine and from your bank or your company's network administration team.

Web Browser Risks

Web browsers work by downloading and displaying web pages, which are, essentially, programming scripts. The script is rendered as a formatted web page by your web browser on your local PC.

The trouble is, at the moment when that page is downloaded, there are numerous opportunities for a hacker to take advantage of the connection in various ways. For example, your requests for pages can be intercepted on their way to the server. This can compromise your privacy, because someone can see what pages you're requesting. More important, however, it can compromise any login information you may be sending to a financial or business site. Scripts can also contain malicious code that infects your system, making it perform unwanted activities like sending your private information to a third party or displaying countless ads. Web pages can also have embedded Flash or Java applications that can do harm in some cases.

Configuring Security Settings

Using the wrong security settings in your web browser can result in a variety of security risks. Fortunately, in most browsers, you can easily set the most common security settings by accepting the defaults.

In Internet Explorer, in the Internet Options dialog box, on the Security tab, you can drag a slider to choose between Medium, Medium-High, and High security presets. Medium-High is the best balance between functionality and security in most cases (see Figure 9.9).

FIGURE 9.9   Use the Medium-High setting for the Internet zone for most browsing

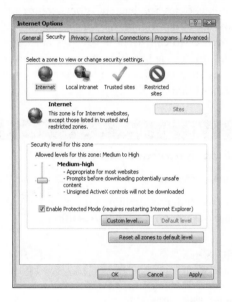

Another prudent security measure is to make sure Protected Mode is enabled for the Internet and Restricted security zones on the Security tab in the Internet Options dialog box. (It's that way by default.) Protected Mode prevents many different security exploits by displaying content in a low-privileges mode.

You may also want to enable ActiveX Filtering. Some websites use ActiveX controls to display content, but ActiveX can also be a security threat. Choose Tools ➢ ActiveX Filtering to toggle the filter on/off. When it's off, ActiveX controls are suppressed.

Controlling Cookies

A *cookie* is a plain text file that a web page (or an ad on a web page) stores on your hard disk for tracking purposes. A cookie can tell an advertiser that you've previously viewed a certain ad, for example, or can keep track of the items in your shopping cart on an e-commerce site.

Cookies are harmless 99.99% of the time, and they may actually perform useful functions that you want. However, there are two risks involved with cookies. One is a privacy threat: a cookie can deliver personally identifiable information to a website. The other is a security threat: a virus or Trojan horse infection may copy a stored password from a cookie and deliver it to someone who can then steal your login information for a site to commit identity theft or some other type of fraud.

Cookies can be divided several ways. A *first-party cookie* is placed on your computer by a website you visit. For example, when you go to www.amazon.com, a cookie provides your name so that the site can welcome you by name. A *third-party cookie* is placed on your computer by an ad on a website, where the ad's parent company isn't related to the owner of the website. For example, as you browse on Facebook, a third-party cookie may record the ads you've clicked, indicating your potential interest in certain products.

A *session cookie* lasts only as long as your web browser is open. When you finish your web-browsing session, session cookies are deleted. A *persistent cookie* stays on your hard disk after you close the browser, either indefinitely or for a certain number of days.

All browsers can be configured to control how your system stores each of the types of cookies. You can create rules for cookie handling, set certain sites from which you'll allow or deny cookies, and delete existing cookies. Each browser does it differently. Exercise 9.6 shows how it works in Internet Explorer 9.

EXERCISE 9.6

View and Delete Cookies in Internet Explorer 9

1. Open Internet Explorer, and choose Tools ➢ Internet Options.

2. On the Privacy tab, drag the slider to Medium if it isn't already set there. Examine the information that appears describing the Medium setting.

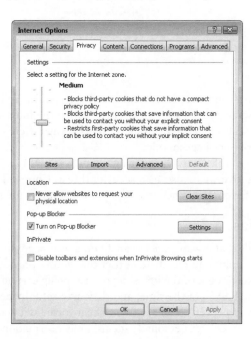

3. Click the Sites button. The Per Site Privacy Actions dialog box opens.

4. In the Address Of Website box, type `www.emcp.com`, and then click Allow.

5. Click OK.

6. Click the Advanced button. The Advanced Privacy Settings dialog box opens.

7. Select the Override Automatic Cookie Handling check box.

8. Under Third-Party Cookies, click Prompt.

9. Select the Always Allow Session Cookies check box.

10. Click OK.

11. Select the Never Allow Websites To Request Your Physical Location check box.

12. Click Clear Sites.

13. Click the General tab.

14. Click the Delete button. The Delete Browsing History dialog box opens.

15. Select the Cookies check box if it isn't already selected.

16. Select the Preserve Favorites Website Data check box if it isn't already selected.

17. Clear all other check boxes, and then click Delete.

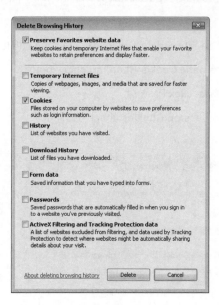

18. Click OK to close the Internet Options dialog box.

19. Click the X on the status message that appears at the bottom of the browser window, telling you that Internet Explorer has finished deleting the selected history.

20. Visit several popular websites until you find one that triggers a Privacy Alert dialog box that prompts you whether to save a certain cookie.

21. Click Block Cookie.

22. Change the setting back to Allow for third-party cookies as you did in steps 6–8.

Controlling Pop-Ups

A *pop-up* is an extra, usually small browser window that appears automatically when you display a certain web page or click a certain button on a page. Pop-ups can serve useful functions, such as displaying the amount of time you've been logged in at a public Wi-Fi location that charges you by the minute. However, pop-ups are more often used to display advertisements or fake dialog boxes that trick you into doing something you really don't want to do, like branching to another company's website.

Most web browsers have a pop-up blocker built into them. You can enable it or disable it, and in some cases you can configure it to be more or less aggressive about blocking pop-ups. Not all browsers' pop-up blockers are very effective, though; sometimes they can miss certain pop-up types. Third-party pop-up blocker applications are also available and are often more effective than the web browser blockers.

EXERCISE 9.7

Configure the Pop-Up Blocker in Internet Explorer 9

1. Open Internet Explorer, and choose Tools ➢ Pop-Up Blocker ➢ Turn Off Pop-Up Blocker.

2. Choose Tools ➢ Pop-Up Blocker ➢ Pop-Up Blocker Settings. The Pop-Up Blocker Settings dialog box opens.

3. Open the Blocking Level drop-down list, and click High: Block All Pop-Ups.

4. In the Address Of Website To Allow box, type *.**emcp.com** and click Add. The asterisk is a wildcard that allows any text in that position. For example, this entry covers www.emcp .com, support.emcp.com, and so on.

5. Click Close.

Working with Secure Sites and Security Certificates

To prevent data from being snooped during transmission, web experts have developed technologies for securely transmitting data to and from web servers. A *secure site's* URL typically begins with https:// rather than http://; and, depending on the browser you're using, there may be other indicators as well, such as a lock icon in the Address bar (see Figure 9.10). *Secure Sockets Layer (SSL)* is one of the technologies used for generating secure connections. Secure connections use a different port than regular browser traffic—usually port 443, whereas regular web browsing is done on port 80.

Sites also employ *security certificates* when communicating via a secure connection that help you know that the site with which you're communicating is legitimate and not a fake out to steal your information. A *certificate* is issued by an *issuing authority*, a company that maintains a website that can tell your browser whether the certificate that a web page is presenting as proof of its identity is valid. A security certificate contains information including a serial number, the person or organization that issued the certificate, and a range of dates it's valid to and from. In Figure 9.10, a pop-up tells you that the certificate issuer for this site is VeriSign.

FIGURE 9.10   Secure URL in Internet Explorer with a pop-up that identifies the certificate issuer

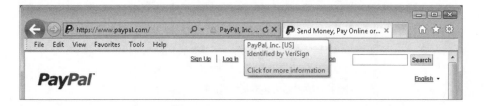

With almost any web browser, it's easy to review and monitor what certificates have been installed, who the issuing authorities are, and what details are held within each certificate. Exercise 9.8 shows where to find security certificate information in Internet Explorer 9.

EXERCISE 9.8

View Security Certificates

1. Open Internet Explorer, and choose Tools ➢ Internet Options.

2. On the Content tab, click the Certificates button. A list of security certificates appears. There are multiple tabs in the dialog box for different certificate publishers and authorities.

3. Click the Trusted Root Certification Authorities tab, and browse the list. These are all companies that issue and verify certificates.

4. Double-click one of the certificates to see its information. Then click OK to close its box.

5. Click Close to close the Certificates dialog box, and then click OK to close the Internet Options dialog box.

Using Phishing Protection

Creating a site that masquerades as a legitimate secure site but actually steals your login information is called *phishing* (or *spoofing*). Phishing employs many tactics, which are evolving all the time. For example, you may get an email that claims to be from your bank, ISP, and so forth, asking you to follow a link to its site to update your details. The email looks authentic, and when you follow the link, the site looks very much like the site of the bank or ISP—except the page probably isn't secure, and some links on the page may not be operational.

Most browsers have some phishing protection built-in. That's part of the role of the different-colored background of the Address bar in Internet Explorer, for example; if it's green, that indicates the phishing filter has determined the site is legitimate. A yellow background indicates caution because there is a problem with the verification; a red background indicates that this site probably isn't what it seems to be and should be avoided.

In Internet Explorer, the phishing filter is called the *SmartScreen filter*, and it can be enabled or disabled. Normally you should leave it enabled, because it provides information and doesn't prevent you from doing anything. Its assessment is fairly accurate, as well. The only drawback (and it's very minor) is that if you leave automatic checking turned on, the browser checks every page you visit, resulting in slightly slower browser performance. If you seldom visit secure sites and you want to check only the specific sites about which you have a question, you can turn off this feature. Exercise 9.9 shows you how to configure the SmartScreen filter in Internet Explorer 9.

EXERCISE 9.9

Use the SmartScreen Filter in Internet Explorer 9

1. Choose Tools ➢ SmartScreen Filter ➢ Turn Off SmartScreen Filter. A dialog box opens with Turn Off SmartScreen Filter already selected.

2. Click OK.

3. Choose Tools ➢ Internet Options.

4. Display the page www.paypal.com.

5. Choose Tools ➢ SmartScreen Filter ➢ Check This Website. A box appears telling you that SmartScreen Filter checked this website and didn't report any threats.

6. Click OK.

7. Choose Tools ➢ SmartScreen Filter ➢ Turn On SmartScreen Filter. A dialog box opens with Turn On SmartScreen Filter already selected.

8. Click OK.

Using InPrivate Browsing

Internet Explorer versions 8 and higher include a highly secure InPrivate Browsing mode that closely guards your privacy. When you start an InPrivate session, none of the history is stored, regardless of your browser's normal history settings. No passwords and login information are stored, and no cookies or temporary Internet files are kept. This mode is very useful when you're visiting a site where safety may be questionable, because in this mode Internet Explorer won't permit the website to affect your computer in any way.

To turn on InPrivate Browsing in Internet Explorer, choose Tools ➢ InPrivate Browsing. A new Internet Explorer window opens, along with a message letting you know that InPrivate Browsing is enabled, and an indicator appears on the Address bar. Close the browser window when you're finished.

Understanding and Preventing Malware Attacks

Malware is a broad term used for many attacks on computer systems. It's shorthand for malicious software, and it covers anything that has been installed on anyone's computer without their consent and is intended for mischief. When thinking about malware, you should consider the following:

Exploits   These take advantage of flaws in the OS or an application.

Viruses   These are used to cause damage and/or disruption.

Worms   These are used to transmit malware.

Trojan Horses   These are applications that mask their true intent.

Adware   These are used to display unwanted advertisements.

Spyware   These are used to report on your computer and possibly steal data.

Rootkits   These conceal themselves on the host OS.

Backdoors   These open ports or other routes into your system.

Keyloggers   These record every keystroke and then use that data for identity theft.

Botnets   These are used to harvest the processing resources of many Internet-connected computers for often-illegitimate purposes.

In the following sections, you'll learn more about several types of malware, and you'll find out how antivirus, antispyware, and antispam applications help you combat them.

 Mac and Linux systems aren't completely immune to malware attacks, but Windows systems run a greater risk of infection. This is partly because some computer-hacking criminals have an axe to grind against Microsoft, and partly because Windows is the most widely used OS, so any financial gain a criminal might get from malware would be maximized by targeting Windows systems.

OS and Application Exploits

All OSs and applications have potential vulnerabilities that criminals can exploit. A *vulnerability* exists when a flaw in the programming creates the potential for misuse, an attacker is aware of the flaw, and a tool or technique that the attacker can use to exploit that vulnerability for malicious purposes is readily available. When criminals use a vulnerability to attack a system, it's called an *exploit*.

Although some OSs are considered to be more secure than others, the reality is that all OSs have weaknesses that, when discovered, are exploited. To guard against exploits, Windows, Linux, and Mac OSs all have mechanisms to update and patch their OS automatically as programmers become aware of vulnerabilities. That's why it's important to download and install all available updates and service packs for your OS promptly. Refer back to Chapter 5, "Maintaining a Computer," and Chapter 6 for details on Windows Update.

Applications can also be exploited, although it happens less frequently because an application is a smaller and less appealing target to a criminal. Widely used applications such as Microsoft Office are most often the targets of application exploit attempts.

As an application or OS ages, more and more security patches become available for it, to the point that rolling them all out individually to users becomes unwieldy. At that point, the OS or application manufacturer typically releases a service pack. A *service pack* is a collection of critical updates (and sometimes minor enhancements) that are released as a group. A service pack is much like a regular update except that it takes longer to download and install, and you can't usually remove it after installing it.

Viruses

A *virus* is computer code that inserts itself into an executable file. When that file is run, the virus's code executes along with the application's code. The virus hides itself inside its host file, so it's not obvious that it's there. A virus's code can cause all manner of mischief, from annoying-but-harmless things like displaying a message, to really destructive things like deleting all files of a certain type or causing your OS to stop working. Most viruses also have a self-replicating component that causes them to spread from one executable file to another. This usually happens via RAM. When the infected file executes, the virus code is copied into RAM, and from there it can attach itself to other executable files.

Many other types of malware are loosely grouped under the banner of "virus" and are detected and removed by antivirus software (covered later in this chapter), but they're actually not viruses because they don't hide themselves in executable files. Instead they may be worms or Trojan horses, explained in the following sections.

Trojan Horses

Trojan horses (often known as Trojans) are rogue applications that may appear to do something useful (and, in fact, may do some small useful things) but also secretly do something malicious, such as damage your system or install a privacy-compromising application. One insidious type of Trojan horse, for example, is a program that claims to scan your system for malware but instead causes system problems (which it tries to get you to pay to get rid of) or installs its own malware, such as a keylogger. A *keylogger* records all keystrokes and sends the information to a file or to a remote location. The hacker can get your usernames and passwords that way and use them to impersonate you. (See the section "Identity Fraud and Social Engineering" earlier in this chapter.)

Trojan horse programs don't replicate themselves, so they aren't viruses, technically speaking. The most common way that Trojan horse programs spread is via worms. (See the next section.) Most antivirus programs can detect and remove Trojan horses.

Worms

Worms are self-transporting applications that carry an active payload, such as a Trojan horse or a virus. Worms can be active or passive: active worms self-transport without human intervention, whereas passive worms rely on the user's innocence to transport themselves from one location to another, normally through email or social engineering. Active worms use email, vulnerabilities in your OS, the Web, and DNS servers to move their payload around a network infrastructure. Most antivirus programs can detect and remove worms.

Adware

Adware is a category of application that displays un-asked-for ads on your computer. The most common type of adware comes in the form of an add-on toolbar for your web browser that supposedly provides "advanced" or "helpful" search services, but that also has the side effect of causing pop-up ads to appear whenever you use your web browser. Adware makers make money when people click the ads they display.

Strictly speaking, not all adware is illegal, and not all adware makers are involved in criminal activity. If you're seduced into downloading a particular web toolbar or application, and then you aren't happy with what it does, or there are too many ads to make it worth the value you're getting from it, you're free to remove it. Removal may not be easy, though; the uninstall option for the toolbar may or may not appear in the Control Panel in Windows, and you may need to connect to a website or go through some extra steps to complete the removal.

Some adware is an out-and-out annoyance, with no pretense of being anything else. Such programs are typically very difficult to remove, much like a virus infection. Your antivirus software may be of some help; you also may need to do a web search on the removal process to find Registry-editing instructions to help you stamp out the adware.

Spyware

Spyware is software that (usually secretly) records your computer usage. Keyloggers are a form of spyware; so are programs that track the websites you visit and what ads you click and send that information back to their owners. Spyware makers get revenue from collecting consumer marketing data, either specifically about you or about all users in general. Most spyware is illegal, works surreptitiously, and can be difficult to remove.

Spyware isn't self-replicating, and it relies on low-level social engineering to spread. The most common way to get infected with spyware is to install a free application from a website. Be very careful what sites you use to download executable files! Another way to get spyware is to run an ActiveX or Java component on a website you visit. A website may seem like a good deal because it's free, but there are many unscrupulous site owners, particularly in the adult entertainment industry, who exploit site visitors by infecting their computers with spyware or adware.

Some antivirus software detects and removes spyware. There are also applications designed specifically to remove spyware and adware from your system, such as Windows Defender (discussed later in this chapter).

Software for Defending Against Malware

Three main classes of applications help protect your system against malware. *Antivirus software* defends against viruses, worms, and Trojan horses; *antispyware* software defends against adware and spyware; and *antispam* software reduces the amount of junk email you receive.

There are also suites available that combine multiple security functions; for example, Norton Security Suite includes antivirus, antimalware, and antispam features, along with identity-protection tools, a firewall, a backup tool, and a PC tune-up tool. In addition, there is some overlap between the types of threats each application guards against; for example, an antivirus program may also target some types of nonvirus malware.

Antivirus Software

Antivirus software attempts to identify virus infections by scanning all the files on your hard disk (or a subset of files that are most likely to contain viruses). Popular antivirus programs include Norton Antivirus and McAfee VirusScan.

The website www.av-comparatives.org/ provides a comprehensive comparison and review of current antivirus applications. Take the time to look through this site and draw your own conclusions about what may be the best antivirus application for you.

Viruses are often concealed by a simple deception. They embed themselves inside an application, redirecting the application's commands and code around themselves while running as a separate task. One way antivirus programs detect a virus is by opening the file and scanning the code, looking for this type of redirection. Some programming languages, such as C++ and Java, generate code in a style that is sometimes wrongly accused by an antivirus program of being infected.

Another way antivirus programs work is to scan the code of each executable file looking for *virus signatures*. A virus's signature is an identifying snippet of its code, sometimes called a *virus definition*. The antivirus program maintains a database of known virus definitions; when it finds a match between its database and some code it finds in a file it scans, it signals a warning that there may be an infection. As new viruses and other threats are discovered, the company updates the virus-definition file for its antivirus program and downloads it to users as an update. Having the most up-to-date definitions is critical for effective virus protection, so you must regularly update your antivirus software (or better yet, set it to update itself automatically).

In addition, many antivirus programs create an MD5 for each application. *MD5* stands for *Message Digest Version 5*, a math calculation that results in a unique value used to reflect the data being checked. If the MD5 changes, this may be treated as a virus attack.

Antivirus applications are normally *resident*, meaning they're continuously running in the background, analyzing your system and any programs when they're opened/closed as well as any files that are opened/closed. Some antivirus programs check incoming and outgoing email too, as well as web pages you visit. You can also tell your antivirus program to do a complete scan of all your files any time you like. (It will probably offer to do one right after you install the antivirus software.)

When your antivirus program finds something suspicious, a message appears, giving you the choice of deleting or quarantining the infected file(s). Deleting a file removes it from your system. Quarantining it places it in an off-limits area so it can't be run, but keeps it on your system. You might quarantine a file that you wanted to share with an IT professional who was tracking virus infections on your network, for example.

EXERCISE 9.10

Install and Use an Antivirus Application

1. If you don't already have an antivirus application, download and install one. For Windows systems, Microsoft's Home Security Essentials program is free, and it will work well for this exercise. You can download it at www.microsoft.com/en-us/security_essentials/default.aspx. Or, if you already have an antivirus application, open it.

2. Using whatever antivirus software you have installed, do the following:

    a. Update the virus definitions.

    b. Run a complete system scan.

3. If any viruses are found, quarantine or delete the files that contain them.

Antispyware Software

Antispyware applications look for known spyware and adware programs and offer to disable them or remove them from your system. Like antivirus applications, antispyware programs look for definitions—that is, code snippets that identify a spyware or adware component. Most antispyware applications also can remove lesser security and privacy threats, such as tracking cookies. Many antivirus applications include antispyware protection too, so you may not have to bother with a separate antispyware application.

Some antispyware applications run all the time in the background, like an antivirus application. Others run only when you specifically open them and initiate a scan.

Windows Defender is a free antispyware tool that comes with Windows. There are also many other free and commercial antispyware programs available, such as Spybot Search & Destroy (www.safernetworking.org).

As with antivirus applications, antispyware applications are most effective when their definitions are up to date.

EXERCISE 9.11

Install and Use an Antispyware Application

1. If you have Windows Vista or Windows 7, open Windows Defender. Or, if you have some other OS, open its antispyware tool if it has one. If not, download and install one.

2. Run a complete check for spyware on your system.

Antispam Software

Spam refers to unwanted junk email. People send spam to try to sell products because doing so is economical—it costs almost nothing to send millions of emails, so even if only a very small percentage of people respond, it's still a money-making proposition. People also send spam to perpetrate fraud, either by trying to sell useless or non-existent products or by trying to trick people into visiting phishing websites or sites where a virus or other malware will be downloaded.

Many email applications include filters and other tools to manage spam. Microsoft Outlook has its own junk-mail filter, for example. However, these built-in filters often fail to catch a lot of the spam because their algorithms for differentiating between spam and legitimate mail aren't sophisticated.

Some antivirus applications include an antispam component, and you can also buy add-on antispam programs or get them for free. For example, *SpamBayes*, available for free at http://spambayes.sourceforge.net/, is an extremely sophisticated email differentiator that uses a ranking system that evaluates each message on multiple criteria to determine its spam probability. It's available for Windows, Unix, Linux, and the Mac OS.

EXERCISE 9.12

Install and Use an Antispam Application

1. Open your current email application, and investigate its antispam features. Look in its Help system if needed to determine what's there.

2. Download and install SpamBayes for your OS from http://spambayes.sourceforge .net, or install another antispam application of your choice.

Diagnosing and Fixing Malware Infections

Even if you have an antivirus application installed, it's not perfect. Occasionally a virus or other malware may get around it, especially a new threat (and especially if you haven't updated your definitions lately). When a system is infected with a virus, a worm, a Trojan horse, or other malware, you may experience some of these symptoms, either immediately or on a particular day or time when the malware triggers itself:

- Your antivirus software may be disabled, and you can't re-enable it. Or, if you didn't already have antivirus software and you're just now installing it, it may not install. This is a very common side effect of virus infection, because it makes it difficult for you to remove the virus.

- Your system may run sluggishly, taking much longer than normal to open windows or applications. Many malware infections bog down a system or cripple it.

- CPU and memory usage may be high even though you aren't doing anything that would cause them to act in this manner. This can happen if the malware is hijacking your system for its own computing purposes.

- A warning or message box may appear onscreen and refuse to go away. For example, there may be a message that your system is infected with a virus and demanding that you enter a credit card to "buy" software that will fix the problem.

- Your friends may let you know that they have been receiving strange emails from you that you didn't send.

- When you use your web browser, you may be bombarded with pop-up ads.

If you start experiencing these symptoms, your own antivirus program may not be much help because a virus may have gotten around it and disabled it. If it's running—great. Do a full virus scan immediately.

If you can't use your local antivirus program, your best bet is an online virus checker. Trend Micro offers a good free one at `http://housecall.trendmicro.com`, for example. Scan your system with that, and then follow the advice the scanner recommends. If the system is infected to the point that it won't operate even to open a web browser, try booting into Safe Mode with Networking. Doing so may disable some of the virus's components temporarily. If you still can't rid of the virus, you may need to consult an IT professional at your local computer shop.

After you've removed the infection, you may need to repair or reinstall your antivirus software and download updates to it.

Summary

In this chapter, you learned about several types of computer security. You learned about measures for preventing hardware and data theft and how to create effective passwords for access control. You learned how to control data and usage permissions including file sharing and encryption and parental controls. You also learned about the risks of using unsecure wireless networks and the importance of using firewalls to block attacks on unused ports. Finally, we discussed web browser security, and you learned about the many types of malware attacks and how to defend against them.

Exam Essentials

Recognize basic security risks and procedures to prevent them. Security risks come in many forms, including physical safety, social engineering, malware, and identity fraud. You should understand each of these threat types and know how to counteract them, both with common sense and with specific utilities and procedures.

Identify security breach prevention methods. User awareness and education is one of the most important prevention methods. Others include wireless encryption, browser security settings, antimalware software, firewalls, and strong passwords that are frequently changed.

Identify access control methods. Passwords and user IDs are the most common access control method used. Make sure you understand how to create an effective password. Other access control methods include locks, parental controls, smart cards, fingerprint readers, and screensavers.

Understand browser safety configuration. A web browser can be made more secure by controlling various features such as cookies, pop-ups, secure browsing (SSL), and ActiveX control downloads.

Diagnose malware infections. Symptoms of malware infection include sluggish-running applications and OSs, disabled antivirus software, and odd messages. Run a full antivirus scan if possible, or use an online antivirus troubleshooter if your antivirus software isn't working. Quarantine or delete any infected files, and escalate the problem to the IT professionals in your organization if appropriate.

Review Questions

1. Which of these is *not* a type of access control?

   A. Fingerprint reader

   B. Password

   C. Biometric device

   D. Pop-up

2. On some Windows servers, _____ is used to manage usernames and passwords.

   A. BIOS

   B. Active Directory

   C. A retina scanner

   D. POST

3. Which of these passwords is the strongest?

   A. password

   B. 123456789

   C. (1776)Independence!

   D. MikeSmith

4. A smart card is a plastic card that contains a(n) _____.

   A. Bar code

   B. Microchip

   C. Serial number

   D. Magnetic strip

5. Which of these is *not* a biometric authentication method?

   A. Fingerprint reader

   B. Retina scanner

   C. Facial-recognition software

   D. Smart card

6. When you are connecting to a wireless Internet connection in an airport, which is the best way to categorize that connection for network sharing purposes?

   A. Home

   B. Work

   C. Public

   D. Private

7. Which of these is a form of wireless encryption?

   A. WPA

   B. WTO

   C. WAP

   D. WSS

8. Firewalls block unauthorized activity on _____.

   A. Passwords

   B. Websites

   C. Drivers

   D. Ports

9. A criminal who calls you, pretends to be from your bank, and asks you for your Social Security number is using _____.

   A. Social engineering

   B. A virus

   C. A worm

   D. A Trojan horse

10. Which of these pieces of information should you never give out to strangers online?

   A. Where you were born

   B. Your Social Security number

   C. Your date of birth

   D. All of the above

11. A(n) _____ is a plain text file that a web page stores on your hard disk for tracking purposes.

   A. Fish

   B. ActiveX control

   C. Pop-up

   D. Cookie

12. What is the prefix for a URL for a secure website?

   A. `https://`

   B. `http://`

   C. `ssl://`

   D. `secure://`

13. How does your browser determine whether a security certificate is valid?

    A. It performs a math calculation on it.

    B. It checks with a certificate-issuing authority.

    C. There is no way to determine whether it's valid.

    D. It makes sure the date of issue is in the past.

14. A site that resembles a secure site such as PayPal but that tries to steal your login information is a(n) _____ site.

    A. Trojan horse

    B. Cookie

    C. Hacker

    D. Phishing

15. How can you minimize the threat of operating system vulnerabilities being exploited by hackers?

    A. Use a pop-up blocker.

    B. Install all OS updates as they become available.

    C. Defragment your hard disk regularly.

    D. All of the above.

16. What type of attack does the SmartScreen filter in Internet Explorer prevent?

    A. Phishing

    B. Pop-ups

    C. ActiveX

    D. Third-party cookies

17. A(n) _____ program pretends to be useful but in fact does something malicious to your system, such as compromising your privacy.

    A. Worm

    B. Virus

    C. Trojan horse

    D. Denial of service

18. A cookie that is automatically deleted when you close your web browser is a(n) _____ cookie.

    A. Third-party

    B. First-party

    C. Session

    D. Persistent

19. A(n) _____ is a self-transporting application that carries an active payload, such as a virus or Trojan horse.

    A. Worm

    B. Cookie

    C. Exploit

    D. Botnet

20. One way that an antivirus program detects viruses is through a database it maintains of virus _____.

    A. Serial numbers

    B. Definitions

    C. Routes

    D. Names

Answers to Review Questions

1. D. A pop-up is a browser window that opens automatically from another browser window. Fingerprint readers are an example of biometric devices, which use physical characteristics for access control.

2. B.   Active Directory is an application that Windows servers use to manage user identities on the network.

3. C. A strong password is long, varied, and unusual, containing no guessable words or predictable number patterns.

4. B. Smart cards contain microchips that can be read by a security system or another chip reader.

5. D. A smart card does not read any biological characteristic of the person who holds it.

6. C. When connecting to a public access point, use the Public option in Windows to turn off file and printer sharing for that connection.

7. A. WPA, or Wi-Fi Protected Access, is one form of wireless encryption for a network. Another is WEP (Wired Equivalent Privacy), which is older and less secure.

8. D. Firewalls prevent network ports from being used by unauthorized programs.

9. A. Social engineering is the technique of tricking a person into providing information that they should keep private.

10. D. All of those pieces of information can be used to steal your identity and should be kept private.

11. D. A cookie stores information a website can reuse when you visit that site, such as your country preferences, name, and buying history.

12. A. The prefix `https://` indicates that the secure HTTP protocol will be used for that connection.

13. B. Certificates are certified by an online authority, which is a company that maintains a database of valid certificates and their identifying codes.

14. D. A phishing site is one that masquerades as a legitimate site in order to steal your private information.

15. B. OS updates are the best way to patch vulnerabilities that can lead to exploits that harm your system.

16. A. The SmartScreen filter is an antiphishing tool.

17. C. A Trojan horse, like its namesake from ancient Greek history, gains your trust by appearing to be something good and then harms you.

18. C. A session cookie lasts only as long as your browsing session. A persistent cookie is the opposite: it remains after you close the browser.

19. A. A worm spreads itself via a network, email, or social engineering. It typically carries some type of malware with it.

20. B. Virus definitions, also called signatures, are used to detect viruses. The antivirus software compares the code in an executable file with the signature of the virus to determine whether the virus is present in that file.

Chapter

10

Safe, Legal, and Green Computer Usage

OBJECTIVES COVERED IN THIS CHAPTER: FUNDAMENTALS OF PC FUNCTIONALITY

✓ **3.3 U.K. Recognize IT related laws and guidelines**

- Data Protection Act
- Copyright Act
- Computer Misuse Act
- Freedom of Information Act

FUNDAMENTALS OF PC TECHNOLOGY

✓ **3.1 U.K. Recognize safety hazards and identify corresponding guidelines**

- Hazardous substances
- Environmental legislation and regulations

✓ **5.1 U.S. Identify environmentally sound techniques to preserve power and dispose of materials**

- Environmentally hazardous substance disposal
- Power Management (power saving features)
- Power management PCs and lower power servers
- Replace large desktops with energy efficient laptops and thin clients

✓ **5.2 U.S. Identify green techniques, equipment, and procedures**

- Define Cloud Computing
- Define VoIP and how it relates to green IT

- Duplex printing and use lower cost per page network printers
- Terminal servers
- Energy Star rating
- Use low power NAS instead of file servers
- Green building infrastructure
- Employee telecommuting

Being a responsible computer user includes understanding and complying with guidelines that ensure a safe, legal, and environmentally conscious computing experience. In this chapter, you'll learn about procedures to follow to make sure you don't pollute the environment or run afoul of the law when using a computer. You'll also learn about some green IT practices that many companies are employing to save themselves money as well as to prevent unnecessary strain on the environment.

Safe and Legal Disposal of Hazardous Substances

Certain computer components and consumable supplies can pollute the environment if you dispose of them along with your regular trash. That's why, in some countries, laws or guidelines require special disposal techniques for certain items. The laws vary depending on the country and state in which you reside, so it's important to familiarize yourself with what's required in your region. In addition, even if your region doesn't require a certain environmentally friendly disposal technique, you may wish to go the extra mile to help the environment and practice that disposal method anyway.

Restriction of Hazardous Substances (RoHS)

In 2003, the European Union passed the Restriction of Hazardous Substances (RoHS) Directive, and it took effect in 2006. This directive restricts the use of six hazardous materials in the manufacture of various types of electronic equipment. These six substances are lead, mercury, cadmium, hexavalent chromium, polybrominated biphenyls, and polybrominated diphenyl ether. (The latter two are flame-retardants used in some plastics.) It's closely linked to the Waste Electrical and Electronic Equipment (WEEE) Directive, which sets collection, recycling, and recovery targets for electrical goods.

Consumer electronic components that may be affected by RoHS include just about anything with a circuit board in it, including computers, cell phones, routers, and printers. RoHS is primarily an issue on which device manufacturers focus; consumers aren't required by law to do anything. However, consumers are strongly encouraged to dispose of items that contain one or more of the six restricted substances by recycling electronic components or delivering them to a hazardous-materials facility rather than discarding them in the trash.

RoHS doesn't require specific product labeling, but many manufacturers have adopted their own compliance marks. Visual indicators may include "RoHS Compliant" labels, green leaves, check marks, and "PB-Free" markings. The WEEE trashcan logo with an X through it is also an indicator that the product may be compliant (see Figure 10.1).

FIGURE 10.1   The WEEE Directive logo

Battery Disposal

All batteries contain toxic substances, such as metals, and can contaminate the environment. Wet-cell (lead-acid) batteries, such as those used in cars and boats, are the most environmentally harmful and have the most stringent disposal guidelines. However, dry-cell batteries, such as those used in PCs and other electronics equipment, are also environmentally hazardous. They contain heavy metals such as mercury, lead, cadmium, and nickel, all of which can contaminate the environment when not disposed of properly, and they can release toxic chemicals into the air when incinerated.

Some of the places where batteries are used in PCs include the following:

- Portable computing devices (laptops, phones, and so on)

- Wireless input devices, such as wireless mice and keyboards

- Motherboards

- Uninterruptible power supplies (UPSs)

Most regions have laws requiring retailers that sell certain types of batteries also to collect them for recycling. The exact rules depend on the battery type and the region. For example, the Battery Directive in the EU (2006) regulates the manufacture and disposal of batteries in the EU. These regulations don't require consumers to recycle; they only require retailers to make that option readily available. The same is true in the United States. Consumers aren't required to recycle most batteries, but vendors are required to take them if consumers want to bring them back.

One way to reduce the environmental impact of batteries is to use rechargeable ones. The U.S. Environmental Protection Agency estimates that one in five dry-cell batteries purchased in the U.S. today are rechargeable. Over its life, each rechargeable battery may substitute for hundreds of single-use batteries.

Computer Recycling and Disposal

Working personal computers can often be donated to charitable organizations that recover and restore them so they can be reused by others in your home town or halfway across the world. Even a nonworking computer can often be repaired to working condition. For that reason, and to protect your privacy, you should erase the data on your hard disk before disposing of a computer.

Nonworking computer parts should be discarded at local recycling or hazardous-waste disposal centers, rather than thrown in the trash, because they may contain components that can be reclaimed. For example, circuit boards contain lead solder, and some of them have coin-style batteries as well.

Monitor Disposal

As you learned in Chapter 2, "Input and Storage Devices," CRT stands for cathode ray tube; it's the older, boxy type of monitor. LCD monitors have largely replaced CRTs, but there are still CRTs in service that are now reaching the end of their useful lives. Therefore, CRT disposal is a very timely topic.

CRTs contain many environmentally harmful elements, including the phosphorous coating on the inside of the monitor glass. Phosphorous is volatile, and it can explode or start a fire when it combines with the oxygen molecules in water. Therefore, in most regions, it's illegal to dispose of a CRT with your regular trash. You must take it to a community recycling or hazardous-waste disposal facility, or pay a recycling company to dispose of it for you.

LCD monitors include circuit boards that contain a small amount of lead, and they're treated similarly to desktop PCs in their disposal.

Toner Disposal

The toner used in laser printers and photocopiers is carcinogenic, so proper disposal of toner is a matter of public safety. Toner cartridges should be returned to the manufacturer or another company that reclaims and recycles them. Handle toner cartridges with some respect to keep the toner from spilling on you, and to keep it out of the air where it could enter a person's lungs. (That's why you shouldn't use a regular vacuum cleaner to clean up toner spills—the air filter isn't fine enough to catch the toner particles, so they get back into the air.)

Cleaning-Supply Disposal

Some of the cleaning supplies used on IT equipment can be hazardous to the environment. Most of the really nasty stuff is associated more with the manufacturing of electronics than with its everyday use, but it still pays to be careful.

You should be able to find disposal instructions on the container of any cleaning chemical. There are different rules in different regions, so check the label. For example, in the U.K., the Control of Substances, Hazardous to Health (COSHH) regulations describe how hazardous substances are to be used, stored, and disposed.

Rather than put complete disposal and handling instructions on the packaging, some products refer you to a material safety data sheet (MSDS) on their website. The MSDS explains what hazards are present in the item, and it dictates the proper disposal and handling of the item.

EXERCISE 10.1

Explore Your Recycling Options

1. Use the Internet or your local phone book to find organizations that will accept old computer parts.

2. Contact the company or agency to find out whether there is any charge for their service, what types of equipment they take, and what they do with it.

IT-Related Laws

Discussing the law is challenging because there are significant differences depending on where you live. Not only do different countries handle IT laws differently, but so do different states and provinces within the same country.

For the U.K. version of the Strata exam, you need to know about some specific pieces of legislation applicable to the EU and the U.K. This topic isn't on the U.S. version of the exam.

Data Protection Directive

The Data Protection Directive is an EU directive that regulates the processing of personal data within the EU. Its purpose is to protect the privacy and human rights of citizens by limiting the ways their personal information may be shared. For example, it ensures that medical professionals are unable to share data with insurance companies.

Some of the key points of this directive include the following:

- Data can be used only for the purpose for which it was collected.

- Data can't be disclosed to anyone else without the permission of the data subject, except where other laws create an exception, such as in crime prevention or detection.

- In most situations, personal information may not be collected without your authorization.

- In many nations, you have a right of access to the information kept on you, again subject to some exceptions.

- No personal information may be kept any longer than it's needed. For example, if you're no longer a customer, a company no longer needs your data. Your data must be kept up-to-date.

- Personal information may not be sent outside the nation (or nation group) in question. (This part has some complex exceptions.)

- In most nations and most cases, organizations that hold personal data must register with a related government department. (In the U.K., this is the Information Commissioner's office.)

- Any organization holding personal information is required to have adequate security measures in place, such as firewalls and staff security training.

- You're entitled to view the data that pertains to you, and to challenge its accuracy and have it amended if needed (unless the data involves personal opinion).

Computer Misuse Act

Computer misuse is a euphemism for hacking. Anything that involves anyone gaining access to systems where they don't have permission is computer misuse. In fact, legislation covers the act of trying to get information to *prepare* to hack (social engineering) as well as the deed itself.

Sections 1–3 of the U.K. Computer Misuse Act of 1990 introduced three criminal offenses:

Section 1: Unauthorized Access to Computer Material   This could include using another person's login and password without permission in order to use either data or an application. This also includes the alteration, deletion, copying, or movement of an application or data, or simply printing out the source code of an application or printing/emailing the data found.

Section 2: Unauthorized Access with Intent to Commit or Facilitate Commission of Further Offenses   This may include accessing system records or databases in order to prepare to commit a crime, or laying a trap to obtain someone's login information or private data.

Section 3: Unauthorized Modification of Computer Material   This includes destroying another user's files, modifying system files, creating a virus, introducing malware locally or on a network, a denial of service attack, or anything that may cause a complete system (or partial system) to malfunction.

There has been some controversy over this act, with complaints that it was hastily prepared and not well thought out, and that it contains significant loopholes and has the potential to lead to unintended consequences. Several amendments have been made to the act via part 5 of the Police and Justice Act of 2006, which helped to clarify the act's intent.

Freedom of Information Act

Generally speaking, legislation related to freedom of information defines an individual's right to access data held by governments and related public bodies on a diverse range of issues.

In the U.K., the Freedom of Information Act 2000 introduces a public "right to know" in relation to public bodies. The act creates a general right of access to information held by public authorities, including legislative bodies, the armed forces, local governments, courts, health services, and public schools, as well as to publicly owned companies. There are many details and exceptions in the full legislation. See http://en.wikipedia.org/wiki/Freedom_of_Information_Act_2000 for a more comprehensive description. At the EU level, a similar regulation permits any citizen of EU countries to request information from the European Parliament, Council, and Commission.

In the U.S., the Freedom of Information Act took effect in 1967, and an Electronic Freedom of Information Act amendment was added in 1996. The act applies only to federal agencies, but all the states have similar statutes that require disclosures by state and local governments.

Copyright Act

The U.K. Copyright, Designs, and Patents Act of 1988 (CDPA) covers current copyright law. It's significant in an IT context because the Internet has made it very easy to share information. Some of that information is protected by copyright, and there may be substantial legal penalties for using it without permission. Works subject to copyright protection include the following:

- Literary, dramatic, and musical works
- Artistic works
- Sound recordings and films
- Broadcasts
- Cable programs
- Published editions

The 1988 act and amendment establishes that copyright lasts until 70 years after the death of its creator (if known), and otherwise 70 years after the work was created or published. For computer-generated works, the limitation is 50 years. For full details about this law, see http://en.wikipedia.org/wiki/Copyright,_Designs_and_Patents_Act_1988.

EXERCISE 10.2

Research IT Laws

Using the Internet, or by contacting your state or local government, find out what IT-related state or local legislation applies to you as an individual consumer.

Energy-Efficient Personal Computing

Saving energy is not only good for the environment, but good for your wallet as well. In the following sections, you'll learn how to minimize the amount of power your computers use while impacting your productivity as little as possible.

Power-Management Plans

Most systems have built-in power-management features that enable you to save energy by shutting down the computer or by placing it in a low-power mode after a specified period of inactivity. The operating system typically controls power management, but some systems also have power-management features available via BIOS Setup.

Low-Power Modes

Different OSs call the various modes by different names, but here are the basic modes. You can set the OS to put the PC into one of these modes automatically after a specified period of inactivity:

Sleep/Standby   All components of the PC except RAM are powered down so that the computer uses only the tiny amount of power required to keep the RAM's content alive. When you resume, all the devices are powered on again. Because the content of RAM remains, waking up from this mode is nearly instantaneous. In Windows and Mac OS, this is called Sleep mode; in Linux it's called Suspend to RAM.

Hibernate   The content of RAM is copied to a special holding area on the hard disk, and then the system is powered off completely, including the RAM. When you resume, the previous RAM content is copied back into RAM, and all the devices are powered on again. Waking from this mode takes a little longer (up to 1 minute), but that's less time than it would take to start up the computer completely after it's been off. In Windows, this feature is called Hibernate. On Linux, it's called Suspend to Disk. On a Mac, the Safe Sleep mode copies the contents of RAM to the hard disk before sleeping, so that if the battery runs out and the computer loses RAM power, hibernation automatically is in effect.

In addition, some OSs enable you to specify a time period of inactivity after which the display dims or turns off completely, and the hard disk stops spinning its platters (if it's a mechanical hard disk, rather than solid state).

EXERCISE 10.3

Put a Computer to Sleep

1. In Windows 7, click Start and click the right-pointing triangle arrow next to the Shut Down command. A menu opens.

2. Choose Sleep. Your computer goes to sleep.

3. Press a key. Some computers may be configured to wake up on a keypress. If yours doesn't wake up, press the Power button to wake it up.

4. Click Start, click the triangle next to Shut Down, and choose Hibernate. Wait for the computer to enter Hibernate mode.

5. Press the Power button to wake up the computer from hibernation.

Choosing Power-Management Settings

Some companies have energy-saving policies, which dictate that employees must place their computers in a low-power mode, or turn them off completely, at the end of a workday. Even if your company doesn't have an official policy, you may want to create one for yourself. You can do this in your OS by setting up a *power plan*. A power plan tells the computer to shut down or to go into one of the power-saving modes from the previous section after a specified period of inactivity. If it's a notebook computer, you can choose separate settings for when it's on battery power versus when it's plugged in. Windows, Mac OS X, and Ubuntu Linux all have similar power-management features.

In Windows, you can choose a standard power plan that includes settings for the display, the hard disks, and the amount of time before the computer goes to sleep. After choosing a plan, you can then customize that plan in a variety of ways, as you'll see in Exercise 10.4.

Mac OS X has an additional power-management feature: it enables you to set the computer to start up and shut down at a certain time every day (see Figure 10.2). In System

Preferences, click the Energy Saver icon, which looks like a light bulb. Then, on the Energy Saver screen, click the Schedule button.

FIGURE 10.2   You can tell a Mac to shut down or start up at a certain time.

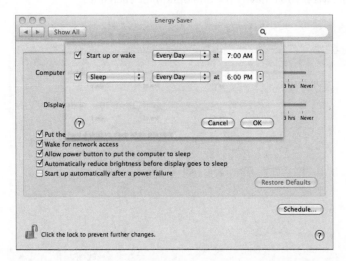

EXERCISE 10.4

Customize a Power Scheme

1. In Windows 7, choose Start ➢ Control Panel ➢ Hardware and Sound ➢ Power Options.

2. Select the Balanced power plan if it isn't already selected.

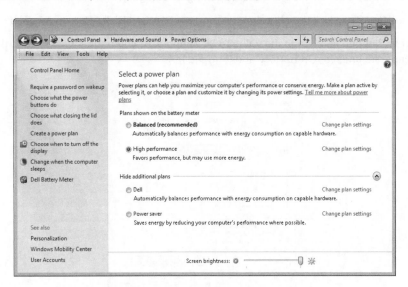

3. Click the Change Plan Settings hyperlink for the Balanced plan. Additional options appear. If you're using a notebook PC, you'll have separate options for On Battery and Plugged In. Otherwise, you'll have only one option for each line.

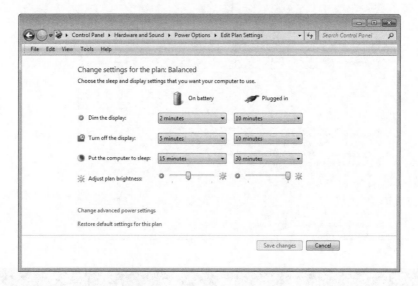

4. Open the Turn Off The Display drop-down list (for Plugged In, if you have a choice), and select 20 minutes.

5. Click Change Advanced Power Settings. The Power Options dialog box opens.

6. Click the plus sign next to Hard Disk, opening its category.

7. Under Hard Disk, click the plus sign next to Turn Off Hard Disk After, opening its category.

8. Next to Plugged In, change the value to 30 minutes. (If you're on a desktop PC, there are no separate lines for On Battery and Plugged In.)

9. Click the plus sign next to Power Buttons And Lid to expand that category.

10. Click the plus sign next to Power Button Action to expand that category.

11. Set the value for both On Battery and Plugged In to Hibernate. (If you're on a desktop PC, there is only one setting.)

12. Click OK.

13. Click Save Changes.

14. Click the Balanced option again, and click Change Plan Settings.

15. Click Restore Default Settings for this plan.

16. Click Yes to confirm.

17. Close the Control Panel.

Shutdown Scripts

On a networked system, the administrator can manage the remote startup and shutdown of any computer connected to the network via shutdown and startup scripts. For example, on Windows systems, you can use the shutdown command at a command prompt to shut down any device for which you know the IP address.

The command is:

```
shutdown -s -m a.b.c.d
```

Where:

- -s is the shutdown option. You can alternatively use -r for reboot.

- -m tells the local machine that this is a remote device.

- a.b.c.d is the IP address of the remote computer. Each letter stands for one of the numbers in the four-section number that is an IP address, like this: 241.55.22.67.

Additional options include the following:

- -t for time (in seconds) to delay the shutdown

- -f to force a shutdown, if you have to do so for urgent reasons

Power-Conserving Equipment

In addition to the OS settings for conserving power, some hardware devices also have their own power savings. For example, notebook PCs use less power than desktops, so replacing as many desktops as possible with notebooks can save a company a significant amount of power. In the following sections, we'll look at some other component savings you can achieve.

Monitors and Energy Savings

The computer display, whether it's built into your notebook computer or a separate stand-alone monitor connected to a desktop PC, consumes the most power of any component in an average system. CRTs consume more power than LCDs, so one way you can conserve energy is to switch over to LCDs for as many computers as possible.

Another way to conserve power is to decrease the brightness of the monitor. Especially on an LCD, doing this can make a big difference; the brighter the display, the more light it generates, and more light means more power.

You can change screen brightness in several ways. One is via the power plan in the OS. Look back at the graphics shown in Exercise 10.4, and notice the Screen Brightness and Adjust Plan Brightness sliders. You can use these to decrease the monitor's brightness under certain power plans.

You can also manually adjust a monitor's brightness. On a standalone monitor, there are typically buttons that open a menu system onscreen from which you can control brightness along with many other factors. On a notebook display, there is usually a brightness control associated with one or more of the keyboard keys plus the Fn key. Hold down Fn, and press the key that is associated with Increase Brightness or Decrease Brightness.

Hard Drives and Energy Savings

Some hard drives are more energy-efficient to operate than others. Solid-state drives, for example, have much lower power needs because there are no mechanical parts. Unless there is a read-write operation, they consume no power. Among mechanical hard disks, drives with lower rotational speeds sometimes use less power than their high-performance counterparts, although the age of the drive is also a factor; newer hard drives use newer technologies that make them more efficient.

Energy Star

Originating in the United States, the Environmental Protection Agency Energy Star rating system for computer technology is now recognized internationally; many other nations use the standard as part of their own power-reduction policies. When you see the Energy Star logo on a PC or a component, as shown in Figure 10.3, you can assume that the device meets certain energy-efficiency standards. For example, an Energy Star monitor puts itself into standby (a low-power mode) when it doesn't detect a signal from the PC, and Energy Star laptops are able to go into Sleep or Hibernate mode when the lid is shut. Energy Star also applies to motherboards, power supplies, and BIOSs that are able to manage power consumption.

FIGURE 10.3   The Energy Star logo

Photo credit: www.energystar.gov

EXERCISE 10.5

Look for Energy Star Hardware

1.   Look for the Energy Star logo on all the computer hardware you have available. Make a list of the items that have it and the items that don't.

2.   For each device that bears the Energy Star logo, find out what power-saving features the device has.

Virtualization and Multiple OSs

One way to save energy is to have fewer computers. If one computer could meet all your needs, you wouldn't need to have all those others, right?

If you need to run multiple OSs on a single PC, virtualization may be the solution you're seeking. With virtualization, you create a separate environment inside the main OS, and within that environment, you can run a virtual computer that has its own separate OS. It borrows memory and storage as needed from the main system, with the virtualization application managing that borrowing so that both OSs remain mostly unaware of each another.

Virtualization has many uses. For example, you can use it to test an application to see how it runs under multiple OSs without having a separate PC with each of those OSs set up. You can also use it to run applications that won't run on your current OS.

Many virtualization applications are available, including these:

- Oracle VirtualBox (free and works on Windows, Mac, and Linux)
- VMware Workstation, a commercial solution
- VMware Player, free for Windows
- QEMU, free for Windows and Linux UK
- VMware Fusion, a Mac commercial solution
- Parallels, a Mac commercial solution
- Virtual PC, a Windows-only solution

This list is by no means definitive; many new virtualization solutions are released every year. Another way to have multiple OSs on a single computer is simply to install them. Place each OS on a separate hard drive. Windows includes a management utility that automatically allows you to select which OS to boot each time you start up. This boot menu is enabled automatically when you install Windows on a PC that already has another OS on it, provided you place Windows on a separate logical drive.

EXERCISE 10.6

Run a Virtual Machine

1. If possible, acquire a version of one of the virtualization applications listed previously. Some of them offer a free trial, and some are entirely free.

2. Install the virtualization software, and then, within that software, install a different OS. It can be a different version of the same OS, or an entirely different OS.

Efficient Printing

You can save both energy and consumable costs by limiting the amount of printing you do. If you don't need to print something—don't. View it onscreen instead.

If you do need to print, you can save paper by printing on both sides of each page. This is called *duplexing*. Some printers duplex automatically; on those that don't, you can re-feed the pages after printing on the first side.

Printer energy cost can also be reduced by having fewer printers, with each printer shared by multiple people. To further reduce the number of pages printed, you can set up psychological barriers to printing by placing the printer a slight distance from the people using it and by placing the printer in a public location where everyone will see what is printed.

Most printers can also be set to use power-saving Sleep modes when they aren't being used. When a printer is in Sleep mode, most of its lights, LEDs, and fans turn off. The printer wakes up automatically when it receives a print job. This type of savings is part of the Energy Star system.

A *multifunction printer* can reduce the need for other office peripherals by combining their functions into a single device. For example, some multifunction printers are also scanners, copiers, and fax machines.

Energy-Efficient Server Usage

Servers are powerful computers, and they consume quite a bit of power. Even a minor reduction in the power consumption of a server has the potential to pay off big in the long run, because a server is on 24 × 7.

Efficient Server Hardware

For a server to be energy-efficient, it should have as few power-consuming components as possible. For example, if it only needs one hard disk, it should have only one; and if it can accept a solid-state hard drive, all the better. A server doesn't need user components like a fancy sound card or a powerful display adapter; these components consume power without providing a benefit to the server. It also doesn't need a large monitor, and the monitor can be turned off when nobody is actively sitting at the server workstation.

You can also make a server more energy-efficient and extend its life by keeping it in a cold room. Computers like to be cooler than humans do, so if you reduce the temperature in the server room to 60 or even 50 degrees Fahrenheit, they will perform better and use less power.

Combining Server Functions

Another way to decrease the power consumed by a company's servers is to combine server functions into fewer PCs. Often, a single PC can serve as multiple types of servers simultaneously. With server platforms such as VMware ESXi and Citrix, system administrators can have a selection of OSs running different roles on the same PC, limited only by the PC's CPU, memory, and storage capacity. The storage can even be on another system, with a virtual server simply processing task-specific instructions.

Terminal Servers

Back in the olden days of computing, a company would have a single large mainframe that served as a *terminal server*. All the users connected to it via *terminals*, which were monitors and keyboards that used the common pool of CPU and memory provided by the server. Terminals connected to the terminal server via a legacy serial interface.

When desktop PCs became affordable enough for all users to have their own, people rejoiced, and terminal servers became much less popular. They're still used occasionally to connect serial-based applications or devices to move data over a LAN.

Remote Desktops

Nowadays, network and Internet bandwidth is high enough that some IT departments are revisiting the idea of providing computer services remotely. This is most often seen with *remote desktops*, where users employ a network or Internet connection to connect to another PC and use it as if they were physically sitting at it. Remote desktops enable multiple users to access the same PC from different locations at different times, which saves the energy and expense involved in maintaining separate identical PCs for people who job-share, for example. Security administration and file backup costs are also reduced.

Some versions of Windows come with a Remote Desktop application. Third-party remote-desktop applications are also available, as well as Internet-provided desktop services such as *GoToMyPC*.

Network Attached Storage

A *network attached storage (NAS)* device is a network-aware hard disk or other storage unit that network users can use to share files. NAS devices are less expensive than file servers, and they're also more energy-efficient to operate.

Inexpensive NAS devices can be attached to a router via Ethernet cable. In addition, some routers come with their own internal hard drives for NAS capability. For example, the Apple Time Capsule is a wireless router and Ethernet switch with a high-capacity hard drive. The Time Capsule works with the Time Machine software included in Mac OS X to maintain a continuous file backup for all users on the network.

Energy Conservation in Business IT

All the energy-saving methods discussed so far in this chapter are small, individual things that together add up to big savings over the long run. But if you're a decision-maker involved in a business's long-term plans, you can make energy-conservation decisions about the company's big picture that can make a significant impact immediately. The following sections explain some of the ways that a business can save on both energy and expense by "going green."

Green Building Infrastructure

Green building is the process of designing and building a home or business so that it's as energy-efficient and sustainable as possible, from choosing the site and constructing the building to operating and maintaining it on a daily basis. The main objective is to reduce the building's overall impact on human health and the natural environment by efficiently using energy and water, protecting occupant health, and reducing waste, pollution, and environmental degradation. *Green IT* refers to environmentally responsible computing, which can be part of an overall green building plan for a company.

Both the U.S. and U.K. versions of the Strata exam objectives include two specific green building infrastructure topics:

Eliminating Cool Air Leaks in Server Rooms   If servers are kept in a room that is significantly cooler than the rest of the facility (which is a good idea, as mentioned earlier, to extend the server's life), make sure the room is well insulated, with tight-fitting seals at the doors and windows.

Proper Spacing for Cooling IT Equipment   When you use fans or air conditioning to keep IT equipment cool, allowing space for the air to flow between items makes the cooling process easier and more efficient. Placing rows of servers tightly in racks is ill advised because they will keep each other hot.

The U.S. version of the Strata exam also includes a third topic under the heading Green Building Infrastructure. It's arguably not really an infrastructure issue, but an issue for individual PCs:

Energy-Efficient Cooling Fans (BIOS Adjustable)   Some PCs include a temperature sensor inside that enables the BIOS to adjust the fan speed according to the temperature it registers. This enables the fan to slow down, so that it uses less energy, whenever the fan isn't needed to keep the system at a safe running temperature.

Cloud Computing

Cloud computing means performing computing activities by accessing the network or Internet, rather than by using applications and data stored on your own individual computer. The term *cloud computing* derives from the fact that a picture of a cloud is often used in network diagrams to signify a wide area network (WAN) such as the Internet.

Many businesses are finding that it's much more economical to buy access to the applications they need, and have employees access them over the Internet, than it is to buy individual copies of the applications for each employee's PC and then pay someone to support them. It's also more energy-efficient, because applications and updates are delivered electronically rather than as boxed software (which uses energy in the manufacture of the discs and boxes, and in the transportation of the boxes to the destination). Microsoft Office 365 offers online access to Office applications for a smaller price than the regular Office product, for example, and many free services like Google Docs and Zoho offer services equivalent to Microsoft Office for free (or nearly free).

Cloud computing can also include using the processing resources of a remote server instead of those of your own PC. For example, if you need to perform a complex sort on an online database, you issue the command to the database program remotely, and then the server on which the database is stored handles the processing burden of that task. Therefore, your local PC doesn't need to have a large amount of RAM and a fast CPU to perform such a task.

Voice over IP (VoIP)

Voice over IP (VoIP) is a technology that uses the Internet rather than a public switched telephone network to deliver telephone services. A company that uses VoIP for its phone system can save money by not having to run separate telephone wires through its building, and it can also save energy by not having to maintain a phone system separate from its network and Internet connectivity.

A VoIP system can also save in hardware costs. A single switch can be used to administer both Internet and telephone services. And employees who work primarily on the phone at a computer can work from headsets that plug directly into the computer's sound card, eliminating the need for a separate telephone for each employee.

Telecommuting

Telecommuting refers to employees working from home rather than reporting to an office building every day. Telecommuting can provide a company with tremendous energy savings because it doesn't have to maintain office space (including lighting, heating, and cooling) for all of its workers. It can also save employees money because they don't have to travel from home to an office every day, and the reduced reliance on transportation systems helps to reduce fuel emissions. Telecommuting can also increase worker satisfaction, leading to a lower attrition rate.

Summary

In this chapter, you learned how to make your computing experience safe, legal, and environmentally responsible. You learned how to dispose of hazardous substances safely, including cleaning supplies, circuit boards, monitors, and batteries. You also learned about some IT-related laws applicable to the EU and the U.K. The chapter also covered how to make personal computers and servers more energy efficient via power-management plans and power-conserving hardware, and by combining server functions. Finally, you learned about some business-related energy-conservation policies such as cloud computing, VoIP, and telecommuting.

Exam Essentials

Recognize IT-related laws and guidelines.   For the U.K. version of the Strata exams, you need to know about several pieces of IT-related legislation: the Data Protection Act, Copyright Act, Computer Misuse Act, and Freedom of Information Act.

Dispose of materials properly.   Almost all electronics contain lead and should be recycled or taken to a hazardous-waste disposal facility. Batteries should also be recycled because of the metals they contain. Placing items that contain heavy metals in regular trash pollutes the environment unnecessarily. Some cleaning supplies should also require special disposal; see a substance's MSDS for details.

Understand power-saving techniques for computers and peripherals. Operating systems have power-saving features, such as power plans in Windows, which place the computer in a low-power mode after a specified period of inactivity. Many peripherals, such as printers, also have low-power modes.

Identify green equipment, techniques, and procedures. A company can save both energy and money by creating IT policies that support power savings. For example, replacing desktops with laptops, removing non-essential components from a server, replacing file servers with NAS, and setting a PC to sleep after a period of inactivity are all green techniques. Using Energy Star–rated hardware can also help.

Understand how business infrastructure affects energy usage. Businesses can dramatically decrease their operational and energy costs by allowing workers to telecommute, by designing their buildings with energy conservation in mind, and by employing cloud computing and VoIP technologies.

Review Questions

1. What does RoHS stand for?
   A. Reuse of Hardware/Software
   B. Rebuilding of Hazardous Structures
   C. Reutilization of Hazards Standard
   D. Restriction of Hazardous Substances

2. What does RoHS limit?
   A. The number of new PCs that can be made and sold each year
   B. The use of six hazardous materials in electronics manufacturing
   C. Heavy metals thrown away in regular trash (not recycled)
   D. Hazardous materials used in building additions

3. Laptop batteries should be recycled because they contain _____.
   A. Electrical charge that could hurt someone
   B. Toxic chemicals
   C. EMI
   D. Circuit boards

4. A CRT monitor, in addition to being a large plastic box that takes up space in a landfill, is also hazardous to the environment because the inside of its glass is coated with _____.
   A. Phosphorous
   B. Lead
   C. Cadmium
   D. Chromium

5. Toner can be _____, so proper disposal of toner is a matter of public safety.
   A. Flammable
   B. Caustic
   C. Carcinogenic
   D. Explosive

6. Which of these is the best description of an MSDS?
   A. It's a safe container in which to place used batteries.
   B. It's an information sheet that tells how to handle a chemical.
   C. It's a type of cooling device that cuts energy costs for a server.
   D. It's a sheath in which to run cables that are susceptible to EMI.

7. Which U.K. or EU law makes it illegal for a utility company to sell your address and phone number to a third-party company that then uses it to try to sell you a product or service?

- **A.** Data Protection Directive
- **B.** Computer Misuse Act of 1990
- **C.** Freedom of Information Act of 2000
- **D.** Copyright, Designs, and Patents Act of 1988

8. What power-conservation mode copies the content of RAM to the hard disk and then powers off the PC completely?

- **A.** Standby
- **B.** Sleep
- **C.** Shut Down
- **D.** Hibernate

9. On a Windows PC, `shutdown -s -m 211.66.82.1` is an example of a(n) _____.

- **A.** Shutdown script
- **B.** Power plan
- **C.** Hibernation script
- **D.** Trojan horse

10. Which type of monitor is the most energy-efficient to use?

- **A.** LCD
- **B.** CRT
- **C.** CPU
- **D.** RAM

11. On a notebook PC, you may be able to adjust the monitor brightness by pressing an arrow key in combination with the _____ key.

- **A.** Ctrl
- **B.** F1
- **C.** Fn
- **D.** Alt

12. Hardware that meets certain energy-efficiency standards has the _____ logo.

- **A.** MSDS
- **B.** RoHS
- **C.** Multiboot
- **D.** Energy Star

13. _____ enables you to run multiple operating systems on a single PC, and it is useful for testing an application on multiple OSs.

    A. Remote desktop

    B. Telecommuting

    C. NAS

    D. Virtualization

14. A(n) _____ connection enables you to control a PC from another location via a network connection to it.

    A. Virtualization

    B. Remote desktop

    C. Telecommuting

    D. Cloud computing

15. _____ is a network-aware hard disk or other storage unit that network users can use to share files with one another.

    A. Virtualization

    B. RoHS

    C. MSDS

    D. NAS

16. Eliminating cool air leaks in server rooms is an example of _____ practices.

    A. Green building

    B. Virtualization

    C. NAS

    D. VoIP

17. _____ means using applications and data stored in a remote network location, such as on the Internet, rather than using applications and data stored on your own computer.

    A. NAS

    B. Cloud computing

    C. VoIP

    D. RoHS

18. _____ is a technology that uses the Internet rather than a public switched telephone network to deliver telephone services.

    A. NAS

    B. Cloud computing

    C. VoIP

    D. Telecommuting

19. _____ refers to employees working from home rather than reporting to an office building.

- **A.** NAS
- **B.** Cloud computing
- **C.** VoIP
- **D.** Telecommuting

20. One way to cut down on printer consumable costs is _____ printing.

- **A.** Duplex
- **B.** Local
- **C.** Inkjet
- **D.** VoIP

Answers to Review Questions

1. D. RoHS stands for Restriction of Hazardous Substances, an EU directive that took effect in 2006.

2. B. RoHS limits the use of lead, mercury, cadmium, hexavalent chromium, polybrominated biphenyls, and polybrominated diphenyl ether in electronics manufacturing.

3. B. Batteries contain toxic chemicals such as lead, nickel, and/or cadmium.

4. A. The inside of a CRT is coated with phosphors that make the pixels light up. Phosphorous can explode or burn when exposed to water.

5. C. Toner is a carcinogen. It is a combination of plastic and metal, so it is not caustic, flammable, or explosive.

6. B. MSDS stands for material safety data sheet. It is a document that dictates the proper handling and disposal of a chemical.

7. A. The Data Protection Directive (EU) prevents data from being used for purposes other than those for which it was collected, and from being shared with another company.

8. D. Hibernate saves the content of RAM to the hard disk and then shuts off all power to the computer. A computer can remain in Hibernate mode indefinitely because no power is being used.

9. A. A shutdown script such as this one can be used to shut down a PC remotely via its IP address.

10. A. An LCD monitor is more efficient than a CRT. CPU and RAM are not types of monitors.

11. C. The Fn key is commonly used along with some other key, such as an arrow key, to change the monitor's brightness.

12. D. The Energy Star logo marks equipment that uses power efficiently and may have special power-management features.

13. D. Virtualization software creates a separate operating system environment within the main OS on a computer.

14. B. Remote desktop enables you to use a computer remotely with the monitor, keyboard, and mouse you have available locally.

15. D. NAS stands for network attached storage, which is a network-capable storage device. Using NAS rather than a file server saves energy.

16. A. Green building practices include methods of keeping cool air from leaking out of a server room, as well as other construction methods that increase insulation.

17. B. Cloud computing means performing computer activities by using applications stored online rather than owning those applications on your own computer.

18. C. VoIP stands for Voice over IP. It refers to a phone system that is implemented over a data network or Internet connection.

19. D. Telecommuting, in which employees work from home and connect to their office via telephone or the Internet, can save a company money and energy.

20. A. Duplex printing means printing on both sides of the paper. This can help you save money on paper.

Appendix

About the Companion CD

THIS APPENDIX COVERS:

- ✓ What you'll find on the CD
- ✓ System requirements
- ✓ Using the CD
- ✓ Troubleshooting

What You'll Find on the CD

The following sections are arranged by category and summarize the software and other goodies you'll find on the CD. If you need help with installing the items provided on the CD, refer to the installation instructions in the "Using the CD" section of this appendix.

Sybex Test Engine

The CD contains the Sybex test engine, which includes the six practice exams, two each for Exam FC0-U11, Exam FC0-U21, and Exam FC0-U41.

Electronic Flashcards

These handy electronic flashcards are just what their name suggests. One side contains a multiple-choice or fill-in-the-blank question, and the other side shows the answer.

Adobe Reader

We've also included a copy of Adobe Reader so you can view the PDF files that accompany this book's content. For more information on Adobe Reader, or to check for a newer version, visit Adobe's website at www.adobe.com/products/reader/.

System Requirements

Make sure your computer meets the minimum system requirements shown in the following list. If your computer doesn't match up to most of these requirements, you may have problems using the software and files on the companion CD. For the latest and greatest information, please refer to the ReadMe file located at the root of the CD-ROM:

- A PC running Microsoft Windows 98, Windows 2000, Windows NT4 (with SP4 or later), Windows Me, Windows XP, Windows Vista, or Windows 7
- An Internet connection
- A CD-ROM drive

Using the CD

To install the items from the CD onto your hard drive, follow these steps:

1. Insert the CD into your computer's CD-ROM drive. The license agreement appears.

> *Windows users*: The interface won't launch if you have autorun disabled. In that case, click Start ➤ Run (for Windows Vista or Windows 7, Start ➤ All Programs ➤ Accessories ➤ Run). In the dialog box that appears, type **D:\Start.exe**. (Replace *D* with the appropriate letter if your CD drive uses a different letter. If you don't know the letter, see how your CD drive is listed under My Computer.) Click OK.

2. Read the license agreement, and then click the Accept button if you want to use the CD.

The CD interface appears. The interface allows you to access the content with just one or two clicks.

Troubleshooting

Sybex has attempted to provide programs that work on most computers with the minimum system requirements. Alas, your computer may differ, and some programs may not work properly for some reason.

The two likeliest problems are that you don't have enough memory (RAM) for the programs you want to use, or that you have other programs running that are affecting the installation or running of a program. If you get an error message such as "Not enough memory" or "Setup cannot continue," try one or more of the following suggestions and then try using the software again:

Turn Off Any Anti-virus Software Running on Your Computer   Installation programs sometimes mimic virus activity and may make your computer incorrectly believe that it's being infected by a virus.

Close All Running Programs   The more programs you have running, the less memory will be available to other programs. Installation programs typically update files and programs; so if you keep other programs running, installation may not work properly.

Have Your Local Computer Store Add More RAM to Your Computer   This is, admittedly, a drastic and somewhat expensive step. However, adding more memory can really help the speed of your computer and allow more programs to run at the same time.

Customer Care

If you have trouble with the book's companion CD-ROM, please call the Sybex Product Technical Support phone number at (800) 762-2974.

Glossary

A

access control   The technologies used to control who or what has access to a computer system or network.

access time   The amount of time that elapses between a PC's request for data from the CD and the drive's delivery of the first part of that data.

active cooling system   A cooling system that contains moving parts, such as a fan.

Active Directory   A user- and identity-management system in Windows servers that controls user login.

ActiveX   A Microsoft technology that uses the Microsoft .NET programming framework. It enables a web browser to interact with the OS to run mini-applications.

ActiveX controls   An ActiveX program that runs a mini-application.

add-on   A browser extension that adds to your browser the capability of handling new content types. Also called a *plug-in*.

ADSL   *See* asymmetric DSL.

adware   A category of application that displays unasked-for ads on your computer.

allocation units   *See* clusters.

amplification   A means of making the sound louder as it comes out of a PC or other device.

antispam   Software that detects and removes or segregates spam email.

antispyware   Software that detects and removes spyware.

antistatic mat   A mat onto which you set a component to drain away any built-up static charge that might result in ESD damage.

antistatic wrist strap   A wrist strap that keeps you connected to a component, constantly equalizing the voltage potential between you and the component so that ESD isn't a problem.

antivirus software   Software that helps protect your system against malware such as viruses, worms, and Trojan horses.

APIPA   *See* automatic private IP addressing.

asymmetric DSL (ADSL)   DSL service in which the upload speed is slower than the download speed.

automatic private IP addressing (APIPA)   A means of assigning IP addresses without a DHCP server on a network within a certain range of addresses.

B

bandwidth   A network connection's ability to send data swiftly and in large quantities.

BD   *See* Blu-ray disc.

binary   A numbering system with only two states: 0 or 1 (on or off).

biometric devices   Devices that identify users by scanning for one or more physical traits, such as fingerprints or retina.

bit   A binary digit, either 0 or 1.

bits per second (bps)   A measurement of data transfer throughput.

Blue Screen of Death (BSOD)   *See* STOP error.

Bluetooth   A short-range wireless networking protocol, separate from Wi-Fi, also known as IEEE 802.15. It's used for cell phones, home theatre devices, and gaming consoles.

Blu-ray disc (BD)   An optical disc that uses Blu-ray technology and is read with a blue laser.

bps   *See* bits per second.

broadband   A wide pathway capable of carrying data at a high rate of speed, such as on the Internet.

broadband router   A router used to help share Internet connectivity. It may come with software, instructions, or other extras.

brownout   *See* sag.

browser cache   A holding area on the hard disk that maintains a copy of some of the files required to display web pages you have visited. When you revisit a page, the browser may be able to reload certain files from the stored cache.

BSOD   *See* Blue Screen of Death.

bubble jet   *See* thermal inkjet printer.

buffer   A simple version of a cache, holding recently used data in case it's needed again.

bus width   The width of a data pathway.

byte   Eight binary digits of data.

C

cache   A temporary storage area for recently used data, located near the processor and connected to it by an extremely high-speed pathway.

carcinogen   A product or substance that causes cancer.

CardBus   An older type of expansion slot and card for notebook computers. CardBus was replaced by *ExpressCard*, the current standard.

case   The rectangular outer shell of a computer, into which everything else connects.

Cat5 cable   A type of UTP cable that can carry data at up to 100 Mbps.

Cat5e cable   A type of UTP cable that can carry data at up to 1 Gbps.

Cat6 cable   A type of UTP cable that can carry data at up to 10 Gbps.

cathode ray tube (CRT)   A type of monitor that is large and boxy, like an old-style television. It uses an electron gun to light up phosphors on a screen to create the image.

CAV   *See* constant angular velocity.

CCD   *See* charge-coupled device.

CD-R   *See* Compact Disc Recordable.

CD-ROM   *See* Compact Disc Read-Only Memory.

CD-RW   *See* Compact Disc Rewriteable.

central processing unit (CPU)   The main processor chip inside a computer or other electronic device. A processor is an integrated circuit containing millions of transistors.

Centronics   A type of connector used to attach a legacy parallel printer cable to the printer. It uses a plastic bar wrapped with metal tabs.

charge-coupled device (CCD)   An array of photosensitive cells that converts light into an electrical charge. Used in a scanner to digitize an image.

CHS   *See* cylinders, heads, and sectors.

clean install   An installation of an OS or application that involves removing the previous version first. Compare to *upgrade install*.

clean uninstallation   An uninstallation that removes any leftover helper or data files that were created by the uninstalled application.

client   A PC that an end user employs to accomplish tasks. Compare to *server*.

client-server network   A network that consists of one or more servers as well as one or more clients.

cloud computing   Performing computer activities by accessing the network or Internet, rather than by using applications and data stored on your own individual computer.

clusters   Groups of sectors that the OS uses to address the storage areas. Also called *allocation units.*

CLV   *See* constant linear velocity.

CMOS   *See* complementary metal-oxide semiconductor.

commercial operating system   An OS that is sold up front, rather than given away for free or shared on the honor system. Windows and Mac OS X are examples.

Compact Disc (CD)   An optical storage disc that stores data in patterns of more and less reflective areas.

Compact Disc Read-Only Memory (CD-ROM)   A read-only CD.

Compact Disc Recordable (CD-R or CD+R)   A CD that can be written to once.

Compact Disc Rewriteable (CD-RW or CD+RW)   A CD that can be written to, erased, and rewritten.

Compatibility Mode   A mode in Windows for running applications that simulates earlier Windows versions.

complementary metal-oxide semiconductor (CMOS)   A chip on a motherboard that stores the BIOS Setup settings; this chip, although volatile, requires very little power and is powered by the motherboard battery. Newer motherboards use flash RAM instead.

constant angular velocity (CAV)   A CD drive that spins at a constant speed, no matter which spot on the disk is being read. The data rate changes as needed. All writeable CD drives are CAV.

constant linear velocity (CLV)   A CD drive that reads data at a constant rate, no matter which spot on the disk is being read. The rotation changes speed as needed.

consumables   Supplies that need to be replaced as they're consumed, such as printer paper and ink.

contention   Competition with other network users for bandwidth.

cookie   A plain text file that stores data about previous web browser activities for reuse in future web browsing sessions.

core   A processor. In a multicore CPU, there are multiple processors operating in a single chip.

CPU   *See* central processing unit.

crash   A situation when an application stops working.

crossover cable   A cable that connects two similar devices, where the order of the wires at one end is opposite the usual order. Also called a *patch cable*.

crosstalk   *See* electromagnetic interference.

CRT   *See* cathode ray tube.

current   A measure of electrical amperage.

cursor   An onscreen mouse pointer.

cylinder   All the tracks that are accessible at a given actuator arm position on a hard disk.

cylinders, heads, and sectors (CHS)   A measurement of hard-disk capacity, derived by multiplying the cylinders by the number of heads by the number of sectors. Also called *geometry*.

D

D-sub connector   A connector with a D-shaped metal ring around a set of pins.

DDR   *See* double data rate SDRAM.

decimal   A numbering system with 10 digits, 0 through 9.

default gateway   The address of the router through which your computer goes out to the Internet or another larger network segment.

degauss   To discharge a built-up magnetic field within a CRT that may be causing the picture to be distorted.

desktop case   A desktop PC that rests on its largest side.

desktop PC   A traditional rectangular-box PC with a separate keyboard, video monitor, and mouse.

DHCP   *See* dynamic host configuration protocol.

digital rights management (DRM)   A system for preventing unauthorized sharing of digital content such as books, movies, and videos.

digital subscriber line (DSL)   A broadband Internet service that delivers Internet connectivity via telephone lines.

Digital Versatile Disc/Digital Video Disc (DVD)   An optical disc that, like a CD, stores data in patterns of more and less reflective areas, but holds more data than a CD.

Digital Visual Interface (DVI)   A successor to VGA for connecting monitors. It's a rectangular plug consisting of 24 pins for digital transmission plus an extra 4-pin block for analog signals for backward compatibility.

digital zoom   The zoom on a digital camera that simulates zooming by interpolating the picture. Compare to *optical zoom*.

DIMM   *See* dual inline memory module.

distribution package   A package that consists of a free OS such as Linux plus a commercial add-on for it, such as a shell like Ubuntu or Red Hat.

distro   *See* distribution package.

DNS   *See* domain name system.

domain name system (DNS)   A type of server that translates between the numeric addresses of IPv4 and the friendlier domain names of the Internet.

dot pitch   The measurement of the distance between one color in a triad on a CRT monitor and the same color in the adjacent triad. The lower the number, the better quality the monitor.

dots per inch (dpi)   A measurement of print output resolution. A higher dpi produces text with crisper edges and more realistic-looking graphics.

double data rate (DDR) SDRAM   RAM that is synchronized with the system bus and runs at twice the speed of the system bus.

double-pumped   RAM that has data pumped in on both the rising and falling of each tick of the internal system clock.

dpi   *See* dots per inch.

drive   A device that reads and writes to disks, such as hard or floppy disks. On hard disks, the disk and the drive are a single unit.

drive bay   A cavity in a computer case where a drive can be mounted.

driver   A file or set of files that contains information needed for the OS to communicate with a hardware device.

drum   In a laser printer, the cylinder on which the page image is written by changing the electrical charge on parts of the drum where toner should be applied.

DSL   *See* digital subscriber line.

dual inline memory module (DIMM)   A RAM module that uses pins on both sides of the circuit board.

dual-boot   The capability of having two or more OSs on the same PC, and being able to choose at startup which one should load. Also called *multiboot*.

duplexing   Printing on both sides of the paper.

DVD   *See* Digital Versatile Disc.

DVI   *See* Digital Visual Interface.

Dynamic Host Configuration Protocol (DHCP)   A protocol that enables a server to assign dynamic IP addresses to computers automatically.

dynamic IP address   An IP address that is assigned to a device on-the-fly, rather than permanently assigned. Compare to *static IP address*.

dynamic RAM (DRAM)   RAM that has to be constantly refreshed to retain its contents. Most RAM on a PC is this type.

E

edition   A certain packaging of a version of an application or OS, containing a unique set of features. For example, Windows 7 comes in Home Premium Edition and Professional Edition, among others.

EEPROM   *See* electrically erasable programmable read-only memory.

electrically erasable programmable read-only memory (EEPROM)   ROM memory that can be erased and rewritten by a burst of electricity.

electromagnetic interference (EMI)   Crosstalk that occurs when electricity passing nearby generates a magnetic field that interferes with a cable or device.

electrostatic discharge (ESD)   Static electricity, which can ruin electronic devices. It occurs when two items of unequal voltage potential come into contact with one another.

EMI   *See* electromagnetic interference.

encrypt   To scramble the content of a file so that it can't be browsed until it's unencrypted (usually via a password).

ESD   *See* electrostatic discharge.

Ethernet   A popular networking technology used for most home and business networks. Can also refer specifically to wired network connections within those networks.

exploit   Malware that takes advantage of flaws in the OS or an application.

ExpressCard   The current standard for expansion slot and card types. There are two types: ExpressCard | 34 and ExpressCard | 54. The latter is L-shaped so that the connector portion is the same as on ExpressCard | 34.

extended partition   An additional partition on a hard disk that has one or more primary partitions. An extended partition can then have additional logical drives.

F

facial recognition   A technique for authenticating computer users by scanning their faces.

female connectors   Connectors with holes into which pins are inserted. Compare to *male connectors*.

File Transfer Protocol (FTP)   A protocol used for moving files between Internet locations.

Finder   The file-management interface in Mac OS X.

fingerprint recognition   A technique for authenticating computer users by scanning their fingerprints.

firewall   A utility or hardware device that prevents unauthorized network activity on particular ports.

first-party cookie   A cookie placed on your computer by a website you visit. Compare to *third-party cookie*.

flag   A marker on a file that indicates its status or the permissions assigned to it, such as Read-Only.

flash drive   A drive that stores data using flash RAM.

flash memory card   A card containing flash RAM that can be inserted into or removed from a card reader.

flash RAM   A type of nonvolatile RAM that holds its data until it's rewritten.

form factor   The size, shape, and orientation of a computer case. Can also apply to motherboards and power supplies.

front-side bus   *See* system bus.

full duplex   Two-way communication that can occur in both directions simultaneously. Compare to *simplex* and *half-duplex*.

full tower   A large tower computer case. *See* tower case.

G

Gb   *See* gigabit.

geometry   *See* cylinders, heads, and sectors.

GHz   *See* gigahertz.

gigabit (Gb)   Approximately one billion bits. Often used as a measurement of data transfer throughput.

gigahertz (GHz)   Billions of hertz, a measurement of CPU speed.

green building   The process of designing and building a home or business so that it's as energy-efficient and sustainable as possible.

green IT   Environmentally responsible computing, which can be part of an overall green building plan for a company.

H

hacking   A variety of computer crimes that involve gaining unauthorized access to a computer system or its data.

half-duplex   Two-way communication that can flow in only one direction at a time. Compare to *simplex* and *full duplex*.

hard drive   A sealed stack of metal platters, each with a read-write head on a retractable arm that reads data from and writes data to the platters by magnetizing bits of iron oxide particles on the platters in patterns of positive and negative polarity.

HDMI   *See* High-Definition Multimedia Interface.

heat sink   A block of heat-conductive metal that draws heat away from a processor or other chip.

hertz   A measurement of cycles per second. One hertz is one cycle. Processor speed is measured in megahertz (millions of hertz) or gigahertz (billions of hertz).

hexadecimal   A numbering system with 16 digits: 0 through 9 plus A through F.

High-Definition Multimedia Interface (HDMI)   A high-speed, high-definition interface used for connecting HD monitors to data sources, including computers, cable boxes, and Blu-ray players.

history   A record of the pages you have recently viewed in your browser.

HomePlug   *See* Powerline Ethernet.

horizontal dpi   The dots per inch that a scanner can record from left to right on a page. Also called *horizontal resolution* or *x-direction sampling rate*.

horizontal resolution   *See* horizontal dpi.

HTTP   *See* Hypertext Transfer Protocol.

HTTPS   *See* Hypertext Transfer Protocol Secure.

Hypertext Transfer Protocol (HTTP)   A basic unsecured protocol used for web traffic.

Hypertext Transfer Protocol Secure (HTTPS)   A secure version of HTTP, used for sensitive data sent on the Web. It combines regular HTTP with Transport Layer Security (newer) or Secure Sockets Layer security (older).

I

IEEE   *See* Institute of Electrical and Electronics Engineers.

IMAP   *See* Internet Mail Access Protocol.

inkjet printer   A printer that produces the image on the page by squirting ink out of nozzles and onto the paper.

Institute of Electrical and Electronics Engineers (IEEE)   The organization that controls, among other things, wireless networking standards.

instruction set   The set of math calculations that a CPU can perform.

instructions per second   The number of instructions that a processor can complete per second.

Integrated Switched Digital Network (ISDN)   An early type of digital networking provided via telephone lines.

Internet Mail Access Protocol (IMAP)   A mail system that uses the interface of a mail program like Outlook, but that stores the mail on and accesses it from a server rather than locally.

Internet Protocol (IP)   A portion of the TCP/IP protocol, most often referred to in the context of an *IP address*.

Internet service provider (ISP)   A company that you contract with to provide Internet service.

interpolated resolution   Resolution that invents extra pixels between the actual scanned ones using a math formula.

IP   *See* Internet Protocol.

IP address   A numeric address that uniquely identifies a network-capable device on that network. IPv4 addresses are currently in use on the Internet; IPv6 is the next generation.

IP version 4 (IPv4)   An IP address consisting of four numbers, each between 0 and 255, separated by periods. The current standard for IP addressing.

IP version 6 (IPv6)   An IP address consisting of a 128-bit binary number written in hexadecimal. The number is broken into four-digit sections separated by colons. The future standard for IP addressing.

IPv4 *See* IP version 4.

IPv6 *See* IP version 6.

ISDN *See* Integrated Switched Digital Network.

ISP *See* Internet service provider.

issuing authority An organization that issues a security certificate.

J

Java A programming language that works across multiple programs. Often used to write mini web applications.

JavaScript A variant of Java designed for inserting code (scripts) on web pages.

K

Kb *See* kilobit.

keylogger Malware that records all keystrokes and sends the information to a file or a remote user.

kilobit (Kb) One thousand bits. Often used as a measurement of data transfer throughput.

L

LAN *See* local area network.

laser mouse A mouse that uses an infrared laser to detect movement.

laser printer A printer that writes an image onto a drum with a laser that neutralizes the electric charge on the drum at the locations where the toner should be applied and then transfers the image to paper.

LCD *See* liquid crystal display.

LED *See* light-emitting diode.

legacy A technology or device that has been largely replaced by a newer technology.

legacy parallel port *See* LPT port.

light-emitting diode (LED) A display or indicator light created by an illuminated diode.

line printer A printer that prints one line at a time. Compare to *page printer*.

liquid crystal display (LCD)   A type of monitor that has a flat-panel screen in which liquid crystals trapped between polarized filters twist to let light through, creating the screen image.

local area network (LAN)   A network in which computers are physically near to each other.

logical drive   A drive letter that has been assigned to a portion of a physical disk.

low-level formatting   Formatting done at the factory to establish a disk drive's CHS values.

LPT port   An older style of printer connection to a computer, using a 25-pin parallel connector. Also called a *legacy parallel port* or *parallel port*.

M

MAC   *See* Media Access Control.

male connectors   Connectors with pins sticking out, rather than holes into which pins are inserted. Compare to *female connectors*.

malware   A broad term used for many attacks on computer systems, such as viruses, exploits, and worms.

master boot record (MBR)   The sector on a partitioned physical drive that contains information about each partition and logical drive.

master file table (MFT)   A table of contents that contains pointers to the starting points of files and folders stored on a logical drive.

Mb   *See* megabit.

MB   *See* megabyte.

MBR   *See* master boot record.

MD5   *See* Message Digest Version 5.

Media Access Control (MAC)   A unique address describing a network adapter. No two network adapters in the world have the same MAC address. It's usually written as six groups of two hexadecimal digits, separated by hyphens or colons.

megabit (Mb)   Approximately one million bits. Often used as a measurement of data transfer throughput.

megabyte (MB)   Approximately one million bytes.

megahertz   One million hertz, often used to measure CPU speed.

memory   Data storage that uses on/off states on a chip to record patterns of binary data.

memory bus   The bus that carries data to and from the DRAM memory on a motherboard.

Message Digest Version 5 (MD5)   A math calculation used by an antivirus program that results in a unique value used to reflect the data being checked. If the MD5 changes, it may indicate a virus attack.

MFT   *See* master file table.

MHz   *See* megahertz.

millions of instructions per second (MIPS)   A measurement of the number of instructions that a processor can complete per second.

mini-tower   A small tower case. *See* tower case.

MIPS   *See* millions of instructions per second.

modem   An analog-to-digital and digital-to-analog converter for sending digital data over a regular telephone line.

Molex connector   A four-pin power connector used for standard PATA devices such as hard disks and optical drives.

monitor   A video display screen.

motherboard   The main circuit board in a PC, into which all components connect.

mouse   A hand-held unit, approximately the size and shape of a bar of soap, that you move on a hard surface to move the onscreen cursor.

MSCONFIG   *See* system configuration utility.

multiboot   *See* dual-boot.

multifunction printer   A printer that includes other functions such as scanning, copying, and faxing.

N

NAS   *See* network attached storage

NAT   *See* network address translation

network   A group of two or more computers that are connected in order to share data and resources.

network address translation (NAT)   A router's technique of translating the individual addresses of the requesting PCs in your network to be sent and received on a single Internet connection.

network attached storage (NAS)   A network-addressable hard disk or other storage device.

network interface card (NIC)   An add-on card, or an interface built into the motherboard, which provides network connectivity, either wired or wireless.

network share   A network location that is made available to network users.

NIC   *See* network interface card.

nonvolatile memory   Memory that doesn't require electricity to maintain its contents.

O

omnidirectional microphone   A microphone that picks up sound in all directions. Compare to *unidirectional microphone*.

online UPS   A UPS that runs off the battery at all times, with the power coming in charging the battery continuously. Compare to a *standby power supply*.

Open Systems Architecture (OSI) model   A seven-layer conceptual model for describing the levels of network communication and its protocols at each level.

open-source operating system   An operating system that is free and whose code is open to the public for modification and sharing. Linux is an example of an open-source OS.

operating system (OS)   The software that maintains the computer's user interface, manages files, communicates with devices, and runs applications.

optical mouse   A mouse that uses a light-emitting diode (LED) or a photodiode to detect movement.

optical zoom   The zoom on a digital camera that uses a real multifocal length lens. Compare to *digital zoom*.

OS   *See* operating system.

OSI model   *See* Open Systems Architecture model.

P

P2P   *See* peer-to-peer network.

packet sniffing   A technique for spying on web traffic by examining packets of data as they're transmitted.

page printer   A printer that prints an entire page in one pass. Compare to *line printer*.

pages per minute (ppm)   A measurement of a printer's speed.

parallel port   *See* LPT port.

parallel printer   A printer that accepts data via a parallel printer cable, transferring multiple bits of data simultaneously.

parental controls   Controls that allow parents to monitor and restrict the computing activity of children.

partition   A section of a physical hard disk that can be assigned one or more logical drive letters.

passive cooling system   A cooling system that contains no moving parts, such as a heat sink.

patch cable   *See* crossover cable.

path   The full address of a file on a disk, such as C:\books\myfile.txt.

PC   *See* personal computer.

PC Card   An older type of expansion slot and device type for notebook computers. PC Cards were replaced by *CardBus*, which were in turn replaced by *ExpressCard*.

PCI   *See* peripheral component interconnect.

PCI Express (PCIe)   An updated and faster version of *peripheral component interconnect (PCI),* carrying data serially on 1 to 16 channels at once.

PCI-Extended (PCI-X)   A double-wide version of PCI, used primarily in servers in the early 2000s. *See also* peripheral component interconnect (PCI).

PCI-X   *See* PCI-Extended.

PCIe   *See* PCI Express.

peer-to-peer (P2P) network   A network that contains no servers, with each of the clients taking on a portion of the burden of maintaining the network. Also called a *workgroup.*

pen computing   A technology that activates a touch screen with a special stylus that comes with the device.

peripheral component interconnect (PCI)   A fast bus on a motherboard that carries data between expansion cards and the system bus. Updated versions are PCI-Extended (PCI-X) and PCI Express (PCIe).

peripheral device   A device that is external to the main body of the computer, or a device that isn't essential to the computer's functioning.

persistent cookie   A cookie that stays on your hard disk after you close the browser. Compare to *session cookie.*

personal computer (PC)   A computer designed to be used by an individual.

phishing   Creating a site that masquerades as a legitimate secure site but actually steals your login information. Also called *spoofing*.

piezoelectric inkjet   An inkjet printer that moves the ink with electricity via piezoelectric crystals, which change their shape when electricity is applied to them.

pin out   A diagram that shows what each wire or pin in each end of a cable represents.

pixel   An individual dot on a display monitor.

platform   The hardware type of a computer that determines the OSs with which it's compatible. For example, an IBM-compatible platform runs Windows and Linux.

Plug-and-Play (PnP)   A technology that allows computers to detect a new device automatically, assign system resources to it, and install a driver for it.

plug-in   *See* add-on.

PnP   *See* Plug-and-Play.

PoE   *See* Power over Ethernet.

pointing device   An object that you move with your hand to control an onscreen pointer. A mouse is the most common type.

POP   *See* Post Office Protocol.

POP3   *See* Post Office Protocol.

pop-up   An extra, usually small, browser window that appears automatically when you display a certain web page or click a certain button on a page.

port   A TCP channel used to transport network traffic.

POST card   A circuit board you insert into an open slot in the motherboard to display a numeric code that tells you where the system is in the booting process.

Post Office Protocol (POP)   A store-and-forward system for receiving email. The current version is 3 (POP3).

POST   *See* Power On System Test.

power conditioning   The ability to correct power voltage flow from brownouts/sags as well as surges/spikes.

Power over Ethernet (PoE)   A technology for using Ethernet cables to conduct electricity.

power plan   Rules you set up in your OS or BIOS to control when and how a computer goes into low-power-consumption mode.

Powerline Ethernet   A technology for carrying Ethernet networking data over power lines in a home. One brand is *HomePlug*.

Power On System Test (POST)   A set of startup diagnostics that run on computer hardware before the OS loads.

prefetch buffer   An extra buffer on RAM that allows quick access to data located on a common physical row of memory.

primary partition   A bootable partition on a hard disk. You can allocate all the space to a single primary partition or divide it further into additional partitions.

printer port   *See* LPT port. Can also refer to any port into which you connect a printer.

privacy screen   *See* screen filter.

processor   The main math calculator on a computer, which takes in data and instructions and outputs the result of those instructions.

prohibition icon   A red circle with a diagonal red line through it, indicating a prohibition against something.

protocol   A set of language rules used between two devices or two points in a process.

R

RAID   *See* redundant array of independent disks.

RAM   *See* random access memory.

random access memory (RAM)   Memory that can be written and rewritten on the device in which it's installed.

read-only memory (ROM)   Memory that can't be changed, once written to.

Recovery Console   A command-line interface for troubleshooting serious problems with Windows XP that cause it to not be able to start. Replaced by the *Windows Recovery Environment* in Windows Vista and Windows 7.

reduced instruction set computing (RISC)   A CPU that uses a smaller than normal instruction set in order to improve performance.

redundant array of independent disks (RAID)   A system that bundles multiple physical hard disks together to work as a team for increased performance, reliability, or both.

remote desktop   A connection to a remote computer via network or Internet that enables you to use that computer as if you were sitting at it physically.

resident   Continuously running in the background. An example is an antivirus program.

resolve   To translate a web URL into an IP address via a DNS server.

RISC   *See* Reduced Instruction Set Computing.

RJ-45 connector   A plastic connector on an Ethernet cable, containing four twisted pairs of wires (eight wires total). Like a telephone cable connector, but slightly wider.

RMS   *See* root mean squared.

ROM   *See* read-only memory.

root directory   The top-level folder on a logical drive.

root folder   *See* root directory.

root mean squared (RMS)   A standard measurement of the wattage a speaker can reliably handle in a sustained manner.

router   A smarter version of a switch, able to direct traffic intelligently not only within your local network but also to other connected networks, including the Internet.

S

Safe mode   A reduced-functionality Windows mode in which only essential drivers and applications load, used for troubleshooting.

sag   A lack of the expected amount of electrical power (under-voltage). Also called a *brownout*.

scanner   A device that digitizes a hard-copy image, converting it into a computer file.

screen filter   A cover over a monitor screen that directs light from it at a restricted angle so that anyone who isn't viewing it straight-on won't be able to read it clearly.

screen resolution   The resolution in pixels of the display. For example, 1600×900 means 1600 pixels wide and 900 pixels tall.

SDR   *See* single data rate.

SDRAM   *See* synchronous dynamic random access memory.

SDSL   *See* symmetric DSL.

sector   A section of a formatted disk where track rings intersect the pie slices made by lines that bisect the disk platter. Each sector holds 512 bytes of data.

Secure FTP (SFTP)   *See* Secure Shell (SSH) FTP.

Secure Shell (SSH) FTP A secure form of FTP.

secure site A website that uses security to ensure the user's data is safeguarded.

Secure Sockets Layer (SSL) An encryption technique that makes web transactions more secure. *See* Hypertext Transfer Protocol Secure.

security certificate A certificate on a website that helps you know that you're dealing with a legitimate site, and not a fake.

server A PC that exists only to route network traffic and provide access to shared files, printers, and services to client PCs.

service pack A major update for an OS or application.

service set identifier (SSID) The name by which a wireless access point is known on the network.

session cookie A cookie that lasts only as long as your web browser is open. Compare to *persistent cookie*.

SFTP *See* Secure FTP.

shell An interface that an OS uses for user input and output. For example, many people use a graphical shell for Linux. In some OSs, like Windows, the shell isn't separable from the OS itself.

shortcut A pointer to a file.

Simple Mail Transport Protocol (SMTP) A protocol for sending email. Usually paired with *Post Office Protocol (POP)*, which receives mail.

simplex One-way communication. Compare to *half-duplex* and *full-duplex*.

single data rate (SDR) RAM that runs at the same speed as the front-side bus.

slimline case A computer case that is thinner than normal. It can be oriented either flat like a *desktop case* or upright like a *tower case*.

small office/home office (SOHO) A category of work environment that resembles a home environment, or one containing very few PCs and people.

small-outline DIMM A DIMM that is smaller than a normal DIMM module, designed for use in notebook computers.

smart card A plastic card, similar in size to a credit card, containing a microchip that a card reader can scan.

SmartScreen filter The Internet Explorer phishing filter.

SMTP *See* Simple Mail Transport Protocol.

social engineering   Tricking someone into revealing personal information.

SODIMM   *See* small-outline DIMM.

SOHO   *See* small office/home office.

solid-state hard drive   A storage device that stores data in flash RAM but interfaces with a computer as if it were a mechanical hard disk.

sound card   A circuit board installed in a PC that controls the sound input and output.

spam   Unwanted junk email.

spike   A dramatic and sudden power surge that results in a quick burst of very high voltage.

spoofing   *See* phishing.

SPS   *See* standby power source.

spyware   Software that records your computer usage. A keylogger is one example.

SRAM   *See* static RAM.

SSH   *See* Secure Shell.

SSID   *See* service set identifier.

SSL   *See* Secure Sockets Layer.

standby power source (SPS)   A UPS in which devices run off the AC outlet when it's available, switching to battery only when it isn't. Compare to *online UPS*.

stateless   A situation in which every exchange starts fresh, with no memory of previous exchanges. HTTP is a stateless protocol, so cookies are used to remember settings from previous exchanges.

static IP address   An IP address that is permanently assigned to a device. Compare to *dynamic IP address*.

static memory   Memory that doesn't require constant refreshing to maintain its contents.

static RAM   *See* flash RAM.

STOP error   A Windows error that appears on a bright blue background with the word STOP in it, which reports a serious error that has caused the system to shut down. Also called *blue screen of death* or *BSOD*.

strong password   A password that is difficult to guess.

subfolder   A folder within a folder.

subnet mask   A code in IPv4 IP addressing used to indicate what portion of the IP address is being used as a prefix and what portion is being used as a unique identifier.

surge   A condition where the voltage in a power delivery system suddenly becomes too high.

surge protector   *See* surge suppressor.

surge suppressor   An extension cord that contains a *varistor* that can absorb any excess power during a surge or spike.

swap file   The file that is used for virtual memory.

switch   (1) A connection box for wired Ethernet that takes in the incoming traffic and directs the data to the appropriate outward-bound lane. (2) An option for a command-line command, preceded by a forward slash (/), such as /w.

Symmetric DSL (SDSL)   DSL service in which the upload and download speeds are the same.

synchronous   When referring to RAM, synchronized with the system bus. When referring to DSL Internet service, refers to the speed of the uploads and the speed of the downloads being the same.

synchronous dynamic random access memory (SDRAM)   RAM that's speed is synchronized with the system bus. It can be single data rate (SDR) or double data rate (DDR).

system bus   The pathway that delivers data to the processor. Also called *front-side bus*.

System Configuration Utility   A utility, also known as MSCONFIG, which allows Windows users to disable certain startup applications and services selectively.

system image   An exact copy of an entire hard disk.

System Restore   A utility for returning a Windows system's configuration files to an earlier version to recover from a recently created problem.

system timer   The timer on the motherboard that determines the speed of the system bus.

T

tablet computer   A notebook computer that includes touch-screen technology, either as a primary or secondary form of user input.

TCO   *See* total cost of ownership.

TCP/IP   *See* Transmission Control Protocol/Internet Protocol.

telecommuting   Employees working from home rather than reporting to an office building every day.

terminal server   A mainframe computer that controls multiple terminals.

terminal   A monitor and keyboard that get their processing power from a terminal server.

thermal inkjet printer   An inkjet printer that uses heat to create vapor bubbles that force out the ink. Also called *bubble jet*.

thermally advantaged chassis   A computer case designed to optimize the airflow inside it to dissipate heat.

third-party cookie   A cookie placed on your computer by an ad on a website, where the ad's parent company isn't related to the owner of the website. Compare to *first-party cookie*.

thumb drive   *See* flash drive.

TLS   *See* Transport Layer Security

total cost of ownership (TCO)   The total cost to own a device, including its purchase price and its consumables, plus the cost of upkeep and maintenance.

touch screen   A pressure-sensitive video display.

touchpad   A pressure-sensitive surface across which you can run your finger to move an onscreen pointer.

tower case   A computer case that is taller than it is wide or deep.

track   A concentric ring on a disk platter.

trackball   A pointing device with a stationary base and a ball that you roll with your fingers or hand.

trackpad   *See* touchpad.

transistor   An electrical gate that either lets power through or doesn't, depending on its current state. Transistors are the basis of binary processing.

Transmission Control Protocol/Internet Protocol (TCP/IP)   An interconnected set of networking protocols used on the Internet and on most other networks.

Transport Layer Security (TLS)   An encryption technique that makes web transactions more secure. *See* Hypertext Transfer Protocol Secure.

triad   A set of three phosphors on a CRT (red, green, and blue) that combine to form a pixel.

Trojan horse   A rogue application that appears to do something useful but also does something malicious.

U

unclean uninstallation   An uninstallation during which the old Registry entries, helper files, and data files left behind aren't removed.

unidirectional microphone   A microphone that picks up sound only in the direction in which it's pointed. Compare to *omnidirectional*.

uniform resource locator (URL)   A web address, such as www.microsoft.com.

uninterruptible power supply (UPS)   A battery backup combined with a surge suppressor.

unshielded   Cable that doesn't contain shielding against EMI.

unshielded twisted pair (UTP)   A type of Ethernet cable that carries data on twisted pairs of wires, with no shielding against EMI.

update   To apply a patch or fix to the current version, usually to correct a problem with it.

upgrade   To replace the current version with a newer, or more feature-rich one.

upgrade install   An installation of a new OS version that involves installing over the old version so that settings and applications are retained. Compare to *clean install*.

upgrade path   A means of getting from one OS version or edition to another. Depending on the versions, you may be able to do an update install, or you may need a clean install.

UPS   *See* uninterruptible power supply.

URL   *See* uniform resource locator.

UTP   *See* unshielded twisted pair.

V

varistor   A variable resistor inside a surge suppressor, capable of absorbing any excess power during a surge or spike.

version   A major release of a program or OS. For example, Windows 7 is a version of Windows. Compare to *edition*.

vertical dpi   The dots per inch that a scanner can record vertically on a page. Also called *vertical resolution* or *y-direction sampling rate*.

vertical resolution   An image's or display's resolution from top to bottom.

VGA   *See* Video Graphics Adapter.

Video Graphics Adapter (VGA)   An analog style of monitor connector that uses a 15-pin D-sub connection.

virtual machine   A simulated processing environment designed to run an application or OS in a closed bubble, separate from the rest of the computer's operation.

virtual memory   A portion of the hard disk that functions as a holding area for swapping data into and out of RAM.

virtual private network (VPN)   A secure tunnel that runs between points on the Internet, creating a secure communication channel using public Internet routes.

virus   Malware that attaches itself to an executable file and modifies what happens when the file runs.

virus definition   *See* virus signature.

virus signature   A snippet of code used to identify a virus.

Voice over Internet Protocol (VoIP)   A set of applications, technologies, and protocols used to provide IP-based telephony services.

VoIP   *See* Voice over Internet Protocol.

volatile memory   *See* dynamic RAM.

volume boot record   A file created via high-level formatting that stores information needed to boot from the drive.

VPN   *See* virtual private network.

vulnerability   A flaw in the programming of an application that creates the potential for misuse; plus a tool or technique that allows an attacker to exploit that vulnerability.

W

WAN   *See* wide area network.

WAP   *See* wireless access point.

weak password   A password that is easy to guess.

webcam   A low-resolution video camera that feeds its images directly into a computer or network.

wide area network (WAN)   A network in which the computers aren't located near each other, such as the Internet.

Wi-Fi   Short for wireless fidelity. A nickname for the collection of standards for wireless networking officially known as IEEE 802.11.

wildcard   A character that stands for one or more other characters, such as ? for individual characters and * for multiple characters.

Windows Explorer   The file-management interface in Microsoft Windows.

Windows RE   *See* Windows recovery environment.

Windows Recovery Environment (RE)   An interface for recovering from serious problems with Windows Vista or Windows 7 that prevent the OS from booting normally.

wireless access point (WAP)   A wireless network switch.

word size   The amount of data that can simultaneously enter the processor in one operation.

workgroup   *See* peer-to-peer network.

worm   A self-transporting malware application that carries an active payload, such as a Trojan horse or a virus.

X

x-direction sampling rate   *See* horizontal dpi.

Y

y-direction sampling rate   *See* vertical dpi.

Index

Note to the reader: Throughout this index boldfaced page numbers indicate primary discussions of a topic. Italicized page numbers indicate illustrations.

Symbols

. (period), file extensions, 192
\ (backslash), Windows folder path, 186
? (question mark), Mac OS X, 315
/ (slash), Mac OS X folder path, 186

A

AC. *See* alternating current
AC adapter, notebook PCs, *145*
access control
  biometric devices, 326
  passwords, **323–325**
  security, **323–326**
  smart cards, 325
  user IDs, 323
access time, 56
Action Center, 203
activation, applications, 248–249, 260
active cooling system, 12, *13*
Active Directory, 323, 363
ActiveX, 122–123
  security, 343
  spyware, 354
Activity Monitor, Mac OS X, 264
add-ons
  Firefox, 120
  speakers, 82
  web browsers, 119–121
  web pages, 119
  webcams, 89
administrative rights
  applications, 242
  OS, 239
administrator account

application installation, 315
  password, 241
ADSL. *See* asymmetric DSL
Advanced Micro Devices (AMD), 7, 28
Advanced Options, 315
adware, 353
AFP. *See* Apple Filing Protocol
alcohol, 38, 165, 212
aliases, Mac OS X, 198
allocation units, 52
Alt key, 33
alternating current (AC), 143
AMD. *See* Advanced Micro Devices
American Standard Code for Information
    Interchange (ASCII), 42, 69
ammonia, 165, 212
amplification, 83
amps, 173
analog *vs.* digital
  microphones, 85
  speakers, 83
anti-phishing, 122
antispam software, 356
antispyware software, 355–356
antistatic bags, 275, *276*
antistatic mats, 174
antistatic wrist strap, 174, *174*, *275*, *275*
antivirus software, 354–355
APIPA. *See* automatic private IP addressing
Appearance, 226
Appearance and Personalization, 206–207
  Mac OS X, 226–227
  Windows 7, 225
Apple Filing Protocol (AFP), 329
applications
  activation, 248–249, 260
  administrative rights, 242

D

worms, 353, 364
WPA. *See* Wi-Fi Protected Access
Write Only, 328
write-protection, 62

X

Xbench, 264
x-direction sampling rate. *See* horizontal
resolution

Y

y-direction sampling rate. *See* vertical
resolution

Z

Zip files, 201
    application installation, 246
Zoho, 383
zoom, 88, 131

John Wiley & Sons, Ltd.
End-User License Agreement

The Absolute Best CompTIA Strata Book/CD Package on the Market!

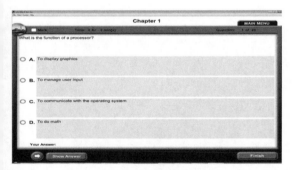
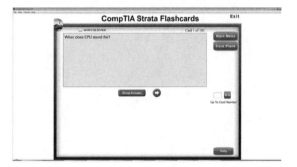